THE JAMAICAN THEATRE

THE JAMAICAN THEATRE

Highlights of the Performing Arts in the Twentieth Century

Wycliffe Bennett and Hazel Bennett

University of the West Indies Press
Jamaica • Barbados • Trinidad and Tobago

CHASE
Culture • Health • Arts • Sports • Education Fund
Working for you

United Nations Educational, Scientific and Cultural Organization
The Jamaica National Commission for UNESCO

University of the West Indies Press
7A Gibraltar Hall Road Mona
Kingston 7 Jamaica
www.uwipress.com

The CHASE Fund, Jamaica
52–60 Grenada Crescent
Kingston 5 Jamaica

The Jamaica National Commission
for UNESCO
25 Dominica Drive
Kingston 5 Jamaica

© 2011 by Hazel Bennett

All rights reserved. Published 2011

A catalogue record of this book is available from the National Library of Jamaica.

ISBN: 978-976-640-226-6

Cover photographs: Ward Theatre by Ian Edwards; Ranny Williams and Louise Bennett by Maria LaYacona; Movements Dance Company by Monica Campbell McFarlane.

Book design by Robert Harris.
Cover design by Communications Services Limited.
Set in Sabon 10/14 x 30

Printed in China by Regent Publishing Services.

The University Singers in concert

Contents

ACT III THE DANCE EVOLVES

ACT IV MAJOR PRODUCTIONS, TRAINING, MUSICAL ACHIEVEMENTS

Foreword

REX NETTLEFORD

This story of the Jamaican Theatre comes with the authority of a particular brand of knowledge rooted in practical experience not only in the shaping of what takes place between proscenium pillars, but also in sustained scholarly observation and analysis of the work done over years by many throughout Jamaica. The authority is further bolstered by the author's active engagement over time, in the building and management of institutional frameworks which guarantee to Jamaican arts and culture the continuing exercise of the creative imagination – individual and collective.

Rex Nettleford

Presentations from village drama, through pageants and national showcases of various performing talents, to the regional Caribbean Festivals of the Arts (Carifesta), have honed the profile of author Wycliffe Bennett. Over fifty years ago someone wrote of Mr Bennett, "It is his faith that the culture of a country should not only keep pace with, but foreshadow its political development; and the great deal of work which he has done, and which is taking fruit because he is a good organizer, will bear testimony to this faith later."

And so it did! He has lived to see Arts and Culture play the central role it has done in Jamaican nation-building and postcolonial development in the quest for certitude – cultural and political. A British Council scholarship to observe the Edinburgh Festival and the Welsh National and International Eisteddfodau and to attend a full-time play production course at the British Drama League certainly paid off, as did his collaboration with such pre-independence cultural activists as W. Adolphe Roberts, J.E. Clare MacFarlane, H.P. Jacobs and Vivian Virtue in the formation of the Poetry League. The later appearance of the journal *Life and Letters*, which helped bring to prominence such Caribbean writers as Vic Reid, Edgar Mittelholzer and George Lamming, merely served to strengthen his understanding of the literary foundations of theatre anywhere.

By the time he entered the academy to pursue formal study of theatre at Yale and Columbia universities, Bennett proved to be as valuable to the exercise of learning as the university programmes were to the deepening and heightening of his knowledge of theatre arts generally, and of the history of the Jamaican performing arts experience in particular. As is the custom in his native Jamaica, his real-life work in a variety of occupations as journalist, customs officer, member of the Agricultural Loan Societies Board and administrator in the Ministry of Mining and Natural Resources, served his theatre experience well, for they provided him ready access to people tenanting every nook and cranny of his native Jamaica, and to the ancestral cultural richness of the island he calls home. That he was able to garner much from these experiences for the Adult Drama Festival and the Jamaica Drama League's Seasons of Excellence series, which he initiated and managed for many a year, has contributed to this welcome survey of twentieth-century theatre and cultural life in a Jamaica which exists as much by its creativity as by its well documented historical struggles out of slavery and colonialism.

Rex Nettleford dancing Kumina

Foreword

DEREK WALCOTT

The not-so-dim figure behind the annual cultural festivals of Jamaica is an urbane, cultivated little man with a charming manner that permits him to make and break appointments with ambassadorial ease. Wycliffe Bennett, the thirty-five-year-old impresario behind the coming of a national theatre, has probably done more than any other person in Jamaica to make the entire country aware of its cultural future, but without the blatant self aggrandisement of the politician.

He has acquired the deftness of management which succeeds mightily where other angels would fear to tread, and despite the occasional air of irritation which his persistence brings to certain workers in the same field, the man himself is a true patriot, a formidable worker, and a very likeable personality.

Where another person's way of achieving things would in some quarters be passed off as effrontery, Wycliffe Bennett's way of talking to common people, without losing the regal touch, has worked miracles and left people gaping.

There are several stories about him which he bears with good grace and absolute confidence. But after the little envies have dissipated into thin air, he is a firm outline behind the theatrical smoke.

He was born on [19 May 1922], and lost his parents by the time he was [four] years old. He was educated at Central Branch Elementary School, and at Normal College. He acknowledges profound gratitude to an adopted mother, Helen Rebertha Mercurius, and to several other tutors and associates in the cultural pockets of Jamaica.

Among his good friends and mentors are W. Adolphe Roberts, J.E. Clare MacFarlane, Vivian Virtue, H.P. Jacobs, all of whom have worked as quietly as Bennett to bring some cultural awareness to the island through the formation of the Poetry League, of which Bennett has himself been secretary. Another lasting debt he acknowledges is to Sir Noel Livingstone.

Derek Walcott

*First published in *Public Opinion*, 13 July 1957.

After leaving school at the age of seventeen, Bennett worked as a proofreader and on the editorial staff of the *Daily Gleaner*, whence he proceeded to an appointment in the Government Service, spending most of his time in the Customs Department.

During all this time he had been working hard in organizing the Island Speech Festivals, of which he had at one time been a schoolboy champion.

In 1955 he was seconded by the governor to manage the speech and theatre section of the great Tercentenary Celebrations, an appointment which met with the complete approval of his colleagues.

There is no doubt that Bennett's enthusiasm matched his achievement. His soft-spoken and assured manner has the ductility of a hypnotist leading people into doing things which they would soberly consider impossible. The success of the Tercentenary Celebrations is on record.

The soundest work which Bennett has done, however, and on which he is still engaged, is the self-sacrificing, unpaid task of spreading the gospel of a national theatre by his arduous trips into remote areas which metropolitan superiority would dismiss. The Adult Drama Festival of which he is chairman is in its third year, and the importance of its appeal to both writers and performers alike is something permanent.

Apart from all this, Bennett has done a great deal in interesting people abroad in the work of Jamaican and West Indian writers. It is mainly through his efforts that *Life and Letters* some time ago published, in two successive numbers, the poetry and prose of Jamaican writers, a break which established Vic Reid and Edgar Mittelholzer, and which gave writers in the Caribbean a sense of dignity and a feeling of being needed.

Bennett has also for some time been compiling, in association with W. Adolphe Roberts, R.N. Murray and G. Coulthard, two anthologies (still in Mss) of the poetry of the Caribbean, and has had articles on West Indian literature published in *Americas*, an international publication, and in *Life and Letters*.

His official job is with the Agricultural Loan Societies Board, a job which takes him to all parts of the country, but his real love and most sincere dedication is the cultural growth of his country.

His faith that the culture of a country should both keep pace with and foreshadow its political development, and the great deal of work which he has done, and which is taking fruit because he is a good organizer, will bear testimony to this faith later. "Never make a timid gesture", he sometimes says. It is good advice, and so far it has brought him respect and given little societies struggling in the rural areas his sense of confidence . . .

Acknowledgements

WYCLIFFE BENNETT AND HAZEL BENNETT

In coming to terms with reality, historians have discovered that, whatever their speciality, other disciplines impinge upon their own. This truism has become increasingly obvious in the Caribbean, where succeeding generations of historians have, of necessity, had to employ an encyclopaedic approach. To this rule the theatre is no exception.

The house a man lives in, what he eats, what he wears, how he gets to work, the people he knows and how he is governed, if and where he worships, will determine the kind of theatrical performances he supports. The theatre historian cannot ignore these considerations if he hopes to be able to reconstruct and conjure up yesterday's theatres and performances; and he is likely to do a far better job if, whenever opportunity allows, he steps aside and invites practitioners and other devotees and eyewitnesses to speak. The theatre historian seems to function best when he tries to create the context in which yesterday's voices and images can have today's immediacy.

Several individuals and institutions have helped to summon up the eyewitnesses who speak through the following pages: the librarians of the National Library of Jamaica, the Jamaica Library Service, the University of the West Indies, the Jamaica Broadcasting Corporation, Television Jamaica, and the Media Technology Institute of the Creative Production and Training Centre of Jamaica; those of the British Museum, the West India Committee, the Royal Commonwealth Society, the British War Office, and the British Record Office in London, among other places; and the librarians of the Bodleian and Rhodes House Libraries at Oxford University, as well as of the Library of Congress, the New York Public Library, Yale University and Columbia University in the United States.

In tracking down elusive Jamaican material, a number of specialists at home were particularly helpful: the late H.P. Jacobs, the late Dr Lucille Mair, the late Clinton Black (government archivist), the late Henry Fowler, the late Professor Errol Hill among others. For more than fifty years, the co-authors worked as a team to continue the research started in 1941 and to see it through to its conclusion. That film and television were added to the study was due primarily to Edward Seaga, then-minister of welfare and culture, who, in 1962, supported Wycliffe Bennett's application for a government scholarship to Yale, and further encouraged him to add these subjects to his studies.

The addition of music to the work was logical, and thanks must be given to Douglas Bennett, past chairman of the Musical Society of Jamaica, Noel Dexter and Marjorie Whylie from the music department of the University of the West Indies, and Ouida Tomlinson (Dunphy) of the Music and Youth series of films and Carifesta '76. Thanks also to Eugene Williams, from the Edna Manley College, and Honor Ford-Smith, formerly of the college, who contributed significantly to the section on the School of Drama and brought to attention some persons who otherwise might have been overlooked. Buddy Pouyat's contribution to the Drama League's Season of Excellence and the vintage years of the Jamaican Theatre was considerable. Thanks also to Dr Maria Smith, who permitted us to include the introductory chapter entitled "Revivalism, Symbolic Language, Memory and the Performance of an Afro-Jamaican Identity" from her thesis; to Cheryl Ryman, who gave permission for the use of her article on the Frats Quintet; to Yvonne Brewster, who contributed the relevant sections on the Barn Theatre and on Carifesta '76; to Jean Lowrie Chin and Lorna Goodison on Carifesta '76; to Professor Rex Nettleford, Barbara Requa and Monika Lawrence on the dance; and to Michael Lorde on set design. The help of many theatre devotees who generously cooperated in the hunt for scarce photographs is truly appreciated.

In the 1980s Errol Hill and Wycliffe Bennett accompanied each other on visits to libraries and other places in England, the United States and Jamaica, and together studied all the available material covering the period since Francis Hanson mentioned *Plays at a Publick Theatre*[1] in Jamaica in 1682. Hazel Bennett, working overseas on another project at that time, also continued to record every item of information on the subject which crossed her path. This enabled her to fill in gaps in the research that Hill and Bennett did not locate. It was agreed that Errol Hill would concentrate on the early years to the end of the nineteenth century and that we would deal with the twentieth century since we were closer to where most of the action would be located and would have personal, on-the-spot knowledge of what was happening. Our research on the early years was made available to Professor Hill. He died in 2005, but had completed his assignment on schedule.

For the chapter on drama at the University College of the West Indies (UCWI) during the 1950s, we must thank Mary Morgan (*née* Brathwaite) and those who assisted her, for their painstaking and meticulous research and documentation. It had to be someone from one of the other Caribbean territories – someone better prepared, on coming into a fresh habitat, to capture the feel, enthusiasm and regional nuances of the young and vibrant students who formed the Drama Society at that time.

This development in drama at the UCWI was greatly facilitated by the pioneer fieldwork of Louise Bennett in folk culture, beginning in the 1940s, followed by Olive Lewin in folk and traditional music in the 1950s, and by Ivy Baxter in dance, beginning in the late 1940s.

We had to allow for the century to run its course, before presuming to be able to complete the study. For reasons which will prove self-evident, the cut-off point is

September 2008, with the play offerings of Trevor Rhone, Lloyd Reckord, Louis Marriott, Patrick Brown, Basil Dawkins, David Heron, Paul Beale and others, among a broad range of end-of-century artists.

The study incorporates the contributions of musicians, choreographers, stage designers, as well as actors, monologists, storytellers, singers, dancers, other performing artists and some technical personnel and critics, who helped to bring important productions to stage, audio, video and the Internet. They are included in the section "Profiles and Biodata". It is the overwhelming support of this great team of devotees, which has given this publication any claim it may have to accuracy, authority and credibility, at this juncture in the highlighting of the performing arts in twentieth-century Jamaica. We thank them for keeping fresh in our hearts and mind their caring voices and images, which bring closure to the study.

For the creation of the book cover we thank Ian Edwards who permitted us to use his photograph of the Ward Theatre. We thank also Monica Campbell McFarlane for allowing us to use her Movements Dance Company's photograph and also her technical staff at Communications Services Limited, to bring William Richards's rough concept to reality.

We must also thank most sincerely the Jamaica National Commission for UNESCO and the CHASE Fund, whose financial contributions made this publication possible.

Hazel Bennett and Wycliffe Bennett, co-authors

ACT I

SETTING THE SCENE

1

Background to the Jamaican Scene

In setting the background to their *Story of the Jamaican People*, Sherlock and Bennett wrote:

> Europe brought Africa to the Caribbean early in the sixteenth century. Europe came as victor, dispossessor, and exploiter. Africa came as victim, dispossessed, exploited. For five centuries the two shaped Caribbean history, Europe through the sugar-and-slave plantation, colonialism and the doctrine of white superiority, and Africa through the African-Jamaican's rejection of slavery, his triumphant struggle for freedom and justice, his resilience of spirit and his creativity.[1]

The British connection with the theatre in Jamaica begins shortly after the commencement of British rule. In 1655 the island was captured from the Spanish and soon became peopled by English-speaking adventurers. Jamaica remained a British colony until 1962 when political independence was granted by the British government. During the early years, the British had intended to establish a colony of small settlers, but by 1700 such efforts were overtaken by other events. In particular, the European craving for cheap sugar led to the introduction of large-scale sugar plantations that relied upon African slave labour.

Theatrical practice has always tended to reflect the outlook of the vital and more articulate elements of society. No art can be conceived in a vacuum: it is the result of a society, of a special way of viewing life at a particular place and time by a particular group of people. There is general exultation when the annual festival of the arts envelops the land – a festival involving, since independence, not only the performing arts (music, drama, dance and speech), but also national exhibitions of painting, sculpture, ceramics, photography, handicrafts and sundry other activities. These include industrial, agricultural and horticultural fairs; culinary presentations; religious services and patriotic proclamations; literary competitions and publications; symposia, lectures and recitals; and athletics, cricket and other sports in which Jamaica has become a world power.

Opposite: The Kingston Theatre, built in 1775 on the corner of North Parade and King Street; daguerreotype by A. Duperly (1831). (*Source*: Errol Hill, *The Jamaican Stage, 1655–1900* [Amherst: University of Massachusetts Press, 1992].)

The Theatre Royal, built in 1840, deteriorated over time, but was rebuilt and reopened in 1897, only to be destroyed by earthquake in 1907. *Courtesy of National Library of Jamaica (NLJ).*

It therefore becomes necessary at the outset to attempt some description of the local habitation and to indicate what would seem to have been the main determining forces in the Jamaican society. This approach should also prove useful for other reasons. In the first place, despite its small size, Jamaica is making a special and much acclaimed contribution to the complex of world culture.

Jamaica has a population of approximately 2.6 million people. It is the third largest Caribbean island in an archipelago that stretches from the Bahamas off the coast of Florida, down to Trinidad at the mouth of the Orinoco river in Venezuela.

Jamaica lies 90 miles to the south of Cuba, and between latitudes 17 and 18 degrees north and longitudes 76 and 78 degrees west. The island has an area of 4,411 square miles. Its greatest length is 146 miles and its greatest width 51 miles.

Chains of mountains give the island a rugged spine. In the east, the land seems to shoot up suddenly out of the Caribbean Sea, and confronts the beholder with a tumbled mass of hidden valleys set deeply between opposing peaks. At the highest point, Blue Mountain Peak rises to 7,402 feet. Steep hills radiate from the spine, but in the west and southwest the land slopes more gradually, and pockets of rolling plains run between the mountains and the white beaches that fringe the sea. As the original Taino name "Xaymaca" implies, Jamaica has an abundance of rivers.

Politically, the island follows the English form of government. It is a constitutional monarchy in that the governor general is appointed to represent the queen of England on the advice of the prime minister in consultation with the leader of the opposition. There are, of course, a judiciary and a civil service. The island is divided into fourteen parishes, each with a capital town.

Kingston, the island's capital and chief port-of-call, along with its environs, has a population of approximately one million souls. Montego Bay, Ocho Rios and Negril are the major tourist centres. From small ports around the coast, shipments of bananas, sugar and bauxite are made. In the deep country among the hills and valleys are hundreds of villages. Here the majority of the islanders eke out a precarious living from the soil or seek employment as craftsmen and unskilled labourers in Kingston and other major towns. If these choices fail, they emigrate. In the past they went to Central America, Cuba and the United States. In more recent times, especially after the Second World War, they have also been going to the United Kingdom and Canada.

The strength of Jamaican society lies in the diversity of its culture. And while simplicity is the goal of this survey, a nuanced understanding is required to address the dynamic nature of this complex society. The theatre and other art forms must reflect not only the different elements that make up the society but also its collective strengths. An important factor that should not be overlooked is Jamaica's relationship with the rest of the English-speaking Caribbean.

With the withdrawal of Jamaica in 1961 from the proposed unification of the English-speaking territories, the Federation of the West Indies that was inaugurated in 1958 collapsed. Trinidad and Tobago, Barbados, St Lucia, St Kitts/Nevis, Antigua, St Vincent and the Grenadines, and Dominica all chose to become independent states within the Commonwealth of Nations. On Jamaica's withdrawal from among the ten units to make up the federation, Prime Minister Eric Williams of Trinidad and Tobago remarked ironically, "One from ten leaves nought."

Nevertheless, it is correct to say that in literature and dramatic art, Jamaica and the other West Indian countries serve each other, and that this practice has included Guyana on the shoulder of the South American continent, and Belize in Central America. At times West Indian plays have been performed in Jamaica even before being staged in their own country. The regional University of the West Indies (UWI) has contributed in no small measure to this practice, as many students from these states attend the Mona campus in Jamaica, and bring their native offerings to the West Indian pool.

Other institutions on the island have increased opportunities for higher education,

The Ward Theatre, built in 1912, as a gift to the people of Kingston from the Honourable Charles James Ward, Lieutenant Colonel, custos of Kingston. *Photo by Ian Edwards.*

Interior, Ward Theatre

and improved the human and technological infrastructure: the University of Technology (UTech), which is physically close to the UWI, the Northern Caribbean University (NCU), located in Mandeville, and the International University of the Caribbean (IUC); and there are other places of higher learning in the United States, Canada and the United Kingdom which have been recruiting students, either to come to their respective campuses or to work for undergraduate and postgraduate degrees via the Internet. In addition, some former teachers' colleges have recently begun to offer degrees in association with the UWI.

The creative energies of the country have been greatly stimulated by the rise of national consciousness and the achievement of political independence. From the vantage point of the present, the following factors appear to have been of the greatest consequence in Jamaica's recorded history:

- The discovery of the island by Columbus in 1494, and the conquest by the English in 1655, which imposed European culture upon the aboriginal Taino culture, and consequently annihilated the native population;

- The introduction into the island of Africans as slaves, East Indians and Chinese as indentured servants, and the later arrival of other nationalities mainly from the Middle East;
- The abolition of slavery in 1834 and full emancipation in 1838;
- The surrender of the old semi-autonomous form of government for a more tightly metropolitan-controlled administration, following the Morant Bay uprising in 1865. (This was because of fear of being outnumbered by black voters who had been encouraged to register by freedom fighters like George William Gordon and Paul Bogle, later designated national heroes);
- Colonial apprenticeship, and the gradual liberalization of educational opportunities;
- The years of unrest in the 1930s, and the development of national consciousness;
- The introduction of universal adult suffrage and internal self-government in 1944, culminating in full independence in 1962, and the creation of the national motto "Out of many, one people";
- The scourge of violence and drugs which has been undermining the reputation of Jamaica as an island paradise with a culture of human rights.

The foregoing factors provide a cornucopia, or endless supply, of themes, ideas and subject matter upon which the creative artists have been feasting: our poets, novelists, playwrights, painters, sculptors and architects; our musicians, choreographers, producers/directors and designers in theatre, radio, film and television.

The phrase *fin de siècle* was often heard at a date when the nineteenth century ended and the twentieth began. W.R. Inge, in *The End of an Age*, remarked, "[T]here was no reason to expect any noticeable change, though . . . the death of Queen Victoria seemed to mark the end of that great period."[2] Some scholars believe that the nineteenth century really continued until the outbreak of the First World War; that, as a form of civilization, the modern world began with the Renaissance and the Reformation and ended in 1914. These same scholars take the view that the new era, our era, began at that time. This is, of course, a macro view, and while we should not ignore such global considerations in trying to place our own concerns in proper perspective, people in the theatre and the arts do not necessarily name epochs in that way. The history of the arts within Western civilization has devised its own system of labelling periods, but within each country across the globe, each discipline will have its own special way of viewing history.

An appreciation of the nature of the Jamaican society at the beginning of the twentieth century is critical to an understanding of the events that followed. The series of monographs and papers, especially at seminars and symposia at the Mona campus of the UCWI (now the UWI), novels and nonfiction works with titles such as *New Day* (1949), *Personality and Conflict* (1952), *A Quality of Violence* (1959), *Mirror, Mirror: Identity, Race and Protest in Jamaica* (1970) would seem to give a clear indication that self-discovery was, in the final analysis, the only true path to development. But another important factor must also be taken into account.

The theatre is often referred to as the art where all arts meet. It is not our view that the history of dance, drama, music or the fine arts can be discussed in any comprehensive way without taking cognizance of developments in other areas. This is

The Little Theatre was built in 1961. The rehearsal room, now renamed the Little Little Theatre, was built in 1958. *Courtesy of Jamaica Information Service.*

what nowadays is referred to as "peripheral vision". It is possible to choreograph without the use of music or decor, but the result hardly qualifies as dance theatre – that is, dance choreographed for and performed on a stage or at a "seeing place" before an audience in which elements of other arts have been supportively and appropriately utilized.

Essentially, what we are talking about, therefore, is the history of the art of performance. And when you attempt to speak about the stage, you have to rely upon eye-witnesses. This is so whether you give your own account, if you are lucky enough to be there, or the accounts, suitably checked, of others who were present.

Jamaica is a multi-racial society in which European and African elements predominate. The demographics supplied by the Statistical Institute of Jamaica (STATIN) in 2008 disclose that, of the total population of 2,600,006 for the year 2001, blacks accounted for 2,378,104; and the remainder (221,902) was comprised of East Indians, Chinese, whites, Jews/Lebanese and others.

The material that follows is organized under the following major headings:

The period up to the First World War: The colonial legacy; touring companies, the death of Queen Victoria (1901); the status of European dance; variety and Christmas Morning concerts; the status of African-derived ritual; ragtime and the introduction of black American expression and experience; first dance schools.

The period between the First World War and the Second World War: The pioneer teachers of ballet: Marguerite Squire, Pansy Alexander, Ermyn Ellis, Herma Dias and others; the continuation of the Variety concert; Buck and Wing and the emergence of vaudeville and the revue; Father Pfister and the Merry Bulbulites; Lindsay Downer and *The Fireflies*, and *Clowns and Clatter*; the Martindale Promenaders; Kid Harold (Harold Smith) and the Butterfly Troupe; Marcus Garvey's operations at Edelweiss Park under the artistic direction of Gerardo Leon and then of Ranny Williams; great performers from overseas. The founding of the Poetry League of Jamaica (1922), the Jamaica Musical Society (1923) and Jamaica Welfare Limited (started in 1936, enacted by law in 1937); the rise of national consciousness.

The period between the Second World War and independence: The Social Development Commission (the work in drama of Louise Bennett, Ivy Baxter, Easton Lee and Enid Chevannes, for example); the seminal work of Hazel Johnston, her tentative enquiries into the possibilities of a Jamaican ballet; Dudley MacMillan and his presentation of *Hot Chocolate*, *Sugar and Spice* and other revues at the Movies (a cinema); the Little Theatre Movement (LTM) pantomime since 1941; the emergence of other ballet teachers; the Ballet Guild of Jamaica; National Festivals of the Arts since 1955; Ivy Baxter and her pioneer Creative Dance Group; national exposure to Jamaican traditional and ritual dances; Eddy Thomas's and Alma Mock Yen's *Once upon a Seaweed* (music by Thomas, book by Mock Yen); the founding of the UCWI and the Jamaica Library Service, both in 1948; the work, since the 1950s, of sociologist Edward Seaga, who has used his positions privately as scholar and music promoter, and publicly as minister and prime minister, to urge and facilitate the indigenization of Jamaica's political, cultural, artistic and spiritual growth.

Since independence: Rex Nettleford and the National Dance Theatre Company of Jamaica; the Cultural Training Centre, first begun by the Institute of Jamaica, with four schools – the Jamaica School of Dance, School of Art, School of Music and School of Drama – later becoming the Edna Manley College of the Visual and Performing Arts, as dynamo, laboratory and outreach. There was also the Creative Arts Centre at the UWI (later the Philip Sherlock Centre for the Creative Arts). Out of these emerged the dance clubs and dance groups. The growth of the Festival Commission which morphed into the Jamaica Cultural Development Commission (JCDC), with Joyce Campbell as moving spirit behind the popular "Mello-go-roun'" community show, part of the finale of the annual cultural activities across the island; Carifesta '76 Grand Gala at the National Stadium which presented multi-cultural offerings from around the Caribbean region; dance in Jamaica as a reflection of our times; our essential eclecticism; the maturity of a Jamaican art and the emergence of "Brand Jamaica".

Later contemporary practitioners: In drama, dance, music, speech and design (lighting, sets, costumes).

Landmark productions of the century, and profiles of leading practitioners.

The impact of technology: Print, radio, film, television, the Internet.

Globalization.

Kapo (Mallica Reynolds) intuitive artist and Revivalist leader

From the early years of the colony, the planters were intolerant of African religious customs and practices. Their intolerance grew with each fresh shipment of slaves, whose cultural baggage they regarded as pagan, fraught with witchcraft and abomination. In their efforts to destroy the Africans' heritage, they all but completely eliminated scores of languages and dialects, and the other constituent arts and practices of those cultures. It was, of course, easier to control the slaves, once speakers of the same tongue were separated from each other and forced to communicate in the language of their masters. From the slavers' viewpoint, this facilitated the detection of conspiracy and thus reduced the incidence of revolt. Less than fifty years ago, Kapo (Mallica Reynolds), acknowledged today as Jamaica's greatest intuitive artist, was arrested on a charge of practising obeah, because he dared to carve an image on the head of his walking stick.

A number of factors account for such African retentions as exist today. They include: (1) the large number of slaves, who brought their cultures to Jamaica over a three-hundred-year period; (2) the Maroon enclaves legalized following the treaties between the British and the runaway slaves, 1738–39; (3) the "Free Villages" for the former slaves, established by some of the churches in the hinterland following Emancipation in 1838; (4) publications and presentations by such folklorists and scholars as Walter Jekyll (1904), Astley Clerk (1913), Martha Beckwith (1922–29), and Louise Bennett (later Coverley), who emerged as poet, storyteller and comedienne in the 1940s; (5) the island-wide arts festival movement, which was inaugurated in 1955 to mark Jamaica 300, a year-long event to celebrate three hundred years of association with Great Britain; (6) the fieldwork of Olive Lewin and Marjorie Whylie for the Jamaica School of Music, of Joyce Campbell for the Jayteens and the Cultural Development Commission, and Cheryl Ryman for the African Caribbean Institute of Jamaica; (7) since 1962 productions of the National Dance Theatre Company of Jamaica under the direction of Rex Nettleford as well as other dance companies which emerged subsequently.

As the country creolized both European and African cultural elements, Jamaican folkways emerged. These folkways are rich in theatrical possibilities, such as Jonkonnu (John Canoe), ring games, Anancy stories, nine nights, wakes, bruckins, tea meetings, mock trials. Even so, a Euro-centred education discouraged black Jamaicans with social aspirations from indulging in African-oriented or folk-derived practices; and even when they knew them, some children were forbidden by their parents to sing Jamaican folk songs at home. It was not until 1939 that the Musical Society of Jamaica reluctantly agreed to create classes for Jamaican folk music in their biennial All-Island Music Festival; and although elocution contests had become a norm, and numbered, for example, national hero Marcus Garvey among organizers in 1913, Jamaican dialect did not become a category in the Poetry League's All-Island Speech Festival until 1950. These and other innovations were eventually made possible by changes that had been taking place in the mindset and basic assumptions of Jamaican society.

The first generation of writers of the twentieth century began publishing before the First World War. Among them were journalist, editor and novelist H.G. DeLisser (1878–1944); poet, historian and novelist W. Adolphe Roberts (1886–1962); and poet and novelist Claude McKay (1890–1948). They had either acquired, or were soon to acquire, reputations as men of letters at home and abroad. There were also a remarkable number of poets, including Tom Redcam (Thomas Henry MacDermot) and J.E. Clare MacFarlane, who were subsequently named poet laureates of Jamaica – Tom Redcam posthumously in 1933, and McFarlane in 1952. The positive attitudes which this generation of writers had inherited from their Victorian fathers were not shaken by the war. Great Britain had won as everybody had righteously expected, and the foundations of Western civilization had thus been preserved.

The return from active service overseas of many Jamaicans of all shades and colours had helped to develop a consciousness of the existence of lands other than Great Britain outside the Caribbean; many went to seek fame and fortune in the neighbouring Caribbean republics and in the United States. World events were making a great impact upon Jamaican and other West Indian thought, and there was now more of a tendency to examine things for one's self.

Other factors were also at work. The Jamaican was developing pride in his ancestry, whether that ancestry was European, African, Asian or a mixing and blending of these races. The acceptance of self as an African Jamaican became, in the oratorical flights of Marcus Garvey, a bold and positive assertion. The masses were beginning to liberate themselves as a creative force; Jamaican intellectuals were now becoming more discriminating in their selection and use of productive elements from other cultures which they could make inevitably their own.

The riots and mass demonstrations that began in St Kitts in 1935, and spread like wildfire to other parts of the Caribbean and to Jamaica in 1938, were symptomatic of a seething discontent with the status quo, and an expression of the irrevocable demands of the masses for such basics as better food, clothing and shelter, and greater opportunities for their families. The dramatic conversion of the intellectuals that followed was to prepare the movement for the rectification of economic ills with the philosophical basis of self-government. In Jamaica, the new dynamic brought to the forefront fresh urges and insights into the island's cultural, artistic and political life. The voices from the poets became more urgent, more immediate and more in consonance with the emotional qualities of the common people. When *Voices from Summerland*, the first anthology of Jamaican poetry, appeared in 1930, the London *Times*, in reviewing the volume, said, "The canon of dominions will not be finally made up even after India and Burma have been added to it."

The year 1936 was an important one for several reasons. Jamaica Welfare Limited was conceived by Norman Manley (later named a national hero) to promote community development throughout the island. The Jamaica Arts Society, under the leadership of Theodore Sealy and Martin Smith of the *Daily Gleaner*, organized a major All-Island Exhibition of Art and Crafts, and Edna Manley, later to be recognized as the "mother" of Jamaican art, produced her monumental sculpture *Negro Aroused*. The Roman Catholic Church staged the great pageant *Jamaica Triumphant*, which traced the history of Jamaica from the days of the Tainos and the coming of Christopher Columbus. In addition, the country proliferated with literary and debating societies.

The following notes should provide a key to the context in which the first plays of modern Jamaica were created, and to the basic assumptions of their writers and audiences. Most of these plays are listed here for the reader's information, and for his later study as opportunity serves:

1. Tom Redcam's poetic play *San Gloria* (a closet drama) (1920)
2. Alexander McGregor James's *A Soul of Sacrifice*, a domestic drama in six scenes (1926)
3. E.M. Cupidon's dramatization of H.G. DeLisser's novels: *Susan Proudleigh* (1930), *Jamaica Bandits* (1931), *Jane's Career* (1933)
4. Marcus Garvey's *The Coronation of an African King*, *Roaming Jamaicans*, and *Slavery: From Hut to Mansion* (1930), and *Wine, Women and War* (1932)
5. Una Marson's *At What Price* (1932), *London Calling* (1937), and *Pocomania* (1938)
6. Esther Chapman's *The West Indian* (1936), and *Travelling Light* (1950)
7. Frank Hill's *Upheaval* (1939)
8. Archie Lindo's *Forbidden Fruit* (1941), *Under the Skin* (1943), and his adaptations of H.G. DeLisser's *White Witch of Rose Hall* (1945)
9. Captain Wayne Reid's *The Maroon* (1947)
10. Roger Mais's *Hurricane* (1943), *Atlanta in Calydon* (1950), and *George William Gordon* (still to be produced)
11. Bim and Bam's *De Burial of A.B.* (1943), *Extravaganza: Comical Mock Trial* (1947), *Mr Ghost Goes to Town* (1948), and *Rhygin's Ghost* (1949)
12. Elsie Benjamin's *One Soja Man* (1945)
13. George Campbell's *Play Without Scenery: A Fantasy* (1948)

Among the more successful of these twenty-eight works in stage presentation were the adaptations of H.G. DeLisser's novels by Cupidon and Lindo, Chapman's *The West Indian*, Una Marson's *Pocomania*, Hill's *Upheaval*, Bim and Bam's *De Burial of A.B.*, Elsie Benjamin's *One Soja Man* and Archie Lindo's *The White Witch of Rose Hall*, which played to overflowing houses at the Strand Theatre in Montego Bay, the general area for the setting for the story.

DeLisser was one of the first West Indian writers of note to treat the lower working classes from their own point of view. He was very happy with Cupidon's adaptations. Cupidon himself played the female title roles; and these productions brought to the boards, to be taken seriously and without apology, the dialect spoken by the vast majority of Jamaicans. A highly polished show, the *West Indian* was Jamaica's first musical, and had a cast of some seventy players. *Pocomania* was inspired by the African-Christian religious cult of that name. The riots of 1938 provided the setting for *Upheaval*. *De Burial of A B* satirized the funeral of a most hated district constable named Arthur Bartley. Those whom he had grievously wronged, and even those who had only heard about him, turned out in thousands to block traffic and to harass the funeral procession on its way to the cemetery. When in concluding the last rites the parson said "Ashes to ashes and dust to dust", the crowd shouted abuse, hurled stones and showered buckets of excrement into the grave.

In producing *One Soja Man*, Elsie Benjamin challenged the theatre establishment to put on an increasing number of shows that were relevant to Jamaican concerns. Bim and Bam's *Rhygin's Ghost* (1949) derives from the same story that inspired the

The Little Theatre, 2011. *Photo by Anya Gloudon.*

Perry Henzell and Trevor Rhone film *The Harder They Come* (1970), and the Michael Thelwell novel of the same name (1980). Attempts were made to cast the productions in accordance with the ethnic types required by each drama. Most of the plays noted were staged just before or during the Second World War (1939–45). Jamaicans contributed generously to the war effort in terms of men and women in service, and cash, but felt that to suspend cultural and artistic activities for the duration of the war would have meant paying too great a tribute to the enemy.

When the second generation of writers came into their own after the Second World War, a revolt had already started against the tradition established by Tom Redcam and the earlier school of poets. Except for the works of writers like W. Adolphe Roberts and Vivian Virtue – who, along with Tom Redcam, have written dramas or dramatic fragments presented on radio (by Wycliffe Bennett and Cynthia Wilmot) but never staged – there were now fewer sonnets, villanelles and poems in blank verse and other traditional forms. Poets – among them, M.G. Smith, H.G. Carberry, George Campbell, Philip Sherlock, Kenneth Ingram, Basil McFarlane and A.L. "Mickey" Hendricks – continued to sing but they did so in *vers libre*. Perhaps the most important talent of the new school was George Campbell, whose strikingly original pieces appeared under the title of *First Poems* (1945). After his *Play without Scenery* (1948) we hear no more from him as a playwright.

Increasingly, the novel was to claim the energies of some of Jamaica's best literary talents: Roger Mais, Vic Reid, John Hearne, Sylvia Wynter, Andrew Salkey. We have already taken note of Roger Mais's dramas. A dramatization by Sylvia Wynter of his novel *Brother Man* (1954) is still to be staged, and another, *Black Lightning* (1955), was adapted by Archie Lindo and given a Barn Theatre production by Trevor Nairne in 1982. Sylvia Wynter's *Ssh . . . It's a Wedding*, a musical, did not survive an unfortunate opening in Spanish Town in 1961. *Under the Sun*, which she adapted from her own novel *The Hills of Hebron* (1962), is a viable piece which still awaits production. Her *1865: A Ballad for a Rebellion*, an epic drama to mark the centenary of the Morant Bay Rebellion of 1865, was given major production by the Government of Jamaica at the Little Theatre in 1965. With Alex Gradussov, she wrote the script for the LTM pantomime *Rockstone Anancy* in 1970. The authors described this show as a magical morality.

Up to about the 1950s, with the exception of the LTM's annual pantomime, most productions played for only a few nights or up to a week at most, and often came off the boards before they had a chance to jell. Support was usually stratified and segmented: productions by the elite had an upper-class following, middle-class offerings with corresponding fans, and Bim and Bam and Ranny Williams, who wrote and produced primarily for and about the lower classes, commanded a decidedly lower-class patronage. Productions like *Upheaval* and *Pocomania* called for mixed casts (blacks, whites and browns) and audience interest widened accordingly.

In any event, the theatre-going public up to that time was rather small. When the Jamaica Arts Society staged Shakespeare's *Twelfth Night* in 1939, in the Ward Theatre under the direction of Joan Grant, an Englishwoman, they were more concerned with considerations of characterization than of colour. Major qualifications were, and should be, that the player should look the part, move well and be able to act, and have the appropriate voice quality as well as speak the verse well – a factor which was to slow down the process of integration for some time. The All-Island Speech Festival, supported by a structured speech-training programme in an increasing number of schools, had begun to meet this challenge. It was the incomparable E.M. Cupidon, who by sheer force of talent had penetrated the colour bar in the late 1920s, who helped to pave the way, as we entered the 1940s and 1950s, for the development of an interracial theatre.

It is generally recognized that the accepted forms of institutional and social life are of European derivation: government, religion, family and kinship, law, property, education, economy and language. But, as the Jamaican educator Reginald Murray, who lived in Africa, remarked:

> African ways are commonly observable – in the fundamental importance of kinship, in diet and eating habits, in the place given to mutual-aid schemes, in economic life (for example, schemes for planting and reaping crops and for assuring decent burial); in survivals of superstitions; in magical rites; in vocabulary, tone and flavour of speech. There are African drum-beats and rhythms everywhere and Anancy, the Ashanti spider-god, is the folk tale hero of Jamaica who performs great feats with astonishing cunning and dissimulation.[3]

2

Overview of Theatrical Activities

The Jamaican Theatre provides an important component of "Brand Jamaica". Powerfully understood and recognized, the "brand" draws upon a broad range of activities in our Jamaican culture: sports, cuisine, fashion, politics, religion, life sciences and the arts.

In Jamaica, such an artist is Robert Nesta (Bob) Marley. He led the placement of reggae music on the world stage and his name has become synonymous with Jamaica's name internationally. At the Beijing Summer Olympics in China in 2008, Jamaica produced Usain Bolt, triple gold medallist, the fastest human in recorded history, who led his team of other Jamaican Olympic record-breaking champions. On their triumphal return home the athletes were given a rousing reception during a ten-day period of celebrations organized by the government across the island. As they visited their schools, friends, families and well-wishers, perhaps the most stirring of responses came from the parents and guardians of the athletes, who demonstrated in their remarks a passionate concern for a more wholesome, crime-free society, and the basic nobility of the ordinary Jamaican.

Marley's *One Love* has achieved the status almost of a world anthem, and his album *Catch a Fire* is a great treasure. Both the song and the album are regarded among the more significant achievements of music in the twentieth century. Other contributors of distinction to Jamaica's image include Louise Bennett Coverley and Ranny Williams, who by sheer force of performance have stamped their authority on national acceptance of the Jamaican vernacular and folklore. Professor Rex Nettleford has shepherded the National Dance Theatre Company of Jamaica, since it was founded by Eddy Thomas and himself in 1962, and has maintained close contact with such institutions as the Little Theatre Movement (LTM), with sixty-seven years of pantomime to date, the Jamaica Cultural Development Commission (JCDC), with its tradition of festival, the Institute of Jamaica, and the Edna Manley College. They have all raised the Jamaican flag so high that, metaphorically speaking, it can be seen both at home and abroad, in the diaspora and beyond, and fill Jamaicans with a sense of self-worth, peace and satisfaction.

This development has been enhanced with the widespread use of radio, film, television and the Internet as tools of creativity and communication. In film there is the potential to accommodate, at the same time, a multiplicity of perspectives that are themselves the aspects of modern sensibility.

There is a paradigm shift each time a new tool is added to the communications spectrum. The old tools are not abandoned. Their use is simply repositioned. Artists of the classical and romantic periods of Europe sought to achieve rhythm, euphony, magic and beauty, and would be imitated by colonials whose living imaginations would at times create enduring "sturdy growths on their own soil", which earned the respect and plaudits of scholars and practitioners at places of higher learning elsewhere.[1] So when, for example the London *Times* said of Vic Reid's *The Leopard* that the author writes as if no one had ever written English before, and that his prose is as fresh as the spring buds unfolding, an observer will note that the reason why the Jamaican artist seems so self-assured is that he knows that his achievement helps to constitute an integral component that is uniquely Jamaican.

Visitors to Jamaica over the last four decades have often expressed surprise at the range and variety of our theatrical productions. Take any year: an observer in 1971 would note that, while the Jamaican theatre continues to reflect international trends, the major emphasis now is on the development of indigenous efforts. During the first half of 1971, the Jamaica Broadcasting Corporation organized a nation-wide "talent hunt". The search was conducted among all age groups, and was designed to discover and display artistic talent. Entries included singing groups, verse-speaking choirs, dancers, village bands, pop singers, magicians, comedians, acrobats, monologists, storytellers – nearly every kind of entertainment. At the final show on television in July, the top award went to a fourteen-year-old boy, Keith Campbell, from the western parish of Hanover, who had told in dialect a folk tale about Br'er Anancy and Poor Patoo.

By the end of October, several groups had staged a variety of shows. In addition to the 1970–71 pantomime *Rockstone Anancy*, the LTM offered an open air presentation of *A Midsummer Night's Dream* at Vale Royal, later the official residence of the prime minister. The National Theatre Trust produced Giraudoux's *Tiger at the Gates* and two plays by the Trinidadian playwright Charles Archibald, *Junction Village* and *Rose Slip*. From the Jamaica Amateur Operatic Society we had *Lock up Your Daughters*, by Bernard Miles, adapted from Henry Fielding's comedy, *Rape upon Rape*; and from the Jamaica School of Music a noble effort at staging Mozart's *Don Giovanni*. The Jamaica Playhouse mounted Bill Manhoff's *Owl and the Pussy Cat*, Peter Nichols's *A Day in the Death of Joe Egg*, and *Othello*. The National Dance Theatre Company introduced into their annual show some new numbers, notably *Kumina*, a possession dance based on the local retentions of a Kikongo rite.

Pauline Stone and Volier Johnson in *Junction Village*, by Charles Archibald

For the Eight O'Clock players, Tony Gambrill and Eddy Thomas created a new musical, *Paradise Street*. The St Lucian dramatic poet Derek Walcott brought his Trinidad Theatre Workshop on a visit and staged his *Ti Jean and His Brothers* and *Dream on Monkey Mountain*. The Caribbean Thespians Dramatic Society celebrated their twenty-fifth anniversary with a production of the *Great Big Doorstep*, adapted from E.P. O'Donnell's novel by Francis Goodrich and Albert Hackett.

The Barn Theatre produced *What the Butler Saw*, and a new local play by Trevor

Rhone, *Smile Orange*. There were thirty-one entries in the Secondary Schools' Drama Festival. In 1971 the National Festival, which embraces all the arts, also included sections for primary and all-age schools, as well as for adult amateur, professional and semi-professional drama productions. An encouraging feature of the primary schools' section was that the most successful productions were both written and produced by the teachers. The Jamaican Folk Singers combined song, dance and mime in their presentation of Jamaican folk songs; and the folk and traditional categories of the national dance finals kept many Jamaicans in touch with this aspect of their theatrical antecedents. This catalogue of presentations for 1971 alone, by no means complete, suggest a robust infrastructure.

Paradise Street, a musical by Tony Gambrill and Eddy Thomas, with Linda Gambrill (*left*) and Grace McGhie, 1970

An important aspect of the theatrical classics lies in the training opportunity they provide for practitioners and audiences alike. Directing on the whole has been good and at times inspired. There was a good deal of magic in Noel Vaz's alfresco production of *A Midsummer Night's Dream* (1943), Carroll Dawes's *The Unravelled Sleeve*, adapted from *Macbeth* (1959), Paul Methuen's *Merry Wives of Windsor* (1971) and Rawle Gibbons's *The Tempest*, set on an isle with enchanting strains of steel band music (1982).

In acting, we can trace a line of landmark performances: Dorothy Blondel Francis's flawed regality as Gertrude (1944), Vere Johns's pathetically obdurate Shylock (1950), Slade Hopkinson's titanic King Lear (1955), Ronald Harrison's Caliban and Barbara Carter's "admired Miranda" (1955), Jean Brown's lyrically moving Juliet (1957), Edward Baugh's "self-loving" Malvolio (1961) and his enviably noble Banquo (1974), Leonie Forbes Amiel's fun-loving and scheming Maria (1966), and Reggie Carter's towering performances in the leading roles of Molière's *School for Wives* and *The Imaginary Invalid* (1982).

In an article entitled "Monster of Anancyism", the Jamaican poet and painter Gloria Escoffery identified a link between Shakespeare and Br'er Anancy:

> Corruption as it is practiced in Jamaica is no simple *ad hoc* bribing of state officials. It is, as designated in the infrequently used metaphor, a cancer; at the heart of it is a bureaucratic system which, being a monster of reality and anancyism, invites further corruption, impinging on the lives of citizens in their commercial and political transactions, and in the very near centre of their private lives . . . Most persons accept this fact cynically as a way of life which surely has the validity of international currency; a few regret the necessity of condoning evil, but weigh the heavy positive benefits of conformity in the system against the disadvantages, deciding like Shakespeare's Launcelot Gobbo that the fiend gives more practical advice than conscience.[2]

In the online editor's forum of the *Gleaner* on 9 October 2006, Colin Campbell, a journalist by profession who over a period of some thirteen years has been sequentially parliamentary secretary, minister of state and minister responsible for various ministries, had this to say: "I am not going to say that there is no corruption taking

A Midsummer Night's Dream, produced and directed by Noel Vaz and Hazel Johnston in 1943 on the grounds of Holy Cross Church, Kingston, with Vaz and Margaret Lauder

place. I would be crazy and stupid to say that . . . But I can tell you that where the allegations have been made, the Government has been quick to make sure that they are properly investigated."

As in Shakespeare's time, today's Jamaican theatre holds the mirror up to life. Plays like Patrick Brown's *Dirty Diana* and Basil Dawkins's *Uptown Bangarang* treat the current drug trade and other dishonesties overrunning Jamaica. Shakespeare has at times assumed the role of the national playwright. This was partially so because every child writing the overseas Cambridge Examinations at high school had to study one or more of his plays as set books. Up to 1962 he was the author most often performed, and has been used to help celebrate special events. When, for example, the British Council in association with the LTM and other groups sponsored the first Drama Festival for Secondary Schools in 1950, the presentations were all chosen from the Shakespearean canon, and the adjudicator was none other than Nugent Monck, English actor and producer, disciple of William Poel, and founder of the famous Maddermarket Theatre in Norwich, England. The British Council was anxious to give as many local actors and directors as possible a chance of working with Monck, and arranged that, in addition to his assignment as adjudicator of the Festival, he would remain on the island long enough to direct the *Merchant of Venice* at the Ward Theatre.

Tony Watson, actor and director

The festival was an unqualified success. Thousands of spectators flocked to the Garrison Theatre at Up Park Camp to see the performances. A refreshing feature was the remarkably high quality of speech and the standard of acting reached by the young performers. Mr Monck was particularly taken with the ability of some of the actors, and was moved to remark on separate occasions that the Caliban in *The Tempest*, and one of the Emilias in *Othello*, were as good as he had ever seen. Tony Lopez of St George's College played Emilia in *Othello*, and Carroll Morrison (Dawes) of St Hilda's High School for Girls, Caliban (poet/beast) in *The Tempest*.

Monck was seventy-three years old when he arrived in Jamaica. A talented young Jamaican director, Maurice Harty, was appointed assistant director. The LTM recruited the cast for *The Merchant of Venice* from all the existing theatrical groups and by public audition. The production contained a number of performances of high quality; for example, C.G.X. Henriques as a Duke, Dorothy Blondel Francis as Portia, Claire Bennett as Jessica, George Lazarus as Lorenzo, Robert Verity as Tubal, Barry and Lloyd Reckord as Old Gobbo and Launcelot Gobbo, respectively, and Vere Johns, whose orchestration of the role of the viciously vindictive Shylock remains legendary. Most of these players have made substantial contributions to the development of a Jamaican acting tradition.

The popularity of the classics, especially of Shakespeare, was based partly upon factors inherent in these dramas – in particular the fact that they were written by poets for an aural tradition – and partly upon the work in voice and speech training that has formed part of the country's cultural and artistic growth during the last one hundred years or more. As in England, "received" pronunciation became more than a badge of social distinction: it was often regarded as the unmistakable sign of a good education. Insofar as the theatre was concerned, you could not expect to be cast in a play that required "good" or "standard" speech, as some organizers then incorrectly called it, if the director felt that your utterance did not belong. "Good" speech was one of the hallmarks of privilege. Whereas opportunities could be based on education, difficulties would continue to be created unless the literate part of the population could be exposed to the same acceptable speech training.

A general assault upon the problem was suggested during the first decades of the twentieth century when a number of public-spirited persons began organizing and

Shakespeare's *The Tempest*, in a 1969 production by Paul Methuen (*centre*, as Prospero), with Roger Roger as Ariel and Pat Gooden as Miranda. *Photo by Maria LaYacona.*

Shakespeare's *The Merry Wives of Windsor*, with Louise Bennett (Coverley) and Peter Hunt, in a 1968 production directed by Paul Methuen. *Photo by Maria LaYacona.*

supporting elocution contests. The Jesuit fathers of St George's College (a high school for boys) and a number of persons, including Marcus Garvey (Jamaica's first national hero), were among the pioneers. Poetry, prose and dramatic pieces are still chosen not only from the English-speaking world and from other literatures in English translation, but also from the Jamaican dialect. It is recognized that candidates who excel in the international pieces usually do as well or better in their Jamaican dialect selections.

During the eighteenth, nineteenth and twentieth centuries there developed a tradition of regular touring companies to the island that was halted during the First World War (1914–18) and from the outbreak of the Second World War in 1939. Historians recall 1745, when the Irish actor John Moody came to Jamaica, produced and acted in a number of Shakespearean productions with amateurs, proposed to erect a theatre in Kingston by public subscription and returned to England a year later in order to recruit resident actors. From 1776 to 1783, the Hallams and Douglasses and their London (later called the American) Company of Comedians settled in Jamaica, and presented almost all of Shakespeare's plays during that period. The company also had in their repertoire a number of traditional English pantomimes, among them *Robinson Crusoe or Harlequin Friday* and *The Genii*, offered as very popular afterpieces. Richardson Wright in his *Revels in Jamaica* notes that in New York it became a feather in a player's cap if he could be billed as late of the Jamaican stage.[3]

The twentieth century opened with remarkable flourish. Errol Hill[4] reminds us that in 1898 the naval and military officers at Port Royal reintroduced the English pantomime in its modern form, when for Christmas entertainment they gave *Aladdin* at their station. That was followed in 1899 by four performances of *Dick Whittington and His Cat*, the last two showings taking place at the Theatre Royal in Kingston, on 16 and 17 January 1900. The British Army and Navy regularly staged theatricals for their own entertainment and that of their friends, right up to the time of their departure following Jamaica's independence in 1962.

Other productions at the beginning of the century included the *Belle of New York*, directed by Madame de Montagnac at the Theatre Royal in 1901. In 1905, Sir Frank Benson's Stage Company toured the West Indies with a company of thirty-five, and during the 1920s and 1930s the Florence Glossop-Harris Company, as well as various other combinations of players, came annually.

Benson's Company played only one week at the Theatre Royal in Kingston, but what a week that was. Every night offered a new play: *The Taming of the Shrew*, *Hamlet*, *Romeo and Juliet*, *The Merry Wives of Windsor*, *Twelfth Night*, *Richard III*, and Goldsmith's *She Stoops to Conquer*. There were several players of worldwide reputation in this great company: Nigel Playfair; Matheson Lang and his wife, Hutin Briton; W.E. Halloway, who had acted with Henry Irving; and Stanley Drewitt, who afterwards brought his own company to Jamaica. Not all touring companies were of this indisputably high quality. But Horace Vaz, a contemporary, spoke lyrically of the Florence Glossop-Harris Company, whose repertoire consisted of three types of offerings: current London and New York hits, Shakespeare, and a miscellany of classical and romantic period pieces. Alongside the offerings of the touring companies were the efforts of local groups, who by the second decade of the twentieth century were demonstrating the bifurcation which was to become a feature of the Jamaican Theatre: in one branch were the imported scripts, classical and modern; and in the other the plays of Jamaican writers.

De Prophet, by "the Negro Ballet from Jamaica", performed before the Queen of England about 1882. *Courtesy of NLJ.*

The first attempts to generate shows locally on a sustained basis were those of Lindsay Downer, who had the social stature and flair to command the necessary support. He began staging variety entertainment in 1917 in aid of the 1914–18 war effort, and followed up with a number of conventional British plays after the war. He devised and staged his aristocratic revues, *The Fireflies* and *Clowns and Clatter*, at Christmastime in the Ward Theatre from 1923 to 1930. His shows had much of the glitter that characterized the *Ziegfeld Follies* of New York – exciting dancing, shapely girls, imaginative decor and attractive costumes, comic sketches and vaudeville specialities – but in spite of all this, they retained a freshness and a spontaneity that were reminiscent of his less pretentious wartime shows. Until 1928, participants in these shows were either white or passed for white. First nights were glittering social events with overflow audiences headed by the governor and his lady. In 1928, *Clowns and Clatter* replaced *The Fireflies* and was jointly produced by Lindsay Downer and Susan Alexander, who invited E.M. Cupidon, a man of colour, to take part.

Cupidon, Jamaica's first great comedian with a national

Una Soutar as Kissie, with two men, in "Conspirators Three Are We", in *Belle of New York*, 1901. *Courtesy of Nicola Mair (Soutar's granddaughter).*

reputation, by sheer force of talent penetrated the colour bar in the 1930s, thus helping to pave the way for an interracial theatre. For the quality of his comic acting, Ranny Williams had very high praise:

> I was greatly impressed at the time watching Stanley Morand, Cupidon and Ableton and Harold and Trim, who were the outstanding entertainers. Stanley Morand was an able one-man comic, as well as a good team player. Sometimes he would team up with Cupes and Abe. Morand often presented the pattern of a "sad face", "dead pan comedian". He would make people laugh, not only from his material, but also from his gestures and facial expression. Insofar as I can remember, he never did any impersonations.
>
> Now Cupes was also a good monologist but he depended more upon his gestures and facial expressions than upon his material. He was an excellent female impersonator, and also a most dependable team player. He was generous in ensemble and the younger fellows felt secure when acting in his company.[5]

The first dances choreographed and staged in a theatre or hall in Jamaica were probably performed by foreigners, because, as we have noted, visits from abroad by touring companies had been a feature of Jamaican entertainment since the early years of the eighteenth century. At least two efforts were made to establish dancing schools before the First World War. By letter and by advertisement in the *Daily Gleaner* of 8 January 1907, Mrs H. MacPherson gave notice of the opening of her Kingston and Half Way Tree Academy, at which music and dancing classes would be given. According to her letter, "there will be facilities for those desirous of acquiring the true art of dancing. Adult classes,

Dance of the Seven Veils, with Ermyn Ellis (*centre*). *Courtesy of NLJ.*

gents & ladies, class course 12 lessons, embracing the latest London ballroom dances, 1 guinea. Fancy dances for children – skirt, tambourine, scarf, flower caprice, dance fantasia, terms according to arrangement."[6] No dance items were presented when the Academy gave its recitals in 1909 and 1910, and soon afterward Mrs MacPherson announced that she would be omitting dancing from her syllabus to concentrate on music. On 5 October 1911, the following notice appeared in the *Daily Gleaner*: "Dancing Classes: Miss Bertram will resume her Children's Dancing classes on Friday, 6 Oct. at Cowen Music Room [Astley Clerk's music room] at 14 King St."[7]

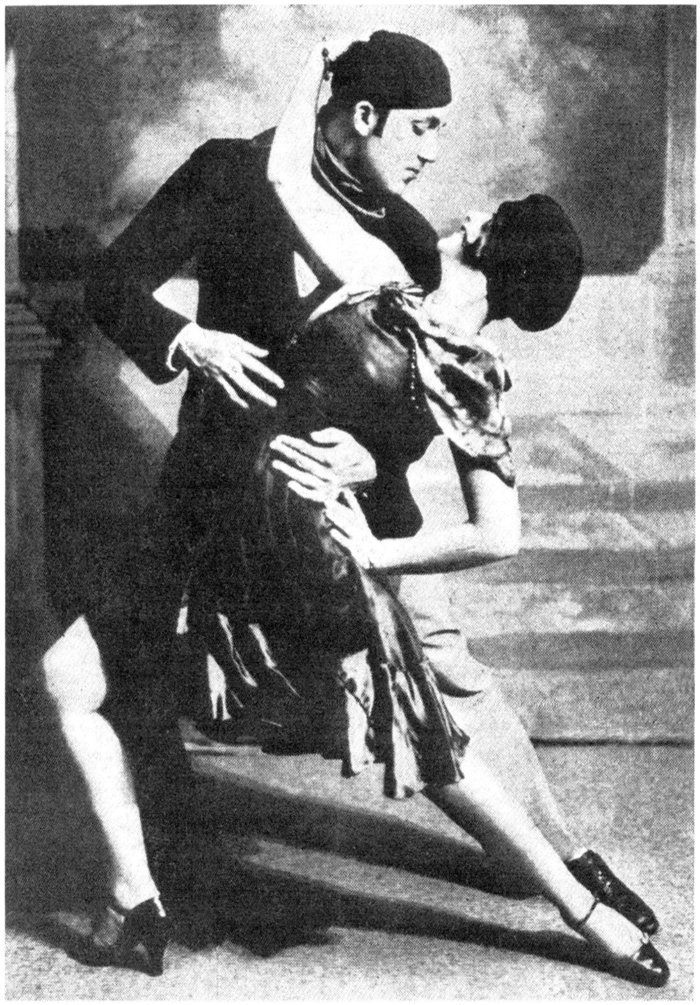

Kathleen McCormack and Eugene Martinez in *The Dance of the Underworld* at the Ward Theatre, April 1928, by the Mayfair Promenaders. *Courtesy of NLJ.*

Up to the First World War, dance had not become a popular offering. The main "carriers" of dance at that time were the circus and vaudeville companies, by which there was a veritable invasion. There were locally mounted musicals, like *Miss Hook of Holland* and *The Manchester Follies*, both in 1911, in the first of which Miss Bertram performed. In the second, Ina Leyden sang beautifully and danced very well.

From these little beginnings and by unflinching efforts, over the century, a succession of dedicated teachers took the art of dance to the masses. Today the island has become saturated with a great many dance groups of all ages, classes and conditions, which, all things considered, is most remarkable. The great exemplar is, of course, Rex Nettleford and his world famous National Dance Theatre Company. There are now four other senior companies: Movements, led by Monica Campbell McFarlane; L'Acadco by L'Antoinette Stines; Stella Maris by Monika Lawrence; and the Company Dance Theatre by Tony Wilson. All the Companies provide training, of course, but the island-wide movement is sustained primarily by the fieldwork of the JCDC and the ongoing training provided by the School of Dance component of the Edna Manley College.

At the opening of the twentieth century the country had a social pyramid with whites at the top, browns in the middle and blacks at the base. It will be noted that the whites have never exceeded sixteen thousand, and that today they constitute less than half of 1 per cent of the population, whereas the blacks and coloureds together over these years have consistently accounted for an overwhelming 95 per cent.[8]

Education, of course, in the early years of the century, meant European education, and the arts continued to be the amiable pastime of the privileged. Participation in European or European-derived practices was controlled by position on the colour scale and by education. Gentlemen players and amateur dramatic societies were mounting shows of considerable polish that invited favourable comparison with presentations of the same works either seen in or on tour from England.

Despite the fact that the theatrical scene continued to be dominated by touring companies from overseas, local enthusiasts ensured that a show produced locally would mark the opening of the Ward Theatre, the keys for which were handed over to the city by the donor, the Honourable Charles James Ward, Lieutenant Colonel, custos of Kingston, in a ceremony on 16 December 1912. The local group called themselves the Amateur Dramatic Club, and chose Gilbert and Sullivan's *The Pirates of Penzance*. The production had upwards of fifty performers and a seventeen-piece orchestra. Publicity advises that the costumes were "from Messrs B.J. Simmons and Company, the same costumiers for the late Mr D'Oyley Carte", and a further note says that "this beautiful opera is being put on the stage at great labour and without regard for expense". Of the performance itself, the poet H.S. Bunbury wrote:

Una Soutar. *Courtesy of Nicola Mair.*

> Were I compelled to compress into the briefest space my impression of Thursday night's performance of *The Pirates of Penzance* I should say it was admirable. Yet in my mind lingers the memory of the *Pirates* as I heard it in London in the year it was produced and acted by the accomplished D'Oyley Carte Company with George Grossmith as Major-General . . . I consider that the Amateur Dramatic Club performers have come as near to the professional standard of efficiency as it is practicable for amateurs ever to attain. Kingston has reason to be proud of them.[9]

The following December, in 1913, the Amateur Dramatic Club produced Oscar Wilde's *The Importance of Being Earnest*, after which they ceased to function. (This is the very Bunbury whom Wilde uses for his absentee character in *The Importance of Being Earnest*.)

In January 1911, while the Ward Theatre was being built, George Bernard Shaw, the Irish playwright, essayist and philosopher, paid a visit to his socialist colleague and friend Sir Sydney Olivier, governor of Jamaica. He addressed a press conference and made observations which were still timely and relevant in 2008. Shaw said that the city wanted for three things: an indigenous theatre with touring companies kept firmly out of it, a first-rate local orchestra, and excellent architecture. When Shaw spoke, Kingston was still recovering from the ravages of the 1907 earthquake, and he thought that the opportunity to rebuild the city in a manner worthy of a national capital should not be missed.

There are three citations on marble plaques on the front of the Ward Theatre building on North Parade. They commemorate the gift by Colonel Ward to the parish of Kingston in 1911 and the erection of the building by the Henriques Brothers, and the third notes that a public theatre has stood on the present site since 1775. The Ward Theatre is the finest theatre of its kind in the English-speaking Caribbean. Until recently it was still at the centre of municipal and civic life. The greatest personalities in the Jamaican theatre and world-famous celebrities have performed on its stage. Jamaica's two major political parties, the People's National Party (PNP) and the Jamaica Labour Party (JLP), were launched there in 1938 and 1943, respectively.

Up to the late 1930s, when, as a teenager, Wycliffe Bennett had been participating in elocution contests and attending plays for some time, the number of black faces in the audience at theatrical productions could be counted on the fingers of one hand. Legally, blacks could attend, but the economic and social considerations – having to find the admission fee, to dress up and make their way there and back home – and the fact that they would feel ill-at-ease in what were essentially all white gatherings, made many take the attitude that such events were not intended for and had nothing to do with them. Some who were devout Christians nurtured a puritanical conviction that the theatre was an ungodly place. In any case, the theatre of those days, with its reliance upon touring companies, or local productions of foreign plays, mirrored a social content and a lifestyle that were, at that time, alien to the majority of Jamaican people.

Productions of Shakespeare by touring companies were among the first plays seen by early Jamaican playwrights. By 1962, however, the local full-length productions of Shakespeare had included *Hamlet*, directed by the Reverend P.W. Gibson (later Anglican Lord Bishop of Jamaica), with the St George's Church Young Men's Dramatic Society, at the Ward Theatre in 1921; *Twelfth Night*, directed by Joan Grant (an Englishwoman) for the Jamaica Arts Society at the Ward in 1939; *A Midsummer Night's Dream*, produced and directed by Jamaicans Noel Vaz and Hazel Johnston for the LTM, in the gardens of Holy Cross Church, Half Way Tree, in 1943; a second *Hamlet*, directed by Molly Ward Johnson (an Englishwoman) for the first Jamaica Drama Festival, organized by Stephen Hill, with Hill in the title role, at the Ward in 1944; and, as already noted, *The Merchant of Venice*, directed by Nugent Monck for the British Council and the LTM at the Ward in 1950. Then there was *The Tempest*, with Slade Hopkinson as Prospero and Ronald Harrison as Caliban, and *King Lear*, with Slade Hopkinson and Hugh Wynter alternating in the title role, for the tercentenary celebrations in 1955; a third *Hamlet*, produced and directed by Jamaicans Wycliffe Bennett and Carroll Dawes, with Reggie Carter as

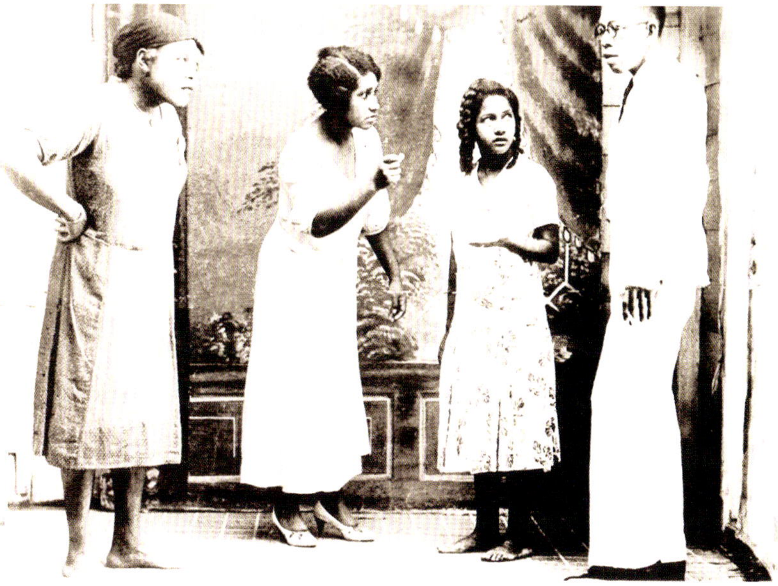

Comedian E.M. Cupidon, Icema and Edna Coverley, and Tom Graham in a dramatic adaptation of H.G. Delisser's novel *Jane's Career*. *Courtesy of NLJ.*

"The Beauty Chorus" of the Mayfair Promenaders, April 1928. *Courtesy of NLJ.*

Kid Harold's Butterfly Troupe of Professional Dancers at the Palace Cinema in Kingston, in *Planter's Punch* magazine, 1929. *Courtesy of NLJ.*

Hamlet and Edward Baugh as Claudius, for the Jamaica Drama League at the Little Theatre in 1961; and a fourth *Hamlet*, produced and directed by Norman Rae, with Alwyn Scott in the title role, Pauline Stone Myrie as Gertrude and Mervyn Alleyne as Claudius in 1994.

Long before Shakespearean productions became so regular on the Jamaican stage, however, the English language had set its seal irrevocably on Jamaica, and had become a standard of reference even for people who could not read Shakespeare. Many a Jamaican peasant would say, "Shakespeare said", and then go on to quote a proverb or some other pithy saying which might not have come from the poet's pen at all. It was felt, as in England, that no major theatre director or actor could enter a claim to greatness until he had measured himself against the works of the man whom Garrick had christened "The Immortal Bard".

In 1941 Greta Bourke (later Fowler) and Henry Fowler founded the LTM and launched its annual pantomime. Until 2002, when the pantomime was moved to the LTM's theatre on Tom Redcam Avenue, the show opened at the Ward Theatre every Boxing Day, 26 December, at 6:00 p.m., except for 1950, when *Alice in Wonderland* had to be accommodated at the Teachers' Hall, Church Street, because the Ward was under repairs.

In 1943 and 1946 the LTM organized the first Primary Schools' Drama Festivals. Together with the later annual Secondary Schools' Drama Festivals and the already existing elocution contests, these efforts provided recruits for adult drama. Theatrical standards had to be achieved, and the right type of play had to be found to give the right opportunity and experience to untrained but potential talent.

Exemplary husbandry of its resources, daring organization and single-mindedness of purpose enabled the LTM to amass sufficient funds to put up its Little Theatre on its own premises on Tom Redcam Avenue in Kingston in 1961. It was evident even before this that Jamaica needed both a large theatre for the community and a little theatre which could act as a nursery for talent and as a feeder for the Ward Theatre. With a grant of £5,000 from the government, the LTM had built a rehearsal room in 1958 beside which the Little Theatre would be placed, to facilitate the rehearsal of shows by all groups. In 1968, the LTM founded the Jamaica School of Drama, and eight years later handed it over to the government to form the drama component of the Cultural Training Centre, which also includes the Schools of Art, Dance and Music. The entire complex is now known as the Edna Manley College of the Visual and Performing Arts.

Since its inception the LTM has mounted scores of productions, but it is the annual pantomime that has captured the imagination of the great majority of theatregoers. Today, one out of every thirty Jamaicans attends the pantomime. Prorated in terms of population, the run would be the equivalent of a success in the West End, London, or on Broadway, New York, for two to three years.

Essentially English pantomimes have been produced from time to time, but the attempt to tap local resources began as early as in 1943, when Elinor Lithgow, the same Englishwoman who had staged *Jack and the Beanstalk*, directed *Soliday and the Wicked Bird*, a Jamaican Anancy story adapted by Vera Bell. When the pantomime *Anancy and Pandora*, scripted by Louise Bennett Coverley, opened in 1967, the few white faces onstage appeared to have slipped in by accident; in fact they were

Hamlet, with Edward Baugh as Claudius and Hope Sealy as Gertrude, produced and directed by Wycliffe Bennett and Carroll Dawes in 1961

brought in as tourists. This is not to suggest that the LTM necessarily set out to "darken" their pantomime or to give it any other colour: they simply wanted to "Jamaicanize" it.

Anancy has lent great distinction to the LTM's Jamaican pantomime, nurtured and kept alive primarily by two women: Greta Fowler, who founded the movement and served as chairperson from 1941 to 1976, and Barbara Gloudon, who succeeded her in the chair and has herself written twelve of the sixty-seven pantomimes, to date. Almost every trained theatre person in Jamaica has at some stage participated in the pantomime. The pantomime has a star-studded sixty-seven-year history. There are names to conjure with, and some of them will be given ampler treatment in the appendix, "Profiles and Biodata". Among them are the following:

Greta Fowler, co-founder of the Little Theatre Movement

- Writers Louise Bennett Coverley, Ranny Williams, Greta Fowler, Barbara Gloudon, Gloria Lannaman, Ted Dwyer, Trevor Rhone
- Actors Louise Bennett Coverley, Ranny Williams, Lois Kelly Miller, Buddy Pouyat, Faith D'Aguilar, Reggie Carter, Barbara Carter, Sheila Carter, Charles Hyatt, Oliver Samuels, Leonie Forbes, Dorothy Cunningham, Lenford Salmon, Michael Nicholson
- Directors Noel Vaz, Maurice Harty, Eddy Thomas, Lloyd Reckord, Carroll Dawes, Paul Methuen, Rex Nettleford, Bobby Ghisays, Yvonne Brewster, Dennis Scott, Brian Heap, Robert Clarke
- Set designers Carl Abrahams and Dossie Henriques, Gil Pratley, Albert Huie, Gloria Escoffery, Eugene Kelly, Colin Garland, Don Bucknor, Richard Montgomery, Henry Muttoo, Laura Facey, Michael Lorde
- Costume designers Doris Duperley, Enid Grunhut, Winnie Risden, Sally Montgomery, Anya Gloudon
- Lighting designers Eric Rumsey, George Carter, Eugene Finzi, Maurice Harty, Rufus MacDonald

Ranny Williams

As yet we have made no more than passing reference to the late Reggie Carter, who as director and actor was one of the giants of the Jamaican stage and screen. Nor have we discussed Lloyd Reckord, whose work as producer and director of the National Theatre Trust has been monumental. We also have to focus on the work of the Jamaica Drama League, which brought drama groups from all over the island together and helped to form new ones. The league not only mounted the annual Adult Drama Festival but also an annual "Season of Plays" and some major productions which, between 1955 and 1965, provided the vintage years of the Jamaican Theatre. And there are other omissions which the authors must rely upon time and other hands to rectify.

3

Some British Influences since 1900

After 1900, the local production of British and American scripts was greatly stimulated by two main factors: the presence of an increasing number of British and American expatriates with expertise, and the growing number of Jamaicans who were being trained at established drama schools on both sides of the Atlantic. The Jesuit fathers set a fine example at St George's College, where they staged a wide range of productions over the years. Father Pfister's colourful versions of Gilbert and Sullivan, for example – first staged with the Holy Trinity Cathedral Choristers and afterwards with his Merry Bulbulites – became keenly anticipated events between 1914 and 1920.

The first four decades of the twentieth century gave a clear indication of the development of a number of elements: the growth and stabilization of British-oriented groups; revue type presentations evolving from Christmas (and other holiday) morning concerts; storytelling, dramatic monologues, dramatic sketches (mainly comedy and mock trials); and folk and traditional song and dance, including ring games. Despite the fact that the theatrical scene continued to be dominated by touring companies from overseas, however, local enthusiasts who formed the Amateur Dramatic Club ensured that they would present *The Pirates of Penzance* at the opening of the Ward Theatre. Unfortunately, after one other performance a year later, in December 1913, the club went out of existence.

Of greater stamina was the Mandeville Amateur Dramatic Society (MADS), which began in 1911 and functioned on and off until 1948 when they staged their last show, *The White Sheep of the Family*, at the Odeon Theatre (a cinema) in Mandeville. After the society had been inactive for some eight years, a number of members, including Basil and Joyce Densham, supported Joan Swaby in founding a new group, the Manchester Players, in 1956.

Before the advent of the large bauxite companies, Mandeville was very English in tone, and was often referred to as "an English village". Planned and laid out during the 1830s, this mid-island town in the parish of Manchester came into being to service the large estates whose inhabitants previously had to travel great distances over bad roads to pay taxes, and to enjoy some of the amenities of civic life. The climate is moderately cool all year round, and many English people, some wealthy, others not so wealthy, settled in or near the town. A few arrived from England on doctors' orders. A few came to assume personal control of nearby estates which had been the main source of their families' income since the days of slavery. A number of professionals – army officers, ministers of religion, educators and the like – retired there. In modern times, the dwellings increased in number and substance, and so did the pleasances and the carefully manicured gardens.

But even more fundamental changes occurred with the discovery and mining of bauxite, bringing a degree of economic prosperity to the local community, and the country as a whole. There has been a substantial rise in the local coloured middle-class population from employment in bauxite, and it has more recently been swelled by returning nationals from England and North America. A distinctly North American quality – in shopping centres, club life, dress, manners and speech – now pervades the town. While some older residents do not resent the prosperity and the attendant bustle, they speak with nostalgia of the passing of the old world charm, of the leisured amplitude of a Mandeville they were accustomed to less than half a century ago.

MADS was, to some extent, characteristic of the typically English and middle-class amateur companies during the nineteenth century and the first decades of the twentieth. Home theatricals had become the rage among such families. Seldom pathfinders, they put on shows for fun, for the social pleasure that comes from taking part in a production with, or before, one's friends and acquaintances. But MADS did even more than this: they also took shows to Kingston, sixty miles to the east, or to Savanna-la-mar, seventy-two miles to the west, for one-night stands. They were a group of highly cultivated, sensitive people, and some of them were widely travelled. Tom Leyden and his wife Ina, who had been a professional in England, spearheaded the earlier productions. Years later they were joined by Vaughan Iver, described by Basil Densham as "a polished actor and producer". Noel and Mary Hughes, and Basil and Joyce Densham, who in 1934 became members, did much to shore up the company.

Older theatregoers recall that Molly Wynne was "equally at home as a duchess or as a charwoman". Her career spanned several generations, and she became affectionately known as Aunt Molly. In the beginning, the group performed by candle- and lamp-light at the Court House in the centre of town, and later, with the aid of electricity, at the Roof Garden Theatre. Surviving members speak, without prompting, of the following productions: *Squaw Woman*, *The Walls of Jericho*, *Lord Richard in the Pantry*, *Lady Windermere's Fan*, *The Cuckoo in the Nest* and *Thark*. They stinted neither in the time, the energy nor the care they put into their productions. It was important to their vanity and to their self-respect that they achieved just the right effect in decor, the leading lady's gown, her hair-do and so on.

Composed of white Jamaicans and English expatriates, the MADS players were taking the theatre they knew to Mandeville, and Mandeville, "an English village", rewarded them with packed, grateful houses. In reminiscing on the production of Ben Travers's *Thark* in 1940, Basil Densham noted:

> As the curtain went up on the dining room scene the applause was deafening. From the chandelier to the beautiful dining table and chairs, the table laid for the dinner party, wine glasses, champagne; and gleaming silver, fox masks, hunting horns; and Noel Hughes and Basil Densham enjoying an after dinner chat.
>
> Terry Mais' first appearance as a flirtatious flapper, and Joyce Densham who was as much at home on the stage as in her own house . . . Edwin Bell played the eerie butler and frightened the life out of us. Auntie Molly was a scream as the charwoman and Henwood had the awkward job not only of producing thunder and lightning but had to have a tree crashing through a bedroom window.[1]

A double nostalgia is implicit here: a harking back to the good old days, and wistfulness for a society that had succoured many English people before they left home to settle in Jamaica. But even in England itself, considerable changes were beginning to take place both in the society and in the theatre.

Few people of obvious colour ever attended these local productions. The content and style of the plays listed above explain why this was so. MADS held a mirror up, but not to the life that the generality of Jamaicans readily identified themselves with. At the same time, a number of well-known British and American producers and directors have paid occasional visits, under the auspices of the British Council and the United States Information Services, respectively. Nugent Monck from England spent a few months during 1950. From America came two other important guests, Reuben Silver of Karamu House in Cleveland, Ohio, to assist the Jamaica Drama League (JDL) in 1957, and Arnold Moss as producer and director of Thornton Wilder's *The Matchmaker*, which marked the opening of the Little Theatre in Kingston in 1961.

People in the theatre have spoken highest praise of the work of these practitioners, but more enduring contributions have been made by other visitors, who have remained on the island long enough to become part of the local scene. An increasing amount of help came from this source after 1935, but before we discuss this we should take cognizance of two other types of contributions to theatre in Jamaica that had a long history: army theatricals (that is, shows mounted by members of the armed forces, which may have been among the first productions on the island after the beginning of the British occupation); and touring companies, whose visits date back to the first half of the eighteenth century, and possibly earlier.

During the First World War, troop ships brought much entertainment. Port Royal, a mere shadow of her former glory, had become a coaling station for ships passing through the Panama Canal and for the British navy patrolling Caribbean waters from time to time. While the sailors were on shore leave they would give variety concerts at the Ward Theatre. Despite their highly improvised character, these shows often contained performances of star quality. Consequently, support for the war effort combined with the possibility of good entertainment to make these events popular, not only among local society people, headed by the governor and his circle, but also among theatre enthusiasts.

The late Gene Martinez used to tell many stories about these shows. He expressed the view that Lindsay Downer, who was head of the Jamaica Standard Fruit and Shipping Company, and was to become the leading producer during the 1920s and the theatre's patriarch in later years, may have improved upon his exposure to show

Lindsay Downer, became the leading producer during the 1920s and the theatre's patriarch in later years. *Courtesy of NLJ.*

business while at school in England. Downer may have learned his more important lessons from close study of the free-flowing nature of these presentations.

Downer began staging variety entertainment in support of the war effort in 1917, and followed this up with a number of straight plays after the war. He launched his Christmastime revues, *The Fireflies*, in 1923. Downer had flair and critical selectivity, and his shows commanded respect because of their considerable polish, freshness and spontaneity, which were reminiscent of those less pretentious wartime shows. Downer continued staging *The Fireflies* until 1930, when increasing responsibilities as top executive of a shipping company forced him to withdraw from active theatrical production. He maintained his interest in the theatre, however, as in 1941 he was listed as financial adviser on the LTM Management Committee. Theatregoers felt a keen sense of loss at Downer's withdrawal because, although there were other groups, some of them doing quite creditable work, most of the city's theatrical fare continued to be supplied by touring companies from abroad.

Another boon from the armed forces was the existence of the Garrison Theatre at Up Park Camp in Kingston after the Second World War. This was a makeshift wooden structure, open on two sides, which made it comfortably cool at night, and equipped with a stage, dressing rooms and lighting facilities. The Garrison served as a temporary home for several dramatic societies during the late 1940s and 1950s, when the Kingston and St Andrew Corporation committed the unpardonable act of leasing the Ward Theatre as a cinema, thereby making it insufferably difficult to rehearse and stage legitimate theatre there. It was at the Garrison Theatre that the Secondary Schools' Drama Festival was launched in 1950, and the Adult Drama Festival in 1955.

Some outstanding events took place during the brief career of the restored Theatre Royal from 1897 to 1907, when it was destroyed by earthquake. Mainly, we must rely upon the newspapers for eyewitness accounts, but there were a few octogenarians still around in the 1940s who recalled having to fight their way into the theatre to get a seat in "the gods", especially when a touring company arrived. Their comments form part of the aggregate drift of response that reaches us today. In 1947 the late Horace Vaz was closer to the time, and would have been able to discuss events with a far greater number of people. Vaz was a critic of remarkable perception. Of the Theatre Royal he writes:

> It was the scene of three great triumphs – "The Belle of New York"; "The Singing Sostegni"; and a visit from the "Benson Shakespeare Company". Mention of these to older theatre-goers brings a gleam to the eye and rapturous reminiscences . . .
>
> "The Belle of New York" was produced by Madame Noel DeMontagnac in 1901, with a cast of seventy Jamaican artists. It was a tremendous success. The press raved; its tunes were whistled by boys in the streets and tinkled on parlour pianos, and Miss Lillie Maynier who played the "Belle" and Miss Una Soutar – "Miss Kissy [*sic*] the dancer", were the toasts of the town . . .
>
> Sostegni was a young Italian girl whose soprano voice is remembered as the loveliest heard in Jamaica. She was touring with an Italian Opera Company; she was only at the beginning of her career when she died in Panama just after her visit here. Her portrait hangs in the foyer of the Ward Theatre.
>
> In 1905 the Frank Benson's Shakespeare Company toured the West Indies with a

> Company of thirty-three strong. They played only one week in Kingston but what a week! Every night a new play . . . Each day the *Gleaner* had an editorial on the night's play. The theatre was sold out for the season. Matheson Lang was the star; he is regarded as the greatest actor ever to appear on the Jamaican stage. He became Kingston's idol.[2]

Benson's company was regarded as a great nursery for talent. Sir Frank had done much to help keep Shakespeare's plays before the public. Nearing seventy years of age, some fifteen years after his 1905 tour, Sir Frank was still playing young leading roles when Sir Tyrone Guthrie saw him as Hamlet and Caliban at Oxford. Guthrie, one of the great theatrical directors of any century, pays a tribute that would have been echoed in Jamaica:

> [F]or the first time I began to see why these plays were considered masterpieces, to realize what great elaborate pieces of structure they were – dramatic cathedrals; to see how interesting they were as narrative, how, over and above and through the narrative were implicit meanings, like the echoes in a cathedral. I began to feel what richness of character was there, to hear what melody was in the lines.
>
> Like thousands of others, I am grateful to Sir Frank Benson and his company. They threw open windows which would otherwise have remained shut. They may have been rather dusty, grubby old casements which creaked open, but they gave onto the foam of perilous seas in faery lands forlorn.[3]

Sir Sydney Olivier had served Jamaica as colonial secretary from 1900 to 1904 and as governor from 1907 to 1913, and was in a position to brief his guest, George Bernard Shaw, on the economic conditions and lifestyles of the three levels of Jamaican society, and on the resilience demonstrated by all classes following the 1907 earthquake. Armed with such briefing, Shaw was able to speak with authority and address his own experience to the Jamaican context when he spoke to the press on 11 January 1911:

> **Shaw said:** But I can tell you what is wrong with Jamaica, if you are willing to admit that there is anything wrong with it.
>
> **Interviewer:** We have our faults, Mr Shaw.
>
> **Shaw:** You wouldn't admit it so complacently if you really believed it. But what is wrong here is that you produce the sort of man who is only a colonial. Please don't misunderstand me. I know perfectly well that it is ten times better to be a colonial than to be a Cockney, because the average Cockney has all the defects of the colonial and none of his advantages. But the fact remains that if a Jamaican wishes his son to be a fully civilized man of the world in the best sense – to belong to a great intellectual and artistic culture – he has to send him to Europe. Now that's not a necessary state of things. On the contrary, it ought to be far easier to build up a Jamaican culture than it is to civilize a Camberwell Cockney.
>
> Just consider a bit. When I speak of culture I am not using a vague general expression which seems to mean everything and really means nothing. I mean a personal equipment, as definite as a Panama hat, a pair of deck shoes and a buggy.
>
> You want three things in Jamaica. You want a first rate orchestra, giving performances at least once a week of the works of the great masters of modern music, from Sebastian Bach to Wagner and Richard Strauss. When a Jamaican knows Beethoven's

> ninth symphony as well as he knows the Ten Commandments, and feels hungry if he does not hear it well played fairly often then he is to that extent no longer a colonial.
>
> And remember it can be done. You can import your band parts as easily as you can import the "Illustrated London News". You can learn the fiddle or the trombone, and play B flat as written by Beethoven just as you can play it in the Gin and Scissors cakewalk. All that is necessary is to believe that Beethoven's music, though you can't pick it up as cheaply as Gin and Scissors, it's enormously more enjoyable and lasts you all your life.
>
> The next thing you want is a theatre, with all the ordinary travelling companies from England and America sternly kept out of it; for unless you do your own acting and write your own plays, your theatre will be no use: it will in fact vulgarize and degrade you. Don't smile incredulously. I tell you the thing can be done fairly easily.
>
> Over the water, when Dublin, Manchester and Glasgow got finally sickened by the trash of touring companies, they started theatre of their own under greater difficulties, and with less money, than you would have to face here. They began by producing Ibsen's plays, Granville Barker's plays, Galsworthy's plays, Hankin's plays, and the plays of Euripides and Shakespeare, not to mention my plays. And now they are producing new plays of their own townsmen, plays of Dublin life by Dublin men, of Glasgow life by Glasgow men – all novices at the game, and all playing it better than the conventional celebrities of Paris, London and New York.
>
> All you want is a band of convinced enthusiasts and an endowment of a few thousand pounds to do that here. And when you have done it and provided your Beethoven orchestra as well, your Kingston man need no longer be a colonial. People will begin to send their sons from England to old Jamaica to get culture.
>
> But a theatre and orchestra are not enough. You must have good architecture and well planned towns.
>
> If you work that vein for all it is worth, and see that your building acts are really enforced, you will produce the first condition of a high civilization, a handsome town. And these three things will cure you of your colonialism . . . [4]

While Shaw spoke, the Ward Theatre was going up. Kingston was just recovering from the ravages of the earthquake, and Shaw thought that the opportunity to rebuild the city in a manner worthy of a national capital should not be missed. He, possibly, also had in mind the fire of London in 1666 and, in its wake, the creation of St Paul's Cathedral by Sir Christopher Wren, and of the other mighty structures that followed. As to producing the sort of man who was "only a colonial", this Jamaica would continue to do for quite some years yet.

When, in 1957, Errol Hill and Wycliffe Bennett sat down with two blank sheets of paper to write a constitution for the JDL, they had not the foggiest notion that such a proposal had been put forward twenty years earlier, in 1937, by Joan Grant. An able director and teacher of speech and dramatic art, Mrs Grant was herself a member of the British Drama League, which, she said, "exists chiefly to encourage and give advice on both the cultural and recreational side of Drama among the people of Great Britain, where the amateur dramatic movement has of late assumed the proportions of a great national force".[5]

Mrs Grant suggested a meeting of heads of dramatic and literary clubs and institutions willing to form such a group, as well as interested members of the general public. She felt that such a representative meeting was most necessary before the scheme could make further headway. Lastly, she emphasized that it was absolutely desirable that the scheme be "all-island". In her view, there was considerable dramatic talent around. The idea was taken up by the Jamaican poet and dramatist Una Marson, producer/director George Bowen and others. Several news items appeared in the press and elsewhere, and meeting after meeting was held to discuss a constitution, but there is no evidence that any fruitful action followed.

Mrs Grant was a graduate of the Guildhall School of Speech and Drama in London, had lectured in dramatic art at University College in Hull, had produced plays and pageants all over England, had adjudicated at speech and drama festivals for the British Drama League, and had worked at the Festival Theatre in Cambridge. She arrived in Jamaica early in 1937, and spent just under three years on the island. She lost little time in becoming involved in the island's theatrical life. In 1937 she directed Una Marson's *Pocomania*, in 1938 J.M. Barrie's *Quality Street* and Ivor Novello's *Fresh Fields*, and in 1939 Shakespeare's *Twelfth Night* for the newly formed Jamaica Arts Society. Along with C.G.X. Henriques and Douglas Judah, she adjudicated at the All-Jamaica Elocution Contest, organized by the Poetry League of Jamaica in 1937. The report of the judges, "Standards of Elocution in Jamaica",[6] remains an important document.

Joan Grant was the wife of an English army officer whose battalion had been stationed in Jamaica. Another wartime resident was Elinor Lithgow, whom we have already mentioned as the director of two pantomimes, *Jack and the Beanstalk* (1941) and *Soliday and the Wicked Bird* (1943). Mrs Lithgow directed the first three shows the LTM produced. In addition to *Jack* (the pantomime), she also staged Esther McCracken's *Quiet Wedding* and Keith Winter's *Shining Hour* in 1941. She was also responsible for the second LTM pantomime, *Babes in the Wood*, in 1942. Although locally written by Pat Worledge, *Babes* was almost completely European in content and style. When Elinor Lithgow mounted *Soliday* the following year, she shared with the director of *Pocomania* the distinction of being among the first foreigners, successfully to apply their sophisticated training to the production of indigenous Jamaican theatre in the twentieth century.

Other gifted practitioners from England included Molly Ward Johnson, Cicely Howland, A.J. Watson and C.W. Fyfield of the British Council, who was the moving spirit behind the setting up of the Secondary Schools' Drama Festival. From America came Doris Hastings (Doris Mitchell of the New York stage) and Father Francis Shea, SJ. Four other Englishmen should also be mentioned: Neil Gibson, Orford St John, Paul Methuen and Harry Milner, the first foreigner to be granted Jamaican citizenship after Jamaica's independence in 1962.

Molly Ward Johnson spent about twelve years in Jamaica, from 1938. She studied at the Bristol and Cheltenham Academies in Bristol, held teacher's diplomas in speech and drama from a number of national institutions in England, and was a superb teacher and craftsman. Her local productions included *Hamlet*, with Stephen Hill in the title role (1944), and the LTM pantomime *The Rose and the Ring* (1946). She acted in several plays, both on radio and on the stage, and taught in a number of institutions, including Wolmer's Girls' School and Shortwood Teachers' College. Some of her private pupils became well-known in the Jamaican theatre: Ralph Thompson, Jennifer Bourke, Joan Swaby, Lois Kelly-Miller and Wycliffe Bennett.

Paul Methuen, actor, director

Cicely Howland had acted in Obey's *Noah* with Sir John Gielgud under the direction of Michel Saint-Denis in London in 1935, and seemed destined for a fine career in the English theatre, when she married a Jamaican, Frank Waite-Smith, and settled in Jamaica. She directed Sheridan's *School for Scandal* for the LTM in 1942, participated in a drama workshop (Sleepy Valley), organized by Knox College and the Extra-Mural Department of the University College of the West Indies, in 1955; and performed with great charm and sensitivity a number of roles on the Jamaican stage. But posterity will know her mainly for the Jamaican plays she wrote, among them *The Creatures*, a play in one act (1954), *Uncle Robert* (1957), *The Ravishers* (1957) and *Africa Sling-shot* (1958).

A.J. (Tony) Watson enabled Wolmer's Boys' School to achieve distinction in the Speech and Drama Festivals during the 1950s. Watson had read modern languages at Oxford, and brought to the theatre a wide knowledge of dramatic literatures, both ancient and modern. For Wolmer's, he wrote, adapted and produced *Forth from Eden* (an old French miracle play, 1954), *Priam's Journey* (from Homer's *Iliad*, 1955), and *Joseph an' 'im Bredren* (in Jamaican dialect, 1957) – all for the Secondary Schools' Drama Festival. In addition, he created an English version of Chekhov's *Uncle Vanya* (1957). Theatregoers will vividly recall his role as Busha Bluebeard in the 1957 pantomime *Busha Bluebeard and Br'er Anancy*. He also played the First God in Brecht's *The Good Woman of Setzuan*, directed by Wycliffe Bennett at the Ward Theatre in 1959.

Doris Hastings served as producer for the ZQI Players, the dramatic group on Jamaica's first radio station. Her radio presentations reflected a catholicity of taste,

Left: Poster for Stephen Hill's Celebrity Concerts, winter season 1947

Right: Programme cover for *The Good Woman of Setzuan*, by Bertolt Brecht, directed for the Library Players by Wycliffe Bennett in 1959

and were well up to international standards. She brought the same expertise to her stage productions for the Theatre Arts Club, among other groups.

Father Shea did bold and imaginative productions of *The Pardoner's Tale* (1962) and *Oedipus Rex* (1963) for St George's College in the Secondary Schools' Drama Festival. During Jamaica's tercentenary celebrations in 1955, he built a stage onto a truck, combined students of St George's College (boys) and Alpha Academy (girls) into a team, and toured the island giving open air productions of *Everyman* and his own Jamaican version of Plautus' *The Twin Brothers*. He returned to Boston College to teach drama.

Library Players in *The Good Woman of Setzuan*, directed by Wycliffe Bennett at the Ward Theatre in 1959

On coming to Jamaica, these practitioners would have worked for, and in fact did work in, whatever theatre or theatres the country had to offer. And, as we have seen, a number of them did much pioneer work. Save where they held teaching appointments, they gave their time and their talent without charge, and the people with whom they first came into contact and met most easily – people from their own country, or of similar backgrounds and upbringings – were the ones towards whose company they gravitated. They therefore quickly found themselves pressed into service by the British-type theatre groups. As in the past, the main ambition of these groups, though not so promulgated, was to provide in Jamaica an extension of the London West End, and they chose and produced their plays accordingly. Their productions often included a number of professionally trained British and Jamaican performers, invariably demonstrated considerable polish, and were usually up to the best British repertory standards.

It was tacitly accepted that Jamaican performers of obvious colour would have been unthinkable in such productions. And the audiences consisted mainly of British expatriates or of Jamaicans with British pretensions. In fact, dark faces were as rare on such occasions as they would have been in the predominantly white cities of London and New York. As long as productions were conceived in this way, plays never had to make a "sea change". Ivor Novello's *Fresh Fields*, produced by Joan Grant at the Ward Theatre in 1937, was warmly applauded by all reviewers, and exemplifies the local approximation of London norms which the sponsors devoutly wished for:

> This is not an easy play for amateurs. It demands subtle acting and swift pace. The acting honours are equally divided by Miss Ena Marchalleck, Miss Dougall, Mrs Bourke [later Fowler], Mrs Worledge, but it is not entirely chance that Miss Marchalleck's name comes first for apart from her convincing portrayal of Lady Mary – and what is acting if not an ability to convey a character other than your own to an audience? – but for the magnificent way she keyed up the whole pitch of the performance and held the cast together from the moment of her entrance. Mrs Worledge gave an unforgettable performance in Minnie Rayner's part of Mrs Pidgeon. If it savoured more of revue than comedy I can pay no higher tribute than that I was forever being put in mind of Cicely Courtneidge. To Mrs Bourke fell the hardest part and if she vapoured and swooned less effectively than Lillian Braithwaite she looked infinitely more Rossetti and in the proposal scene with Mr Blakeley her acting was really good. Indeed like most of the cast she went from strength to strength as the evening went on and here the splendid reception of the warm hearted audience must be held responsible. Miss Dougall played the part as well as it was done in London and was convincing from her first line and subtle in her change of poise and voice in the last act . . .[7]

It should be noted that Miss Marchalleck, Miss Dougall and Mrs Worledge had all been professionally trained in England. The review is not well written, but at least the anonymous critic makes his point. He had also seen the London production, and uses this as his point of departure.

One problem with productions of this genre is that, however good they may be, after the opening and the following two or three nights have creamed off the "smart set", the sponsors find that if they must continue the run, they then have to play to a near-empty Ward Theatre. E.H.J. King, an Englishman who had identified himself with native aspirations, placed the matter in perspective when he reviewed *You Can't Take It with You* in 1945:

> The play was well produced, well acted . . . No one could have anticipated a more appreciative audience.
>
> There was one fault, the fault that Waite-Smith, Noel Vaz and most other producers cannot refrain from making. They expect the theatre-going public of Kingston and Jamaica to appreciate or to pretend to appreciate plays with emotional, factual and dramatic content which lie well without the bounds of anything which the average person in this country has either seen or experienced.
>
> The critics can say what they want about the poorly written, badly produced and incompetently acted Jamaican plays which have so far been produced. They have an undeniable merit. They spring from and are related to the real and emotional experiences of the majority of the audience . . .[8]

King was preaching neither a snobbish exclusivity on the one hand nor a narrow chauvinism on the other. His concern was primarily with the quality and value of the instrument: "But when a serious producer, assisted by a competent cast, takes advantage of the inadequate theatrical facilities which Jamaica can offer, we expect a play which will justify both his own talent and the innate ability of those people who play the leading roles in that drama."[9]

Several Jamaican intellectuals shared these views, but they had neither the prestige nor the influence nor the know-how to make much of a difference at that time. And there came into existence a succession of companies which continued the type of productions exemplified in *Fresh Fields*, in *You Can't Take It with You*, and in the offerings of the touring companies which had visited the island up to the outbreak of the Second World War. The Theatre Arts Club was formed in 1946, New Theatre in 1961, and the Jamaica Playhouse in 1966.

The Theatre Arts Club began staging plays in 1949, and for the next five years provided theatregoers with some of the most highly polished and professionally executed productions ever seen on the island. The producers and directors included C.W. Fyfield and Neil Gibson (England); Doris Hastings (United States); and Maurice Harty and Keith Sasso (Jamaica). They mounted J.B. Priestley's *They Came to a City* (1949); Gerald Savory's *George and Margaret* and Dorothy Sayers's *Busman's Honeymoon* (1950); Shaw's *Arms and the Man* and Noel Coward's *Blythe Spirit* (1951); Emlyn Williams's *Someone Waiting* and Noel Coward's *Present Laughter* and *Still Life* (1952); Patrick Hamilton's *Gaslight* (1953); and Daphne DuMaurier's *September Tide* (1954).

When Her Royal Highness the Princess Alice saw *George and Margaret*, she was so impressed with the performance of this play of gay inconsequence that she thought she was watching a touring company from "home".[10] Sir Hugh Foot, governor of Jamaica (1951–57), who never forgot to send a note of thanks, wrote on seeing *Gaslight*:

> I knew it was a very difficult play and I am ashamed to say that I expected that the parts might be too exacting for amateur actors. But I was proved quite wrong. I thought that the performance was first-rate and I do most sincerely congratulate you and all those who took part in the play on such a success. I went prepared to make allowances and I came away feeling nothing but admiration.[11]

Most of the productions were staged at that time at the Garrison Theatre where the "military thespians" also performed.

New Theatre and Jamaica Playhouse operated with much the same type of theatregoer in mind, but seldom with quite the same artistic success. They continued the production of plays for the "extension" of a London in which "[t]he theatre belonged to the upper and upper-middle classes and the vast army of social climbers, who paid for it and who went to see idealized portraits of themselves".[12]

But even in London itself changes had begun to take place. The Second World War started "the job of jumbling the social classes; post-war prosperity furthered the process of breaking the social barriers. England [had] been extraordinarily prosperous since the war, and its prosperity [had] produced Tory governments and Socialist playwrights".[13] Social mobility had created the possibility not only of larger audiences, but also of widening the areas traditionally given theatrical treatment. The British theatre, therefore, had to begin to change its image, to create new "objects", or remain as stagnant and as inconsequential as it had been after the exuberance brought by Ibsen, Wilde, Synge, O'Casey and Shaw (none of them English) had subsided.

Orford St John, an Englishman, remained one of the few producers and directors in Jamaica during the 1950s who was fully aware of the revolution that had overtaken the British theatre. He saw social mobility in the Jamaican context as an opportunity for interracialism in the theatre. He founded the Repertory Players in 1957 with interracialism as a stated objective. His group demonstrated greater catholicity in choice of plays than any other company either before or since.

Today, for any local group to stage an all-white production of Shakespeare or any other classic would be theatrically suicidal. When, for example, New Theatre mounted *Twelfth Night* in 1960, Sir Arthur Lewis, Principal of the University College of the West Indies, is reputed to have told the university's drama tutor, who was a member of the production team, "I thought *Twelfth Night* took place in Illyria. Not in South Africa?"

Orford St John felt that he had to fight stubborn prejudices, and he was probably right, but interracialism had been becoming the norm from several years earlier; for example: in P.W. Gibson's production of *Hamlet* for the St George's Young Men's Dramatic Society in 1921; in presentations by different groups within the Catholic Church; in 1936 in Esther Chapman's musical *The West Indian*, directed by Burnett Webster with a cast of over seventy; in Joan Grant's *Twelfth Night* in 1939 for the Jamaica Arts Society; in Nugent Monck's production of *The Merchant of Venice* in 1950; and in *Hamlet*, produced and directed by Wycliffe Bennett and Carroll Dawes in 1958.

Vere Johns, elecutionist, actor and journalist, as *Othello*

The visit of Nugent Monck at the invitation of the British Council and the LTM to Jamaica was propitious. His approach to the theatre was an education for those who were privileged to be present to watch. He had had a long association with amateurs. In 1919 he became producer/director of the long-established amateur group known as the Norwich Players. For them he acquired and reconstructed an old, dilapidated building, and gave it an Elizabethan stage, complete with an apron. He had also been a guest producer at the Shakespeare Memorial Theatre at Stratford and elsewhere in England. Monck explained that, despite its fame, the Maddermarket Theatre had remained amateur. He felt that social ambition was curbed by anonymity, and that the theatre had become a most important centre of education and artistic inspiration for the whole of England.

Monck had a canonical approach but would entertain suggestions if they fitted into his plans. Once a decision was made, that was enough. At other times he would say to a diffident actor, "I have myself played that role in several different ways. Go on, let's see what you are getting at", or, "Of course you can do it. I can make a broomstick act." To watch Nugent Monck direct was in fact to watch a performance in which Monck would himself play any number of parts. His production of *The Merchant of Venice* was strong, orthodox and conventional, and contained a number of performances that people in and out of the theatre still speak about.

A tradition of open-air productions of Shakespeare developed with Noel Vaz and Hazel Johnston's *A Midsummer Night's Dream*, which was staged in the gardens of Holy Cross Convent in Half Way Tree. Here to be taken from prodigal nature were some of the very effects that the great Max Reinhardt had wrestled with technology to achieve in his realization of the *Dream* in Germany in 1905. Indeed, Noel Vaz and Hazel Johnston's production was so successful that, when Jamaica decided to celebrate its three hundred years of association with Great Britain twelve years later, the organizers of the Arts Section of the celebrations opted for an alfresco play production as part of the programme. Hugh Morrison and Errol Hill co-directed *The Tempest* on the grounds of St Andrew High School. They gave the play a panoramic setting, with acting areas on different levels covered with moss. The school hall between the tall trees and other foliage provided a backdrop and took on the appearance of a huge white rock. In this rock was the cave in which Prospero and Miranda lived. The building responded to light as effectively as a plaster sky-dome, and the appearances of Ariel from unexpected places helped to heighten the effect of Prospero's "potent art".

A Midsummer Night's Dream, directed by Noel Vaz and Hazel Johnston

In 1964 Gillian Binns directed *A Midsummer Night's Dream* in the garden at Vale Royal, then the official residence of Jamaica's minister of finance. The following year Reggie Carter staged *As You Like It* in the garden at 72 Hope Road, the home of Paul Methuen. This setting then became known as the Garden Theatre, and was improved over the years that Methuen lived there. From 1965 Paul Methuen himself produced and directed a Shakespearean play there each summer for some ten years.

4

Jamaica Triumphant

Creating the Theatrical Object

Father Daniel Lord, director

When the Reverend Father Daniel Lord staged *Jamaica Triumphant* at Winchester Park, Kingston, 11–14 January 1937, he created a great theatrical experience. The production harnessed energies and tendencies in our cultural and artistic growth, and provided a monumental overview of our country's past. Upwards of five thousand people attended each of the four performances. The idea of having the pageant was conceived by Bishop Emmet, who was anxious to commemorate the centenary of the Vicariate of the Roman Catholic Church in Jamaica. But both in writing and performance the presentation accomplished much more.

From the outset the church made common cause with men, women and children of all denominations. In a population of 1,200,000 at that time, there were only about 60,000 Catholics. The pageant master, directors, technical staff, front-of-house management and cast of some 400 players were all determined to create a significant national occasion. Father Lord said of the performers on his return home to Boston:

> They ranged through the whole gamut of nationalities, of ancestries, of colours, of religious and social groups . . . There were English, Irish, Scotch, Spanish, French, Portuguese, Central and South Americans; there were men of coal black and then through the scale to purest white; there were Chinese and one or two East Indians.
>
> And for the duration of the pageant they put aside everything except the desire to make it a success . . . I have never felt community spirit rising to finer heights and more devoted self-sacrifice.[1]

Jamaica Triumphant projected the island's history from the days of the aboriginal Tainos and the coming of Christopher Columbus in 1494, and drew attention to its predominantly African and Afro-European population, which had been a feature of the British occupation since 1655. The presentation specifically called attention to the racial and national elements that came from Africa, Asia and Europe, and were later to give rise to Jamaica's motto, "Out of many, one people."

Fantasy of the Pasion by Father Daniel Lord, directed by Tony Lopez, Holy Cross Church Hall. *Courtesy of George Carter.*

A vast stage rose in tiers from the grassy ground, and provided six major acting areas. The dome of the Cathedral next door towered immediately behind a huge painted backdrop, which keynoted the panoramic production. In the distance, Wareika Hill soared into the open sky and gave further size and depth to the setting. A follow-spot was used in the island for the first time. The skilful manipulation of light and dark emphasized the plastic nature of the staging.

The story unfolded by linear and parallel progression. In the simultaneous passages of scenic summaries, the pageant master employed a technique known as polyscenic staging of juxtaposition. In modern practice the technique may owe something to Japanese theatre, but Father Lord's models certainly went back to the great medieval productions of Valenciennes, Bourges and Renward Cysat at Lucerne. The difference in *Jamaica Triumphant* was that the settings were not necessarily fixed, and that by now the incandescent lamp, introduced in 1922, and the work of the illuminating engineers, had made for greater sophistication. By mounting certain events simultaneously, Father Lord was able to bring ethnological and nascent dramatic forms into counterpoint, as a review of the play from a 1937 edition of the *Daily Gleaner* shows:

> Intense but weary activity greets the eye in the next scene. Black slaves, sweating under the sun and cowering under the lash work as their masters ply them incessantly with vicious whips. The resonant tones of "That's Why Slaves Are Born" sung by an enchained slave, Mr George Bowen, [provide] musical theme for this sight: men, women and children all working, working while the crack of the whip signals their suffering and disgrace. But freedom is coming.[2]

The foregoing event focuses on a group as a whole: incidents are taking place everywhere all the time, but the singing slave remains dominant. In the following section there is multiple staging, but the focus is essentially "double", that is to say, the ex-slaves and their ex-masters perform in counterpoint, thus underscoring the duality that had developed in Jamaica's cultural and artistic life: "The slaves, recently freed, gambol and frolic. 'John Canoe' and his votaries, notably 'Horse Head', jump a merry dance, while matrons and strong men keep time with the general festivity. Representatives of the plantocracy are in frock coats and crinolines, children play at 'Little Sally Water'."[3] Not only the players but also their costumes and the lighting explored the colours of the spectrum: "Crimsons and yellows, greens and blues were there to be sure, but whites and blacks and dainty pastels made them show off all the more. Pretty crinolines, swash-buckling capes, the sombre habits of Holy Orders – worn so well that even the initiates mistook the actors for the genuine thing – all were created not only with a master eye upon colour, but with a true knowledge of period costume."[4]

We may be tempted to question the historical accuracy of designing frock coats (or Prince Alberts) for use at the Emancipation celebrations of 1838, since at that time gentlemen were mainly wearing the swallowtail or cutaway in England, and the frock coat did not become the norm even among the aristocracy in the "mother" country until during the following decade. But this would be to cavil. Quite properly, the reviewer probably ignored the matter as being unworthy of attention, because the all-important point of dramatic juxtaposition had been amply made. Indeed, as we read this eyewitness account, it becomes obvious that the critique is of a high order. Even at this remove in time, the writer is able to recreate the experience for us. He maintains a correct sense of responsibility towards his readers, but is not embarrassed, as a lesser writer might have been, to show how much he enjoyed the performance. On the quality of the overall production, the comments that he makes indicate that, whatever its didactic or other intentions, *Jamaica Triumphant* was certainly show business in the best sense of the term. Note his assessment of the skill and cunning of the practised director: "Drama, sensation, tragedy, music, dancing, comedy, all were woven into a continuity that never palled, and when it did seem to slacken just for a moment it was but to enable a recovery to be the more pleasant, the more startling."[5]

The production provided a showcase for the best talent available at the time: scenario writers and scenic improvisers, directors, choreographers, actors, dancers, musicians and singers, makers of stage properties and costumes, scene painters, stage managers, and so forth. Aside from Father Lord's writing of the narration and the general outline, and his expert overall direction, the production required overseas help in only two other departments: costume and lighting design. Many practitioners have dated their important beginnings in the theatre from this show. C.G.X. Henriques, who was one of the two narrators, crystallized the sentiments of his colleagues in a farewell speech to the American producer: "The verdict of thousands who night after night witnessed the pageant at Winchester Park; the verdict of the ladies and gentlemen whose attainments qualify them to judge dramatic art; the verdict of public opinion in this country – is that the pageant was a spectacle of unparalleled splendour and magnificence, by far the greatest thing of the kind that has ever been done in Jamaica."[6]

Between 1960 and 1972, up to thirty-five years after the event, I checked the tone and substance of the critique and Sir Cyril Henriques's remarks with a number of participants and members of the audience, who still spoke of *Jamaica Triumphant* as one of the most exciting experiences in their lives. They included George Bowen (who played the enchained slave), Douglas Judah, Keith Sasso, Ranny Williams, Greta Lyons – all practitioners who have since died – and George Carter, who started his career as a lighting designer with his apprenticeship to this show, and who at ninety-one (at time of writing) was still very active. Poet and philosopher Ralph Thompson, who took part in the play while still a boy in short pants, recalls:

> I was nine years old, still a student at Alpha Academy, when *Jamaica Triumphant* opened at Winchester Park . . . My memory of the small walk-on part I was assigned is very blurred but I can still feel the excitement of the pageant's overpowering scale – the width of the playing area about as big as the football field, scaffolding and parapets erected to what seemed staggering heights, my first exposure to microphones and speakers, stage lighting so imaginative it defined at the flip of a switch eras and events in the island's history and the sheer numbers of actors, technicians and administrative personnel which Fr Lord commanded with imperial grace. These were the days of short wave radio, faint and scratchy, which could stimulate only a black and white imagination in a boy. The pageant burst upon me and Jamaica in a blaze of colour. I remember especially the armour of the Spanish soldiers, the swords of the pirates; the regalia of colonial officialdom. But my most emotional memory was the pathos of George Bowen, a chained slave, naked from the waist, bathed in moonlight, singing "Ole Man River" in a voice

so rich it seemed to rise and resonate from Africa itself. From that moment on I was literally stage struck.[7]

Thompson's testimony remains overwhelming, and is as it should be, for efforts in the theatre are collaborative, and are concerned with creating an "object". This "object" includes activity which is virtual, not because it does not exist but because the very centre of its existence is appearance. Observed or contributed to, from either side of the footlights, this "object" constitutes both a projection and a response. There is a two-way flow of emotional and psychic energy, in which both those on stage and those in the audience participate and create a single, yet complex, experience. This experience relies considerably upon the faculty of recall, and operates consciously as well as subconsciously.

In building a character an actor must dredge up points of departure from within his own past, be they personal or otherwise, and audiences bring layers of meaning from their own experiences when they attend a production. This explains why no two performances of the same production can ever be the same. Where the actor's and the audience's lines of recall converge, the mimetic intentions of the one and the theatrical expectations of the other come within seeing distance of each other. To the extent that these intentions and expectations are fulfilled, and production comes to fruition, the "object" is created.

All efforts in the theatre are designed to assist the actor and the spectator-participant to achieve this common end. These considerations remain, regardless of our aesthetics: whether we take the primordial, ritualistic approach, or are guided by Aristotle's *Poetics* and the Greek concept of "catharsis"; whether we follow the "rasa theory" of Bharata Muni and the *lokadharmi* (realistic) and the *natyadharmi* (conventional) types of production as conceived by the earliest Hindu theorists, or subscribe to the Brechtian, but by no means new, *verfremdung* (alienation) approach. Because reviews are necessarily written *post facto*, some critics ignore or forget the shared experience and discuss performances as literature. Theatre is essentially the art of performance.

The script remains paramount as the point of departure for the production, but it is never more than a blueprint for action. If the director is worth his salt (and even if he is not) the production will display his personality. The production, nevertheless, owes its form and substance to more than one individual. Actors, designers, even the front-of-house personnel will all have contributed. Theatre issues from communal will. Just as there may be several streams of literature, so may there be several types of theatre operating in a country at the same time.

But a national theatre – that theatre that is most characteristic of a country at a particular time – will derive its shape and substance from psychological dispositions that predominate in the national life. If men of vision, as distinct from mere copyists, take the lead, the national theatre may even go further and be somewhat ahead of current thinking. The national theatre will be among the first groups to perceive ultimate directions and help the society to realize its ideal. Whether practices arise indigenously or are brought in by carrier cultures, it makes no difference. To change the character of any theatre, you must first of all change the basic mindset or assumptions of the people who produce it.

5

Patronage and the Jamaican Theatre

One of the consequences of the British conquest was that, by becoming English-speaking, Jamaica acquired British national memories, ideas, legends and customs that flow from one generation to the next through the English language. To date this has been the single, most decisive factor in the development of theatre in Jamaica; and in this chapter we will look briefly at this heritage. Emphasis will be placed on the origins of the Jamaican attitude to patronage and class in the theatre, on the office of Master of the Revels during the eighteenth and early nineteenth centuries, and how patronage in the theatre has changed from being the prerogative of those of privilege to that of the ordinary citizens of the country.

The first reference to public theatrical practice on this side of the Atlantic occurs in *A Short Account of the Island and Government of Jamaica*, written "in and about the year 1682" by Francis Hanson. Hanson had been living in Jamaica for about twelve years when he addressed his *Account* to the Lords of Trade and Plantations. He was greatly impressed with the colony's affluence: "The manner of living there for Gallantry, Good House-Keeping and Recreations (as Horse Races, Bowls, Dancing, Musick, Plays at a Publick Theatre, etc.) sufficiently demonstrate the flourishing condition of the island."[1]

Jamaica was captured from the Spaniards in 1655 by Admiral Penn and General Venables as a sop to the Puritan Oliver Cromwell for their failure to take Hispaniola. The Commonwealth interregnum began when Cromwell had Charles I beheaded in 1642, and became Lord Protector of England. The Protectorate lasted eighteen years, until 1660. In 1670, Spain finally ceded the island to Britain.

The Puritans had steadily opposed playhouses since the last years of the sixteenth century. They regarded popular stage-plays as "sinful, heathenish, lewde, ungodly Spectacles, and most pernicious Corruptions".[2] Not only did they dismantle the playhouses, they broke into the churches and other religious houses, and destroyed images and other objects of beauty. A similar fate overtook Jamaica when Cromwell's soldiers arrived in 1655. They set fire to the Spanish (Roman Catholic) churches and melted down the bells to provide gunshot.

The Commonwealth ended and the Restoration began when King Charles II signed the Declaration of Breda on 29 May 1660, and re-entered London, "the ways strewed with flowers, the bells ringing, the streets hung with tapestry, the fountains flowing with wine".[3] Politically, the Restoration not only brought back the monarchy; it also restored parliament and law in place of rule "by the sword" under Cromwell. The king's return also restored other norms and brought relief from excessive restrictions. In church affairs, the bishops resumed their ancient office; the Book of Common Prayer was restored; the organs and choirs were heard again in the cathedrals and college chapels of England; and the nobles and gentry returned to their hereditary place as local and national leaders in social life. It was mainly from this class that the governors of Jamaica were recruited.

Charles II re-established, and in many ways built upon, the prestige of former times. His royal court "was also the centre of patronage for politics, fashion, literature, art, learning, invention, company-promoting, and a hundred other activities of the king's subjects seeking notoriety or reward".[4] The Restoration set in train a pattern of conduct that was to be followed with varying degrees of success between then and now, by succeeding governors and governors general of Jamaica.

In the past, whenever royalty wished to see a play they summoned the players to court. Charles broke new ground. He and his brother, the Duke of York, made a point of going to the theatre, and, as is the case today, good houses were guaranteed whenever royalty attended. No detail of management or production was beneath their notice. They even intervened to settle squabbles between actors and between the two London theatres at the time. Members of the royal family acted in the private theatre at court, and invited professionals to give them lessons in the art of declamation, as "good" speech was then called.

With the possible exception of Edward VII, no subsequent monarch has evinced so keen and so personal an interest in the theatre as Charles II. Indeed, as Alexandre Beljame has noted,

> [A]fter the Revolution [of 1688–89] the glory of the Court grew dim. Neither the political position of the Crown, nor the personal temperament of those who wore it was the same as of old. Stern William, invalid Anne, the German Georges, farmer George, domestic Victoria, none of them desired to keep a Court like Queen Elizabeth's. Henceforth, the Court was the residence of secluded Royalty pointed out from afar, difficult of access, save on occasions of proverbial dullness.
>
> Patronage was sought elsewhere in the lobbies of Parliament, in the ante-chambers of Ministers, in the country-houses of the pleasantest aristocracy in the world, finally in the appeal to the educated public.[5]

The king's representatives, nevertheless, continued to exercise considerable royal prerogative in the colonies; and Jamaica was never without people who desired to reproduce, in their new home, some of the delights they had left behind in their old. There is, for example, the story of Henry Moore, who returned to Jamaica in 1735, and later became governor of Jamaica and of New York. Born in Vere in 1713, he was educated at Eton and at the University of Leyden. He then made the grand tour of Europe. When he came back to Jamaica, where he inherited considerable estates, he brought with him a band of musicians, which included Clarke, the violin player who had married and run away from a daughter of the famous actor Colley Cibber.[6]

Another piece of relevant information appears in a letter "from a Gentleman [Charles Leslie] to his Friend", Vice-Admiral Edward Vernon, who was stationed in the West Indies from 1739 to 1742. The letter refers to the kinds of entertainment popular in the island's capital, St Jago de la Vega, in about the 1740s: "They have frequent Balls and lately have got a play-house, where they retain a Set of extraordinary good Actors."[7] It was around this time that the wave of prosperity that produced the powerful West India interests in London may be said to have begun. In revising his first account of *The British Empire in America*, in 1741, John Oldmixon says of Spanish Town: "Tis a very pleasant City, and the inhabitants live in a great deal of Pomp and luxury . . . Here are frequent Balls and Assemblies, a Play-House and a Company of Players; the Jamaican writer assures us there are excellent Actors, which is more than can justly be said of the best Company now in England."[8] What seems remarkable about this development is that, in 1737, the white population was estimated at "not above 8,000", and "not 1,000" of these were "masters of families or [had] any property". Meanwhile the slave population was growing rapidly: it had increased from 9,504 in 1673 to 99,239 in 1740.

Before the middle of the eighteenth century, the need to regulate entertainments apparently arose and, in keeping with the English pattern, the office of master of the revels was created. The introduction of such a functionary would have seemed logical to succeeding governors, who would have been aware of the Licensing Act of 1737 in England. Under this act, the master of the revels was appointed under the lord chamberlain to supervise and pay for particular entertainments at court. We first hear of the master of revels in 1494, and the post was intermittently appointed until 1545, when Sir Thomas Cowarden was appointed master for life. By decrees of 1581 and 1603, the master of the revels was made censor of plays and collected a fee for each play he licensed for public performance.

In Jamaica the appointee assumed authority over theatrical performances and the direction of all balls and entertainments given by the governor. Richardson Wright lists a number of persons who held this office, including "the notorious Teresa Constantia Phillips, about 1757–8",[9] appointed by the Governor Sir Henry Moore. Ms Phillips was born in West Chester, England, sometime in 1708 or 1709, and went to school in London. Seduced by "Thomas Grimes" (the future fourth Earl of Chesterfield) at the age of twelve, she embarked early upon a career of changing one lover for another and "marrying and burying" as a means of getting rich. In 1738 she arrived in Jamaica, escorted by Henry Needham, a member of the House of Assembly and later of the Privy Council. She returned to England in 1747, having written her *Apology for the Conduct of Mrs T C Phillips*. By this three volume publication she attempted to blackmail her friends, but as these efforts did not bring her the hoped-for returns, we find her in Jamaica again in 1754, this time as the wife of a Mr Montgomery, a successful land surveyor, whom she soon reduced to a skeleton. After his death she married a Mr Samuel Callendar and, after the latter's demise, a Monsieur De Lantagnac.

Her position as mistress of the revels secured her much prominence at gubernatorial entertainments. Her appointment by a man of the sensitivity and discrimination of Sir Henry Moore suggests, not alone, a fondness for the vermillion lady on the part of Moore himself, but, more importantly, that the temper of the Jamaican society was in those days still Restoration. Moore's passion for the arts followed him all his life and he acquired the sobriquet of "show governor" because it was felt that he was more interested in giving concerts than in performing his official duties. More than any other of the king's representatives, Sir Henry Moore helped to establish royal or aristocratic patronage of the arts in Jamaica.

Well into the twentieth century the theatre remained the almost exclusive preserve of the privileged. It did not include happenings at the folk level, or attempts in the schools and villages throughout the island to stage their skits, farces, mock trials and playlets, but applied to such productions as would be mounted in the rebuilt Theatre Royal in Kingston, before its destruction in 1907, and at the Ward Theatre after it opened in 1912. For these theatres, amateurs and gentlemen players would put on shows from time to time. Until 1939, when the Second World War made the high seas unsafe for travel, the major theatrical events each year consisted of the offerings of the several drama and musical comedy companies from England, and a number of Italian grand opera companies who visited the island periodically.

As always, the first nights were glittering social events attended by the governor, his wife and the elite of Jamaican society. Until Jamaica became independent in 1962, the king's or queen's representative and his wife remained the arbiters of the island's social life and the prime patrons of culture and the arts. Many of these incumbents actually backed up their exercise of royal prerogative with genuine interest and performance. For example, Lady Stubbs, wife of Sir Edward Stubbs (governor from 1926 to 1931), produced a detective thriller, *The Perfect Alibi*, on 16 January 1932 at the Ward Theatre; and, during the 1940s and the 1950s, succeeding governors' wives (Lady Huggins and Lady Foot) headed the Little Theatre Movement's pantomime committee.

Sir Hugh Mackintosh Foot

Lady Molly Huggins

Lady Marjory Stubbs

Gubernatorial patronage placed the hallmark of class upon certain types of entertainment. This support was especially sought after by those who were anxious to help create a home away from home for the white residents, expatriate or native born. King's House approval guaranteed a prestigious opening night, since all the "right" people would make a point of attending when the governor and his lady were present. The tradition diminished somewhat after Jamaica's independence, but there are still groups who stage plays primarily for this type of theatregoer.

Constitutionally, the governor general, who now represents the queen, is the head of the Jamaican society. His gracious company is sought after by one and all, but King's House is no longer, *de facto*, the centre of patronage. With independence based on representative government, authority has shifted to Jamaica House, the office of the prime minister, and to the chambers of other ministers of government.

But we should give two of our recent governors general their due. During his younger years, Sir Florizel Glasspole was a good elocutionist and a formidable debater, and Sir Howard Cooke was one of the pioneers of the Festival of Arts movement that started in the middle of the twentieth century. He entered and conducted choirs from the schools at which he taught and from the church and community choirs he trained. When Sir Howard arrived at the Ward Theatre to attend a function, he did so not only as the queen's representative: he had his own legitimacy.

Perhaps the clearest indication of things to come was given by Elsie Benjamin Barsoe in 1945, when her People's Theatre presented W.G. Ogilvie's *One Soja Man*. Instead of the governor's imprimatur on the cover of the programme, there appeared a simple statement: "Under the kind patronage of the ordinary people of Jamaica." This is the spiritual and social environment in which native-born governors general and their wives have taken over, with graciousness and consummate ease, as Jamaica's heads of state.

Elsie Benjamin Barsoe, actress and playwright

Sir Florizel Glasspole

Sir Howard Cooke

ACT II

THE JAMAICAN STAGE

6

The Pantomime

Jamaica's pantomime tradition began at the Ward Theatre on Boxing Day 1941 with a performance of *Jack and the Beanstalk* by the Little Theatre movement (LTM). Since that time, the LTM has staged sixty-seven more pantomimes,[1] and pantomime itself has become a uniquely Jamaican art form, quite distinct from British pantomime, from which it derived. The English pantomime tradition, according to *The New Encyclopaedia Britannica*, was begun in London in 1702 by the dancing master John Weaver of the Drury Lane Theatre. Within fifteen years, Weaver and his rival, John Rich of Lincoln's Inn Fields Theatre, were staging competing performances of shows that they called pantomimes. These performances became increasingly elaborate as their popularity grew:

> Weaver's shows were dramatic ballets with several performers (a form that France knew as *ballet d' action*) whereas Rich introduced grotesque scenes of Harlequin and Columbine, often pursued relentlessly by her father Pantaloon. Neither was the art of the solo *pantomimus* of Rome, save in name. Audiences came to demand such pieces before or after (or both) even serious plays. Garrick was to remark, "If you won't come to hear Lear and Hamlet, I must give you Harlequin", and he did. Gradually Harlequin, with his magic wand, was replaced in eminence by the clown, an adaptation of the *zanni* [a clown's partner]. In the nineteenth century the greatest of the clowns, Joseph Grimaldi, with his clown in "Mother Goose" helped bring to this pantomime the wealth of folklore, a repertory that was also tapped by others for "Red Riding Hood" and similar tales. This tradition evolved into the Christmas pantomime, still one of the most popular of English holiday entertainments. Among its continuing conventions is the role of "principal boy" which has been played by many of England's leading comediennes.[2]

Jack and the Beanstalk, the first LTM pantomime, produced by Greta Bourke and Henry Fowler, was scripted by Jack Bruton, an Englishman on the staff of Calabar High School in Kingston. The director was Elinor Lithgow, an English actress and drama tutor who was married to an English army officer stationed at Up Park Camp during the Second World War. Bruton drew upon well-known elements of British pantomime, and upon his recollections of productions he had seen in London since

Opposite: Louise Bennett (Coverley) and Ranny Williams in *Bredda Buck*, 1965. *Photo by Maria LaYacona.*

childhood. Importantly, he knew that, whatever the difficulties, it was critical to the spirit of pantomime that good should always triumph over evil and that it is in such conflict that drama begins. Except for minor concessions to locale, the production aimed at being typically English, and followed the English tradition sedulously. The show had elements of magic, and was mounted with all the sumptuousness local resources could devise.

Hazel Johnston provided the *corps de ballet*, and the local elite of upper St Andrew the chorus of men and women. In addition, the principal boy was played by a girl (Peggy Dougall) and the dame by a man (Mike Campbell), and there was the typical unrelated horseplay between acts. The organizers invited the best acting talent available. For example, Peggy Dougall had been trained at the Royal Academy of Dramatic Art (RADA), and Gene Martinez, who played the Squire, had been a trouper under Lindsay Downer in *The Fireflies* and *Clowns and Clatter*. At the gala opening the audience was primarily British or had British pretensions. In the end, the pseudo-British could not readily grasp the essential Englishness of certain nuances, nor could authentic British viewers understand the local innuendoes. Neither was there that two-way flow of psychic energy, of sufficient force between stage and audience, to make the production an unqualified success. Up to 1953, most productions had similar problems, though probably not quite to the same degree. But there was still enough merit, and sufficient snob appeal, to continue to lure audiences to the theatre.

With its pantomime performances, the LTM has given the Jamaican theatre a spine. When *Jack and the Beanstalk* opened at the Ward Theatre on Boxing Day in 1941, at 6:00 p.m., a black face on the boards was almost an oddity. Actually, there were a token few: Winston White and members of the East Queen Street Young Men's Fraternal in the musical numbers, and Miss Ethlyn Rhodd, a school teacher, who was invited to play the role of the witch. Horace Vaz, who reviewed the production, observed: "Although there are topical allusions in abundance, local political innuendo, which more often than not falls on deaf ears, the witch [played by Ethlyn Rhodd, an uncompromisingly black woman] was the only authentic piece in the pantomime."[3] Vaz's statement notwithstanding, there was at least one other attempt at authenticity in *Jack and the Beanstalk*: an Englishman, the Honourable Richard W. Youngman, chairman of the Jamaica Chamber of Commerce, was a giant of a man, at least seven and a half feet tall, and he was invited to play the giant. The comments about his performance were that he was "so good" and "so natural", but he was immediately recognized by the audience as a caricature of the governor, Sir Arthur Richards, who had been using his wartime defence regulations to detain individuals he felt were a danger to British authority. Youngman became peeved and wanted to withdraw from the production. The producers had to coax him into remaining in order to avoid creating an embarrassing situation.[4]

After *Jack and the Beanstalk*, pantomime productions were, for the most part, splendidly mounted. There were some eight other titles performed in Jamaica in the 1940s and 1950s: *Babes in the Wood* (1942), *Ali Baba and the Forty Thieves* (1944), *Toad of Toad Hall* (1944), *Aladdin and His Magic Lamps* (1945 and 1952), *Cinderella* (1947), *Beauty and the Beast* (1948), *Dick Whittington and His Cat* (1951), and *Robinson Crusoe* (1953). These titles are still among the twelve pantomimes most often performed in the United Kingdom today. The fairytales which formed the

Queenie's Daughter (1963), with Lois Kelly (*left*, later Lois Kelly Barrow Miller) as Ambrozine, the dressmaker, and Louise Bennett (Coverley) as the mother of a returning daughter

bases of these pantomimes had long before come to Jamaica as part of the colonial heritage and were therefore not entirely strange to local audiences.

Productions played for two weeks at most, and were barely able to pay their way. At prevailing admission charges, the elite alone were too small numerically to make longer runs feasible. Up to 1939, when touring companies from overseas visited, they were able to play daily for at least two weeks, but this was only because they usually had a dozen or more productions in their repertoire. Clearly, if the pantomime tradition were to be maintained, fundamental changes would have to take place. And it was to the credit of Greta and Henry Fowler that they had the foresight and the commonsense in those colonial days, to identify the LTM with nationalist and other important extra-theatrical considerations. As one of the authors has written elsewhere: "Once such a decision was taken others followed with unrelenting logic: in the choice of script, of dialogue, music, dancing, and setting, and finally in the choice of cast and the thrust of the production."[5]

As early as in the Anancy-based *Soliday and the Wicked Bird*, written by Vera Bell, and in *Bluebeard and Br'er Anancy*, book by Louise Bennett and Noel Vaz, the LTM began to make use of local folklore and mythology. *Soliday* was an experiment to create a purely Jamaican pantomime. It featured Hugh Morrison in the lead and as main dancer, but, as one critic wrote, there was not a sufficiently trained group of Jamaican actors, dancers and composers to maintain a purely Jamaican musical.

Hugh Morrison, director, dancer. *Courtesy of Alan Morrison.*

The following is an extract from an interview between Wycliffe Bennett and Louise and Eric Coverley:

> **Louise Bennett Coverley:** What happened was that the lady who produced [*Soliday*], Elinor Lithgow, was an English lady. She was a very good director, she had directed *Jack and the Beanstalk* and all that, but she did not get the feel of – she didn't quite understand what she was dealing with in the Jamaican thing, and it became a sort of conglomeration of all sorts of things put together and never really jelled; people liked it, the Jamaican things, but it did not do very well financially.
>
> **Eric Coverley:** She was not well acquainted with the folklore.
>
> **LBC:** [I'll] give you one instance. There was one scene (I'll never forget the scene), where Daisy Riley had just done a torrid dance to . . . "Jama congo in Jamaica", and then I ran in and told a tale of this bird, "Man Crow". "Man Crow, Man Crow da come", [I said,] and everybody [joined in], "Man Crow, Man Crow da come". And then, after all of the excitement, we sang "And did those feet in ancient times . . ." It was a lovely thing, [the song] "Jerusalem". The lady loved "Jerusalem". But I mean to say, at that spot it took the thing [down].
>
> **EC:** From one extreme to the other.
>
> **LBC:** And that was where the curtain came down.[6]

Four years later, in 1947, after a visit to Great Britain, Louise Bennett Coverley noted that *Cinderella* was on the boards at the Ward Theatre, and that the stage did not look any different from what she had left behind in England. "So I was writing in the newspaper", she later recalled in an interview, "and wrote some verse called 'Pantomime'. I can't remember all of it but I remember that I wrote, 'The Pantomime was pretty, pretty costumes, pretty light, nearly everybody white.' "[7] After the interview, the Fowlers were bombarded with calls suggesting that Louise was raising the colour question. Miss Lou responded:

> No, no. All I was saying was that the stage was not reflecting the talent we had in Jamaica. And that we should have a stage that looked like the people we have in Jamaica. So they asked me if I would write a pantomime with a Jamaican theme. They suggested "Busha Bluebeard and Br'er Anancy". I said sure, I would do it only if I had a producer of the calibre of Noel Vaz to work along with me.[8]

Noel Vaz claims that it was he who persuaded Louise to join him in reworking the Bluebeard story into a Jamaican setting. This seems a brilliant example of theatre management on the part of the Fowlers, who finessed both Louise and Noel into believing that each of them had come up with the idea in the first instance. In the words of Eric Coverly (Louise's husband), "You see, they challenged her and she accepted the challenge."

The first scene for this pantomime was written almost totally from a workshop held at Knox College using spontaneous talk by the students. Thus the local themes were resumed with *Busha Bluebeard and Br'er Anancy*. Vera Bell was excited by the progress of Jamaican theatre since the production of her *Soliday*, and, with commendable generosity of spirit, she said in a review that no one could fail to hand the LTM a bouquet for the splendid job they had done in establishing the Christmas pantomime as an integral part of Jamaica's traditions-in-the-making. She added that it seemed abundantly clear that a truly Jamaican show such as *Bluebeard and Br'er Anancy* had evolved only through the gradual breaking down of the traditional English pantomime to suit local needs, keeping what was suitable and discarding what was not.

Now, with Noel Vaz, Louise Bennett Coverley and so many others capable of bringing a professional outlook to the stage, there could be no turning back. The highlight of the show was the combined "Ballet of the Weeds" and "Ballet of Weird Creatures", which must be regarded as a triumph not only for Ivy Baxter and Anatole Soohih, the choreographers, but also for Stella Shaw, who designed and painted the costumes for the weird creatures, Lois Abrahams, who executed them, and Mrs Winifred Doran, who made the papier-mâché masks.

Consistent indigenization brought growing audience support: what started as an annual production with eight or nine performances during the first decade is now a show of between eighty and over one hundred performances each year. Despite the hostility of Jamaican officialdom towards African matters up until the recent past, there are still African drumbeats and rhythms everywhere, and Anancy, the Ashanti spider-god, remains the folktale hero of Jamaica.

Br'er Anancy, superbly played by Ranny Williams for many years, was quick to establish himself as part of the Jamaican pantomime tradition. In 1954 Greta Fowler wrote *Anancy and the Magic Mirror*, the second show with Anancy in the title. With casting along community-wide, as distinct from narrow elitist lines, with stories and

The Honourable All Purpus and the Dancing Princesses (1979), with Ranny Williams. *Photo by Monica DaSilva.*

legends that many had known since childhood, and with themes that everyone could empathize with, pantomime became the show for all Jamaicans at Christmastime. In every department – in writing, directing and acting; in scenic, costume and lighting design, and execution; in music and the dance – almost everybody who was either established or would eventually make a name in the Jamaican theatre became involved. Thus the pantomime became an important training ground for the national theatre.

The pantomime as we know it today is "a strange medley of burlesque, musical comedy, fairy play, music-hall turns and revue which has developed from the highly conventionalized entertainment of the Italian *commedia dell'arte*, of which only the clown and his associates are the relics. No other form of public entertainment has passed through so many changes while remaining the same thing."[9] This statement applies both to the English pantomime, which is over three hundred years old, and the Jamaican pantomime, now approaching its seventieth anniversary. In the case of the Jamaican pantomime, the form remained, for many years, primarily that of the English pantomime, and certain stock elements – such as the unrelated horseplay between acts, and the principal boy being played by a girl, the dame by a man – came to be taken for granted by scriptwriters, artistic directors and audiences alike. It is amazing how Jamaican actors have taken to the style of the *commedia dell'arte* as if they were born to it.

After Greta Fowler's script in 1954, Louise Bennett Coverley wrote the book for the next three shows: *Anancy and Pandora* (1955), *Anancy and Beeny Bud* (1956), and *Busha Bluebeard* (1957), which was in fact a remounting of the 1949 production. A year after Coverley's *Busha Bluebeard* appeared on stage, the Jamaican government sent it to Trinidad for the Arts Festival to mark the opening of the Federal Parliament, in 1958. In the view of Henry Fowler, *Busha Bluebeard* initiated a new type of deliberately West Indian musical. Sir Hugh Wooding, chief justice of Trinidad and Tobago, and later chancellor of the University of the West Indies, told the writers of the present volume that *Busha Bluebeard* was better than anything they had ever seen on celluloid in Trinidad up to that time.

After the production of Coverley's *Busha Bluebeard*, Anancy was given a break, and Ranny Williams, with the support of Louise Bennett, wrote *Quashie Lady* (1958) and *Jamaica Way* (1959). *Quashie Lady* restructures into a Jamaican context the American musical *My Fair Lady*, itself adapted from George Bernard Shaw's *Pygmalion*. *Jamaica Way* (1959) treats the theme of immigration to the United Kingdom. Almost a whole village, so it seems, migrates to London in pursuit of the Busha's daughter Annette and her lover, who have eloped.

In 1960 the LTM staged *Carib Gold*, based on Cecile Nobrega's drama *Stabroek Fantasy*, which dealt with gold prospecting in British Guiana (now Guyana). Then in 1962, the year of Jamaica's political independence from Great Britain, LTM mounted the American musical *Finian's Rainbow*. The choice of an American script for a Jamaican national celebration came as a surprise to most people, who were expecting something spectacularly Jamaican to mark the event. The other production chosen for the occasion was Sam Hillary's *Banana Boy* (1961), which had had forty-eight performances by the middle of February 1962, and was revived for a further thirteen performances as part of the official programme of the independence celebra-

Charles Hyatt as Mrs Uppercrust (the Dame) in *Quashie Lady* (1958). *Courtesy of C. Hyatt Jr.*

tions. The Afro-Jamaican rhythms of Carlos Malcolm's original score for that play and the simulation of the train's passing to Port Antonio by the magic of music, dance and light still linger in the memory.

On reflection, the staging of *Finian's Rainbow* was either an act of defiance or an act of desperation. The producers had wished to signal that, after twenty-one years, it was time for a change, and the American product, "a real musical" albeit on an Irish theme, was to give them a chance to test the waters. Since *Soliday and the Wicked Bird* in 1943, Jamaican folk and original music had been introduced and, as demonstrated by Ivy Baxter in *Bluebeard and Anancy* in 1949, Jamaican dance idioms were being evolved. With the elements of Jamaican story, music and dance, and with the development of a composite style of acting, the pantomime had become immediately identifiable with Jamaican life and thought. Having to create a new show each year called for fresh script-writing, new musical composition and choreography, and originality in costume and stage design and decor.

Evolution into an indigenous Jamaican show meant that the ingredients of the traditional English pantomime were continually being superseded. In *Jamaica Way* (1959) the main surviving elements were those of the dame played by a man (Charles Hyatt), the transformation scene, and the traditional horseplay. In *Carib Gold* the following year, only the transformation scene and the horseplay remained. Thus there had been considerable departure from English practice; and the organizers, while retaining the name "pantomime" for box office purposes, began adding the word "musical" after the word "pantomime", thereby creating the term "pantomime musical". This practice started with *Jamaica Way* and lasted seven years until the second production of *Queenie's Daughter* in 1966.

In 1959, Greta and Henry Fowler, while on a visit to Oxford, saw Rex Nettleford's choreography of a good-humouredly updated musical based on Aristophanes' *Birds*. Mrs Fowler extracted a promise from Nettleford to work with the LTM in the future. On his return to Jamaica a few months later he took over the choreography of *Jamaica Way*, which was being directed by Robin Midgely, then at the Jamaica Broad-

Charles Hyatt and Louise Bennett Coverley in knock-about at a pantomime. *Courtesy of C. Hyatt Jr.*

casting Corporation, on loan from the British Broadcasting Corporation. The idea of the singer-dancer-actor exemplified by Alma Mock Yen as Mantaripa in *Carib Gold* (1960), and Leonie Forbes in a number of other pantomimes, took hold. It was with the 1961 panto *Banana Boy*, with Carlos Malcolm's totally original musical score, that the dance became an integral part of the show rather than set pieces fitted in. (Nettleford both directed and choreographed.) The word "musical" was then dropped as an unnecessary encumbrance, since everybody in Jamaica knew what was meant by the term "pantomime".

In the Jamaican pantomime the story is told directly as well as obliquely; ideally the narrative is as much in the music and in the dance as it is in the dialogue. *Jamaica Way*, *Carib Gold* and *Banana Boy* were in a number of respects watershed productions. Under the direction of Rex Nettleford, for example, dance became an increasingly important component. The performers had been recruited from the membership of the Ivy Baxter Creative Dance Group and from the ballet schools of Fay Simpson, Madame Soohih and others. After working together in these three productions, the dancers decided, in 1962, under the leadership of Rex Nettleford and Eddy Thomas, to form the National Dance Theatre Company of Jamaica.

The next pantomime, *Queenie's Daughter* (1963), was written by a panel consisting of Greta and Henry Fowler, Louise Bennett Coverley, Ranny Williams and Lois Kelly Barrow. The segments were pulled together by Dennis Scott, who edited the final script. Here was a fine example of group authorship. One of the most successful pantomimes to date, *Queenie's Daughter* has had two revivals, one in 1966 and the other in 1973. Each show warrants far ampler treatment than this presentation allows, but a description in some detail of the 1973 production, and some others, will help us to understand the important developments that have taken place.

Jamaica Way (1959), with Charles Hyatt, Ranny Williams and Louise Bennett Coverley

In *Queenie's Daughter*, the plot seems to have been reworked from an American prototype, *Apple Annie*, a short story from Damon Runyon's *More Than Somewhat*, but there is no way in which this production could have come into existence elsewhere. As Harry Milner noted, "The tale of an old apple-seller at the height of the depression, dressed up and financed for a day by her hoodlum friends to meet her daughter from overseas, who does not know of her mother's social position, has been on the whole successfully Jamaicanized."[10] The production was skilfully directed by Carroll Dawes. Eddy Thomas designed the excellent settings and costumes, and was also responsible for the choreography. George Carter plotted and executed the lighting. The production made ingenious use of space, light and colour. The transformation scenes and *a vista* changes revealed, in turn, racecourse, ship, airport, grass-yard, hotel exterior and ballroom. Yet nothing seemed over-contrived and the audience's willing suspension of disbelief was never frustrated.

The director had a great cast: Louise Bennett Coverley, Lois Kelly Barrow (later Miller), Ranny Williams, Oliver Samuels, Leonie Forbes Amiel, and Bobby Ghisays, to name some of those whose performances after so many years still remain fresh in the memory. These players move between the international and the Jamaican styles of acting with ease, but for this production their training could never have been completed on any other soil, or by any other theatrical tradition.

As Queenie, the good-hearted Jamaican matriarch, Louise Bennett Coverley gave Jamaica one of her finest performances; and her scene with Lois Kelly Barrow (later Miller) as the social-climbing Miss Malaprop of a dressmaker, remains one of the gems of the Jamaican stage. Another powerful feature of the production was the relationship between actor and audience. Often the action flowed into and out of the audience, thereby heightening the participatory experience.

The same panel of writers, with the addition of Doris Duperley and the show's artistic director, Derek Boughton, wrote *Bredda Buck* (1964) and, with the addition of Orford St John, *Morgan's Dream of Old Port Royal* (1965). The Anancy cycle returned with a revival of Louise Bennett Coverley's *Anancy and Pandora* in 1967. This was followed by *Anancy and Doumbey* (1968), by Sonia and Don Mills, *Moonshine Anancy* (1969), by Barbara Gloudon, and *Rockstone Anancy* (1970), by Sylvia Wynter and Alex Gradussov. These are trickster tales that follow the popular New World tradition.

Bredda Buck calls to mind the title role in *Le Bourgeois Gentilhomme*, Molière's comic masterpiece. Hugh Moss Solomon looked the part, but did not quite bring it to life. The production, nevertheless, had some redeeming features: dances created and musical numbers staged by Rex Nettleford, sets and costumes designed by Eddy Thomas, and Mapletoft Poulle's orchestration and direction of the original music that he, Hugh Moss Solomon and Lois Kelly Barrow created. There were sensitively realized supporting roles, notably by Inez Hibbert as Grannie, Louise Bennett Coverley as Mirie, and Sheila O'Reilly (later Carter) as the chirpy young heroine, Reggie. But the *pièce de résistance* was provided by Ranny Williams. Norman Rae put it neatly:

> As last year's . . . *Queenie's Daughter* was a personal triumph for Louise Bennett, so . . . *Bredda Buck* [is] . . . a field day for her comedy partner, Ranny Williams. Although his is not the title role, Williams has rarely worked harder nor injected such energy and neat sense of timing as he does into Amos, the samfie man with his eye on a portion of Bredda Buck's new wealth.
>
> As he snuggles up to the comfortable Louise, cunningly feeds Buck's ego, finds himself unable to deliver the social goods to Buck's "soiree", Williams' Amos emerges a delightfully engaging character and one surprisingly far from the Anancy convention which this comedian has built up in pantomime-musicals over the years.[11]

Morgan's Dream of Old Port Royal opens with a prologue. Under the leadership of Alexander Morgan, the Brotherhood of Port Royal is meeting to make plans to restore the glories of their ancient city. Intoxicated by the singing and the euphoria of the occasion, the leader falls into a trance. There the action begins. In his dream world, he becomes Henry Morgan and performs exploits of the famous buccaneer – the sacking of Porto Bello and the City of Panama. We see Port Royal as "the wealth-

Sylvia Wynter, playwright, director

Morgan's Dream of Old Port Royal, 1965. *Photo by Maria LaYacona.*

iest and wickedest city in the world". Here the buccaneers marketed the French silks, Spanish gold, jewels, wines and other booty from the lands and ships they raided. They roistered in the taverns, and in the bordellos met women with whom they would trade their fortunes for a night of pleasure. Not only bawdy wenches and sailors, but also aristocrats and historical figures appear on the play's Rabelaisian stage – Sir Thomas Modyford and Sir Henry Lynch, governors of Jamaica, among them.

This original and historically authentic musical drama marked the twenty-fifth anniversary of the LTM. Never at any time heavy-handed, the production plotted a delicate balance between satire and romance, and served up a heady punch of courage, rhetoric, romance and guile, to which Captain Morgan would undoubtedly have raised his famous cup in approval. Rex Nettleford directed, with music by Sonny Bradshaw. Trevor Rhone was the assistant director. It would have been helpful if in the dream sequence the costumier, Angela Waterlow, had added some suggestions of corpulence to the slight frame of Ranny Williams, who nevertheless played the title role with infectious gusto. Harry Milner gave the production glowing praise. He said: "No play yet put on in Jamaica has been so beautifully mounted and costumed. The script is genuinely original . . . a full scale Jamaican historical musical play, glorifying the past, but with its tongue well in its cheek. It is an odd mixture of glamour, rhetoric and anancyism, which is typically Jamaican and utterly delightful."[12]

The Anancy Cycle

We will now look at the four stories in the next Anancy cycle, but we must begin by asking what or who Anancy is, and what is the source of his power and his hold over Jamaican folk life. In his origins, Anancy, the central Jamaican folk figure, derives from the folklore and religious concepts of the Fanti-Ashanti civilization of West Africa. The 1970 *Rockstone Anancy* programme described him thus:

> Through the Maroons, in particular, central elements of this civilization have survived, transforming themselves into primary aspects of Jamaican folklore and folk belief.
>
> Accompong, the name of the Maroon stronghold, derives from Onyan Kopon and is one aspect of the gods of the Akan-speaking people of this civilization. Nyankopon (or Onyankopon) is one of a triad; the other two are Onyame and Odomankoma. It is the aspect of Nyankopon who is nearest to man.
>
> Nyankopon seems to be at once Creator-god and Trickster hero. His other name is Ananse Kokuroko, which links him in this aspect as trickster to the folk stories which have become central to our experience. These "trickster stories" have been described as "parables of more complex religious thought; parables devised by the learned caste of priests for popular tradition." But apart from these trickster tales of Anancy there is another body of legends and historical myths, in which Nyankopon/Anancy figures as creator-god [and] hero. These are the "sacred and guarded possessions of a few selected elders of the tribe" and have been described as the Old Testament of Africa.[13]

Leonie Forbes and Keith Amiel directed the revival of *Anancy and Pandora* (1967). The show was choreographed by Rex Nettleford, with music adapted by Louise Bennett and Marjorie Whylie, and lyrics by Louise Bennett Coverley and Greta Fowler. Sets were designed by Donat Bucknor and Michael Crosby, costumes by Paul Methuen, and lighting, as usual, by George Carter.

In the play, a village woman named Makeke has a beautiful baby, whom she calls Pandora. Because Makeke suffers a great loss on the day of Pandora's christening, she takes an oath to lock the child away from the sight of all mortal men. She makes a song that only she and Pandora know, and whenever she returns home she sings it as a signal for Pandora to open the door.

Eighteen years pass and the beautiful Pandora, still locked away from the sight of all men, has become something of a legend. From all over the land, men seek her hand in marriage, but Makeke refuses them all. Among the suitors is the Young Chief (played by the youthful Willard White), but he too is turned down. Anancy, who has been monitoring the proceedings, offers to introduce the Young Chief to Pandora but, of course, he must first find the secret to open Pandora's door. So Anancy transforms himself into a spider and waits undiscovered near Makeke's house in the woods. He listens to Makeke singing the song, and soon catches the words and tune, but his voice is coarse and Pandora will not open the door. How Anancy overcomes this difficulty, catches Pandora in his net and carries her to the Young Chief, and what happens afterwards provides light-hearted fun for young and old alike. Forbes and Amiel's production was a well-put-together show.

The following year, Norman Rae directed an Anancy tale, *Anancy and Doumbey* (1968). Don and Sonia Mills composed the music and lyrics, while Marjorie Whylie was the musical director, and Rex Nettleford staged the dances and musical numbers. Unlike *Anancy and Pandora*, in which Anancy won Pandora for the Young Chief, this pantomime portrays Anancy's attempts to claim the hand of the Princess for himself. In order to do so, he must first pass himself off as the hero responsible for ridding the land of the evil spirit Doumbey. This dread monster has been causing fear and destruction on land and sea, and the King is finally persuaded to offer an unlimited reward. As the programme note says, there are three volunteers for the task, "including a most unlikely one, and the contest proceed[s] in most unusual ways to a most unpredictable result, in which national safety is secured, and happy romance smiles on the true hero and his beautiful Princess." Despite its cheerful ending, however, *Anancy and Doumbey* does have its sombre notes. As Verena Reckord has noted, the image of the bird of doom in the play symbolizes "the atmosphere of depression in the island when talks of corruption and graft in high places threatened the stability of the society".[14]

One of the things a theatrical director does in studying a script is to look for those leads that will get immediate responses from an audience. He will use the setting, lighting, music, quality of movement, or speech – anything to clue the audience in. Such intentions are well served when new plays are alive with modern resonances. Achievement lies in finding the right image – visual, aural, psychological – to pull all the factors into focus. When the playwright supplies the image, the director begins his work one or two (or perhaps several) steps ahead. In the case of *Anancy and Doumbey*, Professor John Figueroa, Caribbean scholar and writer, paid Louise Bennett Coverley a wonderful tribute, in saying that she had offered yet another opportunity to remind us, in her kindly way, of how fortunate we were to have her quality of genius living and working with us.

In 1969, Barbara Gloudon, a journalist by profession, entered the pantomime scene with *Moonshine Anancy*. It was directed by Eddy Thomas, who also did the choreography and designed the decor and costumes. In the romantic leads were Harold Brady and Faith D'Aguilar, with Louise Bennett Coverley, Ranny Williams and Lois Kelly Barrow in the other key roles.

Moonshine Anancy was based on a subject that was especially topical at the time – lunar exploration. Even though Jamaica will never be able to land a man on the moon, and no one in his right mind would ever think so, the idea that such launches were becoming the order of the day was precisely the point of the play's imaginative attack. The everyday frame of reference adjusts itself dramatically, and we are catapulted, comic strip fashion, into a fun-filled world of make-believe.

As the pantomime opens, we discover that the prizes that year for Jamaica's national lottery are seats on *Maccafat Three*, the nation's third spaceship to the moon:

> Five have won places: Jan and Robert, two young people trying to bridge the Generation Gap and solve their own personal social difficulties; Miss Tess, a lady who lived and studied in Old Madrid and now heads the Mission to the Moon in search of little green

men; Miss Corpie, a policewoman who has been working for her first stripe for the last ten years and hopes to achieve this with a successful Moon Mission; Bredda Soul (alias Anancy) who is the official pothole "filler-upper", and having heard about the craters on the Moon, is only too keen to get the knack of lunar crater mechanics.[15]

The surprise in store for the space-travellers, and the even greater surprises on their return to planet earth, exploit the comic possibilities of the story.

Moonshine Anancy was to be the start, for Gloudon, of a long association with the Pantomime, and her work thereafter would come to provoke critical controversy as she broke new ground in connecting themes of contemporary social concern with comedy and fantasy. A new feature of production began here: the double-casting of the young romantic leads – Claudia Robinson and Raymond Hill alternating with Eleanor Wint and Buddy Pouyat. The strength of the romantic leads began to shift the weight of the production somewhat from the older stalwarts like Louise Bennett Coverley, who had made her first appearance in 1943 and continued to play the beloved "mother figure" for many years until she retired in 1976. (Ranny Williams, by contrast, started in pantomime in 1942 and continued to perform right up to 1980.)

A third Anancy tale, *Rockstone Anancy* (1970), was directed by Paul Methuen and choreographed by Joyce Campbell. Subtitled *The Rise and Fall of Rockstone Anancy*, the pantomime boasted a script and lyrics by Sylvia Wynter and Alex Gradussov, who have described the production as a tale of "magical morality" based on the assumption that the loss of the creator-god-hero aspect of the Anancy myth is a root cause of psychic disturbance in our society:

> We imagine that most of our ills stem from this personality split and in the working out of the pantomime, the trickster aspect of Anancy – seen through the soul of Jonkonnu, is at last, through the purging of the spirit, rejoined to his Creator-god-hero aspect. Mother Balm, the skilled healer with herbs, is imagined as a descendant of Asase Afua . . . Earth goddess and Goddess of fertility; as the "wife" of Nyankopon, she is Nature in its creative aspect. Hence she is able to carry through the ritual purging of an Anancy whose exile from part of himself becomes dangerous for the survival of his community. The gods appear only to disappear. We take and retrace the lost steps of our past the better to equip ourselves for the way forward.[16]

Programme cover for *Music Boy* (1971)

In the play, Anancy and his crony, Andy, have just settled a strike in Power Square, Babylon City, when they persuade Madame Culture-Vulture to invest all her savings in Anancy's business ventures. Andy's engagement to Blossom, who is the daughter of Madame Culture-Vulture and a close friend of Princess, Anancy's daughter, helps to seal the agreement. As the plot progresses, we witness Anancy's entrepreneurial schemes, his duplicity and evasion of income tax, his "come-uppance" and his spiritual redemption through Mother Balm's intercession. Several sub-plots – the restlessness of the students and their confrontation with the university authorities, the romance of Scorcher and Princess, Andy's *volte-face*, and Blossom's folk research in the village of Look Behind – interweave and enrich the texture of the theatrical experience.

After *Rockstone Anancy*, the next thirty years, from 1971 to 2001, witnessed a further proliferation of the Anancy theme. Even when Anancy was not listed as a role, some aspect of his personality seemed very much present beneath the persona of a villain or "trickster-character", whatever his name, whether as Mr Shifty in Trevor Rhone's *Music Boy* or as Seaside Harry in Barbara Gloudon's *Pirate Princess*.

In Trevor Rhone's chronological development as a dramatist, *Music Boy* (1971) followed his co-authorship of the film *The Harder They Come*. His onscreen depiction of "Shanty Town" spawned the popular cultural entertainment that is reggae, and the genre has produced its own folk heroes: "Dem a loot, dem a shoot, dem a wail in Shanty Town", sings Desmond Dekker; "walking down the road with a pistol in your waist, Johnny you're too bad", warn the Slickers. In *The Harder They Come*, Ivanhoe Martin, alias Rhygin (played by Jimmy Cliff), is an anti-hero buffeted by the hard knocks of a ghetto existence into making a career of crime, before coming to a tragic end.

Rhone's *Music Boy*, however, seeks a triumphantly happy resolution. In the play, we follow the rise to "pop" stardom of young Junior McIntosh, who has to make his way to fame against the machinations of Count Skanker, the promoter, and the manipulations of Mr Shifty, the trickster figure. Junior is succoured by his mother, Miss Mammas, a market vendor who has her own problems to overcome in her old-time romance with the amorous Stripeless. The story has a bittersweet mixture of disappointments, frustrations and successes that leaves a lump in the throat.

Still memorable are the performances of Louise Bennett Coverley as Miss Mammas, Ranny Williams as Shifty, and Keith Amiel and (later) Buddy Pouyat as Count Skanker. Thom Cross directed with flair. The choreography by Rex Nettleford and Jackie Guy made accurate production points, while Boris Gardiner's music articulated the feelings and moods of the story, and Jonathan Porter's settings helped us to believe that what was taking place was real. A supreme achievement was the authenticity of Trevor Rhone's dialogue.

We come now to Barbara Gloudon's *The Pirate Princess*, which ended its record-breaking run of 121 performances on Saturday night, 1 May 1982, at the Ward Theatre. The script treats the exploits of two actual eighteenth-century pirates, Mary Read and Anne Bonny, who haunted the Caribbean with the legendary Calico Jack Rackham, and were captured off the coast of Jamaica in 1726. They cleverly disguised their sex and by some accounts were fiercer in sword-fighting and various other respects than most men of their day. Bobby Ghisays directed, and the production starred Leonie Forbes, Oliver Samuels and Brian Heap, with Marva Gallimore, Faith Nelson, Joan Grant and Paul Anderson in supporting roles. Jackie Guy did the choreography, with additional movement for the fencing sequence by Ronnie Nasralla. Conroy Cooper created the music, and the costumes were designed by Gabrielle Harban. George Carter plotted the lighting and Henry Muttoo had a field day designing and creating the colourful costumes and sets. As the curtain rose each night to reveal the pirate ship floating upon the blue Caribbean, there was an air of expectancy and the audience applauded. Another spontaneous outburst greeted Muttoo's underwater setting. A poet, Neville Dawes, visited the Ward one night with his family, and wrote:

> Every pantomime must have its magic and the sea change in the *Pirate Princess* was fascinating. Under water was blue illusion, sea animals cavort and Rackham continues to

Pirate Princess (1981), with Brian Heap (*left*) and Bobby Ghisays

> clown. The Princess is married to William by the King of the Sea (David Ellis), as the King and the Company sing "Under the Sea", piped back strongly to the audience. Things were sagging in Act 2 and this scene brought the pantomime back to life. We deserved more than the three minutes or so of this scene. Full of life, too, was the music of Conroy Cooper and the efficient pantomime orchestra.
>
> The heart of Barbara Gloudon's book is the presentation of Jamaican "topicalities" (social and political "digs" at current botherations) which have a curious gentleness and never become bitterly satirical. These topicalities kept the audience in cathartic uproar. Sallies and uproar, we feel, should be seen by all intelligent politicians.
>
> Altogether, we had a truly Jamaican night, over-riding the concealed blending of the British music-hall and the American musical tradition. It is Bobby Ghisays's smooth, integrated show of song, dance, farce and enchantment.[17]

The writer feels constrained by the exceptional quality of their performances to add to Dawes's comments brief mention of Brian Heap's Calico Jack Rackham and Oliver Samuels's Seaside Harry. Heap's attention to behaviouristic detail helped him to create a most credible Rackham and provided one of his finest performances. Oliver Samuels appeared after the opening, well up stage, in blue shirt and white straw hat, and without uttering a word opened his mouth, showing his white teeth, and broke into a broad smile that embraced the entire audience. The theatre erupted with thunderous applause. That is genius.

Globalization and the Indigenization of the Pantomime

We have introduced selectively most of the earlier pantomimes of the LTM, as well as the establishment of the Jamaican pantomime tradition and its harnessing of local resources – writing, speech, drama, music, dance, design, spectacle and artistic direction among them. We will now turn to examine how these local talents contributed to the increasing indigenization of Jamaican pantomime, even as Jamaica itself came to face a number of outside influences that pulled it towards the demands of globalization.

During the run of *Fifty/Fifty*, the fiftieth anniversary panto, the writer interviewed Henry Fowler, the then-surviving co-founder of the LTM. In quasi-valedictory tones he said, "What I would like to emphasize is that during the entire period, there was a tremendous body of young people taking part both in the pantomime and other LTM productions." He then listed quite an impressive galaxy of writers, producers, actors, dancers and technical personnel, culminating with Barbara Gloudon, who, he said, was a great tower of strength as a playwright and as chairperson since 1976. He continued: "Now what has happened, and this is a good thing, is that there has grown up around Kingston a tremendous number of small shows with actors and other personnel, many of whom started in pantomime productions or were inspired by this development of drama in Jamaica, and this is exciting."[18]

Costume, set design and their execution are important elements of any stage production. The visual effect they contribute helps to define the story to be told. Over the years the LTM has succeeded in attracting the enthusiastic support of a number of outstanding artists and architects to design and execute its sets and costumes. Among them have been well-established artists as well as younger ones at the beginning of their careers. Gil Pratley (the architect who designed and built the Little Theatre); costume designers Angela Waterlow and Anya Gloudon-Nelson; artists Albert Huie, Carl Abrahams, Eddy Thomas, Colin Garland, Henry Muttoo, Donat Bucknor and Laura Facey – these immediately come to mind.

The pantomime is not merely a postcolonial changeling, or just the hothouse mistress of the elite. It is as familiar and uncompromisingly Jamaican as rice and peas and ackee and salt fish in the national diet. From this secure footing it responsibly firms up its relevance and rootedness as a play-form, whether we go back to pre-independence times or start with mento, reggae or dancehall.

Rex Nettleford, Errol Hill, Noel Vaz, Louise Bennett Coverley and the Fowlers were among the first theatre practitioners in the region to recognize the global nature of this challenge and the response that was necessary. Because of the pantomime's firm Caribbean-wide stance over the past sixty-eight years, the LTM has been able to deal with the demands of globalization that bear so heavily upon all developing countries today, and draw freely upon the riches and civilizations and cultures of Europe, Asia, Africa and the Americas to fashion its own, unique Jamaican model.

Fifty/Fifty (1990), with Fitz Weir (*left*)

For the 2003 revival of *Jack and the Beanstalk*, for example, set designer Michael Lorde had to "recreate elements of Jamaica's past, paying special attention to detail, colour and scale". For this he prepared four main set pieces, including Miss Daisy's house unit, which doubled as the Giant's kitchen cupboard, and the creation of detail for five backdrops, painted very carefully, with shades and shadows added to create the illusion of depth. The greatest challenge was the Macca Tree, which had to grow and be climbed. This was made in the manner

Designing and Executing a Set

MICHAEL LORDE

My own design approach and philosophy as it relates to set design is the creation of a series of stage images that assist the writer and director in telling a story.

The front curtain, to my mind, is the threshold between different worlds: a world of reality and a world of make-believe. As an architect and designer, I feel that it is my responsibility to take the audience on a visual ride in this world. I try to accomplish this by the use of various levels and planes; use of proportion; use of colour; attention to detail and the use of solids and voids which create shade and shadows on three-dimensional forms. I also use shade and shadows on two dimensional surfaces to create an illusion of depth, texture and pattern.

My journey with the LTM started in 1986 with the design and construction of two jangah [shrimp] costumes and a mermaid's tail in *River Mumma and the Golden Table*.

The jangah costumes, although small, required research which saw me catching jangah at the river behind my grandparents' house in the country, dissecting them and studying their shape, colour and movement, and then figuring out a way of transferring this to the human form.

In 1991, having returned from my studies overseas, I was given the opportunity to design the set and fantasy costumes for *Man Deh Yah*. With ideas and sketches starting to flow during initial rehearsals, the long but enjoyable process began. Prior to starting the design, however, I obtained measured drawings of the stage for the Ward Theatre and the Little Theatre, both venues for the production.

As analysis and design are inseparable, I started sketching, looking at the available constraints or challenges of the space, points of entry and exit, circulation, sight lines, views, massing, quality of light and characters. Ideas for this set design came from the Jamaican countryside, the coat of arms and Papine Park (in Kingston). As the main setting was a park, horizontal planes representing grass in planters were sloped to be visible by the audience.

All set pieces were interchangeable for economy and there was only one backdrop, which was used for the "fantasy scene". In this scene the cotton tree opened to reveal the spirits of our ancestors.

In moving the set from the Ward Theatre to the Little Theatre (which did not have a fly tower), this backdrop was split and then hung on traverse lines. The spread of the tree's canopy was designed as a border, which hung in front and above the cotton tree's trunk. An initial design decision was taken to use the white cyclorama lit in scenes by projected clouds in motion. To create a sense of depth, painted sheets of plywood cut out to look like mountains constantly created a silhouette against the cyclorama, which changed with the lighting. There was also coordination with the costume designer, Anya Gloudon, to ensure that colours used were compatible.

---

*Michael Lorde has been the major set designer of the Little Theatre's annual pantomime for more than seventeen years (1986, 1987 and from 1991 on). In this extract, from a paper prepared for Wycliffe Bennett in 2008, he explains the degree of scholarship, imagination and energy that go into designing and executing a set for any show.

of a timber spiral staircase with a crewmember standing behind it for additional stability.

Apart from the creation of recognizably Jamaican set designs such as Lorde's, choreography on the Jamaican stage has also witnessed a gradual indigenization in style, as Rex Nettleford once described in reply to a critic who could find no virtue in the Jamaican modern dance movement. Speaking about the integration of the dance into the pantomime, and of his own role as one of the sustainers of the tradition, Nettleford said:

> The early LTM pantomimes, true to their English model, utilized dancing to add spice to the spectacle. This, indeed, was the way in which dance was used in musical theatre everywhere in the West, whether in grand opera, operettas, or the American musical, though Agnes de Mille had begun to revolutionize its use in the watershed *Oklahoma*. [It] was little more than an expendable diversion to pep up or to hold up the plot, depending on how one looked at it.
>
> Changes on the metropolitan theatre scene were not lost on the LTM producers, as was evident in the evolutions of other departments of the panto. Both Greta and Henry Fowler of the LTM kept abreast of developments in the London West End theatre in particular, and returning theatre artists like Noel Vaz never scrupled to force the form out of antiquity into modernity and relevance . . .
>
> Greta Fowler had that entrepreneurial eye to bring to centre stage not only Louise Bennett [Coverley], the people's poet, and Ranny Williams, the most popular comedian of variety concert and radio fame, but also the music of Jamaica, as against the popular American and British show tunes borrowed and used without compunction in earlier days. It was clear that when we fell back on our own resources, gems like the immortal "Evening Time", composed by Barbara Ferland (with words by Louise Bennett [Coverley]), became possible.
>
> In time, the LTM bowed to the dance of Jamaica when that art form began to show signs of take-off, even if that take-off was to be less counted by veteran critic Harry Milner, who described it as entering after 1960 "a period of prolonged ethnicity, proto-Africanism and folksiness". The truth of the matter is that dance in the Jamaican pantomime, as in the rest of the country's burgeoning theatre, had had its full dose of . . . proto-Europeanism, and a folksiness rooted in the cultures of mid- and southern European peasants dancing the mazurka and the tarantella.
>
> In the process of indigenizing the pantomime, dance reflecting the movement patterns of this part of the world in the body-language of its people, provided an undoubted route to authenticity and artistic credibility. . . It continues to do so to its advantage and, the entire dance movement puts great store by the long process of cross-fertilization, selection and distillation of essences which remain the best guarantee for an enriched and dynamic cultural life anywhere . . .
>
> It was not until 1958 that things changed radically to accommodate the, by then, increasingly definitive developments in Jamaican dance theatre. Ivy Baxter, following her successful "Creations in Dance" show at the Ward in 1954, had gone on to create dances for *Anancy and the Magic Mirror*, to which she brought from her dance-show set pieces suitably adapted. The Baxter dancers, of which I was one, did not rehearse with the rest of the cast. We rehearsed in the Baxter studio at Caledonia Avenue, Cross Roads, and took down the dances to fit them into the production. Such was the way in which ballet studios operated. For the dances could exist independent of the show and vice-versa. It was also the entire group that was engaged by the LTM, not individual dancers just as it was with the classical ballet schools.[19]

Barbara Gloudon

Barbara Gloudon, playwright.
Courtesy of LTM.

Barbara Gloudon is one of those persons in Jamaica whose name immediately strikes a familiar note with people from all walks of life. For some, her name means Stella, the columnist who for years amused Jamaicans with news of local goings on. She has also been a newspaper editor and feature writer, with responsibility for the arts and entertainment sections of the *Daily Gleaner*, and continues to be a prominent talk show host appearing on air (RJR) several days per week. For others, Barbara Gloudon has been one of Jamaica's tourism ambassadors. Over the period when she was deputy director for tourism, she won many friends for Jamaica. She logged many hundreds of miles across the United States and Canada, talking to journalists, conventioneers, Joe Traveller, television and radio audiences, travel agents – telling them about the beauties and strengths of Jamaica, the island that is "more than a beach".

For still others, Barbara Gloudon is associated with the development of Jamaican theatre and the arts. She has been a member of the National Arts Advisory Council, and wrote several plays for children before taking on the mammoth task of writing scripts for the annual LTM pantomime.

She first entered the arena of Jamaican musical theatre in 1969, when she landed Anancy and other Jamaican folk on the moon in *Moonshine Anancy*. In 1972 she created her version of the landing of Christopher Columbus in "Xayamaca" (the original Taino word for "Jamaica") in *Hail Columbus*. Named chairperson for the LTM after the death of founder and former president Greta Fowler, she has continued to write the scripts of other pantomimes. In 1975 she wrote and produced *The Witch*, her depiction of Annie Palmer, the supposed "white witch" of Rose Hall, for Carifesta '76, which was held in Jamaica.

Nobel Prize-winner Wole Soyinka (*left*), with Barbara Gloudon and the cast of LTM's annual Emancipation Day production, *Augus Mawnin*. *Courtesy of LTM.*

The Witch proved to be Louise Bennett Coverley's last pantomime, as she retired after the close of the season and migrated to Florida and then to Toronto. Two pantomime seasons later, Gloudon returned with the amusing and highly successful *Johnny Reggae* (1978), which focused on the popular Jamaican music form with its resultant sorrows and joys for the young performers who hope to achieve stardom without too much work. *Johnny Reggae* proved to be one of the strongest crowd pleasers in recent memory, playing to record audiences in Kingston and Montego Bay.

The Witch (1975), with Bill Blakely and Roma D'Oyen-Fitchett

In 1981 Gloudon again drew on Jamaican folklore. This time the script of the *Pirate Princess* was based on the story of pirate Jack Rackham's two female accomplices, who were captured and eventually executed. This production was staged also at the New Arts Theatre in London's West End – the first and only pantomime to date to be so honoured.

Over the last twenty-five years, Barbara Gloudon has written most of the annual pantomimes, drawing heavily on some aspect of Jamaican life or on folklore translated into a Jamaican image. She continues her efforts to keep the pantomime relevant to Jamaican interests, and has naturally turned once more to sports by saluting the achievements of triple-gold-medallist Usain Bolt, and the other members of the triumphant Jamaican team from the 2008 Beijing Olympics, in the show entitled *Runner Boy*, directed by Bobby Clarke. Pantomimes have, in the past, included scenes from sporting events, as in the two *Schoolers* (1989 and 1995), which reversed the standard gender roles to depict girls playing football. Basketball was featured in *Moonsplash*, where earthlings play basketball on the moon, and cricket in *Howzzat* (2006), when the director managed to compress a five-day game on a regular cricket field onto a proscenium stage, and into a matter of minutes.

According to Gloudon, the LTM has been facing difficulties in obtaining scripts to meet the requirements of a new age. Television has become the main challenge to the pantomime, with audiences wanting more sophistication along with traditional dialogue in Jamaican speech and attention paid to current topicalities. She nevertheless uses the stage as a means of educating people about their heritage while entertaining them. *Jack and the Beanstalk*, written for St Andrew Prep School in 1982, received the Jamaica Festival Award for the best entertainment for children that year. It became the pantomime *Jack and the Macca Tree* in 2002. Gloudon observes:

> There has to be a spareness [*sic*] of language. The audience expects movement – of plot, of people on the stage. They want brisk, exciting movement, colour and fantasy. We try to create another time, another place . . . In writing a musical there has to be balance between all facets – the text, the music, the design elements (set, costumes), and the movement. This works best when there is a mutual understanding between the various persons with special responsibilities – the director, the technical crew, [the] composer.

> Not everyone responds to the sharing of "power" in that way . . . One has to be prepared to edit and re-edit for the overall good of the show. And as a playwright, you have to be prepared for criticism. Critics are not always kind. The challenge also is to be able to learn from criticism, then proceed with confidence as a part of a team. I've been very blessed to have been trained by experience with some great directors . . . each of whom taught me something of value.[20]

As chairperson of the LTM, Gloudon also succeeded Henry and Greta Fowler as the executive producer of the pantomime, a responsibility which places her under pressure to ensure that the show opens by tradition each year on Boxing Day, 26 December, at 6:00 p.m. On several occasions the persons contracted to provide a suitable script have failed to do so by the agreed-upon date – a factor which places a theatre-worthy production at risk.

Baggarags (1997) *Courtesy of LTM.*

When this happens, Gloudon finds that she must create one herself if the country is not to be let down.

Along the way, in 1998, Gloudon partnered with director Brian Heap to found the Pantomime Company, which was designed to provide a base of performers dedicated to the annual show. The company also performs in August at independence and emancipation celebrations to highlight Jamaica's history. Their most celebrated

Miss Annie (2002). Courtesy of LTM.

work is *Augus Mawnin*, a salute to the ancestors, a clever interweaving of song, dance, speech and other theatrical elements. *Augus Mawnin* has played for ten consecutive seasons, 1998–2008, and has been successfully staged in towns across the island, as well as in New York, Florida and Toronto, mainly for Jamaicans in the diaspora.

Gloudon states that she is desperate to find other writers to take on the task of writing for the pantomime. She is willing – for now – to tackle the challenge of work-

Augus Mawnin. Courtesy of LTM.

ing with the production team to build each show from scratch and keep the LTM afloat financially. The organization still regards itself as a voluntary enterprise and has unique arrangements with its members, who willingly give time to the various productions for modest financial returns. As chairman and producer, Gloudon puts in untold hours of coordination leading up to curtain time each Boxing Day, on each pantomime. She is hopeful that new talent will emerge soon, "for the show must go on".

She leads a team that ensures that some sixty years and more of pantomime and LTM records are appropriately stored. The dream includes the building of a small museum so that the material and the process can become more accessible, especially to students, now that theatre studies is included in the local school examinations. Graduate students have been writing dissertations on the pantomime.

Under Gloudon's leadership, a solid core of talent behind the scenes has been encouraged. In Jamaican theatre, the pantomime orchestra is the only live ensemble which accompanies on-stage performances with new scores created each year. The team of stage hands, with technical talents in set design, costuming and choreography, are part of the LTM's accomplishment. As much attention is paid to backstage as to on-stage, front of house and box office.

7

The Development of Drama

The Jamaican theatre reverberates with conditions and practices of other lands and times. Some have been consciously imported; in fact, they have crossed the high seas with texts of plays, and there have been instances, quite misguided though not without some success, in which directors have sought to give facsimiles of London and New York productions. But there are practices that have arisen spontaneously, without conscious reference to prototypes, and parallels have emerged with what we may know, for example, of the dithyrambic beginnings or choric, bacchanalian manifestations of the Attic theatre. Also, there are underdeveloped dramatic forms, traceable on the surface to African practices, but which, upon deeper study, reveal a universality that goes back to the Old Stone Age.

Notions from other cultures have undergone strange transformations in the process of being domesticated, and some traits as we know them today may be stunted relics of practices from another place and time. Aspects of culture once thought adaptive have persisted long after those in authority have frowned upon them, because they still promote the psychological well-being of some group or groups.

Drama arose from the subconscious mind, and testifies to the psychic unity of mankind. In manipulating his environment, man draws upon his cultural heritage, discovers or invents new traits, and, wherever opportunity, need and genius permit, adapts others suggested by diffusion. The theatre has made use of such variables, and from multiple beginnings in different parts of the world has developed distinctive configurations.

Jamaican productions of drama from overseas have ranged from the works of Aeschylus, Sophocles, Euripides, Aristophanes and Plautus, to *Everyman* and other medieval masterpieces, through Shakespeare, Marlowe, Webster, Racine and Molière, and from Congreve, Wycherley and other Restoration dramatists right down to Goldoni, Ibsen, Strindberg, Shaw, Pirandello, O'Neill, Brecht, T.S. Eliot, Samuel Beckett, Arthur Miller, Elia Kazan, John Osborne and more contemporary moderns. This was so up to the 1950s, when, as a result of the activities of the Adult Drama League, indigenous plays and playlets began to emerge.

T.S. Eliot's *Murder in the Cathedral*, directed by Wycliffe Bennett, with Rooney Chambers as Beckett

Rooney Chambers and Barbara Carter in Wycliffe Bennett's production of *Phaedra*. *Courtesy of NLJ.*

Tess Thomas, actress, director and teacher, played *Phaedra*

Today, while the Jamaican theatre continues to reflect international trends, the major emphasis now is on the writing and production of local plays. To see our folk practices for what they are, to relate aspects of the Jamaican theatre to their world setting, indeed to extract the essence of drama from its trappings, two things are necessary: one, we must go back to the ancient roots of the theatre, and two, observe their contemporary manifestations under laboratory conditions. These conditions are provided by societies that have remained in comparative isolation from the spread of the so-called great civilizations, and "have had centuries in which to elaborate the cultural themes they have made their own".[1] This is to postulate neither an evolutionist, nor an environmentalist, nor a racialist approach. There is, however, a consensus as to the primordial origins of the theatre and all the evidence would seem to indicate an antiquity that goes back to the beginnings of community life.

Jamaica's First Playwrights

As mentioned earlier, until the beginning of the Second World War, drama like all other art forms was the purview of privileged locals and expatriates. The Theatre Arts Club, made up primarily of these expatriates, at least for the duration of the war, exposed Jamaicans to the latest English and Irish playwrights, such as Noel Coward, J.B. Priestly, George Bernard Shaw and Sean O'Casey. These productions were presented with flair and excellence, mostly by professionals who were on the island on special assignments or who had accompanied persons on assignments, or had taken refuge here during hostilities. They had access to the Garrison Theatre, a theatre built for the recreation of the English army. The Garrison was dismantled after the war, and after independence the British army and many of the expatriates returned home, and the Theatre Arts Club ceased to function.

By then, the first group of native playwrights had begun to break away from the English tradition and to tell their Jamaican story. Una Marson's *Pocomania* (1938) has its genesis in the Revivalist cults whose influence remains as strong now as it was then. The story treats the entwined lives of Stella Manners and David Davies. Stella, even in her childhood days, comes under the hypnotic influence of pocomania, a ritual dance and Revivalist ceremony that can send participants into a trance, and sometimes has a negative impact on the lives of those who participate. David, closely associated with Stella, is concerned to break this spell. The play incorporates the members of the family – father, sister, Reverend Peter Craig, the dignified husband of Dawn and son-in-law of the deacon – all played by coloured Jamaican actors of the day: Elsie Benjamin, Osmond T. Fairclough, Frank Hill, Newton Willoughby and Linda Edwards, amateurs whose acting was of professional quality, and who occupied important positions in the society from which they earned their livelihood.

As the country creolized both European and African cultural elements, Jamaican folkways emerged. These folkways are rich in theatrical possibilities: the Jonkonnu (John Canoe), ring games, Anancy stories, nine nights or wakes, bruckins, tea meetings, mock trials. Locally originated plays tackled social issues in the country.

In her musical *The West Indian* (1936), Esther Chapman successfully fused talents in acting, dance, music and decor to put on a show with a cast of seventy. Elsie Benjamin's *One Soja Man* (1945), tackled the colour issue and presented a highly provocative social drama. W.G. Ogilvie, with *Half a Fork*, explored "the hidden depths of native life". With each presentation, the Jamaican audiences became more

Remembrances (the life of Edward Jordan), directed by Trevor Nairne, with Hugh Martin and Natalie Thompson (1979). *Photo by Monica DaSilva.*

Louis Marriott, actor, playwright

enthusiastic, and still other writers followed, mostly from the late 1950s onwards, sparked by the Adult Drama Festivals that began about this time and provided a platform for internationally established European and American playwrights, as well as for emerging Caribbean writers.

Along with several European plays, the Caribbean plays produced in 1961 included *Chippy*, *Superstition* and *The Charlatan*. *Superstition*, written, produced and directed by Enid Chevannes, is set in a Jamaican household in which family members and friends meet at a wake to send off the spirit of the deceased to join the company of their ancestors. The play was awarded the Jamaica Broadcasting Corporation Challenge Cup as the outstanding one-act farce in the 1961 Adult Drama Festival. After the festival, the play was presented as the guest performance at the Clarendon Parish Festival of the Arts in May Pen.

Sam Hillary's *Chippy*, directed by Orford St John for the Repertory Players and presented earlier that year, was acclaimed as a significant contribution to the development of an indigenous Jamaican theatre. In 1961, it received three awards at the Adult Drama Festival. The University Players at the same time took another production of this play to the southern Caribbean islands, and it was so successful that on their return home they mounted their production for the benefit of Jamaican audiences.

Scences from the play Bedward (2003).
Photo by Loius Marriott.

The Charlatan, by Derek Walcott, was directed by Ronnie Llanos and produced by Mitzie Townsend. In introducing the play, Llanos noted that Walcott's earlier plays, *Henri Christophe*, *Ione* and *The Wine of the Country*, all tragedies, were ambitious failures in which the tragedy often became melodrama and the dialogue long poems. Nevertheless, in each of them "there was at least one scene that was a vignette of lovely theatre, a sparkling piece of comedy which really delighted". *The Charlatan* was pure farce, a vital gaiety, a joy in the mere fact of living, with all the pranks and jokes conveying serious thoughts, as is the way with all good comedy.

Still others followed: Sam Hillary's *Departure in the Dark* (1963); Slade Hopkinson's *The Onliest Fisherman* (1961); Carey Robinson's *The Runaway* (1960); Easton Lee's *They That Mourn* (1962) and *The Rope and the Cross*; Barry Reckord's *Miss Unusual* and *You in Your Small Corner* (1962); Louis Marriott with a line of critical successes, prominent among them *A Pack of Jokers* (1978), *Playboy* (1980), *Office Chase* (1982) and *Bedward* (1984 and 2003); Sylvia Wynter with *1865: A Ballad for a Rebellion* (1965) and her highly successful *Maskarade*, directed by Jim Nelson for JIS television in 1974 and then at the Creative Arts Centre, University of the West Indies (UWI), in 1979.

In addition to the Jamaican writers already mentioned there are a number of West Indian writers: Errol John and Errol Hill (Trinidadians), the Walcott brothers, Derek and Roderick (St Lucians), and Slade Hopkinson (Guyanese), whose works have enriched the Jamaican stage. Derek Walcott's plays were performed at the University College of the West Indies, where he was himself a student. Errol Hill, extra-mural tutor in drama at the university, was instrumental in promoting Walcott's plays and those of other Caribbean playwrights then unknown to Jamaicans. (The story of the University Dramatic Society during the 1950s and 1960s is told in chapter 8.)

There are, of course, the younger playwrights as well, the bulk of whose works we have seen during the last two decades. They include Patrick Brown, Balfour Anderson, Basil Dawkins, David Heron and Pat Cumper.

Winston Bell as title character Bedward, looking into the sun, in Louis Marriott's play. *Photo by Loius Marriott.*

Jamaica's Younger Playwrights

Among Jamaica's younger generation of playwrights, Patrick Brown authored a series of "yard" revues leading up to *Yard 99*. In these productions he pokes fun at contemporary issues and helps us to laugh at ourselves. His comic offerings include *Cornflakes*, *Friends*, *Guava Jelly*, *Love Games* and *Puppy Love*. He has written nine episodes of the television series *Oliver at Large*, and has developed and written the television series *Titus in Town*. His *December*, directed by Trevor Nairne, with Leonie Forbes in the leading role, won the award as the best Jamaican play in 1991. And his pantomime *Breadfruit Kingdom*, mounted by Jambiz Productions at Center Stage, was an overwhelmingly popular, island-wide success in the year 2000. Keith Noel directed Brown's *Cornflakes*.

All of Brown's other works have been staged by Trevor Nairne, who has developed an author-audience chemistry at Center Stage and elsewhere, and produced a substantial corpus of plays, at least two each year since 2000. Brown joins the main-

Patrick Brown's *Cornflakes*, directed by Keith Noel, with Rosie Murray. *Photo by Monica DaSilva.*

Oliver Samuels, the actor and producer around whom Patrick Brown wrote the popular television series *Oliver at Large*. *Courtesy of NLJ.*

stream of landmark comedic writers who, since classical Greece, have set the stage by establishing their own parameters – expanding, pushing back, tightening or otherwise adjusting the boundaries of the genre by adapting it to native needs. This is especially so of his *Breadfruit Kingdom*, *Oliver Large Abroad* and *Love Games*. His titles since 2000 have sent special messages to his fans and have piqued the curiosity of an increasing number of theatregoers.

Balfour Anderson has written and directed some twenty-three "roots" and comedy productions over the last two decades. At the heart of the roots play is the sexual experience of the ordinary Jamaican, treated farcically. It borders on the vulgar and is played with gusto and relish. His scripts have included the pantomime *King Root* for the LTM; *Browning*, which deals with the subject of skin shades in Jamaican women; *Rip Off*, which deals with the housing situation and wicked landlords; and *Two-to-One*, about the ganja traffic. His subjects are always topical, and he uses music to help illustrate his themes. Roots plays evolved from the Bim and Bam slapstick comedy of the 1940s and 1950s. The term was coined by Ralph Holness, one of the pioneer producers. Other such practitioners include writer-producers Paul Beal and Luke Williams and writer Michael Denton.

Basil Dawkins has had an imposing list of successes over the last two decades: *Flatmate* (his first play, 1980), *Couples* (1984), *Champagne and Sky Juice* (1986), *Same Song Different Tune* (1991), *Toy Boy* (1996), *Feminine Justice* (1998) and *Uptown Bangarang* (2007). *Feminine Justice*, directed by Buddy Pouyat, with Munair Zacca and Ruth Ho Shing in the leading roles, is among the more satisfying local productions these authors have yet seen. It received several Actor Boy awards in 1998 for best production, best drama and best new Jamaican play.

Basil Dawkins's *Uptown Bangarang*, with Ruth Ho Shing (*left*), Maylene Walton (*centre*) and Sakina. *Photo by Basil Dawkins.*

David Heron's *Against His Will*, with Douglas Prout and Margaret Young

Still in his thirties, David Heron is one of the youngest of the established playwrights. Between 1994 and 2005, Heron produced six hits: *Ecstasy*, *Intermission*, *Against His Will*, *Love and Marriage and New York City*, *Redemption*, and *4Play*. His writing is remarkably sure-handed, and when his scripts are handled by experienced directors like Trevor Nairne and Norman Rae, there are moments of magic.

Pat Cumper's first play was *The Rapist*. She has participated in the preparation and creation of other scripts, including *Fallen Angel and Devil Concubine*, and

Guess Who's Coming to Dinner? with, from left, Bettina Macauley, Lois Kelly (Barrow) Miller, Oliver Samuels and Bari Johnson

provided the concept for the LTM pantomime *The Honourable All Purpus and the Dancing Princesses*, the script for which was written by Michael Reckord. She has also adapted for the stage Claude McKay's short story "Crazy Mary", and Erna Brodber's novel *Jane and Louisa*. She devised *Bennie's Song*, adapted from Shakespeare's *Romeo and Juliet*, within the context of Jamaica's tribal politics.

Drama Clubs

In addition to the achievements of Jamaica's native playwrights, a number of drama clubs have made significant contributions to the development of the local cultural and dramatic scene. Among the most outstanding have been the Ivory Club, the Coke Drama Group and the various incarnations of the Barn Theatre group.

Enid Chevannes and the Ivory Club

Enid Chevannes, playwright, director

The Ivory Club, a social and cultural club, was founded on 16 February 1951, by a group of music enthusiasts – all officers of His Majesty's Customs in colonial Jamaica – who were seeking an avenue for the development and exposition of their talents. The initial group comprised Vance Lannaman, Con Allison, Delroy Mendes, Copley Johnson, C.V. Tulloch, Lloyd Adams, Sandy Grant and Welton Tapper. In the early years, meetings were held at the Young Men's Christian Association situated then on Hanover Street, and the main focus was jazz. Interest in the club rapidly grew and it was soon clear to the founders that to harness the multiplicity of talent demonstrated, there was need to expand the club's vision and mission.

This gave birth to a choral group, which had the distinction of having the respected and much sought-after Eglon Fairweather as its first director. By 1953, a drama group was formed under the leadership of Enid Chevannes, educator, playwright, director and producer. She had worked for most of her life in primary schools in Jamaica, where among other subjects she specialized in speech and drama, and for which she created her first little plays and skits. There were evenings when the Ivory Club's audience would be treated to the performance of selections from greats like Shakespeare and George Bernard Shaw, various other writers, as well as West Indian writers such as Derek Walcott, Errol Hill, Louise Bennett Coverley and Chevannes herself.

Chevannes wrote and produced most of the Ivory Club's entries in the National Drama Festivals in the 1950s, and several of them won prizes. For her success in the National Drama Festival, she was awarded a government grant, which enabled her to receive advanced training at the New York Academy, and to observe stage and television productions in New York and California.

Chevannes's *Root of all Evil* won the Drama Festival award for adults in 1956. The following year, a visiting American adjudicator, Reuben Silver, gave her play *Turned Tables* high commendation, and in the Adult Drama Festival of 1960, *Superstition* was adjudged the best West Indian Farce. In the 1962 festival, the club was invited to present Chevannes's play *The Vision* as its major presentation. In 1966 and 1967 the group was awarded two cups and two silver medals as well as a cash award for the performance of an English play, *All on a Summer's Day*, by Howard Agg. Chevannes's own *Superstition* (1960), also earned awards for best comedy in the Festival. *Turned Tables* was runner up that year. Her *Camilla of the Great House*, a pantomime, is still to be staged.

Individual members of the club's drama group also received awards for best actress, best supporting actress, best actor and best supporting actor for their performances in various plays. The group included names like Pearl Ashman (a gold medallist), Joyce Logan, who won a best actress award for her portrayal of Jama in *The Vision*, and best supporting actress for her performance as the maid in *Root of all Evil*, and later, best actress for her portrayal of Sugar in Carey Robinson's play *The Runaway* based on the life of a rebellious slave. Chevannes also wrote several episodes of the radio serial *Life in Hopeful Village*, which in 1966 was voted the most popular radio programme in the island. Members of the Ivory Club performed in the radio drama serial, and in *Dulcimina*, a long running radio serial by Elaine Perkins, and *Shadows of the Great House*, another radio serial by Carmen Manley.

Barbara Chevannes (*seated*), in an Ivory Club production

The Ivory Club welcomed, nurtured and yielded many of Jamaica's fine artists; it never closed its doors to applicants who could neither play an instrument nor sing, nor participate in speech or drama. The organizers knew that every individual could make a contribution of one kind or another, and that they needed a diversity of gifts to ensure achievement of their loftiest goals. Hence, persons not having artistic talents but who had other skills such as organization were encouraged to become members. And still at other times members would engage in lively structured debates. Indeed, the club provided a springboard for many young musicians, singers, actors and actresses of the time. Among such persons were the celebrated Byron Lee and the Dragonnaires, Leonie Forbes, Charles Hyatt, Calvin Foster and Stanley Irons.

Some time after its commencement, the Ivory Club shifted its operation from the Young Men's Christian Association to the Young Women's Christian Association on North Street, but maintained the same meeting day. Thus Thursday afternoons saw entertainment highlighting one or more of the club's special interests. The executive often arranged performances in jazz that featured artistes such as George Moxie, of international acclaim, as well as Foster on piano, Don Drummond on saxophone, Ernest Ranglin on guitar, and singers like Totlyn Jackson, Louise and Blossom Lamb, among others.

On other evenings there would be classical music – instrumental as well as vocal – featuring young pianists of promise like Maxine Franklin, Oswald Russell (both of whom later achieved international distinction); and popular singers like David Reid, Mercedes Kirkwood, Jimmy Tucker, and Sheila Reckord. Other sessions featured choral performances of classics and spirituals under the baton of Eglon Fairweather and his successors: Frank Hart, Kenneth (Ken) Blake, and David Reid (who developed

Basil Dawkins's *Hot Spot*, with Charles Hyatt and Zandrian Maye, directed by Buddy Pouyat. *Courtesy of C. Hyatt Jr.*

into a fine choir master and tenor soloist). The choral group boasted male voices drawn mainly from the Kingston Male Voice Chorus and included Jacob Taylor, Carl Fuller, Hugh Faulkner, May Foster, Helen Clennon, Joyce Logan (later Archibald) and Barbara Chevannes.

Whenever there was a fifth Thursday in a month, the committee arranged a social evening, in which members got together and shared in dance, fun and fellowship. On such an evening it was not unusual to have entertainment provided by well-known bands led by Byron Lee, Sonny Bradshaw, Eric Deans and Baba Motta.

The club's major fundraising activity was an annual barn dance at the Bournmouth Club, Rockfort Gardens, where featured bands and artistes were engaged, and attracted wide support.

During the more than twenty-five years that the Ivory Club existed – between 1951 and the late 1970s – the club made a significant impact on the cultural life of the island, and proudly acclaimed all those artistes whom it spawned, discovered and nurtured, and whose sterling performances subsequently earned for them fame and fortune.

On retirement from teaching, Chevannes joined the Jamaica Festival Office as drama officer, where she shared her skills in theatre arts with groups across the island, and organized presentations of plays and speech items for their annual festivals. In recognition of her contribution to cultural development in Jamaica in the field of drama and speech, Enid Chevannes was awarded the Bronze Musgrave Medal (1966), and the Centenary Medal (1979) of the Institute of Jamaica. She joined the adult literacy programme, JAMAL, and had to retire finally, when her health began to deteriorate. She managed to complete the writing of a pageant for the Methodist Church to celebrate its two hundredth anniversary in Jamaica. Chevannes died of a heart attack in late August 1988.

Enid Wynter and the Coke Drama Group

Enid Wynter (*née* Walker), born 16 April 1913 in Kingston, holds a teacher's certificate from the Ministry of Education. One of her lifelong interests has been drama. She was one of the founding members of the Coke Amateur Players, later renamed the Coke Drama Group. In the early days, plays by the Coke group were presented at the Ward Theatre and included a Russian comedy, *The Proposal* and *This Desirable Cottage*. When the Jamaica Drama League was established in the 1950s, Enid Wynter attended training courses offered by the league, and her group very enthusiastically entered plays in the drama festivals and staged Easter and Christmas plays at the Coke church. The Coke Drama Group has been in existence for over fifty years, and for all of that time Mrs Wynter has been the artistic director.

Enid Wynter, playwright and director

She taught for some eight years at Ardenne High School, specializing in speech and drama. Through her insistence, a stage was made at the school, with proper flooring, flats and curtains, as well as other amenities. Those who attended the Schools' Drama Festival over the years cannot fail to remember the many delightful performances presented by Ardenne, which included *Anancy and Mancrow* (traditional), *Tarshan Lace and Velvet* (Easton Lee), and *The Runaway* (Carey Robinson). As a result of public response, Mrs Wynter took these plays on tour to other parts of the island.

Ardenne excelled also in the National Speech Festivals, which, after 1962, formed part of the National Festival of the Arts. During Mrs Wynter's tenure, the school distinguished itself by obtaining three gold medals, twenty silver and some twenty bronze. In her nineties at time of writing, Enid Wynter was still directing and producing plays for the Coke Drama Group.

Forty Years in the Garage

The Barn Theatre, Kingston, 1965–2005

YVONNE BREWSTER

"The greatest explosion of new writing in the history of Jamaican theatre was concentrated in the Barn Theatre", says Trevor Nairne. The development of the Barn Theatre movement can be divided into distinct phases, some longer and more intense than others, but each phase has been important to the growth of contemporary Jamaican theatre, which has seen over one hundred productions in its forty-year history.

Theatre 77

In 1965 a number of young Jamaicans, some of whom had been trained in Theatre Arts either in Britain or the United States, came together in an alliance cemented by a shared sense of frustration they had experienced upon returning home. They had met with little welcome and almost tangible hostility, and were offered virtually no opportunities by members of the existing theatre establishment. This group became Theatre 77.

The name was significant, as it encapsulated the primary aim and objective of the founding members: to establish a fully professional theatre company in Jamaica in twelve years (sixty-five plus twelve makes seventy-seven). The group, led by the late Sidney Hibbert, counted Patricia Priestley, Billy Woung, Grace Lannaman, the nineteen-year-old school drop-out Munair Zacca, Trevor Rhone and Yvonne Jones (now Brewster). Leonie Forbes Amiel was to have been the eighth, but somehow this did not materialize.

Theatre 77's introductory programme of work was a double bill of Edward Albee's *Zoo Story* and August Strindberg's *Miss Julie*. In spite of its social relevance to Jamaican society and some fine performances, this programme of work failed miserably because of over-optimistic audience projections, inflated egos and a complete absence of financial and logistic planning. The first performance, presented in the Old Dramatic Theatre building on the Mona campus of the University College of the West Indies, played to four persons. Audience numbers fell after that. The run ended prematurely.

The Barn Theatre 77

In a post-production night of long knives and bitter recrimination, Theatre 77 died and the Barn Theatre 77 was born. This successor company, while adhering to the original principles of its precursor, also actively sought to explore ways of engaging with the culture and experience of the Jamaican "man in the street". For its first production, the group began rehearsals for one of J.B. Priestley's time plays on Yvonne's parents' veranda, but rehearsals were soon banished to their garage. The spirit of theatrical adventure led to the conversion of the large garage into a basic rehearsal and performance space with the help of George Carter, who gave the group an ancient lighting board, and Kathleen and Claude Clarke (Yvonne's parents), who were not only willing enough to allow them to take over their building, but helped with the technical adjustments necessary to transform a garage into a performance space. Having a safe place in which to

*Adapted from text prepared for Wycliffe Bennett in 2007. All quotes in this section have been taken from personal communication with Yvonne Brewster in the course of researching this article in 2007.

work made the choice of a Priestley play seem uninspired and inappropriate, and rehearsals were abandoned. The search for work more in keeping with the aspirations of the group began in earnest.

As, at the time, so few scripts existed which either interpreted or explored the contemporary political and social concerns of Jamaicans, the company looked abroad in the first instance. Noel Vaz suggested Roger Milner's *How's the World Treating You?*, which was having a successful first run at the Arts Theatre in London, and which was quite cutting-edge politically at the time. The cast list called for fourteen persons but they managed with eight. The entire original company, with the inclusion of Vincent McKie, was involved in this production, which, happily, enjoyed a marked improvement in audience attendance, upgraded production values and inspired sufficient confidence to request each audience member to "Bring Your Own Cushion".

Vincent McKie and Yvonne Jones (Brewster) in *How's the World Treating You?*

The Barn Theatre 77, 1965–1974

This happy state of affairs did not last long, however. Tempers flared, personalities clashed and a major exodus of members left the triumvirate of Munair Zacca, Trevor Rhone and Yvonne Jones to carry on the search for theatrical self. Successful as *How's the World Treating You?* had been, it was clear that relevant, topical local work had to be found. Since there was nothing that caught their collective imagination, Trevor became playwright, Munair honed his skills as actor and Yvonne turned her hand to directing.

Early Rhone plays, such as the excellent five-minute curtain-raiser *Look Two*, led to a splendid collaboration among Daryl Crosskill, Sonia Mills and Trevor Rhone, which delivered *It's Not My Fault, Baby*. This was followed by *The Gadget* (later to become *Old Story Time*), *School's Out* and *Smile Orange*, which holds the record for the most performances of any play at the Barn in its history, and which heralded the beginning of commercially viable and successful independent theatre in Jamaica.

Although early productions at the Barn Theatre 77 are often correctly associated with Rhone, it is important to stress that there were many other Jamaican playwrights – including Roger Mais (*Rolando and Rosamund*, in which Lennie Little-White had his first acting role), Sam Hillary (whose *Koo Koo* was the theatre's first really big success), Dennis Scott (*The Inquisitors*, a one-act play), Stafford [Harrison] Ashani (*The Quickie*, directed by Munair Zacca) – who all had work produced. Carmen Tipling's first experience of the Barn was as a member of the audience for *Ask Your Mama* in the late 1960s. She remembers that "the context and ambience of the Barn Theatre, the performance, as well as the enthusiasm of the players, convinced me that I should be associated with this theatre. And, many years later, my plays *Straight Man* and *The Skeleton Inside*, both Bronze Medal winners in the Jamaica Festival, were showcased there in 1974 and 1976."

The Barn provided wider opportunities for its members to extend their individual theatrical expertise. For example, Munair Zacca, who had hitherto been associated with acting, "was instrumental" in getting Carmen Tipling "to first

Forty Years in the Garage: The Barn Theatre, Kingston, 1965–2005 (*cont'd*)

finish the script, and then trust him to direct *Straight Man*"; and Trevor Nairne, known for his direction, acted in *The Skeleton Inside*. The theatre even played host to the revolutionary Sistren Collective productions when they could not find accommodation elsewhere.

Alongside original Jamaican productions, work from other parts of the Caribbean, most notably *Dem Two* from Guyana, involving Ken Corsbie, Marc Mathews and Henry Muttoo, were hosted. African-American work did not play as large a role as it might have: Ed Bullins's *The Electronic Nigger* caused some intellectuals to picket the theatre because of the title. The Barn's production of Langston Hughes's tone poem *Ask Your Mama*, however, directed and designed by George Carter, created before a spellbound audience a perfect evening's entertainment, with visually delightful physical theatre that used movement, mime and music in an evocative soundscape designed by Del Weller.

Although many of the Barn's plays were relatively serious in content, they also made forays into the world of satirical revue with, for example, *I'm Human, Right?*, directed by dancer and choreographer Neville Black, and Ken Maxwell's *Soon Come, Please*, which brought down the wrath of Prime Minister Michael Manley, who thought the script had gone too far in its criticism of him and threatened an injunction. Undeterred, the Barn's cultural confidence abounded to the extent of producing the radical Joe Orton's last play *What the Butler Saw* (described at the time as "licensed insanity") only months after it had premiered in London.

The company did not confine itself within the walls of its garage home but travelled far and wide into the Jamaican countryside. One important result of their touring was the first-ever schools' tour of fully rehearsed excerpts from the three Shakespearean plays on the examination syllabus – *Hamlet*, *A Midsummer Night's Dream* and *Julius Caesar* – which the group performed in the majority of secondary schools in the Corporate Area and other parishes. Directed by Sam Walters, who was on loan from the LTM, the production used a minimal concept to maximum effect with a travelling company which included Joanna Hart, Janet Bartley, Andrew Garbutt, Ed "Bim" Lewis, Peter Ashbourne, Trevor Rhone, Munair Zacca, Yvonne Jones (Brewster) and others. The Barn rode out objections from some teachers who thought Ed "Bim" Lewis should not have been included in the cast, because he was not the right "type" and would surely ruin the Bard's words. In fact he elucidated them and made them relevant to Jamaicans in his inspired portrayal of Bottom the Weaver.

Regular Saturday-morning drama classes for children took place in an attempt to train audiences of the future. A small industry of training young people in all the arts of theatre, both physical and practical, developed almost by default. The late George Silvera was a classic graduate ambassador who, at the time of his death, was the longest serving resident technical director in Jamaican theatre.

The Barn became a meeting place for many creative artists from all disciplines. Yvonne recalls: "When Gene Pearson was invited to take up residence in the first years of his life as a ceramicist in a makeshift studio at the 'Back-of-the-Barn', this development was blessed by Edna Manley, who showed us how to fire pots in the kiln we purchased." Karl Parboosingh was a regular visitor at rehearsals and painted a mural for the theatre auditorium; John Hearne, Basil McFarlane, Dennis Scott and Mervyn Morris performed their work in a theatrically devised evening of poetry. Fine artists Christopher Gonzales and Dawn Scott used to hang out and help out, too.

The demographic of the Barn's audience shifted noticeably over time. The uptown theatregoers continued to turn up, but then so did their staff, who returned with their friends on Saturday nights, to the delight of those who believed that theatre must relate to and engage its audiences before it can hope to influence them. Rhone's *School's Out*, directed by Yvonne Jones (Brewster) and starring a young Oliver Samuels in his first leading role in a Jamaican comedy, was among the plays which brought this initial period of the Barn Theatre 77 to a rousing end. Ten years of exhausting, intensive work of writing, administering and in general creatively leading the project, had taken its toll on the strong, artistic leadership of Rhone, Zacca and Jones (Brewster). They stepped aside, devolving much of the artistic control of the programming to other creative practitioners, such as Trevor Nairne.

Forbidden, by Basil Dawkins, with Charles Hyatt and Karen Harriott.

The Barn Theatre, 1980–1995: The Playwright-Producer Era

The Barn Theatre ceased producing the work presented on stage, and the era of the playwright-producer was born by inviting promising, new, young, creative playwrights and other artists to present work there so that they might develop the skills necessary to produce their work. This change of emphasis allowed writers the hands-on opportunity of controlling, exploiting and maximizing their profits, while making sure their work remained accessible and trail-blazing. The playwright-producer who invests exclusively his or her own work may not be unique to Jamaica, but it has become the norm here. Actively encouraged and facilitated by Trevor Nairne, the theatre kept faithfully to the original tenet of the founding members, working steadfastly towards professionalism and the creation of a Jamaican canon.

Foremost among the many new names to Jamaican theatre who wrote and produced work during the period of playwright-producers was Basil Dawkins. He encapsulates the significance of what had by now become known as the Barn Theatre:

> My first play, *Flat Mate*, won a Bronze Medal in festival in 1978 but I couldn't find anybody to put it on. I was basically locked out of the system. When you are a black boy from the country and nobody knows your father, you didn't come up through pantomime, you didn't train in England and you didn't go to school with anybody big . . . well! It was the Barn that said "Come". I was afforded my first opportunity in theatre substantially by the Barn. It allowed me to become a producer as well as a writer.
>
> The Barn opened up theatre in Jamaica as a popular form of entertainment and enlightenment. It wasn't closed off for upper St Andrew folk. The humility of the setting was important; it didn't terrify anybody. I remember plays that ordinary people could relate to, plays that told our story. I don't remember a Molière but I do remember *Smile Orange* and Hugh King's *Night Work*! The Barn encouraged young people like myself to continue to dig and find stories out of ourselves and the success was reflected in the faithfulness of the following in this whisper of a theatre setting.

Trevor Nairne insists:

> The Barn made theatre into one of the popular "going out" choices for the "man in the street" audience, vying with the night club and the pop concert. In providing a facility for the exposition of new writing and for the exposure and establishment of a core of new writer-producers to the possibilities inherent in live theatre, the Barn was unique. Think of the people who cut their teeth at the Barn, Trevor Rhone being the father of them all. There is Basil Dawkins, Hugh King, Patrick Brown, Aston Cooke, Alwyn Bully, Stafford Ashani, Carmen Tipling, David Heron, to name but a few. These names represent much of professional theatre in

Forty Years in the Garage: The Barn Theatre, Kingston, 1965–2005 (*cont'd*)

Jamaica today, as does the list of directors who also did foundation work at the Barn, such as Keith Noel, Eugene Williams, Trevor Rhone, Munair Zacca, even you yourself, Yvonne, . . . and me!

The Barn, 1995–2005: The Ethos Changes

Stringent enforcement of fire regulations by the authorities, carried out at the Barn in punctilious detail, resulted in a reduction in the seating by twenty seats. In a theatre that had previously seated one hundred and forty-four persons, the reduction had a significant effect. Some producers found fewer seats uneconomic, and one must not forget the growing competition which the numerous other small, independent theatre spaces, such as the Center Stage Theatre, the New Kingston Theatre and the Little Little Theatre, provided. Many of these venues now attracted the attention of people such as Basil Dawkins and Patrick Brown, who virtually abandoned the Barn as a venue.

The Barn's initial goal of encouraging first-time writers was still important, but, with the departure of Trevor Nairne from the artistic overview, the product at the Barn sometimes suffered. Valerie Chuck, who now managed the operation, found that balancing the books, although always a significant factor, became an overwhelming consideration, as some producers did not fully appreciate the necessity of paying their bills. The Barn's mounting deficit made it impossible to continue with a project which relied on fair play, in light of the fact that it received no public subsidy whatsoever.

Despite the presentation of some rather substandard, trite work, this period did see a few revivals of older Rhone (*Old Story Time*) and Dawkins (*Couples*) classics. In 2003, a production of the autobiographical *Bellas Gate Boy*, written by Trevor Rhone and adapted for the stage by Yvonne Brewster, was mounted as a farewell production for these two founding members. The Barn notably ended its life on a high note with one of the most successful Jamaican revues ever, *Jamaica2 Rahtid*, by the faithful Aston Cooke in March 2005.

Will there be a successor to the Barn? Is there a need? A conversation among several of the Barn's former members revealed their thoughts on the likelihood that Jamaica will see the establishment of another theatre like the Barn.

Basil Dawkins: I'm starting to panic that the lifespan of the small theatre spaces is now threatened. We need to move forward to a position where we begin to assess not only the aesthetics but the economic opportunities which theatre can provide if we aspire to become the theatrical capital of the Caribbean region. I am saddened that a society which allows the Ward Theatre to rot, might not take up the challenge. However, I feel sure that sufficient sensitivity exists in the country to make it happen.

Trevor Rhone: One of the important decisions we made at the Barn was to take off a play which was raking it in at the box office but which no longer gave us any joy. Do you remember that, Yvonne?

Yvonne Brewster: I certainly do.

Trevor Nairne: Theatre in Jamaica is not about to turn back. We are heading for a major place in the cultural industries of this country. Jamaican theatre has had good and successful diasporic exposure and the experience learned at the Barn of managing, producing, writing the work is a basis of this new trend.

Munair Zacca: I don't know if I am that enthusiastic about the future of theatre in Jamaica. The audiences for anything not pre-digested, predictable, with big crowd-pulling comedy names as the attraction, have shrunk considerably. Tickets for benefit performances are sold out and yet you find the auditorium half-empty because people buy the tickets to support a cause but are not interested in the less banal plays. I will make an analogy with reggae which descended into dancehall similarly. Too much of Jamaican theatre has descended into Roots and serial shows. Selah!

YB: Time will tell who is correct.

The National Theatre Trust

The National Theatre Trust, founded in 1968, was the vision of Lloyd Reckord. He wished to provide Jamaican audiences with international and West Indian plays of quality and to use this opportunity to highlight the indigenous drama of the region by constant training and theatre activity. He predicated the success of his efforts on major financial support from the government in expectation that, eventually, a professional theatre with paid personnel would emerge.

Reckord's ideas were not new. The White Hall Players had tried to do the same in Trinidad in 1946; so had the Georgetown Dramatic Group in British Guiana (now Guyana) in 1948, the Green Room Theatre Club in Barbados, and the Little Theatre Movement in Jamaica in 1941. There was also the Federal Theatre Company (1957) at the recently founded University College of the West Indies. Reckord's National Theatre Trust was determined that it could maintain a company of professionals. Other groups accepted the fact that they would have to rely on amateurs, to a very large extent.

What was significant about the Federal Theatre, however, was its efforts to introduce West Indian plays using very talented students at the University College of the West Indies and other young Jamaicans interested in the theatre. Their productions included *African Sling-shot* by Cicely (Howland) Waite-Smith, *Junction Village* by Charles Archibald, and *Ione* by Derek Walcott, who went on to acquire fame and fortune as a Nobel Prize winner. The leader of the group was the extra-mural tutor Errol Hill from Trinidad, who also arranged to have West Indian plays copied and distributed in the only form affordable to the department at that time, mimeograph.

Prior to establishing the National Theatre Trust, Lloyd Reckord had himself started the Actors Theatre Company in the 1950s, and succeeded in mounting plays like Arthur Miller's *The Crucible*, Barry Reckord's *Della*, Cicely (Howland) Waite-Smith's *The Sudden Guest* (later renamed *Starboarder*). But Reckord soon learned that the take from the audiences was not sufficient to keep the company going. He could not afford to pay a stage manager, a technical director or a set designer. And it was impossible for him to carry the load alone. The company was dissolved when Reckord accepted a part in his brother's play *Flesh to a Tiger* (formerly titled *Della*) in England in 1954.

In 1968, on his return to Jamaica, Reckord made another attempt at forming a theatre company. When the National Theatre Trust began, Lloyd Reckord was the only theatrically skilled member of the group. He formed a registered company with some distinguished Jamaicans on its governing council: G. Arthur Brown, governor of the Bank of Jamaica; Dr Aubrey Phillips from the UWI School of Education; Michael Sloly, a lawyer; Tony Gambrill, in public relations; Ed "Bim" Lewis, a popular comedian; Joan Swaby, a member of the Manchester Players group in Mandeville; and Aaron Matalon, a wealthy businessman.

The National Theatre Trust wished to include outstanding foreign plays as well as West Indian ones. Its first production was Barry Reckord's *You in Your Small Corner*. The play was set in London but dealt with West Indians and university life in

Tony Gambrill, producer

England. The playwright was drawing upon his experiences as a foreign student in post-war colonial England. The play attracted capacity audiences at the university's New Arts Lecture Theatre for several runs.

The programme for *You in Your Small Corner* set out in no uncertain terms the aims and objectives of the National Theatre Trust: to attract professional Jamaican artists living abroad for short-term contracts; to carry live theatre to schools and to persons in rural communities; to serve as a feeder for the television and radio stations then just coming into being on the island, as well as expressing the need for strong government and private support.[2]

Reckord saw the role of the director as being concerned solely with directing, but he soon found himself taking on all the roles of directing, producing and set designing almost single-handedly. He approached the appropriate government ministry for assistance, and although he received promises, funds were never forthcoming, except for the sum of two hundred pounds sterling for rental of a rehearsal room. He therefore set out to raise funds to pay the director. The profit from productions was shared with the cast and other personnel.

Even despite the lack of funding, Lloyd Reckord continued to pursue his dreams. His *No Place to Be Somebody* was directed by Noel Vaz, now UWI staff tutor in drama. Under the auspices of the National Theatre Trust, a group from the Virgin Islands staged Jean Genet's *The Maids* in Jamaica in 1972. The following year, Carroll Dawes directed *Macbeth* at the Ward to good houses and put on performances for school children and students from teachers' colleges and the UWI. But the National Theatre Trust continued to struggle.

Jean Small in performance

Lloyd Reckord's dream to educate while entertaining, to take theatre to the masses, inspired his next move. He gave tickets to the municipal bus company, to factories and to young people in the inner city. He organized a ten-week theatre workshop for fifteen young people, among them Stafford Harrison (now Ashani), who has become an established playwright. The next move for the National Theatre Trust was to commission Thom Cross (a teacher with training in drama) in 1970, to write a musical with a Jamaican theme. Out of this came *Long Ago, Sometime*. It required the minimum number of props and so could move from place to place with comparative ease. It played in a number of schools in the Corporate Area and also to schools in the rural parishes, free of charge so long as sponsorship was available. Reckord made another attempt at providing free theatre when he convinced the government to sponsor the revival of *The Rose Slip*, but the support dried up after only fourteen performances.

In 1974, the National Theatre Trust moved to what was called Children's Theatre, shows for children and acted by children. It presented *Puppets and Other Small People*, written and directed by Dennis Scott (then employed at Jamaica College) and Jean Small, using members of the Jamaica College Drama Club. The show was staged at St Andrew Preparatory School and was well received. The next effort was *Androcles and the Lion*, staged at the Ward; it played to children not only from schools but also from the Mona Rehabilitation Centre and the Alpha and other orphanages in the city. Again Reckord ran into financial problems, as the island was facing an economic crisis. He turned to staging plays set for the General Certification of Education syllabus, and these he took to schools all over the island. But by 1976 the government was actively involved in establishing the Cultural Training Centre and once more funds dried up.

Reckord persuaded the government to assign some twenty Youth Service workers to the National Theatre Trust to be trained in theatrical skills, but no funds were provided. He therefore instituted a charge of thirty or forty cents per child attending performances. Immediately the audiences dropped to half, and once again he set out to raise funds to keep the project afloat. Reckord was paying tutors five dollars per fifty-minute session, and even that was a strain.

The Youth Services group did manage to stage one play, Barry Reckord's *I-Man*. The theme was relevant to the situation in Jamaica at the time. A report in the *Daily Gleaner* noted that "*I-Man* hits at a school system that gears its graduates to meet neither individual adult needs nor societal needs. It suggests that the education machinery . . . is deliberately programmed to produce a 60–40 ratio in favour of failure, because the society is fully aware that it cannot cope with the demands of even the 40 per cent success."[3] The show perhaps cut too close to the bone, for it did not receive the audience support expected. In December 1977, the National Theatre Trust sponsored the visit of the Dance Theater Company of Harlem to Jamaica, and Reckord once more used this occasion to boost the trust, but without too much success.

In spite of these disappointments, Lloyd Reckord could not be deterred, and he turned to developing a one-man show, *Beyond the Blues*, which was comprised of selections of poetry, drama and prose very well delivered. It featured works from the Caribbean – including poems by Claude McKay, Evan Jones and Louise Bennett Coverley of Jamaica, Derek Walcott of St Lucia, and Kamau Brathwaite and Frank Collymore of Barbados – and one or two American poets. His emphasis was on brotherhood across the globe. The show opened in Nassau, Bahamas, in November 1980, and the local *Guardian* newspaper called it "an excellent performance, universal in its appeal". Today Reckord has performed *Beyond the Blues* across the Caribbean, in the United States, in Canada and in England. With private sponsorship, he has performed this show to some hundred schools and other non-paying audiences in Jamaica. His dedication to the theatre is unquestionable and, in spite of disappointments, he keeps soldiering on.

The Montego Bay Little Theatre Movement

The crowds who normally flock the Strand Theatre or the ballroom of the Holiday Inn Sunspree Resort in recent years practically shunned the Fairfield Theatre when it was first begun, because they thought the venue was only for "aristocrats". And maybe it was, when the Montego Bay Little Theatre Movement (MLTM) opened its doors in 1975 with plays by Shakespeare, Neil Simon and Noel Coward – plays that the "little man" could not relate to, written in language he could not understand. These productions gave local people the feeling that indigenous material would not be highlighted at that venue. Over the years, however, the Montego Bay Theatre Group has consistently produced more and more works by Jamaica's and some of the Caribbean's top playwrights.

Paul Methuen (as Lord Capulet) and the late Gay Hodgkins (Lady Capulet) in *Romeo and Juliet*

According to chairman Douglas Prout, the Fairfield Theatre, as founded by Paul Methuen, a Scottish Jamaican, catered mainly to expatriates.[4] Fairfield was originally a venue for the elite to watch and play tennis, before Methuen had the pavilion covered and converted into a theatre in 1975, through donations from friends at the Tryall and Round Hill Resorts. Methuen had introduced garden theatre (that is, open air theatre) to patrons of Round Hill and Tryall in the late 1960s and early 1970s, and had created a garden theatre at his residence at Hope Road in Kingston before moving to Montego Bay.

Now, with a total of three productions per year, and poetry readings the first Sunday of each month, there has been a change from plays geared towards "foreign" aristocracy to local and contemporary plays such as David Heron's *Against His Will*. Consequently, the audience base has shifted drastically: the average person will now take a taxi from downtown Montego Bay to the Fairfield Theatre, which is just seven minutes away from the town square, enjoy a good laugh, then go home. Ten years ago this would not have happened; today there is a wider cross-section of patrons.

The MLTM boasts a cast of well-rounded, seasoned professionals of the calibre of Douglas Prout, who was one of the first persons drawn to the movement, while he was still a student at Cornwall College; Lloyd B. Smith, broadcaster, director, playwright, publisher, actor and journalist; actress, dancer and radio presenter Makeda

The Fairfield Theatre, founded by Paul Methuen in May 1975 as the Montego Bay Little Theatre Movement (MLTM). It is the only full equipped, purpose theatre outside of Kingston. *Courtesy of MLTM.*

Solomon; dramatist and teacher Jane Crichton; accomplished actress, dancer and scuba enthusiast Anne Bernard; dramatist, actress and businesswoman Fleurette Harris; and Paulette Spence of the Tourism Product Development Company, among many others.

Although the MLTM often boasts high-quality performers, it is not a members-only movement. Its doors are open to anyone who is talented and willing to work for little or no money. A broad spectrum of actors and actresses grace the set each time there is a production. "At one time we had two doctors, one lawyer, one teacher and an unemployed", says Douglas Prout. The MLTM attracts students, the average man and even people who are only functionally literate but who want to be part of an active group. "We have no artistic director, but a management team of Jane Crichton, Lloyd B. Smith, Diane Girvan and myself, all direct plays at intervals", says Prout. The MLTM's most recent production, at the time of writing, was Patrick Brown's *December*, which was directed by Jane Crichton. "We embrace anything that is indigenous, but we will not put on anything that is laced with bad words, nudity or crassness . . . Plays must be tasteful, we have done risqué things, but they had a message, which was the real focus", says Prout. Intellectually stimulating, entertaining and classic plays are at the forefront of the productions put on by the MLTM. Jamaican and Caribbean works such as *Man Better Man*, *Same Song Different Tune*, *Old Story Time*, *Play Boy*, *Toy Boy*, *Feminine Justice* and *Against His Will* are part of the list of an estimated fifty plays that have been staged by the group to date.

"Financially viable" is probably not the best term to describe the MLTM, although there have been improvements since 1975, and the movement has not lost any money. It has broken even following each production. At the box office, tickets cost J$500 for each play. Set construction, advertising, costuming, lighting, sound and a small incentive for the cast can run into as much as J$700,000 per production. "A play can cost J$600,000 to put on and make only J$580,000", says Prout. Sponsorship

Patrick Brown's *Hurricane Lovers* directed by Christopher Daley, 2009

thus plays a pivotal role in the existence of the theatre, and the Montego Bay business community has really embraced the group. Prout dreams of the day when members of the MLTM can state their professions as actors or actresses because they earn a livelihood from plays. "Right now we can't say this, but it will come as the community becomes sensitized and more culturally aware", he adds.

The MLTM is an offshoot of Kingston's LTM. The latter's co-founder, Greta Fowler, was very involved in charting the course of the MLTM, and the present chairman, Barbara Gloudon, is constantly in dialogue with her Montego Bay counterparts. The MLTM has performed many times at both the Little Little Theatre and the Little Theatre in Kingston.

In 2006, the group took Basil Dawkins's *Feminine Justice*, under the direction of Douglas Prout, to the capital city. The MLTM has also successfully staged *Count Dracula*, *Man Better Man*, and *Romeo and Juliet* in Kingston. "We have an understanding that once we have a play that may do well in Kingston, we have their blessings to take it there", Prout commented. In fact, he says, Barbara Gloudon, who did *Augus Mawnin* at the Little Theatre in Kingston, brought the production to Fairfield and then took it to Negril in the neighbouring parish of Hanover. Along with removing the perception that the Fairfield Theatre is an exclusive place, Prout says his life has been enriched by many of the people who have walked through the theatre's doors.

On Saturday 23 February 2008, the MLTM organized the inaugural Paul Methuen Award for Excellence at the Fairfield Theatre. Douglas Prout was awarded best director and best actor in a leading role for his performance in the play *Redemption*. He also received the award for best original song for the lyrics of "More Than You Ever Know", with vocals by Karen Smith. According to Prout, Smith "lifted it off the paper and made it into something enjoyable".

At the same ceremony, actress Makeda Solomon was nominated for best actress for her performance of the leading role in *Redemption*. Actor Tony Rodney, who co-starred in *Redemption*, received the award for best actor in a supporting role, and actor David Tulloch won the awards for best lighting design and best costume design for his productions *Should I Kill Him?* and *The Narrative*, respectively. The awards ceremony, which is expected to be an annual event, is named in honour of Paul Methuen, veteran actor and director, chairman of the Fairfield Theatre and founder of the MLTM. At the 2008 awards ceremony, Methuen, who now resides in Scotland but was specially invited to attend, received a special lifetime award for his contribution to the development of theatre in Montego Bay, and for laying the foundation for a culture of theatre in the Second City. He was recognized as a living legend in the Jamaican Theatre, and as a consummate professional.

Jambiz Productions

In 1998 Jambiz International commissioned into service the newly constructed Center Stage Theatre in Kingston, which formally introduced the company to the theatre-going public. The occasion was marked by the staging of Theatrefest, a festival of four plays: *Ecstasy* and *Against His Will*, both written by David Heron and directed

Class of '73, Oliver Samuels and Glen Campbell, by Patrick Brown and directed by Trevor Nairne. *Courtesy of Jambiz International.*

by Trevor Nairne; *Guava Jelly*, written by Patrick Brown, directed by Lenford Salmon; and a monologue, *Halley's Comet*, written and acted by John Amos, a well-known American film and television actor. *Halley's Comet* tells the story of the US Deep South over a seventy-six-year period.

The establishment of Jambiz was the culmination of previous attempts by directors to determine a partnership with the requisite balance between sound administrative management and artistic expertise, in order to capitalize on the tremendous potential for commercial theatre across Jamaica and in the diaspora. The team assembled for this venture was comprised of Lenford Salmon, actor, director and management specialist; Patrick Brown, playwright, civil engineer and company director; and Trevor Nairne, freelance producer and director, former actor, and cultural administrator. Brown and Nairne had worked on a number of theatre projects prior to Jambiz: the defunct Mass Productions Ltd, which produced the comedy revues *Yard 89* and *Yard 90*, and the plays *December* and *Guava Jelly*. Salmon and Nairne later partnered under the banner of Better Theatre Productions to produce David Heron's debut play *Ecstasy*, and the British farce *Run for your Wife*, by Ray Cooney.

Salmon, Brown and Nairne came together initially to produce Patrick Brown's *Puppy Love* at the Barn Theatre in 1996, and they transitioned into Jambiz later that year with the production of Brown's comedy revue *Irie* (1997) and Frances Coke's

Lenford Salmon, actor, playwright, director, Jambiz International

Patrick Brown, actor, playwright, director Jambiz International

My Son's Friend (also in 1997). Inevitably, the combining of the three kindred spirits led to the forging of an important dream: the provision of a theatre to facilitate the staging of productions. Nairne immediately approached the Barn Theatre with a Jambiz proposal for a lease of that facility. He had been responsible for booking productions at the Barn for several years, and thought that, with the uncertainty of the future existence of the most popular theatre space in Kingston, an inspired Jambiz could help to guarantee a productive future for the theatre. The first Jambiz initiative proved unsuccessful but the relentless search for space continued. It resulted in an historic lease agreement with Life of Jamaica Properties, a rare example of involvement from the private sector in the arts at that level. This, of course, opened up an era of exciting theatrical possibilities. Patrick Brown, in his capacity as construction engineer, reconstructed the former Life of Jamaica New Kingston Drive-in Cinema concession-cum-projection building into a two-storey, 250-seat proscenium theatre.

Center Stage has become synonymous with Jambiz and is the centre of the company's production activities. It is here that the company's theatrical policies have been shaped. Each year Jambiz stages a major family-oriented comedy executed by a small but committed and dynamic cast, and each year the show opens its run on 26 December, the unofficial opening date of the Jamaican theatre season. This production has three phases: the show in residence at the Center Stage, New Kingston, followed by weekend tours of rural Jamaica, culminating with an overseas tour. In addition, there are one or two other productions staged during the year, one of which is its summer production. The company has been able to sustain this policy, creating and staging productions that have become staples for the theatre-loving public.

Jambiz' successful cycle of annual theatrical activities is due in large measure to the versatility and proven production and artistic skills of the Jambiz directorate, which now includes seasoned actor Glen Campbell. Additionally, there has been a tight, loyal production network, comprised of a secretariat, set construction, front-of-house, technical personnel and actors led by Oliver Samuels, who has been particularly advantageous to the development of Jambiz. Samuels is the most renowned actor in the Caribbean and is extremely popular at home and abroad. He and a core of other actors, including Glen Campbell, Claudette Pious and Dahlia Harris, have developed an aura of respect for the Jambiz theatrical fare throughout the company's existence. Samuels retired from stage acting in 2008 but has not abandoned his contact with the theatre.

Veteran actors of stage and screen Oliver Samuels and Teddy Price. *Courtesy of Mediamix.*

Theatre is the company's core business, but the directors have made brief excursions into television and film. Serious initiatives have resulted in a joint-venture television project created by Patrick Brown and involving all the Jambiz directors as actors and directors. There are two television pilots awaiting sponsorship marketing: *13*, a conflict resolution sitcom, and *Changes*, a soap opera. Brown has been preoccupied with screenplay development for film projects, while the team has been researching funding opportunities. The company has also extended itself beyond the boundaries of production activities into training. A Jambiz Bursary has been in progress at the Edna Manley College Drama Department, and the Center Stage Theatre Workshop has been established to expose adult theatre enthusiasts to a rounded appreciation of theatre crafts. Some of these emerging talents have appeared in Jambiz productions.

8

Drama at the University College of the West Indies in the 1950s

MARY MORGAN

"Bliss was it in that dawn to be alive,
But to be young was very heaven!"

Students at the University College of the West Indies (UCWI), like Wordsworth in 1809, felt that they were part of a new dawn, a new West Indian morning to be shared with the West Indies cricket team and the bright, brief Federation of the West Indies (1958–62). Life at the fledgling university reflected the golden dawn of light rising from the west, as described in the motto *oriens ex occidente lux*: the light of higher education rising, shining bright, here in the West Indies. It echoed the triumph of Arthur Hugh Clough's poem (so often quoted by Winston Churchill in war-torn 1941) that begins "Say not the struggle naught availeth . . .", which gave rise to that motto:

And not by eastern windows only,
When daylight comes, comes in the light,
In front the sun climbs slow, how slowly,
But westward, look, the land is bright.

Before 1948, only a fraction of a fraction of an infinitesimal few in the West Indies could even think about going to university. Since then, countless students in the region

*This chapter was prepared by Mary Morgan (*née* Brathwaite) for inclusion in this book, and it was a collaborative undertaking with input from her surviving colleagues from the University College of the West Indies (UCWI) from those first challenging and exciting years of the 1950s. Her account explores the activities of a brilliant group of young people from across the Caribbean: they developed intellectually, artistically and creatively at the UCWI and became what might be referred to as the melting pot of Caribbean cultural understanding and exchange. Through this interchange, Jamaican students and the wider Jamaican community began the process of integration with our neighbours in the region.

have shared this gift of a lasting bond: a university in the Caribbean for Caribbean people.

The University College was fully residential. The two West Indians appointed by the colonial secretary to the Irvine Committee of the Royal Commission on Higher Education in the Colonies – Philip Sherlock of Jamaica and Hugh Springer of Barbados – had seen to that. They both considered it vital for the development of a true Caribbean spirit that the students should not only study together, but also live together. The committee endorsed this, and a mixed population came together to live among the ruins of two sugar estates at Mona, Jamaica, in the foothills of the Blue Mountains. Long-lost memories of slaves touched those of a more recent war-time camp for refugees from Gibraltar, and merged with lively students, young and mature, from all over the region; academics and staff from all over the world; a potpourri of cultures, a mix of races and colours. Everyone knew everyone else in those halcyon days. The students lived like one large family, thankful for the incredible beauty and blessing of their rosary of islands bastioned by two mainland territories and pearled across the Caribbean Sea.

Our Pelican Light: Westerly Rising

Vitality and energy flowed through the college's societies and clubs, and none more so than the Dramatic Society, where the rich diversity of Caribbean cultures could have full expression. Two first-comers – medical students Owen Minott from Jamaica and Denise Mitchell from Grenada – had started the society in 1948. One afternoon they walked along the concrete pavement between Hut 24 (where the ten female students lived) and Hut 19 (where the men lived) and Gibraltar Hall, summoning anyone who was interested. The first meeting was held in one of the unused huts.

The group honed its skills with play-readings, some dramatized – Kathleen Drayton (*née* McCracken) recalls making costumes (including hats) for a play directed by English lecturer Dr Robert LePage. Members used to attend performances of drama groups in Kingston, including the Thespians and the Little Theatre Movement (LTM). They had practice runs with the pre-Christmas *Words and Music* programme started in December 1949 by Carlton Patrick, of Trinidad, and Owen Minott, who took the Junior Common Room gramophone down to the old gym near the playing fields and staged a fabulous open-air presentation on the old lawn tennis hard courts. The production was enthusiastically received by the entire campus community (led by the first principal and his wife, Dr and Mrs Thomas Taylor) and several invited guests, friends of the university college. Keith Tang of (then) British Guiana and Cleo Drakes of Barbados directed the 1950 *Words and Music* programme. In 1951 young St Lucian poet Derek Walcott of the first arts class (1950) "was inspired to write a Nativity Play";[1] Tang led the choir.

Trinidadian arts student Kathleen McCracken and Barbadian medical student Rosemary Weatherhead coordinated the behind-the-scenes team that worked on costumes and decor for the early *Words and Music* productions, while medical student Earl Been from the Turks and Caicos Islands (who sometimes played the small pump organ for Sunday services) was involved in the music.

Launch of the University Players

On Tuesday, 3 June 1952, the Dramatic Society launched the University Players with two plays: Derek Walcott's *Harry Dernier*, a tense drama written for radio and directed by Walcott himself, and A.P. Herbert's farce, *Two Gentlemen of Soho*, directed by Jamaican Joan Swaby. Both directors were second-year arts students. The audience of undergraduates, staff and friends was small, but this production was significant: a successful presentation by a vibrant, talented group, with one of the plays the work of a member of the group, and the old wooden stage of the Dramatic Theatre rescued from decay by a coat of paint. Ronnie Llanos, a science student from Trinidad, was outstanding as Harry, the last man on earth. Kathleen McCracken and Jamaicans Mavis Arscott and Al Cotterell were among those who made their mark as actors that evening, while Jamaican medical student Eric "Rixie" Munroe, who had been tutored by LTM's George Carter, worked wonders with the second-hand single-handled lighting equipment.

Ronnie Llanos, actor

The writer remembers Saturday mornings downtown Kingston in the 1950s . . . Exciting times for the Dramatic Society (one of the chief links between the university and the public). Backstage teams busy arranging for the next production at the Dramatic Theatre, soliciting ads, collecting props, getting advice from the many businesspeople willing to support a venture of the young university college; slipping into Stanley Motta's or running across the road to BWIA, down to the Gleaner Company or up the narrow stairs to Evon Blake's office or into Doris Duperley's Phoenix

Terminus, written by Dennis Scott (twenty years old), directed by Peter Maxwelll for the University Players, 1959. *From left:* Donald Harris, George Henry, Neville Bramwell and Sheila Hill.

Library at the corner of Harbour and Port Royal Streets. Members of the front-of-house team, armed with seating plans, posters and ticket rolls, sat at the entrance to Times Store and Nathan's Department Store on King Street, and in front of Sangster's Book Store on Harbour Street, persuading shoppers and passers-by to purchase tickets. And all were welcome for lunch and complimentary ice cream at Kinkead's Drugstore.

Prof Hugh Wynter, elocutionist, actor

"Everyman, I will go with thee and be thy guide, In thy most need to be by thy side", Mavis Arscott's clear voice sang out, ringing with the promise of knowledge, at the beginning of the morality play *Everyman* (March 1953), and it still echoes in the mind today. The play was directed by Trinidadian James Lee Wah and Jamaican Sheilah Evans-Smith. New faces – freshmen who had come up in October 1952 – appeared in this production, which was favourably reviewed by *Gleaner* drama critic Harry Milner: Hugh Wynter, who had been an elocution champion in the Jamaica Schools Drama Festivals, showed, in the title role, "a fine sense both of the music of the verse and its meaning"; Slade Hopkinson as Fellowship was "good, but with an appalling pair of tights"; Carroll Morrison played Good Deeds; Wilfred Cartey was terrifying as Death. Milner found Trinidadian arts student Chris Osborne "quite excellent" as the Messenger, and commended Mavis Arscott's Knowledge. A tough critic, he made it a point of duty to attend most of the UCWI productions, sometimes accompanied by young *Gleaner* staffers Barbara Goodison (later Gloudon) and Lettice Small. The society respected Harry Milner's reviews; members would carefully read his column at breakfast in hall, holding points for in-depth discussion later at the Students' Union or at rehearsals.

Errol Hill on Staff

Errol Hill, playwright, director and historian

When Errol Hill joined the university college staff in Trinity Term 1953, as drama tutor in the Department of Extra-Mural Studies, he brought technical expertise and professionalism, plus vision and a sense of confidence to the young dramatic group. In a little under five weeks, the players were ready with *Six Scenes* (from Shakespeare to Shaw), directed by Hill; and on 22 May 1953 a packed Dramatic Theatre was delighted with the production. The variety of scenes – from *Hamlet*, *The Merchant of Venice*, *The Importance of Being Earnest* (Wilde), *The Stronger* (Strindberg), *Winterset* (Maxwell Anderson), and *Village Wooing* (Shaw) – gave several undergraduates with varying talents the opportunity to be involved, either "treading the boards" or working backstage: sets, costumes, make-up had to be changed quickly and efficiently.

Joan Swaby's last appearance on the UCWI stage was memorable in *The Stronger*, in which she acted against Mavis Arscott. Senior medical students Owen Minott and Hal Clarke, a Barbadian, proved their mettle; first-year students Thelma Lawrence (arts, British Guiana), Handel McFarquhar (science, Panama–Jamaica) and Slade Hopkinson (arts, British Guiana–Barbados) came on the scene. Slade, excellent as Hamlet, showed his dominance in this production. The *Pelican Annual* recorded: "Errol Hill showed the group how easy it was to manipulate the stage, and *Six Scenes* proved how much could be done in a short time with some imagination and hard work."[2]

Hard work there certainly was, from the beginning. For instance, Derek Walcott was not only poet and playwright, but also a demanding director, skilled stage manager, artist and creator of his own sets; he used to spend hours at the Ward Theatre with Phillip Morris, master set-builder of the LTM. Rixie Munroe imparted his lighting skills to first-year Trinidadian science student Ancile Gloudon. Mavis Arscott was showing interest in production. Backstage talent was developing: Thelma Lawrence, Jamaican Pam Morris and Barbadian Mary Brathwaite in make-up and props; Jamaican Carroll Morrison in costumes; Barbadian James Williams in sets. The society set itself the goal of presenting at least two productions each academic year, with the expectation that three would be possible – one in each term.

Lilieth Nelson, former musical director of the University Singers and member of other choirs for over fifty years. She has played lead roles in over fifteen musical/ theatrical productions

In December 1952 Jimmy Lee Wah directed *Words and Music*, with music composed by Jamaican science freshman Hugh Moss-Solomon, who created and led the first orchestra on campus. First-year arts student Vincent "Brongo" Brown from Montserrat (who organized and led the first campus band) was also involved, and second-year arts student Austin Clarke from Barbados led the choir. In 1953 Hugh Wynter staged an expanded version of *Words and Music*, making it into a spectacular pageant by adding scenes from the birth of Christ and relating them to the Caribbean; nearly a hundred students participated. In 1954 Mavis Arscott (later Lee Wah) presented an impressive dramatization of the *Fourth Wise Man*.

The element of drama in *Words and Music* was gradually reduced and evolved into the carol service, the Festival of Nine Lessons and Carols. This remains a sublime offering each Christmas by the University Singers, enjoyed by an overflowing congregation in the University Chapel (opened 1956).

Voices in the Night

Students from that time remember – off-stage, after midnight – Ronnie Llanos and Slade Hopkinson projecting their voices across the campus. Llanos's mellifluous tones could be heard from a Taylor Hall balcony, echoing through Irvine Hall and the space that would soon become Chancellor Hall and down Gibraltar Camp Road, trumpeting the lines of his current play or *The Song of Solomon*. And Hopkinson – quiet, shy at school in Barbados – more than fulfilled the promise he had shown as Brutus in the last Harrison College/Queen's College production before coming up to university in September 1952, where his powerful voice would often ring out from Gibraltar Hall, across Gibraltar Camp, through the other halls and down the Mona Road, reciting John Donne or T.S. Eliot, or pitting his voice against the elements with Lear's "Blow, winds and crack your cheeks! . . ."

Slade Hopkinson, actor

Training

Soon after his arrival at UCWI in 1953, Errol Hill started training the group by theory and example. Rehearsals often lasted until well after midnight, with the company walking back from the theatre to rooms in hall, in those days without fear of assault or attack. Hill mounted workshops on theatre craft, bringing knowledgeable theatre personalities to run short courses and to address the group. The idea was to train members in the techniques of production through play-readings and make-up classes, as well as by attending the performances of other groups, where they could observe the importance of front-house management, watch the other groups rehearse and see the realities of stage management – problems encountered by the stage crew, the intricacies of lighting and the significance of set, costumes and good prompting. Students were encouraged to specialize, according to aptitude, in lighting, stage management, directing or reviewing. Hill always emphasized teamwork, punctuality and knowledge of the stage.

During the 1955–56 academic year, Derek Walcott (then teaching at Jamaica College) lectured on "The Problem of Poetic Drama in the Twentieth Century", and Barry Reckord spoke on "The Dramatist and His Art". In later years, Harry Milner and others also lectured to the group. Training has remained one of the society's key activities. The present-day Dramatic Arts Society occasionally invites persons to speak on aspects of drama – one such satisfying visit having been made in March 2008 by Keith Noel, Amina Blackwood-Meeks and Jean Small (*née* Thomas).

Learning from the Irish Theatre

The society's interest in creating a West Indian national theatre led to study of the development of the Irish theatre. Identifying with the Irish struggles against the English colonizers, members started reading Sean O'Casey and John Millington Synge. The University Players' first full-length play, directed by Errol Hill and Jimmy Lee Wah, was O'Casey's *Juno and the Paycock*, staged on 28 November 1953 in honour of the visit of Queen Elizabeth II to the college. Because of the occasion, the walls of the old theatre were painted and the society was given funds to construct a complete set of flats and to procure a new front curtain.

Juno was a landmark production. It made a deep impression on all in the group. Although the company was very nervous, the acting was good, the stage management sound. But in his review the British Harry Milner was critical of the players' failure to attempt the Irish accent and to play for more comedy. The society agreed with many of his other criticisms, however, and fully endorsed his comment that "a week's more rehearsal would have worked wonders". Indeed, the second performance, on 1 December, was much better. Without royalty in the audience, given the few extra days and having overcome their first-night jitters, plus having taken Milner's critique to heart, the cast did itself proud.

On the production, Harry Milner commented: "The University Players, save for Kathleen McCracken, sacrificed the accent [perhaps, he found McCracken's Trinidadian accent nearer to the Irish?], and it was 'Joxer Daley', played by Slade Hopkinson, who alone caught the Irish rhythms and mood." Milner thought that Richard Morris "did well in the part of Captain Jack Boyle, 'the Paycock'", the drunken husband who constantly flinches at work. But he felt that Juno, "who surely must be a large and motherly type, full of . . . rough humour", was miscast, although he conceded that Mavis Arscott – small, slim, intense – "worked hard and sensitively" and "was most moving in the emotional final scenes". Indeed, Milner found that the whole cast improved as the play progressed – "everyone was pretty nervous at the start", he declared.

Harry Milner saved his strongest plaudits for Jamaican Rex Nettleford as Johnny, "the most difficult role of the play . . . the neurotic, terrified crippled son awaiting execution from the terrorists he has betrayed". A freshman in November 1953, Rex gravitated naturally to the Dramatic Society and excelled in this production. Milner wrote: "Most young amateurs in this part that does not relax in mood for a second would have inevitably 'fluffed' and drawn wrong laughs. A constant state of fear is one of the hardest things to put across on the stage. Rex Nettleford succeeded and seldom overacted."[3]

The Dramatic Society felt that *Juno* represented "a major stage in the evolution of the society". Milner reinforced this opinion in the recommendation at the end of his review: "This play should be seen: . . . it does show a way for the West Indian Theatre to follow if it is to get in contact with the mass of the people."[4]

Nucleus of West Indian Theatre

Derek Walcott directed the University Players' next production: *Henri Christophe*, his verse chronicle in seven scenes, portraying the rise and fall of the black king of Haiti. The production was eagerly anticipated in Jamaica. It coincided with the observance of Haiti's 150th anniversary, and it followed Errol Hill's much-publicized pro-

A scence from *Henri Christophe* by Derek Walcott

duction of the play in January 1954 in Hans Crescent, London, with Errol John in the title role. Also, the governor of Jamaica, Sir Hugh Foot, was expected to speak before the opening performance, on 12 March 1954, about his recent visit to Haiti and on that country's ties to the rest of the West Indies. The University College's public relations officer, Cedric Lindo, worked with the society on advance publicity, and brought to attention the spirit of West Indian independence and the challenge to all West Indians of a man who rose from slavery to be a king.

Archie Hudson-Phillips in Soyinka's *The Road* (1968). *Courtesy Noel Vaz collection.*

On stage, Jamaican Lloyd Stanford had a commanding presence as Christophe; Rex Nettleford was electrifying as the witch doctor, dancing portents of doom before the king to the sound of drums and his own choreography. A note of dangerous comedy was introduced by co-conspirators Lance Lougheide (Trinidad) and Vernon Royes (Jamaica) when they planned the king's murder. After three years backstage or in small parts, Archie Hudson-Phillips (Trinidad), made his debut as an actor of great promise in the role of the secretary Vastey – suave sentinel – and Slade Hopkinson gave a terrific performance as Dessalines, the usurper emperor. It was a memorable production.

The 1950s are regarded by some as the golden years of theatre at the university. The UCWI Dramatic Society played a seminal role in the development of theatre in the West Indies, not only by leading the way with quality West Indian (and other) productions, but also through the work of UCWI graduates in the communities and schools of the region. In this respect it is not an exaggeration to call the UCWI Dramatic Group the nucleus of a future West Indian theatre.[5]

Slade Hopkinson took over the presidency of the society from Mavis Arscott in October 1954, and in that academic year the society began working on an open-air theatre between the Old Works Farm and the Mona Still House Ruins (an area now called the Oriental Gardens). The next few years saw some of the players' finest productions: *Oedipus Rex* (December 1954), *The Lady's Not for Burning* (March 1955), *The Glass Menagerie* (June 1955), *King Lear* (January 1956). Hopkinson produced and acted in *Oedipus Rex* and *King Lear*, and was unforgettable in both. Ronnie Llanos and Mavis Arscott directed the Christopher Fry play *The Lady's Not for Burning*, rated as the society's most polished offering in which newcomers to the UCWI stage appeared: Barbadian Cynthia Alleyne; Jamaicans Edward Baugh, Mervyn Morris and Helen Saunders; and Sybil Blair from British Guiana. James Williams came into his own as stage manager with an attractive set; Ancile Gloudon was brilliant on lights, the society having by then acquired more sophisticated (six-handled) lighting equipment.

Harry Milner adjudged the University Players' production of Tennessee Williams's *The Glass Menagerie* to be "quite the best they have done to date . . . very nearly up to good repertory standard". Directed by Ronnie Llanos and Sybil Campbell, the play, which opened on 23 June 1955, was Mavis Arscott's farewell to the UCWI stage. Milner felt that she "gave a very competent touch to the part of the mother, Amanda . . . Miss Arscott played the role both intelligently and sensitively". But he could not help comparing the play with the film, finding that Arscott tended to underplay the role and "her own very likeable personality obtruded". He considered Hopkinson, as the son, Tom, "agreeably ironical, . . . with a nice sense of humour, phrased well, . . . in his final speech very moving". But he felt that Hopkinson also tended to

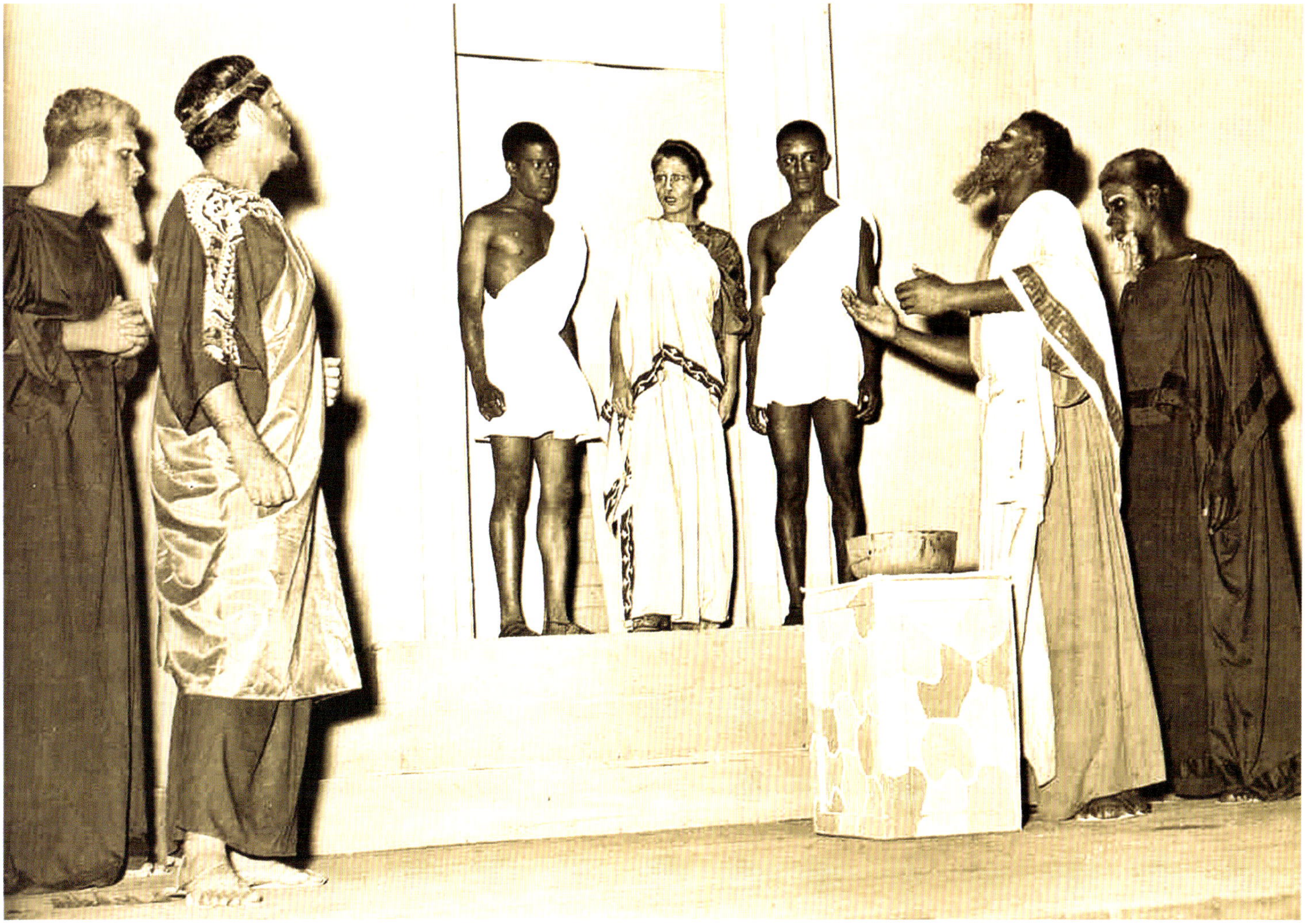

Oedipus Rex, 1954

under-act, as did Owen Minott, the "show off", the visitor, Jim. Minott could not compete with Harry Milner's memory of Kirk Douglas in "what might really be the hardest role". Milner found the scene between Jim and Laura "a little flat", but he held that Helen Saunders "had a soft glowing loveliness as the crippled Laura", and her performance will long be remembered by theatregoers of the 1950s. Milner ended his critique with a recommendation and an observation: "This is an effort that any person who considers himself the slightest bit cultured should . . . see. But half the trouble of the theatre in this island is that those who should know better decry the absence of a local stage and never support it on the few and fewer occasions it does appear."[6]

1956: A Splendid Year

January 17, 1956: opening night of *King Lear*, with Slade Hopkinson, assisted in production by Mary Brathwaite, alternating with Hugh Wynter in the title role. The *Gleaner* preview on 21 December 1955 had revealed that, as the University Players were determined to do well, the date of the production had been postponed. Difficult as it was, *Lear* turned out to be one of the University Players' best productions. The actors were well cast, lines well learned, costumes (taken over by Trinidadian Margaret Stewart) and set apt. Newcomer Julian Anderson from British Honduras played a valuable Edgar, Hugh Moss-Solomon a capable Duke of Gloucester, and Lloyd Stanford a good Earl of Kent, placed in the stocks for his loyalty to the king. Jean Thomas Small as Cordelia was poignant, gently strong. Wynter's Lear was magnificent; Hopkinson's was colossal. The play moved swiftly – through the scenes with the king's sons-in-law, played by Vincent McKie and Al Cotterell; Lear's gifts to his two elder daughters, Goneril (Jeanne Hill) and Reagan (Sybil Blair); the bittersweet vignettes between Lear and the fool (Edward Baugh) – to the climax, with Lear cast out, and to the tender scene with Cordelia, the only one of Lear's three daughters to show him true love, though he had rejected her. To this day, Hugh Wynter still greets Jean Thomas Small as "Cordelia", and the writer of this chapter, while attending a Royal Academy of Dramatic Art production in London some two or three decades after Hopkinson's *Lear* (like Harry Milner with *The Glass Menagerie*), could not resist the strong currents of memory from the incomparable UCWI production which swept over and into that of the Royal Academy of Dramatic Art. Meanwhile, in 1956, Harry Milner wrote that Slade Hopkinson's Lear "has come within fighting distance of the great Lears, which I have witnessed in London's West End".

West Indian Scripts

As Errol Hill travelled through the region in the capacity of extra-mural drama tutor, and as Caribbean plays became available in the territories through extra-mural offices, drama groups began selecting more and more West Indian plays, and the University Players led the way. Youthful exuberance and authentic Caribbean tone made the difference in the productions of the University Players. *Four West Indian Plays* opened at the Dramatic Theatre on 20 April 1956, attracting fairly large audiences, "and awakened the interest of the public in West Indian drama", according to the society's records. The four plays were *Now for Now* by Wilfred Redhead of Grenada, *Ping Pong* by Errol Hill, *Bond of Matrimony* by J.S. Barker (a retired English colonial civil servant who had settled in Trinidad), and Derek Walcott's *The Sea at Dauphin*. Producers were, respectively, Mary Brathwaite, James Lee Wah, Thelma Lawrence and Slade Hopkinson. The society was encouraged by new talent – Jamaicans Joyce Walker, Dwight Whylie, Winnie Blackwood and Althea McPherson; Trinidadians Osmond Downer, Ossie Morris and Kenny Small – while "oldsters" like Lance Lougheide and Cynthia Alleyne (later Wilson), the new lighting trainee, gave memorable performances.

Hopkinson's production of *The Sea at Dauphin* was the *pièce de résistance*. The lilt and cadence of the Trinidadian and St Lucian accents, and the "difference" the French creole made to the dialogue, captivated the audience, as it had in *Henri Christophe*. Archie Hudson-Phillips was outstanding as the fisherman Afa, who refuses to take Hounakin, the uncle of his young assistant Augustin, to sea with them even though the old man's wife is ill and he needs to make some money – "don't want no old man to bring bad luck, and to-besides, bad weather coming". Afa and Augustin (Barbadian Warren Thorpe) put out to sea; old Hounakin (played by newcomer Sam Ramdial from British Guiana) wanders off, depressed, and falls (or jumps) off the cliff at Boileau, where the sea foams angrily. When the fishermen return, there is a confrontation on the beach between Afa and the priest, Father Lavoisier (Dave Wildish, English-Jamaican medical student), who responds to Afa's curses with a blessing. Derek Walcott stage-managed the play, painted the backdrop and supervised the building of the boat, *Our Daily Bread*.

The second production of Walcott's *The Sea at Dauphin*, at the Ward Theatre on 28 July 1956, the University Players' entry in the Adult Drama Festival, ended the year in a blaze of glory for the Dramatic Society. Hopkinson was not available this time as producer, so Brathwaite (who had assisted him in April) directed. There were also changes in the cast because some of the original actors were not in Jamaica that summer. Thus Dominican Eustace Royer convincingly became the old man Hounakin, Jamaican John Stockhausen was the priest and Ancile Gloudon, persuaded by the new director to take the part of Augustin, left the management of lights to Cynthia Alleyne and played an intuitive Augustin. The performance was superb, with awards going to Archie Hudson-Phillips for outstanding actor (as Afa); Brathwaite for the most imaginative and satisfying production; Derek Walcott for the best West Indian play; and Ancile Gloudon, honourable mention.

The University Players were ecstatic at the decision and honoured by the judges' tributes, especially the reference to the "sensitive handling" of the production: "*Sea at Dauphin* is beautifully done, always a pleasure to look at and to listen to. Excellent acting, fine costumes and painstaking production are evident and the pleasing result must be ample reward for the hard work it has involved on the part of every member associated with it – on stage and off."[7] The players agreed that the kudos should be shared with Slade Hopkinson, director of the April production. After the Festival, the players were invited by Mr Patrick Delapenha to take *Dauphin* – set and all, with LTM's Phillip Morris accompanying the group – to Mandeville for a Sunday afternoon performance at the Odeon Theatre. Players and audience alike appreciated this "repertory" experience.

In 1956–57 Robert Henry took over the presidency of the society from Mary Brathwaite. The University Players had by that time established a tradition of good, regular, on-time productions, and Jamaican audiences looked forward to the colour and flair of their presentations, particularly of West Indian plays.

After the success of *Sea at Dauphin*, Norman Rae, writing for the *Daily Gleaner*, pointed out that the players' production of Errol Hill's *Man Better Man*, which opened on 1 March 1957, was not one of the Dramatic Society's best productions; he was uneasy with the storyline and the handling of the crowd scenes. Whatever he may have thought of the plot or of the production, however, he was intrigued by the pace of the dialogue, the peculiarly Trinidadian turn of phrase, and the French creole. In effect, *Man Better Man* was a lively performance, full of movement and colour and verve, and the stick-fight was classic, flawlessly executed to the accompaniment of expert drumming and *kaiso* rhythms and women's brightly swirling skirts. Although at the heart of the play is rivalry to the death, with a beautiful woman the prize, the performance was a celebration of life and youth and music and skill. This drama of old Trinidad showcased the deadly artistry of stick-play, the passionate superstition of the "jamette" life in a nineteenth-century barrack-yard underworld community, where men, armed with stout "pouis", risk their lives and drain their life-blood away over the "blood-hole" after every wound.

Before the fight, of course, each contender has to take his "*bois*" (same as pouis stick) to a good obeahman "to get it mount".[8] Final-year English honours student David Williams from Barbados reviewed the play for the March issue of the undergraduate magazine, the *Pelican*. Unlike Rae, Williams felt that "the manipulation of the crowd in the stick-fighting tent" was adequately handled: "one did not get the impression of a congested stage." In addition, he liked the set: "What I found particularly interesting was the immediacy of effect of the design of Diable Papa's house . . . The design of the stick-fighting tent was colourful, the back-cloth depicting an authentic setting of trees and board-houses."[9]

Errol Hill himself was to have presented the play in the Michaelmas (first) term of 1956–57, but he postponed and then cancelled the production as backstage work was moving too slowly and people were coming late to rehearsals. But the cast liked the script and, wanting to go ahead, prevailed on assistant producer Mary Brathwaite to take over, with Hill's blessing, and with first-year student Bernice Lake from Antigua as assistant. St Lucian Angela Lewis, coached by Cynthia Alleyne, proved an apt pupil in lights; a good team from British Guiana (Christobel Deane, Desirée Shackleford and Hazel Campayne) worked on costumes and make-up; and Ancile Gloudon, who played the challenger Tim Briscoe, held classes in the theatre in the art of stick-fighting.

Archie Hudson-Phillips dominated as the obeahman Diable Papa, who takes silver from both contenders to mount their sticks (so each expects to win) and sends two accomplices to place bets on the two men. The village beauty Petite Belle Lilly (Trinidadian freshette Marina Archbald-Critchlow), having announced that she is only interested in a champion, changes her mind when Briscoe is felled by a *bois-zaygwee* from the reigning champion, Tiny Satan (Barbadian Cecil Crawford); she falls weeping on Briscoe's body. Briscoe (who has not died after all) appears at his wake, terrifying the mourners; Diable Papa and his henchmen confess to double-dealing and fraud and are chased from the village.

Three women played good supporting roles: British Guiana-born Ada Thompson as Minee Woopsa, Diable Papa's medium; Trinidadians Anne Marie Stewart as Briscoe's precocious daughter Marie; and Daphne Pilgrim as Alice Sugar, Man Man DaSilva's woman. The Portuguese shopkeeper was well played by Ralph Araujo, a newcomer to the UCWI stage, as were many of the other Trinidadian men recruited for the large cast, which included accomplished steel-band players and calypso singers Bertie McNeil (the chantwell Hannibal) and Murchison Wilson. The *Pelican* review conveys some of the excitement of the production: "The two men meet and fight with the music of the drums and kalinda rolling in their ears and Hannibal the renowned 'chantwell' singing them to death."[10]

The academic year 1956–57 ended with the production at the Ward Theatre of William Saroyan's *Hello Out There!*, a sensitive study of the loneliness and frustration of a young man wrongfully imprisoned in a small western town in the United States. Archie Hudson-Phillips and Ada Thompson were the protagonists in Brathwaite's last University Players production, which received special mention for its starkly simple set of prison bars and lights and won Ada Thompson the Sir Alexander Bustamante Cup for best actress in the 1957 Adult Drama Festival.

University Players–West Indian Players

Most of the West Indian scripts brought to life at the Dramatic Theatre in the next four years were directed by Slade Hopkinson, who was then working in Jamaica. These included Derek Walcott's *Wine of the Country*, a contemporary tale of middle-class rum-drinking (rum being the Caribbean equivalent of wine in the Mediterranean), with Archie Hudson-Phillips; Errol John's *The Tout*; and Walcott's morality/folk play *Ti Jean and his Brothers* (1959).

Walcott directed his *Ione* (the Oedipus story), which drew large audiences, perhaps because of the newspaper controversy between himself and Norman Rae. In his *Daily Gleaner* review of 18 March 1957, Rae took the playwright to task for failing to appreciate the purity of Greek drama and for trying to Caribbeanize a masterpiece like Sophocles' *Oedipus* by setting his *Ione* in the West Indies. Walcott hit back in a letter to the editor, indicating that he had created a play; he had not set out to make a modern Caribbean audience think like ancient Greeks: "I cannot imagine a crowd of Elizabethans eating whatever was the Elizabethan equivalent of popcorn, listening to Lear and keeping one eye on the lectures on Seneca by T.S. Eliot. I also cannot imagine the Greek audience checking on their Aristotle before they entered the theatres. The thing is that the theatre is made by creative people, and both Aristotle and T.S. Eliot knew when to make their remarks."[11] The correspondence continued trenchant on both sides until it ended with a tacit agreement to disagree.

The Tout was staged at an Adult Drama Festival in 1957, but not in competition. It fulfilled a 1956 recommendation of the judges that a well-produced West Indian play be used as a demonstration on one of the festival nights. The production starred Lloyd Stanford and Jamaican newcomer Neville Hall, and featured Winnie Blackwood and Ossie Morris, with Charles Thesiger as the grandfather in a wheelchair, unable to prevent the assault. The play was meticulously directed by Hopkinson.

Errol Hill left on a Rockefeller grant to the Yale University School of Drama for the academic year 1958–59, and Noel Vaz, appointed to act as drama tutor, invited Franklyn "Chappy" St Juste (then with the Jamaica Film Unit), a St Lucian, to work on lights for the University Players. St Juste was already doing lights for Hopkinson's new group, the West Indian Players, who had started work on Derek Walcott's *Ti Jean and his Brothers*. Thus St Juste came to be associated with the University Players and took part in joint productions at the Dramatic Theatre. The 1959 *Pelican Annual* reported that "The most important play produced in our dramatic theatre during the year . . . was directed by Slade Hopkinson during February, with a cast including many of the undergraduates. *Ti Jean and his Brothers* is a morality play with the personified issues of good and evil worked out in terms of West Indian folklore."[12]

In the title role of Ti Jean (little John), St Juste contested against Ronnie Llanos's Old Man/the Devil, winning where his brothers, Gros Jean (big John, played by Charlie Thesiger) and Mi Jean (middle-sized John, played by Stanley Iton from St Vincent),

Mitzie Townsend

had failed. Mitzie Townsend of the Caribbean Thespians played the mother, and Hopkinson, in addition to directing, acted the part of the Bolom, the spirit of an unborn child. The writer of the *Pelican Annual* report thought that the play had gained something from Jamaican pantomime, and concluded "that a drama that includes singing, dancing and music is best equipped, in some secret way, for attaining that elusive goal – a truly 'West Indian' theatre".[13]

Parallel Theatre in the 1950s and early 1960s

Members of the UCWI Dramatic Society appeared from time to time in other productions as well. On 14 May 1955, first-year French student Jean Thomas and second-year student Lloyd Stanford, were featured in Jean Anouilh's *Antigone* – with Thomas impressive in the title role, and Stanford stately as Creon, a role he had played (in English) in the Dramatic Society's *Oedipus Rex* the year before. *Antigone*, produced by Professor Manfred Sandmann, Head of Department of French, also featured freshman Sammy Rudolph Insanally from British Guiana as the Chorus, and second-year Trinidadian Mervyn Alleyne. The programme contained a detailed analysis of the play, written in English, to enable all spectators to follow the unfolding of the plot with ease.

Members of the society were involved in diverse activities off-campus. Slade Hopkinson's performance as Prospero in *The Tempest* for the Jamaica 300 celebration (May 1955) was spoken of for years. Rex Nettleford joined the Ivy Baxter Dance Group and started performing with them. Derek Walcott wrote and directed the spectacular celebratory pageant *Drums and Colours* for the inauguration of the Federation of the West Indies in April to May 1958 in Trinidad. Errol Hill took Jamaicans Easton Lee, Lloyd Stanford and Neville Hall to Trinidad to represent the University Players in the pageant, and to act in his play *The Ping Pong* – with Ossie Downer, who had starred in the UCWI production in 1956.

"*Qwik Qwak!*", "*Crik Crak!*"

Like the anancy spider in Jamaica and the monkey in Trinidad, the frog and the cricket are significant creatures in French Caribbean folklore. Thus, when persons gather around the old folk in St Lucia or Dominica, for instance, the children know it is story time when a voice croaks, "*Qwik qwak!*" The circle choruses back, "*Crik crak!*", and the story begins, "*Qwik qwak!* Once upon a time . . ."

Near the end of the 1950s, Slade Hopkinson produced two folk-based plays by Roderick Walcott, Derek's twin brother – *Mal Finis* and *The Trouble with Albino Joe* – and directed two one-act performances under the umbrella title *Poets and Pariahs*. They were *The Onliest Fisherman*, his own work, and *A Door Opens*, by David Williams, drama critic for the student publication the *Pelican*. *Mal Finis* was based on an actual obeah incident (a grisly tale) in St Lucia, and was entered in the 1959

Adult Drama Festival at the Ward Theatre. The other plays had brief runs between 1960 and 1961 at the Bournemouth Theatre, off Windward Road. Gerald "Buddy" Pouyat from the Pantomime was one of those who joined Hopkinson's cast; Noel Vaz made the lights available and St Juste was lighting manager.

The University Players in the Golden 1950s

The group was now clearly in the position to be considered the nucleus of a West Indian Theatre. Members of the UCWI Dramatic Society were moulded by participation in wide-ranging discussions at the Students' Union with young lecturers, staff members and their friends – people like Roy Augier, E.V. Ellington, Aston Preston, Leslie Robinson, writer John Hearne and, of course, Errol Hill. Sometimes, with friends of the society like Barbara Goodison (later Gloudon), students would be taken to visit the riverside Gordon Town, home of Louise (Bennett) and Eric Coverley, or Lois Kelly-Barrow, where the discussions continued. Regular topics were federation and the West Indies as a viable unit, the role of the university in an independent Caribbean, and the responsibility of the players to lead the way in the formation of a West Indian theatre.

Slade Hopkinson took the players to the summit; he and Derek Walcott continued their association with the Dramatic Society long after graduation. Hopkinson, the quintessential dramatist, was lead actor, leading producer, trainer of voice, and shared his talents with other groups and with schools (through Noel Vaz, who, as drama tutor after Errol Hill, brought the society into the 1960s and the university's independence). Walcott continued to write for production after he left UCWI at the end of 1955. And guiding the players in those formative years was the firm hand and incisive mind of Errol Hill, master drama tutor.

Many of those who trod the boards at the old wooden Dramatic Theatre and sat in the director's and critic's chairs then have passed on, leaving a legacy of glorious theatre behind them. They are remembered with love and respect: Earl Been, Winnie Blackwood, Vincent Brown, Wilfred Cartey, Neville Hall, Errol Hill, Slade Hopkinson, Stanley Iton, Robert LePage, Cedric Lindo, Ronald Llanos, Vincent McKie, Hugh Moss-Solomon, Chris Osborne, Eustace Royer, Vernon Royes, Manfred Sandmann, John Stockhausen, Joan Swaby, Denise Thwaites (*née* Mitchell), Dwight Whylie, Dave Wildish. So too are associates in the craft, among whom are Greta Bourke Fowler, Enid Chevannes of the Ivory Club, Patrick Delapenha, Harry Milner, Phillip Morris, Mitzie Townsend.

Theatre at UCWI in the 1950s was, as good theatre always is, exhilarating, inspiring, demanding. West Indian playwrights were encouraged by the UCWI Department of Extra-Mural Studies; aspiring producers, actors and stage technicians were trained and provided with opportunities in the UCWI Dramatic Society. Graduates leaving the UCWI (and later the University of the West Indies) to teach in schools and work with drama groups in their communities throughout the region (and in the university itself) have benefited, then and down through these sixty years, from the experiences of those golden 1950s. Today's students, who work with the tutor and coordinator at the Philip Sherlock Centre for the Creative Arts (PSCCA), Carolyn Allen, and Brian Heap, the current drama tutor, continue to hold the University Players aloft. In September 2007 Jamaica Youth Theatre (born of the Schools' Drama Festival) produced *Man Better Man*, directed by Carolyn Allen at Mona's cultural hub, the PSCCA.

Acknowledgements

Mary Morgan acknowledges with grateful thanks the cooperation of the following: Valerie Fraser of the National Library of Jamaica; Evadne McLean and others in the Elsa Goveia Reading Room, University of the West Indies Main Library, Mona; the staff in the Jamaica Methodist District Office. She is also grateful to her family and friends for nudging memories: Kamau Brathwaite, Joan Brathwaite, Anderson Lake; Carolyn Allen, Jeanne Barnes (*née* Hill), Edward Baugh, Sybil Campbell, George Carter, Kathleen Drayton (*née* McCracken), Ancile and Barbara Gloudon, Robert Henry, Archie and Angela Hudson-Phillips, James and Mavis Lee Wah, Kenneth Magnus, Owen Minott, Mervyn Morris, Buddy and Cissy Pouyat, Jean Small (*née* Thomas), Kenny Small, Peter and Gloria (*née* Barrett) Sobers, Franklyn St Juste, Lloyd Stanford, Charles Thesiger, Hugh Wynter, and Althea Young (*née* McPherson).

9

The School of Drama

HONOR FORD-SMITH AND EUGENE WILLIAMS

The School of Drama is part of the Edna Manley College of the Visual and Performing Arts, which is a publicly funded and accredited tertiary institution, offering a range of programmes in the arts and related disciplines. The college continues to be the signal institution of its kind in Jamaica and the anglophone Caribbean, with curricula informed by the cultural identity of the region.

The school formerly known as the Jamaica School of Drama (JSD) grew out of the work of the Little Theatre Movement (LTM). In 1969, the LTM set up a part-time evening school, then called the Theatre School, to teach basic theatre skills to potential cast members of its annual pantomime. It later developed a drama in education programme for teachers who wanted to use drama as a part of their activities within the school system. In 1976, the JSD moved into the new, government-funded complex called the Cultural Training Centre (CTC), which also housed schools of art, dance and music. The new JSD opened to full-time diploma students and also offered evening classes. It consisted of three classrooms and two theatres – an amphitheatre shared with the other schools, built in white cut stone (which recalls the foundations of "great houses" and the forts of the British), and a studio theatre, which opens onto an abandoned colonial firing range. It was built on part of the land where British colonial military (the Garrison, later Up Park Camp) had its headquarters until as late as 6 August 1962, when Jamaica was declared an independent nation. (Up Park Camp remains the headquarters of the Jamaica Defence Force.) The CTC's location was a physical statement of cultural decolonization and creolization.

The curriculum was conceptualized from the outset as a combination of theatre, social research, community service and education. When the CTC was established in 1976, an exploratory committee on the arts, set up by the prime minister's office –

*This chapter was written by Honor Ford-Smith, a former member of the staff at the School of Drama at the Edna Manley College, and Eugene Williams, head of the School of Drama at the Edna Manley College.

the prime minister then being Michael Manley – developed a brief for the training of the students. It had input from many of the country's cultural agencies. Chaired by Professor Rex Nettleford of the University of the West Indies and Mrs Jean Smith of the Office of the Prime Minister, the committee conducted a study of the forces that determined the use of leisure in Jamaica. It specifically analysed the needs of the youth, focusing on ideas about the role which the government, the mass media, public organizations and existing cultural groups should play. Significantly, it also asked, among other things:

> 1. Are there specific anti-social attitudes in our culture which should be faced? What are the principal agents affecting them and the cultural agencies that can help us overcome them?
> 2. How can the various arts, crafts and cultural agencies be strengthened so as to have maximum appeal to the community?
> 3. Are there some activities which should be nourishing our culture which have not yet received adequate recognition (African Studies, Jamaican publications . . .)
> 4. Are our museums or galleries, etc. playing a sufficiently significant role?[1]

The committee advised the government to act as a catalyst for cultural development linked to social and economic development, through the country's educational policy on adult education, youth and community programmes, as well as through direct assistance to national cultural groups. The CTC was to "provide the country with a cadre of trained cultural agents, art teachers and creative arts practitioners as well as to foster field research and analysis".[2] Social problems of the country were to be addressed through the arts, just as the social creativity of the Caribbean people was to be addressed through the arts. This relationship among art, community service and nation-building formed the basis of the framework for training at the School of Drama.

The school's curriculum was theorized at the outset as an interdisciplinary combination of cultural research, performance and education, but there was no "manual" for explaining how the implementation of this curriculum should take place, given the unique approach to drama education. Where did the limits of the three areas lie? What were the methodologies for making this innovative overlap? How were these ideas to be made concrete in a drama school, which works with the voices and bodies of people? Inevitably therefore, heuristic learning and experimentation was at the core of the work of lecturers and students.

In 1961 Wycliffe Bennett, who had been chairman of the LTM Theatre School since 1958, volunteered to give a one-year course in voice and speech and drama, culminating in a production of Goldoni's *Servant of Two Masters*. At the same time, the LTM school was renamed the Jamaica School of Speech and Drama, and entered the production in the Adult Drama Festival conducted by the Jamaica Drama League. The cast took to Goldoni's *commedia dell'arte* style of acting like ducks to water. The production proved an outstanding success, with a number of award-winning performances and displays of technical excellence by practitioners, who afterwards became celebrities, carrying the professional theatre to new heights: Fae Ellington, Ruth Ho Shing, Oliver Samuels, Trevor Nairne, Lloyd Brown (now deceased), Michael Everett and Turnell McCormack among the actors, storytellers, and direc-

Ruth Ho Shing, actress

tors; and among the technical staff and teachers, George Carter (lighting), Richard and Sally Montgomery (set and costumes), and the late M.G. Robinson (sound effects).

In the following decade, important groundwork was laid for a link between Caribbean theatre and pedagogy. In 1977 Dennis Scott was appointed director and leader of the team at the JSD. He brought to bear on the work of the school his considerable reputation as a published poet, dancer, playwright and critic with cross-disciplinary connections. In keeping with the Nettleford brief, then under constant discussion and interpretation by the staff of the CTC, all of the work undertaken at the JSD had a broadly educational intent. This extended beyond the usual training of actors' instruments, the learning of dramatic traditions and the specifics of theatrical division of labour associated with conservatory programmes. The pedagogical work was linked to the needs of the newly independent nation and the anglophone region, and to the question of cultural identity.

Owen "Blacka" Ellis as Ariel in *The Tempest*, directed by Rawle Gibbons, 1981. *Courtesy of Edna Manley College.*

Scott identified the central organizing concern of the work of the school as that of Caribbean creolization. Questions of creolization and hybridity are themselves much contested and there are differences between the use of the terms in Jamaica, Trinidad, the Leeward and Windward Islands, Cuba, Haiti and Martinique. Nevertheless, this theoretical "cat's cradle", in practice, linked theatrical responses to questions of transculturation. It also informed many of the methodological approaches to work with language, improvisation and scripts, and the commitment to performing narratives of the anglophone Caribbean. Orality, the written tradition and the issues raised by their combination are themselves central elements in debates on creolization and national identity. The teaching of speech is linked to these questions and to the development of inter-generic forms of representation. The dub poets, developing as they did in the 1970s, had an informal home at the school, and their work grew independently within the space provided by the school. Their work attests to the potential of the school's attempts to work with popular culture and the oral and written continuum.

The school has consistently presented new Caribbean scripts or creolized European and North American scripts. In the 1970s and 1980s, up to fifteen scripts were presented per year.[3] Many of these were not vehicles for commercial theatre, but they were cheaply produced and were able to attract small but committed audiences. Until the lack of resources and personnel which seriously undermined theatre production in the mid 1980s, the school worked to build an audience for a season of Caribbean theatre as well as for plays and performances from elsewhere. Until the 1990s, under difficult financial conditions, the school continued to stage plays from the region. It has since turned to minimal use of sets as a design strategy.

Between 1977 and 1989, the school, in association with other agencies, presented original productions of new scripts such as *Dog*, *Under a Sky of Incense*, *Live and Direct from Babylon*, *Agnes of God* (world premiere), *Masqueraders*, *Shepherd*, *Ilawah* and many others. It showcased Jamaican productions of Derek Walcott's *Pantomime*, and remounted scripts by Errol John and Douglas Archibald. Experimental plays such as Pablo Hoilett's *Journey*, a collective creation about life in Jamaica's prisons, *Di Yard*, by Michael Smith, and a poetic drama called *Foreday Morning*, were also produced.

Beverly Edwards and Andrew Brodber in *Playboy of the West Indies*, directed by Eugene Williams, 1991. *Courtesy of Edna Manley College.*

Agnes of God, by John Pielmeier, received its world premiere in 1979 at the JSD, with (from left) Hertencer Lindsay, Honor Ford-Smith and Jean Small. *Photo by Monica DaSilva.*

The school's theatrical work took as an important theme the project of critiquing colonial and postcolonial versions of history and memory, as in the case of *An Echo in the Bone*, *Ilawah* and *Shepherd*. These efforts critiqued colonial discourses through mimicry and satire while retaining elements of tragic structure. Given these thematic intentions and the lack of resources for productions, the school developed a particular style based on minimal staging, rapid role-changing by actors, music and an emphasis on ritual form. The aesthetic approach of the school in this period involved turning the institutional scarcity of resources into a design strategy. Bare stages and sets made from abandoned car tires, boxes and cardboard exemplified minimal and sometimes highly symbolic approaches to representation. Students were encouraged to stage their work in diverse settings.

Caribbean Lab, a course designed by Jean Small, supported experiments with the structure of traditional forms and their implications for actors. Testimonial autobiographical work, which drew on Jamaican orature, was also encouraged. Improvisation as developed by Hertencer Lindsay encouraged a journey of self-discovery and the awareness of personal strengths as a therapeutic response to psychological development in the context of colonial systems of knowledge. Work with the School of Dance on Jamaican vocabulary further developed students' awareness of Caribbean forms and helped to give voice and validity to their identity and inherent aesthetic sensibilities.

In the process of development, the school introduced a formal curriculum in community drama which sought to extend the cultivation of the cultural agent. Director of studies Thom Cross devised a programme that stressed theatre's potential for adult and youth education and for the release of what was called "community voice". He fused elements of social analysis, child drama, and theatre and performance skills. In his words, "the essence of [the work] was that you'd have to select the appropriate form or dramatic media for the objectives that you had, within that group, at that time, in the social setting that you found yourself. There was no one-way, no single 'halleluiah path' to success. You had to select. You and the participants had to select the appropriate form."[4]

This work was supplemented by philosophies and practices inspired by Paulo Freire and Augusto Boal, as well as other examples of collaborative social research and performance. Gradually, from the experiments in the classroom, and the outreach work of lecturers, students and graduates, popular theatre and community drama companies evolved in various locations in the island. The major ones were Sistren Theatre Collective, Groundwork Theatre Company and Oomph. The non-governmental sector drew on these groups as a means of promoting participatory adult education and of supporting community members who found "development" work tedious and needed new strategies of intervention. Recently, since the dawn of the new millennium, these early approaches have been reapplied in Jamaica in projects that address the needs of inner-city youth in communities at risk. The Area Youth Foundation, which was spearheaded with the skills of graduates of the school, is a prime example.

A major outreach arm of the drama school in community drama, and theatre in education, was the Graduate Theatre Company (GTC), established in 1981. Staffed primarily by graduates of the school and financed by international funding, the company was engaged in two decades of work in communities and schools as well as an annual commercial production. The community drama work of the GTC significantly enabled and facilitated community development and empowerment in the communities that were targeted. The company also established meaningful linkages with non-governmental organizations, popular theatre, and companies in Africa, Canada and Latin America. Its Theatre in Education work was in demand in schools as a major support for the CXC curriculum, while the annual theatre production engendered much social and political discussion through its aesthetic innovations and the political concerns incorporated in the productions.

One of the best-kept secrets of the school is its achievement in the area of drama in education. Since the start of that programme twenty-two years ago the school has successfully trained many teachers for the primary and secondary school system. More than this, its approach to teacher training has drawn on the strategic importance of performance in Caribbean culture and has used this as the basis for the development of personal autonomy, language arts and critical skills.

Thom Cross, Brian Heap, Hertencer Lindsay and Dennis Scott introduced process-oriented drama into Jamaican schools in the early 1970s, stressing its importance for personal autonomy as well as for exploring other subjects. Their work adapted the British approach to the needs of the local context. In a system which, since emancipation, has stressed external modes of evaluation and normalization by examination, and which rigidly represented the pyramidal structure of Jamaican society, drama in education was a highly liberating innovation. It was a space where popular culture,

A production of the Area Youth Foundation

Area Youth in *Beatification*

signs and images could enter the curriculum and where students could freely link their concerns to formal curriculum, and explore their own voices without fear of giving the wrong answer. The initial diploma offered at the school, therefore, came to be an integration of conventional theatre training, community drama and drama in education. In 1989, this curriculum, in response to the need for accreditation, specialization and a more realistic response to the emerging market conditions, was redesigned to provide for two diplomas: a diploma in drama in education, and a diploma in theatre arts, as well as a studio certificate in theatre and a technical certificate in theatre arts.

The Joint Board of Teacher Education now accredits the diploma in drama in education. Graduates with this diploma are regarded as trained teachers, and posts for drama teachers are being made available in schools. Students who would like to pursue a career as theatre artists opt for the education diploma, as it is the only one accredited. Subsidized fees for teacher trainees and the guaranteed job market have disappeared and, as a result, since 1989, there has been only a sprinkling of applicants to the theatre arts programme. It is expected that the Bachelor of Fine Arts in theatre, at present being designed, will address this imbalance.

In the first decade of its development, the JSD was able to travel from its infancy at the LTM to being what can be called, in the jargon of organizational life cycles, a "go-go organization". This is the phase when the work of an organization is marked by innovation and a strong sense of community among those involved, as they work

Area Youth Foundation. Dancing with Prince Charles, 2001

to win acknowledgement for their institution. It is a phase of institutional development often marked by enthusiasm, which offsets the difficulties of its beginnings. Whereas the socio-cultural backdrop for this period in the Caribbean was one of tremendous cultural optimism and postcolonial self-affirmation, the 1980s and 1990s saw the emergence of major structural adjustments in the socio-economic sectors of the region.

These shifting paradigms created much dislocation in the school, which gradually led to the collapse of the academic team that chartered the early course of its development. A new phase in the journey then evolved, which saw the emergence of graduates as the new leaders. While the umbilical connections with the past remain as the driving force behind the programmes, however, this inevitable period in organizational life cycles (often called the adolescent phase), which is currently still being experienced, has been focusing the energies towards the administrative infrastructure and academic systems being clearly defined and strengthened, as well as the refining of techniques of performance and the systematic training of drama teachers.

Consolidating the administrative base and updating the academic thrust has been a major objective of the entire Edna Manley College in this period. A universal consequence of this evolving phase in the evolution of organizations is the training of the creative energies that are so prevalent in the early phase, towards administrative development in this period. It is, however, realized by all involved in the school that the rekindling and sustaining of the creative fire must be engendered by research, documentation, programme development and the imaginative capitalization on the local and global marketplace. This is the challenge and the target for the next phase of the school's development.

ACT III

THE DANCE EVOLVES

10

The Ballet

We can approach the history of dance theatre in Jamaica in any of several ways: we can discuss chronologically the work of the several dance groups, of the different teachers, choreographers and dancers, or of the musicians, designers, producers and promoters; we can trace trends and movements with a view to discerning patterns in human development; or we can look at the themes or icons which have remained consistently emblematic over the changing years. It is also important to remember that Jamaican dance has antecedents in other countries – primarily in Europe, North America and Africa – and that many of our practitioners have been trained at internationally famous centres in ballet, modern and national dance, and in methods developed by some of the world's most outstanding teachers. To achieve a comprehensive overview, due regard must be paid to these factors as well as to the political, social and cultural realities of the times.

It might prove salutary to bear in mind that, in the history of the dance, some of the most influential figures have not always been practitioners. For example, from 1835 and for nearly forty years in Paris, often the views most sought after and most highly prized were those of Theophile Gautier, poet, novelist and critic. Likewise, the man who gave western Europe a vision of imperial Russian Ballet and had such a revolutionary impact upon subsequent developments in the art, was the legendary Serge Diaghilev, an impresario who was neither dancer, musician nor designer.

In Jamaica dance has become a valid expression of a specific time and place, for the unique quality of any people is the distillation of their common experience over time. Their art derives from thought, sight, sound and rhythm of their experiences and it is this unique vision that our artists must give back to the world, if they are to project a Jamaican art. But what may now be seen by some as the realization of a dream could only have been an act of faith when Rex Nettleford, Eddy Thomas and their colleagues founded and named the National Dance Theatre Company in 1962. Of those initial members, only five were actively performing after twenty years – Rex Nettleford, Pansy Hassan, Barry Moncrieffe, Monica McGowan and Joyce Campbell. The descriptive name "dance theatre" emphasized from the very beginning the positive theatrical intentions of the company. And before they started to rear the super-

Opposite: Pupils from the Rowe School of Dancing. *Courtesy of NLJ.*

structure over four decades ago, many other people had already done some solid work and begun to lay necessary foundations.

Jamaica's First Dancing Schools: Mrs Melton Adams, Pansy Alexander and Ermyn (Ellis) Lyons

It is probably correct to say that the first dances choreographed and staged in a theatre or hall in Jamaica were performed by foreigners visiting from abroad. At least two efforts were made to establish dancing schools before the First World War: Mrs H. MacPherson's music and dancing classes were advertised in the *Daily Gleaner* of 8 January 1907, and Miss Bertram announced on 5 October 1911 the reopening of her dance classes (for both, see chapter 2). The latter appears later in our account of dance as Mrs Melton Adams and subsequently as Mrs Marguerite Squire.

The former Miss Bertram gave an interview to the *Daily Gleaner* in 1941, in which she compared the opportunities she felt existed at that time with the attitudes and problems she encountered when she had tried to launch out as a professional teacher of dance thirty years earlier. She expressed her hope that ambitious, talented teachers would seize the opportunity then presented by the tide of culture to make the most colourful and vibrant contribution to West Indian art – the ballet:

> The freedom of their opportunities, increased by the presence of really good musicians here, is in contrast with my own youth . . . When I came from college in England with a Teacher-Performer's Diploma which I had studied and practised hard to possess, the dismay of my parents at my proposal to open a Studio of Dancing, makes a fantastic story. Like all the men of that era, my father felt himself disgraced at the very thought of my accepting money for teaching. It was through the sympathy of a friend who understood my craving to express myself and who pleaded with my father, that I held my first dancing classes in Jamaica, in her drawing room.

Ermyn Ellis (later Lyons), founder of the Mayfair School of Dancing. *Courtesy of NLJ.*

After this small victory in feminine freedom, she went on a visit to her brother in Toronto, where for some time she was a member of the Hapsburg Academy and the Canadian Academy. When, finally, in 1916, she settled in Jamaica as Mrs Melton Adams, she opened her studio again; and her periodic visits as dancing instructor to the island's leading girls' schools, such as Hampton and Wolmer's, and the performances of her children's group, "The Little Mummers", became important contributions to the island's cultural life.

Mrs Adams taught classical ballet, national and character dances, and several other kinds of dance. Jamaica owes the beginnings of its tradition of classical ballet dancing to her and to two other women: Pansy Davis, later known as Pansy Alexander and as Mrs Arbuthnot; and Ermyn Ellis, later Mrs Frank Lyons. Both women were born in 1903, Pansy Davis Alexander in Demerara (British Guiana) and Ermyn Ellis in Jamaica.

Wycliffe Bennett spoke with both women on the telephone in 1976. Pansy Alexander (then Mrs Arbuthnot) resided in London and Ermyn Ellis (Mrs Frank Lyons) in Miami. They had both trained in London at the Royal Academy of Dance. Miss Bertram had also taught some ballet, but she had tended to concentrate more on the freer forms of dance and, in any event, by 1920 had become much too heavy to demonstrate the art herself. She preferred to function through youngsters whom she had taught – Phyllis Morais at Hampton School, for example – if any were available.

Pansy Alexander began teaching around 1921, and soon became a much sought-after artist, working eventually with Lindsay Downer, the most eminent producer of theatre in Jamaica during the 1920s and 1930s. She also produced a great many shows for charity, and was the most outstanding exponent of the ballet in those days. (There used to be a photograph of her on points hanging in the foyer of the Ward Theatre.) In 1928 Mrs Alexander assumed responsibility for the artistic direction of Lindsay Downer's *Clowns and Clatter*, which succeeded his *Fireflies*. Downer himself took charge of general and stage management. The show was widely acclaimed: one critic praised the costumes and scenic effects, especially the silhouetted forms of the six dancers in the Eastern scene, and although the chorus was extremely original and effective, the costumes did not harmonize perfectly with the blue and green of the very talented *première danseuse*'s beautiful gown. Of Mrs Alexander's dancing, the only criticism was that "there was not enough of it".[1]

Downer's company was very creative. While the costumes for the rest of his cast were made in Jamaica, Pansy Alexander's dresses were imported from New York. For one segment – the Russian dance scene – Russian boots were made locally by Mr Morin of Handal and Company. There were fourteen Russian ladies and fourteen Cossacks in the dance choreographed by Mrs Alexander. The programme for the December 1928 to January 1929 season noted that the proceeds were devoted "to provide new curtains, lights and scenery, and to provide the nucleus of a fund for the Ventilation of the Ward Theatre". Some of these programmes also included a topicalities section, *Kingston Mends Her Ways*, which included recognizable characters like the Foreman, Time Keeper, Lunch Woman (played by E.M. Cupidon), Water Boy, the Mayor, Coolie Watchman, Engineer and Labourers – all figures from Kingston's city life.

Ermyn Ellis taught ballet, tap and acrobatic dance, as well as other types of dancing, privately and in high schools such as Wolmer's and Hampton from 1924 to 1928, until she married wharf-owner and shipping agent Frank Lyons. He built her a studio at Mayfair, their home on Hope Road, where she continued her classes until 1939. Wartime conditions and lack of petrol for travel to Mayfair, which was then on the outskirts of the city, made it difficult for her pupils to come to classes. Mrs Lyons and her husband organized a troupe, the Mayfair Promenaders, which made its debut in 1928. She, with assistance, designed and made all of the costumes, which were said to be quite beautiful. Rehearsals, however, proved a problem because of the difficulty of arranging practice sessions with members of the Military Band, the orchestra for the occasion. This group also mounted several shows to raise funds for charity, and during the war years was continually called upon to contribute in this way to the War Fund.

Both Pansy Alexander and Ermyn Ellis Lyons catered to a somewhat aristocratic clientele, and so in fact did Lindsay Downer, who would use whites with "black face" for black characters. The colour of the performers on stage mirrored in large part the colour of the audience, since few blacks attended those kinds of shows in those days.

Hazel Johnston

Hazel Johnston, dancer, dance teacher, choreographer and producer. *Courtesy of NLJ.*

Certainly, one of the most influential figures in Jamaica's history of dance theatre was Hazel Johnston. Much activity has stemmed from her seminal work. Some of her students provide an imposing array of names in the Who's Who in Jamaica's history of dance theatre: Ivy Baxter, Barbara Fonseca, Dorothy Fraser, Punkie and Betty Rowe, Fay Simpson. Hazel Johnston's career as a dance teacher, choreographer and producer spanned only the last six years of her short life. She was born in Kingston in 1908 and died in 1944 at the early age of thirty-six. A daughter of banana tycoon and shipping magnate Charlie Johnston, she was sent in 1919 at the age of eleven, along with her two sisters and her brother, to Great Ayton Public School in Yorkshire, England, where she remained until 1926. Feeling that the long absence from Jamaica during their impressionable years could have caused some degree of alienation, "Maas Charlie", as her father was affectionately known, arranged for the children to be taken, on their return, on a tour of the island, spending a few weeks at a time in each parish.

Hazel Johnston started a kindergarten school, but in 1935 she suffered a nervous breakdown and gave up the little school. She needed a change of occupation, something to challenge her. So, as an adult of twenty-six, she went to see Herma Dias, who had been trained by Pansy Alexander and was now teaching ballet at Mrs Squire's studio. Herma Dias introduced her to the teaching of dance, and after a period of twelve months she left Jamaica again, this time for London. She entered the McLaren School of Dancing, run by Scottish ladies, Miss Euphan McLaren and her two sisters, all three of whom had been trained by an Italian dancing master and were by then well-known in theatrical circles as choreographers for some of London's biggest shows.

With a group of students from the school, Hazel Johnston performed in Coleridge-Taylor's *Hiawatha*, which ran for two weeks at the Royal Albert Hall. She studied ballet, character and tap dancing, and, recognizing the need to learn more about these types of dance, took a year's course in Greek dancing at the Ginner-Mawer School. After a year at McLaren's, she passed the qualifying examination for membership of the Imperial Society of Dancing, with which the Cecchetti Society was incorporated. She was, however, awarded the associate's certificate "not having had the necessary three years experience as a Teacher of Dancing in a responsible position, to qualify for membership".

On returning to Jamaica, Miss Johnston set about opening her own studio, and after just over a year, the school gave its first recital on 26 November 1938, at the Ward Theatre. She was assisted by Mrs Joan Turner, the talented wife of a British army captain at Up Park Camp. The programme incorporated classical ballet, Greek, character, national, acrobatic and musical comedy pieces, some of which she recreated from productions she had seen by her former teachers. Edgar Stewart did the decor. Hazel Johnston designed all the costumes; her sister, Leila, an accomplished musician, assumed responsibility for the music, and her other sister became business manager. The reviews were favourable. She and her two sisters became a formidable production team.

Commendable though this effort was, it was really her next show at the Ward Theatre, in 1940, in aid of the War Fund, that set her on an unfaltering path to high critical esteem. She arranged all the dances herself, and her sister Leila organized a thirteen-piece string ensemble. The varied and balanced programme demonstrated the in-depth training that had been achieved during the past three years, and ranged from *Baby Academic*, through *The Artist's Dream*, to several pieces of character work – *Greek Frieze*, *Acrobatic Waltz*, *Patriotic Jazz* and three scenes from *Sleeping Beauty*. Not only were the critics ecstatic, but so were producers and other theatre practitioners of repute.

In *The Artist's Dream*, an artist visits an art gallery for the purpose of painting a copy of one of the pictures. Growing weary as he works, he falls asleep and dreams that the portraits have come to life. One by one they descend to the floor of the gallery and join in a dance. When the dance is over they return to their frames and the artist awakens. The critic from the *Daily Gleaner* wrote that, for sheer beauty and almost startling realism, *The Artist's Dream* was perhaps the most outstanding item. Of *Sleeping Beauty* another critic wrote that the ballet was in its infancy in Jamaica and so the success achieved in its presentation must be recorded as a notable step in the advancement of classic dancing in this country, and that proper credit must be given to Miss Johnston and her pupils.

Sleeping Beauty, based on the Grimms' fairytale, was presented in three scenes, the first depicting the birth of the princess and the gifts of the fairies, the second describing the fulfilment of the curse when the princess falls asleep for a hundred years, and the third featuring her awakening after the coming of the prince. The author of the review from the *Daily Gleaner* made special mention of Phyllis Cardoza, "who made a charming Princess", and Geraldine Kelly, "who danced diabolically" as the Wicked Fairy. Phyllis Cardoza's dancing in the final act, with Patrick Vermont as the prince, was the personification of grace and poise.

In addition to the review in the *Gleaner*, Greta Bourke (Fowler), founder of the Little Theatre Movement (LTM), said of Miss Johnston's success: "Through the medium of Hazel Johnston Jamaicans are discovering ballet – the unprecedented queues at the box office prove this. Her genius for costumes, her arrangement of music and movement ensures her a continued appreciation."[2] Lindsay Downer, in a private letter to Hazel Johnston, wrote: "It is really the best show I have seen in Jamaica, and the standard maintained from start to finish was of a uniformly high level."[3]

Patrick Vermont in the role of the prince marked the first appearance of a male ballet dancer on the Jamaican stage, and some people were taken aback. Greta Bourke let go another salvo:

> Hazel Johnston has a direct dramatic narrative [which] demands a male dancer; in any case female movement is the complement of male movement. Hazel Johnston does pioneer work when she introduces a Jamaican audience to its first experience of a male dancer in ballet – and for the benefit of those in our audiences who seemed to be so surprised, it is interesting to note that Ballet originated with men and is in no way incompatible with virility.[4]

Hazel Johnston's Children's Group. *Courtesy of NLJ.*

Hazel Johnston's next studio recitals were given at the Ward Theatre in December 1942, and at the Carib Theatre in December 1943. She did one further show in support of the war effort. She provided the ballet for the first LTM pantomime, *Jack and the Beanstalk*, in 1941; and co-produced, with Noel Vaz, that landmark 1944 alfresco production of Shakespeare's *A Midsummer Night's Dream* on the lawns of the Holy Cross Convent at Half Way Tree.

Hazel Johnston was a highly intelligent and articulate woman, and wrote lucidly

Hazel Johnston's dance group: *Les Sylphides* (round shot) at the Carib Theatre (1944). *Courtesy of NLJ.*

on the subject of the ballet. Some of her views on the evolution of a Jamaican ballet may come as a surprise to many today, but it should be remembered that she was expressing herself in 1939. She was coloured but she was brought up as an English upper-class aristocrat isolated from the Jamaican peasantry – a situation which her father tried to correct when he took her on an extended tour of the island. Some of her writings in *Public Opinion* showed her alienation from the Jamaican folk when she noted that "Jamaican native dances consist of improvisations which, however, bear some similarity to each other" and that while this was proof of the spontaneity and natural aptitude of the people it presented "almost insurmountable difficulties to the choreographer".[5]

Eddy Thomas and Jeanette Nasralla from the Rowe Studio of Dancing. *Courtesy of NLJ.*

After Hazel Johnston's death in 1944, some of her students provided the nucleus of a studio for Joan McCulloch, formerly of the Ballet Russe. An Englishwoman married to a Jamaican doctor, Joan McCulloch could speak with the full authority of experience both as a teacher and performer in England and Jamaica. In 1946 she made an assessment of the situation *vis-à-vis* jobs and the possible future of those who would wish to take up the art seriously. She observed that Jamaica was awakening politically and trying to find its feet, and that one of the most important changes was the people's increased interest in things artistic. Painting, music and writing had shown signs of improving while the ballet was still in its elementary stage. She gave credit to the work of the late Hazel Johnston, who was instrumental in raising the artistic and technical standard of dancing in Jamaica, and had made the public realize that dancing was something worth waiting for. Her dream was that, in a few years' time, there might be a real ballet school and a ballet company where students from the other West Indian islands could be trained. The late Hazel Johnston had set Jamaica dancing and the country owed many dancers and teachers to her influence.[6]

Among some of Hazel Johnston's pupils who had returned from training overseas and begun to make their contributions were Ivy Baxter, Barbara Fonseca, the Rowe sisters – Betty and Punkie – and Fay Simpson. In addition, there was Hazel Doran, pupil of Italia Conti who had attended the Royal Academy of Dancing, the Imperial Society and Bruneschelli.

Barbara Fonseca, dance teacher, choreographer and producer. *Courtesy of NLJ.*

Madame Soohih, Ivy Baxter and the Ballet Guild of Jamaica

Finally, there were Anatole and May Soohih. Anatole brought to Jamaica the teachings of the Imperial School of Russia through its professors, who, following the Russian revolution, had fled to China. Before settling in Jamaica in 1947, Anatoly had himself lived in Manchuria, China and Japan.

Madame May Soohih, Ballet Teacher. *Photo by Maria LaYacona.*

The LTM soon sought his assistance, and in 1948 and 1949 he produced ballet vignettes for the pantomimes *Beauty and the Beast* and *Bluebeard and Br'er Anancy*. After his death in 1950, May Soohih continued to participate in several pantomime productions, *Dick Whittington* (1951), *Anancy and Pandora* (1956), and *Busha Bluebeard* (1957), which also went to Trinidad in 1958. Madame Soohih identified two young Jamaican dancers who were to become famous – Clive Thompson, then at the Martha Graham School, and Washington Chen, who was at the time dancing professionally in Germany.

During Jamaica 300 in 1955, dance schools run by Ivy Baxter, Barbara Fonseca, Fay Simpson, Hazel Duran, Anatole and May Soohih came together to form the Ballet Guild of Jamaica, and offered their first and only presentation in 1956. That they were able to pool their resources and present three major works is an event of some artistic importance in Jamaica. That some of the major works are well-known masterpieces is akin to challenging the thunder, but the comparisons were never made. Orford St John wrote of the guild's performance:

> I have seen *Les Sylphides* done by all the great companies and am inclined to avoid it unless it is done by the masters, so it is greatly to Madame Fonseca's credit that I soon succumbed to the magic. The solo work of Shirley Jackson and Sheila McNaught was thoroughly finished. Joyce Blondel Francis dances with grace but her extension is poor. Neville Cardoza is a neat dancer but lacks the attack for the great Mazurka; an excellent support, he was far better in the Boutique Adagio.
>
> Though one cannot compare the performance of Shirley Jackson and Neville Cardoza with the Massine–Danilova enchanted partnership, they nevertheless evoked smarting tears of nostalgia and brought a well executed ensemble to a fitting climax. Clive Thompson shows signs of developing into a good romantic lead and there were nice performances too from Margaret Lewars and Eddy Thomas.
>
> In *Danse Elementale*, Ivy Baxter has made a welcome departure from folk and pro-

Opposite: Melanie Graham (*née* Robinson) and Barry Moncrieffe at a Madame May Soohih Dance Company recital (1970). *Photo by Maria LaYacona.*

Melanie Robinson (Graham) and Washington Chen, from the May Soohih School of Dance. *Courtesy of NLJ.*

> duced a ballet of ideas having some kinship with Massine's symphonic ballets. It was an interesting and well disciplined piece of teamwork to a Beethoven score, with Ronan Critchlow once again emerging as the best male dancer in Jamaica. His backdrop design was suitable and effective: A production of which Jamaicans may be proud.[7]

Danse Elementale was the most memorable of the Ballet Guild's 1956 presentations. Ivy Baxter choreographed and the *corps de ballet* moved with an authority that paralleled the music of Beethoven.

Of the guild's production of *Once upon a Seaweed*, Vic Reid wrote:

> The strings, brass and wind instruments in the pit strike up a tap-teasing number; the lights fade out; the audience, filling nearly all the 900 seats in the Ward Theatre, settle back with the big question mark . . . What is this going to be like? – This musical something, that Choreographer Ivy Baxter and her dance troupe have strung together to celebrate their tenth year in amateur show biz? This offering with the out-of-this-world title "Once upon a Seaweed"?
>
> Three hours later the audience is on its feet applauding lustily . . . the curtain is going up and down, then up again to reveal the cast, 50 of them, all happy, excited and breathless as they take bows, bows and still more bows. *Seaweed* was worth the box office price.[8]

The book and lyrics were written by Alma Mock Yen, and the choreography was shared by Ivy Baxter and Rex Nettleford. Noel Vaz was the artistic director, and leading roles were played by Easton Lee, Clive Thompson and Marina Maxwell.

While Hazel Johnston made the ballet the focus of development in dance, and identified that something had to be done to create a sturdy Jamaican product, Ivy Baxter, one of her former students, came along and set out to creolize the ballet and

Bert Rose and Pauline Malek, of the Rowe School of Dancing. *Courtesy of NLJ.*

to initiate a modern creative dance that draws upon the traditional and the indigenous as well as upon the vast European, African and American heritage that was available. It was not until the 1950s after Ivy Baxter founded her group that Jamaicans began to practise modern creative dance as a serious art form.

The Ivy Baxter Creative Dance Group began in 1949, and shares with Hazel Johnston's school a reputation as one of the seminal forces in the development of dance as Jamaica approached independence. Miss Baxter was primarily concerned to find a strategy, a mode of expression that would be eloquent of Jamaica's needs and aspirations, and in doing so she became the mother of Jamaica's modern dance movement. Outside of classical ballet, most of the senior practitioners of dance in Jamaica

Dennis Scott and Pauline Malek, of the Rowe School of Dancing. *Courtesy of NLJ.*

received their initial or important early training at the hands, or rather at the feet, of Ivy Baxter – Rex Nettleford, Sheila Barnett, Joyce Campbell and Eddy Thomas, to name but a few. Some of her former students have also gone on to hold significant positions abroad. She not only trained members of her company to dance, she encouraged them to choreograph. Her great strength as a teacher lay in her generosity of spirit. Her mission was to produce an ever-increasing number of people who could take dance and what dance stands for, into every corner of the land.

Rat Passage, choreographed by Ivy Baxter for the Jamaica 300 Bandwagon, with Alma Mock Yen and Ronnie Nasralla. Set designed and painted by Albert Huie. *Courtesy of George Carter.*

11

Two Influences on Jamaican Modern Dance

Almost all students of modern dance in Jamaica have been greatly influenced by Revival, folk and other ethnic types of music. The latter of these incorporate survivals of African music and dance – which go hand in hand – and manifest themselves as recurrent themes in Jamaican culture. All of these forms have significantly influenced Jamaican dance, theatre, music and rhetoric (including speaking in unknown tongues), and Jamaican audiences respond to them spontaneously.

Although some study of Jamaican folk culture was done in the nineteenth century, the subject was only seriously researched in the twentieth, when the country, while not completely shedding its European antecedents, made a positive effort to affirm its African ancestral roots. Started by Ivy Baxter in the 1950s, Jamaican dance has, since the 1960s, increasingly drawn upon and adapted the rhythms and techniques, both African and European, practised today in rural Jamaica. Because the influence of Revival and ethnic music has been so great on the island, we present here an extract from Maria Smith's dissertation on Revival iconography,[1] as well as the text of an interview on the Laban dance method, as an introduction to the modern dance segment of this book.

Dr Smith follows the path that Hazel Johnston had identified and was about to explore when she was suddenly struck down in 1944 at the still-early age of thirty-six. Ivy Baxter took up the challenge somewhat later, after she had been able to undertake the necessary research and develop her own familiarity with Jamaica's rural lifestyles. Through dance Baxter inspired her students – Alma Hylton (Mock Yen), Rex Nettleford, Eddy Thomas and Clive Thompson among them – to bring their own fresh insights to the creation and use of modern dance forms. Her goal was to equip her students to understand better the influences of the panoply of Ghanaian art, culture and dress and the pervading pan-Africanism, not only in Jamaica but also throughout the Caribbean, as they sought to draw upon their folk heritage to enhance the expansion and development of the Jamaican theatre.

Laban and his pupils influenced posture and movement, especially of Jamaica's early teachers of modern dance, including Ivy Baxter (a student of Sigurd Leeder, who was influenced by Laban) and Sheila Barnett. The interview on the Laban influence which follows was with Barbara Requa, one of the practitioners of the method and (at the time of writing) principal of the Jamaica School of Dance, a component of the Edna Manley College.

The Laban Influence

Rudolph von Laban, born in Hungary in 1879, was a philosopher of music and dance who taught in Munich, Zurich and Hamburg before eventually becoming choreographer at the Berlin Opera. He emphasized expressive gestures of rhythm and movement because, to him, this was the means of conveying feeling, and therefore at the root of all dancing.[2] Today, modern Expressionist dancing is based on Laban's theories. During the Second World War, Laban fled to England. First he introduced a system of remedial exercises for factory workers. He also invented a system of dance notation known as *Cinematography*, which has been applied in the United States and Russia.

Two of all Laban's pupils who became important practitioners of his ideas were Mary Wigman, who developed a career parallel with, and in many respects as important as, Martha Graham's, and Kurt Jooss, who worked for three years as assistant and "premier danseur" under Laban. In 1924, Jooss was employed by the Municipal Theatre, Munster, and there he met three artists who shared his views, Aino Siimola, Sigurd Leeder and Fritz Cohen. With them he formed a dance group, *Neue Tanzbuhne*. In 1932, Jooss's group from the Essen Opera won first prize in a choreographic competition organized by the Archives de la Dance in Paris. The piece was *The Green Table*, set to music by Sir Frederick Cohen, a composer born in Jamaica in 1852. The ballet was a "send-up" of a group of bald-headed diplomats arguing and shouting at each other around a conference table and finally firing their revolvers. The National Dance Theatre Company's (NDTC's) send-up of Jamaica's parliament in *Rockstone Debate* (1981) immediately comes to mind.

Sheila Barnett, dancer, dance teacher, choreographer and producer

Of Jamaican dance teachers who have been exposed to the Laban method through their pupils, there have been Ivy Baxter, who studied at the Sigurd Leeder School; Sheila Barnett, who studied at Chelsea College of Physical Education; and Barbara Requa, at Dartford College of Physical Education. (As mentioned earlier, Leeder was a member of the group of enthusiasts with whom Laban had worked in Munster.) Much later, in the early 2000s, Marlon Simms from the NDTC was exposed to Laban's methods in his studies at Texas Southern University. Wycliffe Bennett spoke to Barbara Requa in 1982 about the Laban method as it was taught to her at Dartford, and as she practised and taught it in Jamaica:

Wycliffe Bennett: How would you describe the Laban technique?

Barbara Requa: Well, it's not so much a technique as a concept. You know, it's a concept that dance is a free movement to be participated in by everyone. It tends more to think in terms of the mass participation . . . rather than specific skills. They [practitioners of the Laban method] have, over the years, been changing the concept

The Revival Iconography

MARIA SMITH

My interest in Revivalism began when I was a little girl growing up in the parish of St Andrew, the home of two famous Revival sites: Hope River and August Town, the site of Alexander Bedward's church and the famous "healing stream".

During the 1950s and 1960s it was not unusual to be awakened on a Sunday morning about 5.00 [o'clock] by scores of people travelling on Hope Road to attend a baptism ceremony. Revivalists from all over the Corporate Area of Kingston and St Andrew would join the procession along Old Hope Road during the early hours of the morning. The procession would travel on Hope Road through Papine down through Kintyre to the point of the river called "Three Hole" . . . Here three big rocks meet around a large hole that looks like a pool. As the legend goes a "River Mumma" (mermaid) lives in this hole.

During the procession the people danced, sang and clapped their hands, sometimes to the beat of drums. Most of the people were dressed in full white with colourful head-dresses, cords and waist bands . . . The different "bands" were distinguished by their flags as well as the styles of their uniform. The flags and accessories added colour to the occasion. The drumming, hand clapping, feet stomping and singing were infectious. People lined the streets to watch, move to the rhythms and sing along with the bands. There were those who followed the bands joining in with the singing and movement.

In the 1960s I had the privilege of spending some time with my grandparents in a district called Walker's Wood, in the parish of St Ann. In this setting I was able to watch and listen to Revival Bands singing and dancing as they made their way through the hills coming from the adjoining parish of St Mary to hold a street meeting at the Walker's Wood crossroads. As they journeyed through the hills they carried a lamp called a "kitchen bitch" and candles to light the path. At this meeting they would be joined by Revivalists from the area and other sympathizers or onlookers. They would also solicit new converts for baptism. The meeting would have at the centre a table with a Bible and a vase with croton leaves. Near the table there were two drummers, an old man and a small boy. The bands would stretch from each side of the table in the horseshoe or U formation, leaving a clear opening at all times. I later learned that this opening . . . was not only to facilitate the people going to place their offering on the table but also to facilitate the entrance of the "unseen guest". This was a very colourful scene – the uniforms were combinations of red and white, [and] pink and white, as well as green and yellow.

After the meeting, the people in Walker's Wood provided accommodation for the visiting bands. The following day the bands continued on their journey to Ocho Rios, where the new converts would be baptized at the historical site at Roaring River. This baptism site has been in use since slavery and is said to be rich in healing properties. The site in August Town is also said to be rich with healing properties . . .

I was also privileged to be able to sit and listen to the most fascinating stories about [Jamaican Revivalist preacher Alexander] Bedward from a number of persons, one of whom was my grandfather, Earnest Gordon, a Baptist deacon, who travelled from St Ann to Kingston with scores of their people to be baptized by Bedward. Another person I learned from was Roland Boyd, a Bedwardite. He was one of the "saints" who lived in August Town at the Bedward community. It has always remained with me how deeply moved they were, each time they told their stories or recalled events like the healing ceremonies and the march to Half Way Tree Court House with the saints all dressed in white [and] singing the hymn "Onward Christian Soldiers, Marching as to War". I knew by the expression on their faces and the fervour with which they spoke, that these events meant much to them and that in retelling these stories they were affirming the things that meant most to them.

The Revival Iconography (*cont'd*)

My career path has always kept me in touch with Revivalism. As a teacher in West Kingston I became aware that many of the students and their parents were Revivalists. The only church inside the community, situated just a few blocks from the school, was a Revival one. Many of the school's ancillary staff who lived in the community worshipped at this church. It was not unusual for a child to "catch Myal" [that is, become possessed by a spirit] during devotion or to be absent from school because he or she was "under Myal". Most of the funerals in the community took place at the church. It was at one of these ceremonies that I first noticed the practice of the releasing of the deceased spirit before burial . . . The church also played a part in the healing and care of members of the community.

In the late 1970s my studies at the Jamaica School of Dance took me on field trips to two famous Revival centres – to Blakes Pen in Manchester, the healing centre, and to Watt Town in St Ann, the spiritual Mecca of Revivalism in Jamaica. My visit to Watt Town was the beginning of a long and interesting relationship with this site and the people who visited it. From my first visit to Watt Town in 1978, I was intrigued by the setting and the mystique that surrounded the ceremonies and the people. I never could have imagined a gathering of such magnitude, style, colour and sense of order in the hills of rural Jamaica. The welcome was different. They greeted us with a bunch of croton while singing "Come in, my little one, come in", as soon as we stepped on the pavement in front of the church. We were then taken through a welcoming ritual. Without any warning or verbal instructions we just "moved" as we were led anti-clockwise around the seal (the sacred space). This ritual was repeated with all who entered.

The day was packed with excitement and information gathered on tape recorders, in notebooks and on cameras by the different groups. When we were leaving, our group was invited to receive gifts. My gift was a bunch of mint (bush used to make tea). On leaving the site and entering the bus we tried to play the tapes that we made on the site. To our astonishment they were all blank. I was told that the reason for this was that we never got permission to record. This reminded me of a story Katherine Dunham told about her visit to Maroon Town. She made the point of the importance of getting permission from the ancestors before any information [was] shared.

My post as national dance coordinator at the Jamaica Cultural Development Commission has allowed me the privilege to observe Revivalism in different parts of the island. As I travelled to and from workshops and seminars held in the different parishes I noticed an abundance of small churches made very conspicuous by their names and, very often, groups of people colourfully dressed singing and dancing. The occasion could be a baptism, a funeral or just waiting to go on a "journey".

A most memorable learning experience for me was an assignment to assist with the coordination of the National Revival Ceremony held at Jamaica House during the 1980s. The then-prime minister and minister of culture, the Honourable Edward Seaga, who has done extensive study in Revivalism, presided over the occasion. This event, held over three days, brought together Revivalists from all across the island. Although the bands [of worshipers] had many variations in expression, colour and performance, they had enough in common to be grouped under the same name and to fit on the same continuum between the poles of Africa and Europe. There were more than two hundred bands from the fourteen parishes. The first night of the "table" was led by Kapo [pseudonym of Jamaican artist Mallica Reynolds] and all the other bands joined in. The second night saw the bands grouping according to the "orders". One large group remained with Kapo and the large table with candles, bread, drinks, flowers and other paraphernalia, while others went in small groups around ground tables. There was one band that worked around a maypole.

In 1986 I did the choreography for Louis Marriott's play *Bedward* and was forced to look in detail at the Revival dance vocabulary and to attempt to put this vocabulary in the context of the play. The play was remounted in 2003 and I was able to bring even more to the chorus work through the dance. In October 2003, I had the privilege of going to a conference at the University of Cape Coast in Ghana to present a paper. While there, I was able to visit a number of sites, including Kumasi, the Ashanti Palace, Elmina Castle,

The Revival Iconography (*cont'd*)

the Castle of Cape Coast and the Old Koromantse Castle. I also paid a visit to the Koromantse chief and his council. After the offering of libation they shared with me stories about their history and culture and we discussed possible Jamaican connections. I was also taken on a tour of the village – both the old section and the new. The slave market Assinmanso was another very important connection. This is the market from which many of our ancestors would have been shipped to the Caribbean. While at this site, I saw the graves with the remains of two slaves: Cristal from Jamaica and Samuel Carter from the United States. Their remains were shipped to Ghana in 1998 on the 160th anniversary commemoration of Jamaica's emancipation – the first celebration of its kind. On the same site was the Slave River, where the slaves were given their last bath before being shipped to the New World. After leaving Cape Coast I went to Nankopong, the village on which the Jamaican Accompong was patterned. It was there that I attended a funeral, [and] visited two spiritual churches and a settlement where the descendants of Jamaican ex-slaves who [had] returned to Ghana lived.

My study of Revivalism is undoubtedly influenced by my past experiences. I bring to the academy a body of knowledge gained from my years of working in the field with Revival people and insights of how this form has been sustained across the island. Over the past four years I have gone back to the field investigating this religious form of operation from a cultural studies perspective. I intend to use the ideas gained from the cultural studies programme to look at their ideological principles and practices. This will be done mainly through visual representations of symbols and icons, discussions of concepts of identity, cultural reversals, cultural resistance and wellness. Ancestorism and performance will also form part of the discussions.

The body is a site for recording social and religious practices; therefore all forms of structured movements both by the body and its extensions (for example, clothes and props) that form part of the movement concept will be treated as primary text.

because they feel that it is as important for a dancer to be a performer as it is to be a general participator in dance. Laban really concentrated on the art of movement and we studied that. His concept was that creativity was very important . . . that was a very strong part of his dance concept.

WB: It seems to me that a number of influences entered into the Jamaican dance movement . . . the Laban method or approach being one. Could you comment on that?

BR: Yes, I think that Ivy Baxter was exposed . . . well, I am not sure; she was exposed to the Jooss/Leeder dance method, which is in actual fact not the same as Laban, but pretty similar in this idea of free dance movement, not tied down to specific skills as the classical ballet was, and some of the modern dance techniques became. They had their own style. I think Laban was a little more free-form . . . because he definitely insisted on the creative aspect as being probably the more important . . . participation and pooling of ideas.

WB: When you say creative, what do you mean?

Barbara Requa, dancer, dance teacher, choreographer and producer

BR: Well, you know that you go into a technique class in a studio and the teacher gives you instructions . . . they teach you exercises, they teach you steps, they put the movements together . . . everything comes from the teacher . . . the students really give you little. Now this is what Laban was against, because he said that everybody is creative in their own right, and therefore everybody should be given the opportunity to create . . . in movement. So that the teacher, as well as doing [assigned] exercises [with students] . . . [teaches that] exercises can come out of creative activity, especially for small children. You don't want to throw skills at a small child . . . they first have to learn to use their bodies. So he built up sixteen movement themes which train the body, so that you became aware of the body in space and effort – qualities and stuff like that – and once you have attained this, you then can go on to learn specific skills. Also, you feed into this the creative ideas from the dancers. It's like role playing . . . you suggest something, they give you back something, you like what they give you along with your ideas, and you pool everything to create dance movement.

WB: That's how you work?

BR: That's how I try to work in the school and that's what I teach students in my dance education course, and it has helped. It's a challenge . . . it's much more difficult to work that way than go into a studio and teach exercises . . . you go into the studio with a preconceived idea . . . but you must remember that you are going in there as a trained person, dealing with students who are at different stages of coordination . . . there are the well coordinated, there are the not-so-well coordinated and the totally uncoordinated. You can't expect an uncoordinated person is going to get a movement that you as a trained teacher may find easy to do. But if you try to motivate them . . . letting them find the movement you suggest out of their own experience – it's really something they are capable of doing. The movement . . . it's not wrong . . . you as a teacher can't say . . . "This is wrong", because it's their movement, they found it, you understand. So that the frustration that some people get from trying to master a skill that they can't [master] and [that they] find very difficult . . . is not there, you know, and [until] they become more confident and they learn to relax (because a lot of uncoordinated people are un-relaxed) . . . they lack confidence. As they become more relaxed and more confident, they find it much easier to master the specific skill.

WB: Who else uses the Laban method around here?

BR: You mean in other studios? I don't know of anybody else who uses it.

WB: But you do it in the school?

BR: We do it in the school and . . . we hope the students who leave here . . . some of them will use it, some of them won't. I know some of them won't because, as I say, . . . it's not easy . . . it's not easy . . . because you have to do more work, you have to do more preparation. It's harder, harder work.

WB: When you come to a class and you give the children a basic idea and say, "Work on that", that's what you do? And then you have to use what they give you and build on that . . . so that the whole thing comes from them. Am I right?

BR: That's correct . . . and you use experiences, their own experiences to work with, environmental experiences to work with, because in learning, you know, in the learning processes, you have to start with the known and move on to the unknown. But you take a five-year-old and you try to teach her to do a *battement*, that's totally outside of her experience. But if you can break it down into something that the children understand, they are much more able to get the idea of what you want. So you use the environmental experiences and you build on that, to get the technique and to get the body awareness and the understanding; and you take it from there.

WB: To what extent do you apply this method, or are you allowed to . . . in developing your own roles in the dance?

BR: My roles as a performer? Well . . .

WB: That's difficult?

BR: No, I will tell you what. I have found that it has been very useful for releasing your . . . what is the word, now?

WB: Inhibitions?

BR: Right! Inhibitions . . . because when you have a class where people are exploring, improvising movement, you tend to forget yourself if you can leap and shout and roll . . . They use a similar kind of method in drama, because I have had to work with . . . and I have spoken with Dennis Scott . . . [S]creaming, rolling, doing these things that we know about, it helps to build a sort of dramatic experience, and I find it works a lot with small children . . . they don't have any inhibitions, so that's cool; they work very well with it. With teenagers also, it's very, very useful because they can release themselves in the idea that they are working on.

WB: To what extent are you able to use your own methodology in developing your own roles?

BR: Well, we are back to that again, aren't we? That's what I am saying. With my experience over the years working in this form I found that I could, first of all, through exploring and improvising movements, I could get a visual picture of my kind of character through movement and it becomes much clearer, both for choreography and for performing, you know, if you get the mental picture of what you are . . . in your head . . . the visual thing in your head of what it's about, it's much more easily portrayed.

WB: In terms of the movement?

BR: In terms of movement and character, you know, bringing out the character of whatever your role is.

WB: So when you are cast in a role as a dancer, any role, you do a certain amount of exploration of movement for yourself and dance in that role, not just what is given to you by the choreographer?

BR: Right! It's absolutely essential because, well, let's say, if you're doing something that's pure dance, not anything dramatic, all movement has its specific quality. I have learned to understand the quality of movement through my Laban training, and this way I have learned to express and conserve the energies used in dancing, right? You know that if you want a light movement you use less energy, if you want a strong movement, you increase the energy . . . part of the control which some people instinctively have and some people have to be taught, ok? Also again, if you are doing a dramatic role you have to sit down and think about it and work it out in your head, and decide what you would do in such a situation, you know, and really become part of the role.

But I have run ahead of the years, for although from time to time there were intimations of things to come, it was not until the 1950s when Ivy Baxter founded her group that Jamaicans began to practise modern dance as a serious art form.

Ancestral Echoes Bush Spirits of Jamaica and the Caribbean, NDTC. *Photo by Maria LaYacona.*

12

The Ivy Baxter Creative Dance Group

In the words of Rex Nettleford, "Ivy Baxter can be described as the mother of contemporary Jamaican dance theatre." She was born into a very scholarly Jamaican family on 3 March 1923. Around fourteen years of age she had to decide whether to choose music or dance. She chose dance but was too old to start ballet training. Nevertheless, she was accepted by Hazel Johnston, Jamaica's premiere ballet teacher of the day, and eventually took part in two of her shows. She danced with Hazel Johnston from 1941 to 1943, and later said that Miss Johnston "showed Jamaica what ballet was like, and she made us learn how to rehearse and get on stage and how to organize music as she did".[1] During the seven short years that Miss Johnston worked as a teacher of ballet and national dances, she had begun to make tentative enquiries into the possibilities of developing a uniquely Jamaican product, but did not live long enough to bring her ideas to fruition.

Ivy Baxter, mother of contemporary Jamaican dance theatre

In the 1940s Ivy Baxter came under the influence of Phyllis Stapells and Breta Powles, two Canadian teachers at Wolmer's Girls' School who also taught modern creative dance at the Young Women's Christian Association. (This period overlapped with Baxter's training with Hazel Johnston.) It was possibly through their influence that Baxter received a scholarship to the University of Toronto, from which she graduated in 1946 with a major in physical health education, having studied dance as part of that programme. She returned to Jamaica in 1946 and began organizing the first modern dance group (as distinct from "folk dance") in Jamaica. She recruited some members from among persons with whom she had worked earlier and some others who had attended the University College of the West Indies Extra-Mural Drama Summer School in 1949. Her original dance group included Hugh Morrison, Eddy Thomas, Garth Fagan, Sheila Barnett, Barbara Requa, Monica McGowan, Joyce Campbell, Alma Mock Yen, Ronan Critchlow and Neville Black. Others, like Rex Nettleford and Clive Thompson, joined later. All of these foundational members went on to make a significant contribution as dancers and choreographers, both locally and internationally.

Ivy Baxter, dancer, dance teacher, choreographer and producer. *Courtesy of NLJ.*

Ivy Baxter's *L'Rev Di La Petit Creole*, with Clive Thompson and Joyce Campbell, Jamaica. *Courtesy of Clive C. Thompson.*

After her return to Jamaica, Baxter was invited back to the University of Toronto to teach Caribbean dance for eighteen months, and, during her holidays there, she continued her studies at Columbia University and eventually received a master's degree in physical education. In her absence, Cynthia Wilmot, Herma Dias and others kept the Jamaican dance group going. She was next awarded a one-year British Council scholarship to Britain, where she attended the Sigurd Leeder School. Here she refined her ideas on free movement of the body to accommodate the meaning and interpretation of the dance, rather than the structured set movements around which the ballet was choreographed.

Prior to her departure for Britain, Baxter took part in pantomimes, first *Jack and the Beanstalk* and later *Busha Bluebeard*, for which she choreographed the "Dance of the Weird Creatures" (not to be confused with the "Garden of Weeds" by Madame Soohih for that same show). She returned to Jamaica in 1951 and continued her experiments in modern dance. Until that time very little attention had been paid to Jamaican dance forms. According to Baxter, "Nobody said there was anything other than a little quadrille or a little shey-shey; then little by little I began to understand that Jamaican folk dance existed."

Neville Black, choreographer and dancer, a member of Ivy Baxter's original dance group. *Courtesy of NLJ.*

In 1956 Baxter joined the staff of the Jamaica Social Welfare Commission, where she and Louise Bennett (Coverley) were employed as recreation officers. Baxter's position was as all-island dance and creative officer. This gave her the opportunity to get to know the rural folk culture. She recalls that at first she would choose a Jamaican theme and use Jamaican music, and little by little the actual folk dances began to emerge. In time, twelve authentic folk dances were identified. She recounts hearing kumina drums for the first time in St Thomas: "Then my real Jamaican eyes were opened." This exposure to the folk culture allowed her dance group, along with the children she trained, to participate in national and civic events, especially when the Ministry of Education requested shows by school children in honour of royalty and other dignitaries. In 1960, fourteen years afer she had graduated from Toronto, the university invited her back for an academic year and the following year offered her the post of head of the dance department, but she turned down the offer to return to Jamaica.

This exposure is reflected in the Ivy Baxter Creative Dance Group's specific objectives, which, in addition to widening the knowledge and experience of its members, was to develop a dance idiom suitable and adequate for artistic expression in keeping with life and culture in the Caribbean. Baxter also hoped to collaborate with other West Indian groups, and soon struck up a very productive relationship with Beryl McBurnie of Trinidad and Lavinia Williams, who, at the time, was researching Haitian dance forms.

Baxter's first dance recital, "Litany", was held in 1950 at Anderson House on Brentford Road in Kingston, which was at the time being used by the University College of the West Indies Extra-Mural Department for its classes in drama. The performance was based on a poem of the same name by George Campbell, and the poem itself was included in the programme to enable viewers to understand the interpretation of the dance better. Several years later, in 1954, the group's first major performance, *Creations in Dance*, played to full houses and enthusiastic audiences at the Ward Theatre. One work for which the group has received lasting acclaim is the Eddy Thomas and Alma Mock Yen musical *Once upon a Seaweed*, produced by Rex Nettleford and Noel Vaz at the Ward Theatre in 1960. Even the uncritical still remember the magic of the underwater scene with seaweeds and sea animals dancing behind a scrim. One of the most memorable dances was the "Dance of the Jewels" in the cave. Baxter recalls, "The people danced as if they were amethyst or topaz or diamonds . . . and then when the pantomime began to become Jamaican . . . when they had Anancy and this, Anancy and that and *Anancy and the Magic Mirror*, I created the 'Dance of the Cane Cutters', and that was a high point when the kids were in the cane . . . and you had the fellows dancing around them – Clive Thompson and all those people."

Baxter's most memorable performances were in the Coronation Tattoo, organized by the military in Jamaica; the mammoth pageant *Joy for Jamaica* (1953), organized and produced by the late Father Daniel Lord; and *Rat Passage*, based on a Jamaican theme on stowaways, with music by Eddy Thomas and with Ronan Critchlow as lead dancer. *Rat Passage* was a major contribution to the Jamaica 300 bandwagon, which swept across the island during 1955.

Young dancers with drive and enthusiasm used the opportunities created by Jamaica 300 – an island-wide celebration of three hundred years of Jamaica's history – and, after 1962, by the National Festival movement, to discover African-Jamaican traditional dance retentions such as kumina and etu, which they later brought to the national stage. According to one critic, "By utilizing folk themes and hammering this raw material into shape on the anvil of theatricalism, [Ivy Baxter] managed to create something new and vital in the theatrical world."[2]

Somewhere in the late 1940s and early 1950s, Baxter converted to Roman Catholicism, and for many years gave devoted service to the church, sitting on school boards and committees and encouraging the use of dance in the liturgy. She saw the arts as a positive force for good; hence her parallel commitment to formal education and community development. During the 1950s and 1960s, the country witnessed a remarkable upsurge of creative energy. As the group expanded, senior members, notably Enid Douglas and Cynthia Lee Gittens, helped with class teaching. The group worked in roadside concerts, in performances at teachers' colleges, and in Jamaica Social Welfare shows, and they also gave group demonstrations and judged seminars and competitions arranged by the Jamaica Festival Committee.

In 1952, while Jamaica and many of the other Caribbean islands were recovering from the major hurricane of the previous year, Ivy Baxter's group participated in the Festival of Dance and Folklore in San Juan, Puerto Rico. She described the experience as follows: "For Jamaicans mentally and physically isolated from the surrounding small countries, the Caribbean Folk Festival was an education." The group also performed at the West Indies Festival of Arts in Trinidad in 1958, and in Cuba in 1959.

Clive Thompson, an original member of the Ivy Baxter Dance Group, as lead dancer (with Judith Jamison) of the Alvin Ailey American Dance Theater, New York. *Courtesy of Clive Thompson.*

For twelve years, from 1950 to 1962, the Ivy Baxter Creative Dance Group was the flagship for the modern dance movement in Jamaica. Its achievements facilitated the formation of the National Dance Theatre Company (NDTC) in 1962. The founding members of this company came mainly from the Ivy Baxter group. To this day, after forty-seven years, the NDTC, which has achieved excellence and acquired international fame in its own right, still acknowledges the debt the company owes to Ivy Baxter. She was an indefatigable and energetic teacher and choreographer, and provided the opportunity for young Jamaicans to develop their talents as performers and as choreographers in their own right.[3]

In the early days, Baxter's style of dancing was not accepted by traditionalists with backgrounds in ballet because she had introduced what was then frowned upon as "barefoot dancing", at a time when dancers' wearing of ballet shoes was thought to give status and legitimacy to the art. Asked if there was anything in her career that she would have done differently, she replied:

> Yes . . . if I had the opportunity to keep my people with me or get new people or actually work with people who are presently learning dance right now, I'd do it. I think I would

Eddy Thomas, foundational member of the Ivy Baxter Dance Group, and Jeanette Nasralla in a 1958 photo. *Courtesy of the Gleaner Company.*

> like to teach choreography to people who could learn it. I think far more people who are in the educational field should learn how to create dance – school teachers, school children . . . [T]he School of Dance should be full every day and I think this is the only way you can do this and people can have little pantomimes all over Jamaica if necessary, or little shows.

For her pioneering work in modern dance, Ivy Baxter was awarded the Member of the British Empire (MBE), and made a Commander of the Order of Distinction (CD) by the Government of Jamaica. She was also awarded the Silver Musgrave Medal by the Institute of Jamaica. Her book *The Arts of an Island*[4] demonstrates the importance of dance in the study of Jamaica's social development. She died on 9 January 1993. In his tribute, Prime Minister P.J. Patterson concluded with these words: "She has bequeathed to us the appreciation of the dignity, the beauty and the authenticity of our Jamaican spirit and culture through the dance."

13

Modern Dance

The National Dance Theatre Company

The spirit and motto of the Jamaican people, "Out of many, one people", represented in dance form and depicting Jamaican life, formed part of the independence celebrations in 1962. The show, *Roots and Rhythms*, devised and directed by Eddy Thomas and Rex Nettleford, featured some of Jamaica's top dancers, choreographers and musicians, and opened at the Little Theatre on 1 August at 8:00 p.m. Special music was composed by Carlos Malcolm, Oswald Russell and Eddy Thomas. Thomas also designed the costumes and the sets. George Carter designed and executed the lighting, with special new effects from England. The full title of the show was *Roots and Rhythms for Independence 1962*.

Rex Nettleford, dancer, dance teacher, choreographer and producer. *Photo by Maria LaYacona.*

In addition to the works of Nettleford and Thomas, the following well-known choreographers and teachers contributed: Ivy Baxter, May Soohih, Betty and Punkie Rowe, Barbara Fonseca, Glen Gordon and Barbara Kerr. Guest artists included Lavinia Williams of Haiti, who came to Jamaica from British Guiana (Guyana), Neville Black, the Haitian drummer Tiroro, and the Canboulay Singers. Principal Jamaican dancers included Maureen and Bridget Casserly, Joyce and Shirley Campbell, Yvonne DaCosta, Barbara Grant (Requa), Monica McGowan, Pansy Silvera, Bert Rose, Dudley Bitter, Ken Mock Yen (now Monsignor Mock Yen), Micky Gallimore, Rosalie Marks and Gertrude Sherwood. It is important to name them here because they provided the pool of dancers who were to help man the National Dance Theatre Company (NDTC) when it started.

The dances featured a wide range of themes depicting different aspects of Jamaican life. For the occasion, the following ten items were presented:

- *A Time to Rejoice (Out of Many, One People)*, choreographed by Eddy Thomas and the Rowe Ballet Studio. Appropriately, this study was in the nature of a prologue, showing the different cultural influences in Jamaica.
- *Legend of Lovers' Leap*, by Eddy Thomas, a tale of two lovers in the parish of St Elizabeth, who jump to their deaths from a high cliff into the sea rather than face the wrath of their slave owners.

Madame May Soohih, dance teacher and choreographer, and students Monica McGowan and Melanie Robinson (Graham) to her right. McGowan was a foundational member of the NDTC, and Graham later joined the group. *Courtesy of NLJ.*

- *Jazz Sequence*, by Eddy Thomas, a study of the African-American jazz influence on dance and musical life in Jamaica.
- *Jamaicana*, by Ivy Baxter, a number of dances done to Jamaican folk tunes and in a style developed by Baxter, showing the free and lyrical movement patterns of people in the rural areas. In this number the Canboulay Singers contributed folk songs and street cries that enhanced the authenticity of the presentation.
- *African Scenario*, by Rex Nettleford, a sequence based on African movement patterns and showing basic elements in Jamaica's traditional rural culture. It echoes kumina, Jonkonnu and Maroon dancing.
- *Legend of Old Port Royal*, by May Soohih, a reminiscence of the glories of Jamaica's buccaneering past, with magical underwater scenes.
- *Ballet Suite, Tropical Delight*, by Betty and Punkie Rowe, Barbara Fonseca and Barbara Kerr, the classical idiom adapted to deal with common Jamaican themes.
- *Maypole Suite*, traditional European dance adapted by Glen Gordon.
- *New Web*, by Ivy Baxter, a new slant on an old theme: Br'er Anancy's encounter with Br'er Eagle and Br'er Bear.
- *Seven Ages of Man*, conceived of and choreographed by Ivy Baxter as a parallel to Jacques's "Seven Ages of Man" in his "All the world's a stage" speech, in Shakespeare's *As You Like It*.

Of the items listed, *African Scenario* and *Legend of Lovers' Leap* still remained in the company's active repertoire at the time of writing.

The 1982 Season

Every July to August since 1962, the NDTC of Jamaica has presented a season of dance at the Little Theatre, under the guidance of artistic director and co-founder Rex Nettleford. The 1982 season climaxed the celebrations that marked the company's twentieth anniversary, with a symposium dubbed "Celebration and Challenge". These festivities confirmed this writer's view that, in Jamaica, dance has become a valid expression of a specific country and time.

More than forty years after the first *Roots and Rhythms* performance, dance has become an established Jamaican art form, owing largely to the efforts of the NDTC. In order to understand fully the nature of these achievements, it is necessary to place the NDTC's work in proper perspective, to look at the company's sources of growth, to examine its strengths and weaknesses, and to note some of the challenges that lie ahead. Of special interest is a week-long symposium in May 1982, organized by the Jamaica School of Dance, to salute the collaboration between the NDTC and the school, which was itself founded by the company in 1970, with Sheila Barnett, Barbara Requa and Bert Rose as founding tutors. (The school has now been incorporated into the Edna Manley College, which serves the entire English-speaking Caribbean.) For those who attended, the 1982 symposium proved an enriching experience. It subjected the company's work to the most rigorous scrutiny, so that, by the time the season of dance opened that July, many questions had been answered and other issues identified for further examination.

Events leading up to the 1982 twentieth anniversary celebrations included, for example, a "meet the press" evening that February; the thanksgiving service in March at Scots Kirk, where, in 1968, the company had performed for the first time in a place of worship; and the second Easter Sunday *Morning of Music and Movement*, put on at the Little Theatre. The *Morning* brought the company's religious repertoire into focus and resulted in a tradition that has continued throughout the years. It included such seemingly ageless pieces as *Misa Criolla*, choreographed by Rex Nettleford (1967), and *The Rope and the Cross*, by Sheila Barnett (1974), as well as some later works by Nettleford – *Back to Bach, Viva Bach* (1979) and *Gospel According to . . .* (1980).

A proper study of the company must recognize also the contribution of the NDTC Singers, whose songs are certainly among the highlights of each season's programme. Under musical director Marjorie Whylie, who succeeded vocal soloist Joyce Lalor, they have played an indispensable role, augmenting the orchestration where necessary, as well as performing in their own right. The NDTC choir of about ten to twenty individuals has always been an integral part of its performances. Under the guidance of its musical director, the choir continues to unearth African survivals and links in the Jamaican society as well as in Spanish-speaking and francophone countries. They have faithfully transcribed and arranged old folk songs and rituals without losing the feel and quality of the music. They are also continually reworking and rearranging the ever-changing modern music forms of ska, reggae and dancehall. Marjorie Whylie claims that a great deal of research is being undertaken into religious songs – be they orthodox Christian, African-derived or Creole creations – which accompany and energize work, social activity and socio-religious observance. The musical perform-

Joyce Lalor, vocal soloist, NDTC Singers. *Courtesy of NLJ.*

Plantation Revelry, an early work of the NDTC, choreographed by Rex Nettleford. Painting by Susan Alexander (oil on canvas).

ances in between dance numbers complement the dances, melding the event into one very refreshing whole.

Since *Roots and Rhythms* in 1962, the NDTC's repertoire has grown to some two hundred forty-six works. Rex Nettleford remains the major choreographer, with more than seventy-five works. Others include Eddy Thomas, who created twelve works before he left the group in 1966; Neville Black, who had done eleven up to 1969; and Sheila Barnett and Bert Rose, with nineteen and thirteen, respectively. From time to time other members of the group will produce an isolated piece, or the company will have a guest choreographer for the season. The 1982 season added five new works: *Litany* and the allegorical tale *The Visitor*, both by Rex Nettleford; *Fantasy* (a young man's dream of the ideal woman), by Barbara Requa; *Just Time* (a solo dedicated to Barry Moncrieffe) and *Phases: Part A* (a dance in four movements dedicated to Sheila Barnett), both by Tony Wilson. Since then the company has endeavoured to perform more than one new major work each season. And in addition to their annual season and mini-season at home, the sixty-member troupe has also performed in many other parts of the world, including the United Kingdom, the United States, Canada, Australia, the former Soviet Union, Germany, Mexico and other Caribbean lands.

Barry Moncrieffe, dancer and choreographer

During the 1982 season, one of the nights was given the status of a gala affair and named "Founders' Night". By then, only five of the sixteen founding members were still dancing with the company: Rex Nettleford, Pansy Hassan, Joyce Campbell, Monica McGowan and Bridget Casserly. As the curtain came down at 11:00 p.m. that night on *Kumina*, Barbara Gloudon, the Little Theatre Movement's (LTM's) chairperson, came on stage and invited the overflow audience, despite the lateness of the hour, to remain behind so that due tribute could be paid to those whose unstinting efforts and dedication over the years had raised the NDTC to the level of a cherished national institution. The audience responded with resounding applause as founding members, some of them no longer performing, came forward to receive certificates and other tokens of esteem.

For the NDTC, 1982 was a great year. But things were not all that rosy twenty years earlier. The company had to overcome many obstacles, prejudices and downright hostility at home, and misunderstanding and, at times, arrogance abroad. Even as the country ushered in political independence in 1962, many Jamaicans who pretended to any kind of status disapproved of "barefoot dancing", and of the presentation of anything that savoured of Africa. Some upright men and women dismissed the company's production of *African Scenario* as "a piece of obscenity and a disgrace". And some members of the Jamaican middle-class audience were disturbed by the work and walked out of the theatre in protest when it premiered in *Roots and Rhythms*.[1]

Some early critics overseas had difficulty finding a ready-made category to which they could comfortably assign the company, and were tempted to dismiss the troupe as another of those artistic aberrations that wander into their domains from time to time. If, at this remove in time, some of the NDTC's earlier works can be classified as derivative, it should by now be recognized that, from the very outset, the foundations were being well and truly laid for what has become, stylistically, one of the most eclectic of major companies operating today.

Joyce Campbell, dancer and choreographer

The Influence of Ethnic, Folk and Ballet Forms

Several influences remain identifiable in the NDTC's repertoire: the ballet from Europe; ritual dance from Africa; jazz and modern creative dance from America; and traditional folk, national and contemporary dance from the three continents. Of course, all of these ingredients have become creolized, and the company is more rooted in the Jamaican and wider Caribbean experience than in anything else. Over the past four decades, the NDTC has become synonymous with talent, discipline and achievement in Jamaica, and has helped to bring praise and prestige to Jamaica abroad.

Prior to national independence in 1962, the African drum was never brought into prominence on the stage because it was linked to superstitions and African cult practices. It was the NDTC that broke this taboo. *African Scenario* was Nettleford's first major work for the NDTC and in it he set the tone of future productions, celebrating Jamaica's African past through the introduction of non-orthodox rites and rituals from survivals such as pocomania, kumina, myal and etu, in which song and dance are intricate elements of ceremony. Other pieces, like Sheila Barnett's *Mountain Women*, brought a sense of dignity to the Jamaican woman struggling up the hilly slopes with her load of ground provisions on her head, her back erect, with a sense of dignity even in her humble circumstance.

Either by design or circumstance, the company will in the future possibly absorb additional ethnic traits. Perhaps in a few years' time we shall note that the NDTC has also assimilated elements from Asian or Far Eastern cultures. This has been happening at the folk level in Jamaica, for example, in hosay, Jonkonnu and pocomania, in which Jamaicans of both African and East Indian ancestry participate. When Beryl McBurnie of Trinidad and her Little Carib Group came on a visit in 1955, they introduced Jamaica to what the exploitation of such additional multi-ethnic resources could mean. Over the past forty years the NDTC has gone on to forge a language, building a vocabulary and a syntax where need and opportunity allow, and has achieved a consistency in form, rhythm and dynamics, which is one of the touchstones of style.

Masterminded by Rex Nettleford, himself a dancer and choreographer, the NDTC's repertoire reveals a deep sense of history, a broad knowledge of ethnic forms and an understanding of theatre arts and literatures from other cultures. But the company's prime concern is with the human condition. This motif is often presented within a matrix of great themes – mythical, legendary or biblical – and ranges from subjects of epic dimensions to the immediate and commonplace.

During the celebrations of 1982, some twenty pieces were staged, including five new ones. Absent from the list were such pieces as Eddy Thomas's *And It Came to Pass* (1964); Sheila Barnett's *Mountain Women* (1972) and *I Not I* (1977), a picaresque piece on Pitchy-Patchy, a Jonkonnu character; Bert Rose's *Switch* (1977), based on the legend of the white witch of Rose Hall, and Rex Nettleford's *Myal* (1974) and *Court of Jah* (1975). These would have added perspective to the programme. There was, nevertheless, a rich feast, and the offering was wide in range, and provided some of the finest nights of theatre it has been the writer's privilege to attend, either at home or abroad.

Critics have to remind themselves that the company is continually refining and polishing its repertoire, and that even within a single season an old or new work will improve almost beyond recognition. This is especially so, it seems, where there are alternating casts which, in a competitive spirit of the best type, pace each other on the road to excellence. This happened to a marked degree in 1982, with the revival of Nettleford's *Dialogue for Three*, and one of his new works, *The Visitor*, as well as with Barbara Requa's maiden offering, *Fantasy*. The same cannot be said of Tony Wilson's solo piece, *Just Time*, in which the choice of inconsequential music led to inconsequential choreography.

But even *Dialogue for Three* would have been a stronger composition had the music been more in consonance with the twists and tensions of the eternal triangle. Joaquin Rodrigo's *Concierto de Aranjuez* did not always have the densities when the choreography needed it. Often there were exciting moments when music and dance were in conjunction; and we saw some inspired performances with Barry Moncrieffe as the Man, Judith Pennant or Jacquie Smith as the Wife, and Melanie Cooke-Graham or Sandra Minott as the Other Woman.

The writer did not see Jacquie Smith, but saw Judith Pennant, who brought a warmth and simplicity to the role of the Wife. Her cradling of the baby could have been just a bit more positive, within the rhythm set up by the music, as Sheila Barnett's was in the film of that performance years before. Sandra Minott demonstrated star quality as the Other Woman, fiery and sensuous; and when it was thought that Cooke-Graham was being rather too cold to be taken seriously as a contender for that role, she pulled out all the stops on the closing Sunday afternoon. When, during the *denouement*, Cooke-Graham in a dramatic reversal turned her back on the scene and brought down her hands in final rejection of the Man, she made a statement that will certainly remain one of the more memorable moments of that season.

Nettleford set his allegorical tale *The Visitor* in New Orleans. Susan Alexander's decor, with white wrought iron furniture and crimson tapestry, created the setting for this house of assignation, in which the madam and her two assistants have decked themselves out in garish finery for such guests as fortune might bring. Enter the Visitor, elegant, commanding, a fine catch for any of the three ladies of the night. He goes into the bedroom, and soon pieces of clothing are flung back into the salon. The Visitor returns to the stage, a cadaverous figure of a man.

A more macabre atmosphere would have been realized in the production, had the designer introduced a strong tinge of green into the lighting at this stage. Aaron Copland's *Danzon Cubano* provides scope for those voluptuous movements and gestures that characterise the denizens of such a milieu as the madam's house. More importantly, the music has a trajectory that parallels the development of the choreography, which would have been helped by a stronger suggestion of *rigor mortis* before the figure of Death, with great flourish, orchestrates that final note.

Duran Hylton and Tony Wilson alternately brought their special qualities to the title role, Duran Hylton essentially dramatic, Wilson the more lyrical. Hylton's elevation and simulation of height were amazing. Cooke-Graham as the Madame had the technical proficiency. If she could have given herself more to the inner demands of her role, she would have been an even greater asset to the performance.

Barbara Requa had of course choreographed for the juniors at the Jamaica School

Gerrehbenta, the Company.
Photo by Maria LaYacona.

of Dance, but *Fantasy* marked her debut as a choreographer for the company. It was indeed an impressive beginning, demonstrating a fluency of style, knowledge of characterization, and use of the stage that would prove to be great assets to her in the future. It was a source of delight to watch alternating teams perform this work, and how they apparently benefited from observing each other. She used Chick Corea's music well. In *Fantasy*, a young man dreams of his ideal woman. Three different types appear in his dream, each having some attractive features, but the more he probes what he sees, the more elusive becomes all that he most desires. The deft use of scarves by the women underscores the fragile nature of each encounter, and the choreographer leaves with us the gossamer texture of a dream.

The remaining two new works were Wilson's *Phases: Part A* and Nettleford's *Litany*, both of which employed the full or almost full corps of dancers. There can be no doubt that Wilson's dance, in four movements, pushes the NDTC beyond its ordinary range of sensibility, and brings fresh nuances and body accents to the company's experience of dance. A product of the NDTC himself, Wilson showed the benefit of his North American sojourn, his exposure to another milieu: the black and white jazz traditions, the concrete and steel of Chicago, the sharp movements of the windy city. He chose music from Leonard Bernstein, Duke Ellington and Herbie Hancock, all within the genre of his composition. The impact of the dance would have been considerably increased by cutting at least eight minutes off the twenty-three minutes' playing time. There were, however, more serious problems: the often too facile use of the melodic line or rhythm without a feeling for the corresponding texture of the music, and the failure to exploit his own rhythm without losing contact with the musical peaks and valleys.

Within the company itself there are superb models to follow. Note, for example, in *Misa Criolla*, how Nettleford's shimmering line expands the aesthetic range of Ariel Ramirez's music or the fabulous fusion of the two muses when he calls upon Quincy Jones's score for *The Crossing*. Nettleford has, over the years, continued to build his expressive vocabulary and syntax, exemplified in *Folk Forms* (1968), *Celebrations* (1972), *Homage* (1973), *Elements* (1978), *Drumscore* (1979) and in *Litany* (1982), which is intended to be a biographical piece on the company. The programme note reads: "From those who sow and will not nurture, Good Lord deliver us! (A dedication to those who sow as well as reap.)"

For any audience, the company's performances require one of three approaches: either that you come with the innocence of a child (and the group is highly successful when playing to children in different parts of the world), or that you come with an open mind (whether you are an occasional theatregoer or a devotee of dance) or with a global perspective (if you are a critic or have aspirations to be one). There should never, of course, be a complete disengagement of the critical faculty. Indeed, the more one can apply the brain to what the heart feels, the more textured the experience becomes. The viewer should be a participant in the best tradition of theatre-going, and should give each performance a chance to demonstrate that, whatever the origins of what is presented, essentially, one is in the presence of a sturdy native growth that will not be dealt with except on its own terms.

As a celebration of growth, *Litany* had the potential to become a great work. At its initial mounting, some of the metaphors were not clear and at times, surprisingly, we got what seemed an unintentionally messy floor pattern. It was not clear whether the four dancers who formed a circle at the beginning were nuns or mother figures; and except in the ring game section, which was joyously portrayed, the directorial image which would have been necessary to indicate each phase of growth did not have the customary Nettlefordian authority. The music seemed somewhat hollow. This is not intended as a stricture on the musical director, who is expected to, and often does, perform musical miracles with limited resources each night. But if good old-fashioned hymn-singing was required, this too should have been theatricalized into something transcendental, and imbued with modern resonances. Above all, the final epiphany should have enthralled, as *Kumina* did, when it first went into orbit in 1971. And here lighting and decor would have helped, say, had the cyclorama been radiant with heavenly hosts, joining with the celebrants on stage in jubilant thanksgiving.

But the company's considerable reputation does not rest upon five or more new pieces per season. Even before the 1982 celebration there were over a hundred works in its repertoire; and often the range of programming is so wide that one gets the feeling the group can and will do almost anything. What one might still ask is: What is so special about the NDTC? What are the ingredients of its style? What was remarkable about the twentieth anniversary season? What were the highlights and in what respects, if any, did the company not meet its own high standards?

The company has drawn primarily upon Jamaican traditional forms, African-American forms, European classical ballet and American modern dance, but it was in the European folk and classical ballet traditions that the first formal training in dance was conducted in Jamaica. Indeed, Europe has contributed much via the ballet, in terms of aesthetics and a base of technical support, to what is an essentially composite structure for Jamaica.

To begin with, you will find in the company – the *école*, that is to say – the kind of physical stance, arrangement of limbs, and easy and unforced grace of manner that are regarded as endowing dancers with authority. You will find also several ballet or ballet-derived steps and features: attitude (position of the body indicating a particular mental state), arabesque (posture in which the body is bent forwards and supported on one leg, with the other leg extended horizontally backwards, and arms extended, one forwards and one backwards), *ballon* (the ability to appear effortlessly suspended while performing movements during a jump), *entrechat* (a vertical jump during which the dancer repeatedly crosses the feet and beats them together), *fouette* (a pirouette performed with a circular whipping movement of the raised leg to the side – a quick shift of direction of the upper body, performed with one leg extended), and *plié* (a movement in which a dancer bends the knees and straightens them again, usually with the feet turned out and heels firmly on the ground). These turns, lifts and elevations, and the sense of line, timing, pace and weight, as well as the split-hair precision in ensemble-playing, show the company at its best. Such a base of support was comparatively easy to assimilate from the very beginning. Many of the founding dancers had previously had years of ballet training, among them Yvonne DaCosta, Mavis Lai, Monica McGowan, Pansy Hassan and Bridget Casserly.

The company has made conspicuous use of this background in such pieces as Eddy Thomas's *Concert Suite* (1964), Neville Black's *Waltz Suite* (1965) and Rex Nettleford's *Dance Andante* (1965), which all contained strong ballet forms. Even in the earlier work *Footnotes in Jazz* (Thomas, 1962), where the music is chosen from Leonard Bernstein and Dave Brubeck, and the movements are syncopated in parallel with the music, the dance structures and the sense of line rely upon an earlier ballet idiom. There are echoes of ballet in Sheila Barnett's *Ring Hunt* (1968), set to the jazz score *Black Saint and Sinner Lady*, by Charlie Mingus; and the company's indebtedness to its own ballet background helps to inform its approach in such semi-classical pieces as *Murals* (1971) and *A Question of Balance* (1972), both by Barnett, John Jones's *Resurrection* (1972) and Nettleford's *Homage* (1973).

Both Nettleford and Barnett will insist that they have had no formal training in ballet; nonetheless, Barnett moves on stage with all the authority and grace of the well-honed ballerina. Note, for example, her roles in Nettleford's *Dialogue for Three* and in her own *The Rope and the Cross* (1974), the latter role being danced in succeeding years by Patsy Ricketts, Sheila Graham, Judith Pennant, and by Monica McGowan (1994 and after), who was trained in ballet. And in whatever mode Nettleford chooses to work, whether he is creating *African Scenario*, *Misa Criolla*, or *The Crossing*, one of his great assets as a choreographer is his lineal power.

Choreographer and dancer Rex Nettleford as the Healer in *Myal*. *Photo by Maria LaYacona.*

In addition to using ballet forms, the company has culled steps from regional and traditional European dances, among them the maypole, the quadrille, the polka, the jig, the schottische and ring games. Often these dances have been creolized; that is, they appear today in African-Jamaican forms with the same step patterns, but with modified use being made of the body, the knees and the feet. Nettleford and Barnett have picked these forms apart, set up fresh kinetic linkages, and have given them a stylization while retaining the essence. Eventually, whatever the NDTC uses, it makes inevitably its own. But however violently the company may depart from classical European precepts, it will nevertheless insist upon a good *port de bras*.

It would not necessarily be a profitable exercise to attempt to establish with any great accuracy the extent to which the several influences have enlarged the resources of the NDTC. The precise mix at any given time will be determined by the product intended. But the NDTC is, above everything else, a modern dance theatre company and, *ipso facto*, the modern dance input is considerable enough to "ratif[y] the branding of the talented Jamaican ensemble as a Caribbean company with a modern dance impulse".[2]

American Influence

Ivy Baxter founded the first modern dance group in Jamaica in 1949, over half a century after the movement had begun in America. Her work was of seminal importance, and it was from her group that Rex Nettleford, Eddy Thomas and several other founding members of the NDTC emerged. Baxter herself had been trained under the Sigurd Leeder method in England; later, two other members of Baxter's group, Sheila Barnett and Barbara Requa, who trained under the Laban method, also helped to found the NDTC. But the major modern dance component of the NDTC came not from England but from North America.

Even before the NDTC was formed, modern dance had moved away from the codified and stylized ballet technique, and sought to rediscover natural movement in the use of the body in its rhythmic, dynamic and linear functions with an enormous amount of gesture.[3] To date, a number of NDTC members have trained under some of the most famous exponents of the modern school in America. To Martha Graham's School, for example, have gone Eddy Thomas, Bert Rose and NDTC associate director Barry Moncrieffe, among others.

Much of what we take for granted today came into Western dance via, or directly from, Martha Graham: the earth-awareness; the use of the ground; the kneeling, squatting, rising and sinking which she derived from Oriental dancing; the balancing on bent knees, with the thighs as hinge and the spine cantilevered and suspended backwards in counterbalance; the spirals or turns with the changing and swinging body axis; the continuous unfolding movement from a central core; the contraction and release of the spine; the breath quality and the flow of movement to a climax, and its ebbing away in relaxation.

A few of the NDTC's earlier works were Grahamesque in exposition. Eddy Thomas, who was the first member of the NDTC to go to the Martha Graham School, used the method in his *Legend of Lover's Leap* in the *Roots and Rhythms* show of 1962. Graham's teaching was evident in the contraction of the pelvis, the spiral of the torso or back, and in the breath quality. But Thomas was not only dancer and choreographer. One of the more gifted of practitioners ever to have worked in the Jamaican theatre, he was also a musician and a designer of sets and costumes, and he brought the Graham approach to his Jamaican work in all departments, perhaps sometimes a bit too literally. This input remained among the more obvious features of the NDTC's repertoire right up to *Omegan Procession*, which Thomas created in 1966 just before he left the company.

But it would be unfair to leave Thomas's contribution without noting that he often used Caribbean folk idioms without even the briefest discussion, as in *And It Came to Pass* (1964). This dance featured Sheila Barnett as Mary, Dennis Scott as Joseph, and Bert Rose as the Archangel. The music, by Darius Milhaud, was well chosen, though in those days the company had neither the numerical nor financial resources necessary to match the majesty of certain of the composer's passages. But Joseph's frequent use of a walking , the journey on camel back across rough terrain, the adoration and the birth of the holy child – all conveyed by symbolic movement and gesture – linger in the mind as one of the fine achievements of Jamaican dance theatre.

Bert Rose, who returned to the company in 1970 after a five-year stint at the Graham School, acknowledges the use of the Graham method in his productions of *Thursday's Child* (1973) and *Switch* (1977). But, by this time, whatever had been taken from Graham had been Jamaicanized. Rose used the same ingredients that Thomas had imported, but he extended them, for example, by adding the ripple of the back to the spiral, and the bounce in the rhythm of the Jamaican walk, to move-

NDTC dancers, early years. *Courtesy of Jamaica Tourist Board*

ment across the stage. Based on the story of the white witch of Rose Hall, *Switch* remains one of the most exciting of the shorter works produced by the company to date, and it received a standing ovation at its premiere in 1972. In the lead roles for *Thursday's Child* and *Switch*, Rose was well served by Barry Moncrieffe, who was his contemporary at Graham.

Both the international ballet and modern dance have had considerable impact on the NDTC's stylistic repertoire. Exposure to these dance forms have enhanced the company's vocabulary, increased its artistic options and strengthened its convictions in the correctness of its own path. The company is now unassailably Jamaican. As Sheila Barnett, who was at the time director of the Jamaica School of Dance, says, "We are ourselves, in the way in which we move and release energy, neither too controlled nor too relaxed."[4] And Bert Rose, who also taught at the school, asserts: "You can identify a Jamaican girl in the crowd on Fifth Avenue on Christmas Eve night by her rhythm – from the way in which she walks and moves."[5]

Caribbean and African Influence

Drumscore was performed during the 1982 anniversary celebrations. The drums are the protagonists in the work, and each night two youthful drummers control the proceedings from centre stage. This is the opening number on the programme whenever it is performed. *Drumscore* not only emphasizes the centrality of the drum in the company's work; the number seems to have become the NDTC's signature. But there are other reasons why this could well be so. Rooted in Caribbean folk, *Drumscore* is an authoritative piece with a broad panoramic sweep. Multiple entries and rapidly

Afro-West Indian Suite. Photo by Maria LaYacona.

succeeding diagonals mass, dissolve and reappear. The piece creates a joyous coming together of different peoples. The male and female leads – Adrian Fletcher and the two alternating women, Cheryl Ryman and Pansy Hassan – perform with infectious fun.

In *Drumscore*, music and movement support what approaches total theatre, with the dancers at times contributing to the sound. The number opens with the *Yen Valou* of Haiti, a dance of Dambala. Then there are two Jamaican rhythm games, with interplay between the voices and the drums when the girls come in. Next there are two *tambu* rhythms from Trelawny in Jamaica, the *saliung* and the *mabumba*. This is followed by a Cuban-derived piece in which gyrating hips speak to that familiar style. Next there is a drum pattern put together by Marjorie Whylie based on steps devised by Rex Nettleford. This leads into a carnival-type finale, loosely based on the Cuban *conga* from the Oriente province of that country. The trumpet signals the climax. The boys and girls again make their timely vocal intervention in what is a joyous commingling of peoples.

The triumphant return of *African Scenario* (1962) vindicates the artistic integrity with which the company started out twenty years before. Many who left the theatre in disgust then have now returned to praise it. The choreographer, Rex Nettleford, had seen aspects of the dance among the folk in rural Trelawny, where he was born and spent his boyhood years. A visit to Ghana in 1961 confirmed both his youthful recollections and what he had been able to intuit. He brought back on tape from Ghana five songs: *Momi Opete*, *Oola Kala Kame*, *Aiwayeye*, *Wofa* and *Ayaye*. Marjorie Whylie arranged them appositely for the NDTC Singers, adding the drums, but the tempo and effort quality necessary were indicated by the cowbell, played by Nettleford.

According to the programme note, "A young girl enters maturity and is betrothed, then loses her Loved One to war. She invokes the gods for his safe return. He returns in safety and rejoicing. The action takes place against traditional African scenes of puberty, fertility, war, fetish and masquerade."[6] The part of Initiate was performed by Arlene Richards, the Warrior by Barry Moncrieffe, and the Witch Doctor by Adrian Fletcher. Discrete parts with matching music make up a delicately balanced structure; the well-judged variety of pace introduced, in turn, Prelude, Preparation and Induction, War Preparation and Invocation, Fetish Dance, and Triumphant Finale.

The decor and setting as designed originally by Eddy Thomas are West African, but not exclusively Ghanaian. They admit us unmistakably into an African village, and remind us of one of the many ways in which Thomas had proven himself an asset before he left the company. The costumes in particular enhance the quality of movement and emphasize the use of different parts of the body. This production is the seminal piece in the African orientation of the company: the hip-saw movement of the pelvis, the bent knee; the long-release back, the rippling spine, the vibrating shoulders, the arms that pull down and define space between the body and the extensions; the multiple rhythms; the leaps that hover in the air.

The dance uses all these resources in expressive floor patterns, and fuses them with a lineal quality that is both African and European. All the segments are exciting in their own way, but to this writer the prelude provides a special joy: there is a dignity and subtlety in the movement, nothing ponderous, not just bump-and-grind, but a disarming innocence and a sensuous grace that gives the presentation its timeless quality. The work achieves throughout a sense of celebration. Observing the performance, one might feel like a participant in as well as a spectator of a ritual whose antecedents go back to a dateless antiquity. By virtue of its position in the company over the first twenty years, its triumphant return and the fact that no other piece choreographed before 1982 has survived – except for the performance of *Legend of Lover's Leap* at Stratford, England, in 1963 – *African Scenario* has become, in our time, the first classic of Jamaican dance.

At the centre of the NDTC's being is the approach to dance as an act of celebration – a celebration of life. This spirit suffuses everything the company does, and it comes across as the NDTC's full enjoyment of its own work, an infectious enjoyment, in fact, which seduces the spectator, willingly or unwillingly, once he begins to suspend his disbelief. We may trace this approach back to the African survivals and the Caribbean commonalities which are the company's deepest roots: hence the primacy of the drum, supported by other instruments, and the orchestral use of the voice. The multiple rhythms of the drums set up correspondences of multiple rhythms in the human bodies, as in *African Scenario*, and there is sometimes a feature which masses bodies, not as individualized characters in a tableau, which of course is sometimes done, but as moving blocks of people, at once formidable and compelling, as, for example in *The Crossing*. There is a whole range of African-derived and other Caribbean steps which constitute a large part of the company's enormous stylistic vocabulary.

Elements (1978) appears to have been the company's most taxing work. Somewhat of a laboratory, it brought together the idioms in which the company works, and has provided the widest single review to date of the company's development in the art of dance. Although it was listed for performance at the twentieth anniversary celebrations in 1982, *Elements* had to make room for *Litany*, which draws upon much the same material but links the kinetic units in a different way. The decision to drop *Elements* from the season was probably based on the fact that the public expects to see new major works each season, in addition to renewing their acquaintance with old favourites.

Perhaps the only other explicitly African piece is *Sulkari*, mounted for the NDTC by Eduardo Rivero, by arrangement with Danza Nacional de Cuba. The composition was first performed in Jamaica in 1976 when the Cuban company participated in Carifesta '76, the second Caribbean Festival of the Arts. The Jamaican version made its debut in 1980. We are told in the programme that "the forms of the dance were inspired by, and originate from the sculpture, carvings, headdresses, masks, stools and other elements and details of African sculpture, as well as the movement of the Yoruba peoples of Arara". The choreographer, however, must have studied and absorbed far more than the programme states in order to have been able to produce such a philosophically consistent and artistically satisfying work. First, he and his collaborators, dancers and musicians had to get both the spirit of the work and the enormous tradition behind it right.

The music is pre-literate African-Cuban (Yoruba), collected and arranged by Rivero himself, and transcribed phonetically as well as scored and adapted by Marjorie Whylie for the NDTC Singers. The *oriki* (or praise-chants) hark back to Yoruba creation myths, and celebrate Orisa-nla and Oluwa. Orisa-nla is the god of soul purity. It is he who moulds human beings, into whose forms the supreme deity, Olodumare, breathes life.

The harmonic structure of the music seems strange to Jamaican ears. The sopranos carry a descant, and the melodic line is sung by the contraltos and doubled by all the males. It must have been quite a task to get today's Jamaicans to reproduce with such seeming authenticity the open-throated vowels of the African-Cuban Yoruba dialect. The rhythms had to be transposed from the double-headed *bata* drums to single-headed instruments. Some of the players had to be redeployed on cow bells, sleigh bells and specially constructed bamboo instruments, in order to approximate the percussion of the original. There are three movements, the first in 4/4 time, the second in compound duple, with a switch back to common time in the third, in which some of the musical ideas are reprised.

Rivero also designed the lighting and the costumes, which remain as close to nature as possible – flesh-coloured, with the three men in the briefest of briefs, and the women with their hair high off their heads, copper-banded and puffed. The women adorn their necklines with several strands of pearls. Each uses a five-foot rod as prop, weapon and staff of office, but primarily as phallic symbol. No adult is expected to miss the intended eroticism, but the use of the rod could possibly also have specific African reference: among the Akamba, for example, on the third day of the second initiation rites, during which initiates rehearse adult life, the boys are each given a special stick with which they perform symbolic sexual acts upon the girls.

As J.S. Mbiti's study of African religion points out, "in African societies sex is not used for biological purposes alone, but . . . it also has religious and social uses", and "there are African people among whom rituals are solemnly opened and concluded with actual or symbolic sexual intercourse between husband and wife or other officiating persons".[7] They reaffirm the regenerative principle in the natural ordering of society, and venerate the genitals as the gates of life.

Sulkari speaks powerfully to this tradition. Artistically, it is a symbolic treatment of a man and woman making love. First the women enter. Their expressions are mask-like, cool. In a series of symbolic gestures and movements, they glorify the body of woman and her sexual possibilities, which they place at the service of the gods. Two notable examples will suffice.

In one flowing movement, the hands start just above the waist and follow the line of the body upward. As they pass the breasts, the palms turn up, as if they are now supporting the breasts. The elbows move out bringing the up-turned palms on a level with, but slightly forward of the head. The imagination completes the picture. Held up in offering for all the world to see are the breasts, which in the fullness of time will proclaim the state of motherhood. In another sequence, the women go down in full *plié* on their toes, with heels and metatarsal areas of the soles together, and, when still in this position, as they turn slightly away as if to protect "the gates of life", they reveal yet another aspect of their sexuality. Indeed, there is a suggestion of coyness, but this too must be seen as a symbolic offering to the deities. From time to time, the heads pivot sharply on the necks, now this way, now the other, without disturbing the verticality of the torso. On other occasions, the women produce an undulating, snake-like movement. This usually begins in the solar plexus, and by alternating contraction and release, moves up through the torso, through the shoulders and then through the arms, finally ebbing away through the fingers. Each of the three women performs a solo portraying a different style of sexuality: toughness, gentleness and in-between. Thus, they indicate a state of knowledge and their preparation for motherhood.

A rhythmic thudding approaches. The men enter, each with his five-foot rod adorned with ribbons. They present these phallic symbols to the women, who raise their arms in acknowledgement. They then perform a corresponding sequence. The last soloist puffs and blows, nostrils distended, seemingly overwrought.

Early in the final segment, the men and women pair themselves off into couples, with the men standing in front of the women, who stoop with legs apart. The men bring down their rods in a thud between the legs of the women, who respond with a resounding closure of their legs. The women caress the rods and slide up and down them, and they mimic different sexual positions with the men. Afterwards, there are several other bits of love play. Towards the symbolic climax of the performance, the men are puffing and blowing violently, eyes protruding, nostrils distended. The women, their responses somewhat delayed, soon display a similar ecstatic possession. The men hoist the women in a sitting position onto one shoulder and, astride their rods, they and their partners make their erotic departure from the stage.

Sulkari is a successful exercise in organization, structure and form. The power of the work lies as much in the integrated use of myth and imagery as in the relentless build-up of the erotic experience. The production makes no concession to European notions of line or weight. There are, for example, a great many lifts, and a stress upon the arms and thighs is always evident. Effort revealed seems more of a plus than a minus. The production proclaims an essential Africanity that expects to be judged on the basis of its own aesthetics, and the results are achieved with economy and impeccable taste.

The only pieces from Sheila Barnett offered during the anniversary were *The Rope and the Cross*, based on a play by Easton Lee, which formed part of the "Morning of Movement and Music at Easter", and *Ni: Woman of Destiny*, which was one of the highlights of the season. Deeply schooled in the theories and practices of dance, Barnett uses her position as principal of the Jamaica School of Dance to help young dancers, choreographers and teachers to find their own ways in this demanding discipline. Her artistic work is informed by a lively intelligence and careful research, which she often transmutes into magic. Already in the company's development, some of her compositions are regarded as watershed pieces: *Mountain Women* (1972), *Ni: Woman of Destiny* (1976) and *I Not I* (1977). In these works she draws upon folk, myth and legend for content, rhythm and form. There is a clear trajectory over the four-year span between *Mountain Women* and *Ni*. In *I Not I* the protagonist is Pitchy-Patchy, the character out of Jonkonnu or masquerade. *I Not I* traces the odyssey of this bush figure out of Africa, through time and space across the middle passage to Jamaica, and his survival through changing times and customs. The treatment is picaresque, and takes on the mode of each milieu in which Pitchy-Patchy finds himself.

Mountain Women derives its name from and is in part inspired by Edna Manley's sculptural masterpiece of the same name, which was carved the year before the production. In Barnett's office there is a picture of the carving, which shows, in Barnett's words, the mountains "anthropomorphized into three female heads, building up from, at the base, a young girl's head, then a mature woman's and finally at the summit, the large, dominant head of an old woman".[8] The suggestion of female power present in Manley's sculpture and Barnett's dance piece reflects the fact that, among the Jamaican folk it is usually the mother who fathers the family. Strong and tender, she has to be breadwinner, disciplinarian and comforter. Her multifaceted role often causes her children to develop a love/hate relationship with her. This woman icon is further reinforced in the society as a whole by more universal associations of motherhood, and from colonial history by the position Queen Victoria held for over sixty years as "Missis Queen" of Jamaica. Thus, the woman icon has become a powerful tool in Jamaican artistic production – in literature, theatre and the plastic arts – and Barnett has shrewdly observed that "the gestures, stance and movement of these archetypes have become a recognizable, readily understood kinetic unit". Within this overriding directorial framework, there is a wide range of roles and possibilities, but it is the hardworking, enduring hill woman who dominates *Mountain Women*.

Parallel with the carving, the dance produces three stages in the life of one woman. When the curtain opens we see her coming in, tired and weary, in a pool of light. She passes a huge, mountainous formation in silhouette against the cyclorama. When the lights come up, we discover that the huge mountain that we thought we saw was something else: her extended family huddled together, awaiting her homecoming. In dress, they create a composite of the Jamaican landscape: the slate colours of Brown's Town, the bluish greens of Portland, the honeys and nut browns of St Ann, the bauxite red of St Elizabeth, the mossy patina of Bog Walk Gorge are petrified and time-weathered now. The costumes are not shapeless but blousy, able to respond to the movements and contours of the body, with the skirts slit at the sides to facilitate movement.

Barnett fills the landscape with activities and concerns from the life-cycle of these women – pounding the mortar, washing and other forms of toil, going to market, the nine nights, the ring games – all of which throw up characteristic gestures and stances: the back and head kept upright for load-bearing, the bent knee and strong thigh to support the forward or backward tilt of the trunk, the eloquent use of the hands. These actions, however, are not reproduced exactly as in life. The essence is preserved, but the movements and gestures are stylized, and, as is appropriate, they are sometimes bigger than life and sometimes there is just a nuance or an even more subliminal use. These resources are pulled together effectively in the conversation piece with the three women, in which body accents, nuances, gestures and stance are present, but resonate with modern overtones.

Barnett has been well served by Marjorie Whylie with the music for this piece. They first worked together on *Shadows* (1970), but it was with *Mountain Women* that they firmed up a collaboration that was to come to flower with *Ni* four years later. Jamaica's heroes are strong and resilient mountain people, and this is typified by the Maroon woman Nanny, who defied the redcoats from her mountain village and who, according to legend, was able to absorb in her capacious backside the musket shots fired against her people, and so protected them from harm. She was an Ashanti warrior, and because of her courage and her successful strategy in the First Maroon War (1720–1739), she became a symbol of unity and strength. Besides her prowess in jungle warfare, Nanny passed down legends and encouraged the keeping up of customs, which had come with her people from Africa, so that they would remain confident and proud. She was declared a national heroine of Jamaica in 1975.

Imaginatively, this is a subject with epic possibilities, and in her work *Ni: Woman of Destiny*, Sheila Barnett presents Nanny as priestess, warrior leader, woman and heroine. Three different dancers have appeared in the role of Ni: Patsy Ricketts, Cheryl Ryman and Monica McGowan, all good in their respective ways. Patsy Ricketts's body was the clay upon which the choreographer modelled the role, and Miss Ricketts is a dancer of exceptional talent, but the definitive performance, in this writer's view, was given by Monica McGowan, one of the founding members of the NDTC.

Barnett draws upon African-derived and Creole traditions in creating the styles to articulate her unique world of the heroine. She makes prime use of "bruckins", a

Patsy Ricketts performing *Court of Jah*. *Photo by Martin Mordecai.*

form evolved around Emancipation time in Manchioneal out of the older Jonkonnu. Bruckins is in fact a highly stylized and formal dance. The movements are characterized by long dipping and gliding steps with the body bent alternately backwards and forwards. Barnett contracts the glide but not completely, and keeps the body's axis constant, with minimal backward incline. The stress remains in the thighs, and the result is a gliding, bobbing movement that seems, if not to defy, at least to ignore the forces of gravity. When McGowan uses the step in her solo pieces, the effect is hypnotic and magical to a degree that suggests that forces other than natural have taken over.

The NDTC Singers serve an ancient theatrical function. As chorus, they link the action with the natural ordering of the society, and help to give the production its world view. They also expand the range of the orchestra. Significantly, also, we hear them as ancestral voices, and they come on stage to act out the roles of village elders expressing communal grief. The abeng (a horn) opens a brief commemorative prologue in which Maroons pay tribute to Ni, who is now numbered among the ancestors. Three huge shields or masks are mounted on the ground at stage right, and on the backdrop there is the outline of a mountain with a rugged escarpment. The stage itself represents a clearing in the forest upon which footpaths and less obvious entrances open onto a wide area. The prologue strikes a formal note and sets up expectations for a production that is stylistically emblematic, ritualistic and presentational. Romantic scenes provide naturalistic interludes, and as the villagers disperse the enactment of the story of Ni begins.

We meet Ni as a young woman happy in the company of Johnny, her lover. A thumb piano and other sounds delicately echo the harmony of their souls. The pace of the duet suggests that they have all the time in the world together. There is a moment at the end – held just long enough for us to feel the tenderness of their love for each other – when Johnny takes leave to go about his chores. Left alone, Ni dances herself into a daydream. The flute and martial drums help to conjure up a spell. History passes by and we see the chapters unfolding in her mind: in pantomime upstage, trek upon trek of chiefs and tribesmen in defile, high-stepping, bearing trophies, purposeful and proud; lower down, slaves with long rhythmic steps pulling back upon a rope, their rib cages disengaged, rotating unevenly, grappling with burden . . . A chorus of ancestral voices interrupts her reverie. Herbs fall upon the ground around her from nowhere. She receives the call of destiny. To the throbbing of drums, male and female voices chant, "Kaya Katumbe", and counsel in call-and-response. They reveal that the herbs are a source of power that she must use in the service of her people.

She collects the herbs, holds them aloft with both hands, and we see her becoming more and more possessed with supernatural strength. This is reflected at first in great steps to voice and drum. We also sense the growing power in her arms, in her thighs, in her hips; and as she dances from downstage to upstage, we get from this small, almost diminutive dancer, a view of that powerful, capacious bottom that virtually fills the stage and had been the terror of British soldiers.

Suddenly the drums take over and direct the pace of the proceedings. A wounded Johnny and another Maroon are catapulted onto the stage. A British soldier follows them, overbearing, in control. He pulls Johnny, who has lost the use of one arm, first one way and then another. Ni watches from upstage. She dashes forward and brings down the Englishman. The chorus chant, "Anjooma", meaning "stranger". Ni and the intruder roll over several times in their scuffle, but she finally dominates him. There is a subtle musical transition, in which Johnny's pain is expressed by flute and drums. By now the villagers have arrived. Two of them take the wriggling soldier away. The singers sing in four-part harmony accompanied by full orchestra, "Et scheo a odi a fufan hutseo". Ni begins a dance of defiance. Johnny tries to get up but collapses. Ni must restore Johnny. She collects her herbs. Flute and drums power a rhythmic exercise in which she is joined by the villagers. They are now at one in body, mind and spirit. They move as if they are pumping life out of the earth with their feet and bodies. Their communal will puts strength back into Johnny. He rises and goes off with Ni. The villagers disperse. Martial music fills the air, and voices cheer: "mayombe ears a ring O". In the general euphoria, Ni makes a triumphal entry, borne aloft – the acknowledged leader of the Maroons, who follow in the run-walk steps of the Jonkonnu. They process around the stage and go off.

We are then startled by the sound of the abeng, which warns of coming trials. Maroons dash hither and thither. A hand-clapping chant prepares the village for the struggle ahead: "idée, idée, ghebe bii ashemo lala". They have been summoned to the ritual in which they prepare for war. Ni stands tall in the centre of a group of women who are kneeling, squatting, rolling on the ground. She turns to the north, the south, the east and the west. They dance to extract energy from the earth, whose motive force they then locate in the solar plexus. They are joined by the men, who form an outer circle. In changing formations they rehearse the actions of jungle warfare – the searching, the stalking, the hunting. Johnny, not yet recovered from his injuries, brings on the spears and gives them to Ni. She hands them to the women, from whom the men take them with great leaps. The men go off dancing to the tune of "Oh Masumba", a Maroon song that celebrates the navel as the source of manly strength. The dance is a shuffle forward on both feet well apart, with knees bent and body well back, more or less on a level with the navel and parallel with the ground.

The ritual is over, but the mood of preparation is still with Ni. The women left behind have their chores to perform but they must will their men to victory. In the meantime, the drums return the scene to its domestic mode. There is a brief evocative piece in which they clap their hands: "alkee akasu kane ta bee asumoo n henyeloi". Ni gives instructions and directs the affairs of her mini-state. The dance reflects the body sob and the *yanga* (a slight shrugging motion of the body while walking or dancing). But news comes thick and fast. We get a glimpse of the theatre of war; detachments of threes and fours report to Ni and are redeployed. We see others in the distance in flight or pursuit. Johnny returns but keeps a respectful distance. He bides his time.

Her duties discharged, Ni moves downstage, her little body tired and worn out. She sits, feet apart, and bends forward, elbow on thigh, chin in hand. With one hand still in a sling, Johnny comes forward silently. He touches her from behind, with a knowledge of that other side of her body that only he knows. She shivers with delight, and her response fills the theatre with an immediate sense of comfort. They go into their second duet to the music of "Edo, Edo", a Maroon love song, sung with great empathy by the Singers, accompanied by the orchestra.

After forty-five years, the NDTC continues to be active and dynamic. A new generation of dancers, "many of whom are the beneficiaries of the Company's vision of elevating dance into the mainstream of educational life", now perform with excellence and continue to exalt the Jamaican dance theatre through performance and choreography.[9] Principal dancer Arlene Richards emerged in the 1990s as lead dancer in a number of important works, including *Sulkari* and *Tribute*, also choreographed by Cuban dancer Rivero; *Dream on Squatter's Mountain*, *Children of Mosiah* and *Praise Songs* by Nettleford; *Of Prophecy and Song* and *Phases of the Three Moons* by Clive Thompson (who returned from years of performing in New

Blood Canticles, with Arlene Richards, Arsenio Andrade, Deroi Rose, Natalie Chung, Elaine Grant and Abeldo Gonsales (1996). Choreographed by Rex Nettleford. *Photo by Monica DaSilva.*

York to contribute to the training of younger dancers). Richards herself is a choreographer of several pieces, including *Coroon* (1994), *Side by Side* (2001) and *Sacred Ground* (2001). She is also the company's manufacturer of costumes.

The NDTC continues to draw upon Caribbean traditions and rituals, such as Jamaican kumina, pocomania and gerrehbenta, as well as Zion Revivalist ceremonies and chants, Cuban Santeria, Trinidadian Shango, Haitian Vodun, Spiritual Baptist songs and tunes (Sankeys), and some African dance survivals still performed at wakes and funeral celebrations. Other younger dancers are given the opportunity to develop their choreographic skills, and their best works are often incorporated into the annual programmes. In this way the company continues to grow.

Where, in the earlier years, audiences were mostly persons with Jamaican or West Indian connections, today the company attracts a more catholic audience as its reputation for quality and excellence has grown. According to the fortieth anniversary brochure, it combines "the versatility of the African/West Indian pelvic movement with the bodily composure of the flowing peripheral movement and extended footwork of the European Christian influences". In the 2002 programme, the company described itself as the manifestation "and living monument to those countless, voiceless millions [of] dead who made their mark unmarked before this could be so". And even today the NDTC continues to explore, experiment, create, disseminate, entertain and educate "while rippling like snakes and promenading like flamingos".

14

Other Dance Companies

Monica Campbell McFarlane and the Movements Dance Company of Jamaica

Movements Dance Company of Jamaica is an eclectic experience of Jamaican modern contemporary dance – a gala of rhythm, energy and moods. Launched in March 1981, Movements emerged from the vision of four dancers who desired a particular expression of their art form, inspired by innovation, ingenuity and a deep appreciation of Jamaica's rich cultural heritage. The four were Monica Campbell (later McFarlane), Pat Grant-Heron, Michelle Tappin-Lee and Denise Desnoes. They envisioned a creative institution that would revolve around the collective efforts of its members, offer an avenue of training and performance for dancers and dance students to develop their discipline, and introduce what they considered to be an even higher standard of technical and performance excellence.

Monica Campbell is a communication consultant by profession, and is co-founder and executive chairperson of the advertising and public relations agency Communication Services Limited. Her expertise in the field of communication has, over the past three decades, seen her direct and develop wide-ranging communication projects throughout the Caribbean, from the election of political parties to helping shape spheres of economic influence for various private entities. Her success in this field has helped to fuel parallel success in the arts, to which she has contributed significantly. She has helped to nurture a generation of dance artists through the acclaimed Movements Dance Company of Jamaica – the company for which she serves as artistic director and chief choreographer.

Monica Campbell McFarlane, artistic director of Movements Dance Company of Jamaica

Campbell was born in Jamaica, and at the age of six she joined her parents in England, where she remained for nine years before returning home in 1969. Her early training in dance was in ballet, tap and ballroom dancing, which she studied as a child in Birmingham, England. After returning to Jamaica, she began to study modern dance with Eddy Thomas, choreographer, designer, dancer and co-founder of the

Opposite: Clive Thompson Dance Co. *Courtesy of Clive Thompson.*

Ceremony, choreographed by Neville Black for Movements Dance Co. *Photo by Monica Campbell McFarlane.*

National Dance Theatre Company of Jamaica. Still later she studied with Neville Black, a Jamaican who had established the first black dance group in Chicago, and who, on his return home, immersed himself in whatever dance forms were operating. Black worked with the NDTC, taught at the Rowe Ballet Studio and became a major tutor and choreographer of Movements from its formation in 1981 until his passing in 2000.

Black brought precision and detail with his choreography. There were no boundaries to what he could do on the floor and, through the laboratory he created, he passed these skills on to an eagerly responsive group of young people. Black's contributions to Movement's repertoire include *Adagio* (1982), *Genesis* (1984), *Ceremony* (1989) and *Take Two* (1996).

Jackie Guy is another early NDTC dancer and established choreographer. He now resides in England but returns home annually to work with the Movements company. Among his works with Movements, Guy has choreographed *Ruth* (1984), *Missioner* (1988) and *Transitions* (1991). His latest and highly successful work, *Only Fi Yuh* (2006), makes use of recorded spoken-word recitals from the late Louise Bennett (Coverley) collection, set to the music of two Jamaicans, Ernie Smith and Dennis Brown. The dance opens with performers dressed in white huddled together, and as the music begins they gradually spread across the stage, depicting the emergence of the new nation, Jamaica. As the dance progresses, the audience is treated to brief and often humorous dramatizations of Miss Lou's recorded works. Movements continues

Pressure, at the Shaw Theatre, London, in 1986. *Photo by Monica DaSilva.*

to refine this number and expects it to become one of the most lasting contributions to its repertoire.

Movements works with a number of other local and international artists as well, including Michael Holgate, who choreographed *The Mood, The Muse, The Music* (2002) and *Doorways* (2004). Patrick Johnson, principal dancer and founding member of Movements, choreographed *Pathways* (2001) and *Semi Colon* (2004). International award-winner Christopher Huggins, a former member of the Alvin Ailey American Dance Theater, New York, choreographed *Tears of War*, an introspective piece inspired by the causalities of war, and *Rendering* (2005). The Cuban-Jamaican national Arturo Castillo's latest work with Movements was *Point Zero* (2007). With these and other internationally known choreographers, the company has consistently retained artists of a high calibre, despite the fact that its management committee is comprised only of volunteers from the business and professional sectors. These volunteers set the company's broad policy, coordinate its annual schedule of activities and organize fundraisers to sustain the efforts of the ensemble. Movements' main sponsor for a number of years has been the Jamaica National Building Society.

Monica Campbell McFarlane's teaching style and choreography blend reggae and traditional African-Caribbean influences with modern jazz and classical. She draws upon international directors, including the Japanese Ray Tadio, a Third Generation Horton Technique Master, for *Tikka* (1993); Vince Collins, soloist from the Dance Theater of Harlem, for *Lotus Flower* (1996); Jamel Gaines, artistic director, Creative Outlook Dance Company of New York, for *Autumn Breeze* (1996) and *Cutting Edge* (1997); and Cubans Estaban Delgado for *La Vida* (2002) and Narziso Medina, who

Baraka, choreographed by Monica Campbell McFarlane for Movements Dance Company. *Photo by Monica Campbell McFarlane.*

has also choreographed in Europe, for *Metamorphosis* (2007). Since 1994 a Cuban dancer has always been in residence with Movements.

Metamorphosis was inspired by Franz Kafka's book of the same name. This is how one reporter described the dance when it premiered in 2007: "We see three 'male beings' – seemingly trapped in a barrel-like structure – who manage to free themselves from the confines and later evolve into erect figures. The body contortions and writhing on the floor to some stormy sound effects and sometimes vivid lighting made the piece one of the night's unforgettable offerings."[1]

The more than one hundred dances created by Mrs Campbell McFarlane and her choreographers over nearly three decades have consistently drawn on social issues and spiritual themes. Movements is shaped by a rich cultural heritage that has made Jamaica and things Jamaican special and unique in the world. Some of Monica Campbell McFarlane's works include *Pressure* (1984), *Flashback* (1993), *Baraka (I am beautiful, you are beautiful, we are all beautiful)* (2003) and *Ushindi* (2006). The success of Movements can be readily ascribed to her unwavering leadership and the solid commitment of her team of dancers, management committee and production personnel, many of whom are leaders in their respective professional fields. (There are very few dancers who are full-time professionals.) Today, Movements is a thriving ensemble recognized for its freshness and distinctly Jamaican style. Its energy and texture sets it apart from other dance groups, especially in North America. "It seems to shine a little differently with the mix of cultures, mix of spirituality and Africanity, that make us a people", says Campbell McFarlane.

Under the infinite inspiration and meticulous eye of its artistic director, Movements' performances are an intimate exchange of experiences and emotions set against a tapestry of diverse musical compositions ranging from the classics to the rhythms of the Caribbean, but always with the vibrations of Jamaica. Its dynamic repertoire reflects the dedication of a troupe that must satisfy full-time professional and personal obligations and still make time for intense rehearsals and scheduled performances, which climax each year with an annual season of dance that begins in November. Overseas performances have taken Movements to the United Kingdom, the United States, Canada and several Caribbean countries.

In 1992, Mrs Campbell McFarlane co-founded DanceScape Jamaica Limited, along with Sheila Barnett, Maria Smith, Alison Symes and Cheryl Ryman, in an effort aimed at promoting greater collaboration in the dance, and she served as editor of *DanceScape* magazine from 1992 to 1994. In May 2008 Movements acquired a home on Haining Road in New Kingston, and in time plans to expand, by reintroducing workshops as a feeder for the group.

L'Antoinette Stines and L'Acadco: A United Caribbean Dance Force

Dancer, actress, teacher and lecturer, administrator, founder, artistic director and choreographer of the L'Acadco Dance Company, L'Antoinette "Osun Ide" Stines studied classical ballet with the Royal Academy of Dance and the Dance Theater of Harlem, and modern dance at the Martha Graham School of Dance and the Alvin Ailey American Dance Theater. She is also an author and visionary. Her early training in dance was with the Alma Mock Yen Dance Company. Stines tells the story that, as a child, she was passing a gate in the Harbour View community one afternoon when she heard music and saw young people dancing. She stopped to watch and heard a voice inviting her to come and join the group. The person was Alma Mock Yen, dance

L'Antoinette "Osun Ide" Stines, founder, artistic director of the L'Acadco Dance Company

teacher, dancer and choreographer. Here began her lifelong fascination with modern dance.

In 1978, Stines founded Miami's first primarily black dance company, L'Acadco. As a choreographer, she has worked with the Netherlands Dance Academy, the Florida School of Dance and the Grove Dance Theatre of Florida. She has directed sessions at the Barbados Dance Workshop, the University of Miami and Howard University, the Aruba School of Dance, and at the Jamaica School of Dance. She has also functioned as movement director and lead choreographer for the Cricket World Cup opening ceremony in Jamaica in 2007.

Stines is best known for creating and developing a distinctive contemporary Jamaican dance technique that blends reggae, kumina, gerrehbenta and nyabingi. In 1994, after ten years of experimentation, she unveiled a new modern Caribbean dance technique called "L'Anyah reggae technique", in which she fuses the anglophone Caribbean contemporary technique into what is now known as "L'Antech", a synthesis of classical ballet and the anglophone Caribbean's indigenous traditional and popular dances. For this work she has received both local and international commendation. According to Stines, she gives the audience choreography embodying a wholeness of body, mind and soul. At the present time she is working on the codification of this dance technique towards a doctorate at the University of the West Indies. The project is entitled "Dance Is Language".

Stines is also founder of YARD, a dance conference focusing on Caribbean techniques. She hopes to preserve the remnants of a Caribbean tradition jeopardized by modernism, and, in the process, to educate students about the rich and vibrant culture of Jamaica and the Caribbean. The company draws upon local customs, folk songs, survivals of African rites, and social issues, as reflected in "No Justice, no Peace", a Peter Tosh song which declares that justice has many colours and is consistently inconsistent. Stines incorporates nyabingi rhythms and movements, as well as other forms expressed in the dancehall music of present-day Jamaica. There is much emphasis on rediscovering African sounds and rhythms.

One of the company's most renowned pieces, *Satta* (meaning "give thanks to the Most High"), produced in 1985 to the music of Third World's "Satta Masagana", glorifies the strength of women in a sensual tribute that draws its vocabulary from the Egypto-Yoruba Orisha dances. *Freedom Time Bruckins* is a bruckins celebration in memory of Jamaicans' own ancestors, the former slaves who adapted the dances of their European masters in their own peculiar ways. Jamaica's lost African heritage is a source of grief in *Stolen Verses* (2004): "You stole our ancestral philosophy and told us we had none!! Alas our philosophy lives in the reverence of our being."[2] *To Haiti* was commissioned by UNESCO in commemoration of the two hundredth

Divine Unity, L'Acadco Dance Company, choreographed by Antoinette Stines. *Photo by Antoinette Stines.*

anniversary of Haiti's revolution, which made the country an independent nation in 1804. There are many other items which examine some of Jamaica's social embarrassments, like *Zinc Fence*, based on live conversations with tenants in an inner city "yard".

L'Antoinette Stines explains that her vision is to unite music and dance from a spiritual space where the ancestors live; in doing so, she aims to inspire through her breath and her dance. L'Acadco's mission is to present the rhythms of the Caribbean people on the world stage as one method of building bridges through the arts. The company continues to expand and grow intellectually, as it tours countries overseas and addresses the social issues of the day. Its membership includes dancers from across the Caribbean – Jamaica, Trinidad, Barbados, Guyana, the Bahamas and Suriname.

L'Acadco dancers are exposed to international techniques through scholarships to parts of Africa and Cuba, as well as being gainfully employed by internationally acclaimed companies, productions, institutions and practitioners such as Alvin Ailey and Garth Fagan. With the aid of the Rita Marley Foundation, one member of the drumming team was afforded the opportunity to spend a year in Ghana perfecting his skills in African drumming.

Tony Wilson, founder, artistic director of the Company Dance Theatre

Tony Wilson and the Company Dance Theatre

The Company Dance Theatre, founded in 1988, was the lifelong dream of artistic director Tony Wilson, a former member of the NDTC who studied with the Alvin Ailey American Dance Theater, the Martha Graham School and the Dance Theater of Harlem. In 1991 Wilson was awarded the Caribbean Academy of Arts and Culture bursary, which enabled him to refine further his dancing technique and to choreograph for the Inner City Ballet Company of Buffalo, New York, as well as the New Breed Dance Company of Chicago. Wilson launched the Company Dance Theatre in 1989 with seven dance works – three by guest choreographers and four by himself. As artistic director, he choreographed, costumed and mounted his own works.

To date, the Company has produced thirteen critically acclaimed seasons of dance. The 1992 season included *Red City*, Jamaica's first full-length modern ballet. The fifth anniversary (1993) saw Wilson's ground breaking *Rose Hall*, another full-length dramatic ballet, based on the life of Anne Palmer, the fabled white witch of Rose Hall. Again he choreographed, designed, staged, costumed and mounted the performance. That same year, the Company produced *Dancescape*, one of three presentations by Jamaican companies, at the gala of the Black Dance Theatre performance held in the United States. The Company's 1996 presentation, *Breaking the Mirror*, was their most challenging performance. It explored the social taboos of rape, incest and prostitution, and was based on an original script created by Wilson and other senior members of the company. The choreography, sets and costumes were all his work.

The Company Dance Theatre has developed a distinctive repertoire of unique style and artistic creativity that has received critical acclaim. Tony Wilson has delighted

Rosehall by the Company, choreographed by Tony Wilson. Dancers are Janela Kassem and Tony Henry. *Photo by Monica DaSilva.*

and excited Jamaican audiences with his originality and energy. He is a dynamic teacher with innovative ideas and the ability to impart them. His love and appreciation of music forms a strong base for his works. His sense of theatre is apparent in his staging, costume and set designs. Wilson feels that dance should expose Jamaica's rich and multicultural society, and urges other dance companies to take up that challenge. Wilson also choreographs regularly for the NDTC.

The Junior Ensemble, formed by Wilson in 2002, is comprised of a group of talented students registered at the School of Modern Dance. Since its inauguration, the group's performances have included the Glory Concerts alongside the Company Dance Theatre in the Emancipation Park series of Christmas concerts, the Ministry of Foreign Affairs Concerts for the diplomatic corps, and the annual Youth in Concert performances. There is also the Annual Dance Concert Season held at the Courtleigh Hotel Auditorium. Many members of the Junior Ensemble also participate in the Jamaica Cultural Development Commission's (JCDC's) annual Festival of Arts competitions and regularly earn medals.

Colours, by the Company, choreographed by Tony Wilson. Dancers are Chris-Ann Steele and Lee-Ann Steele

The Junior Ensemble is adapting to various dance styles and techniques as a result of being exposed to teachers and choreographers with different training and backgrounds. The dance styles incorporate traditional dance forms – from reggae, folk and Afro-Caribbean to American jazz, modern contemporary, ballet and the Cuban technique – to create an exciting and arresting amalgam of movements. The Ensemble also serves as a feeder for the senior company. Each year, selected young dancers are invited to attend classes with members of the Company in the hope that they too may become future members.

Monika Lawrence and the Stella Maris (Young Adult) Dance Ensemble

Monika Lawrence began dancing while at school. She started with Noelle Chutkan, a dancer with the NDTC, before moving on to the Jayteens Dance Workshop conducted by Joyce Campbell. From the Jayteens she was introduced to the NDTC, where at first she served as an usher, hoping one day to be invited to join the group. While at the University of the West Indies in the 1970s she joined the Eddy Thomas Workshop, later named the Jamaica Dance Company, before that company was dismantled by Thomas later in the 1970s. She then joined the Jamaica School of Dance and worked with Bert Rose, who was the artistic director of the school's workshop. At the time of writing, Monika Lawrence had completed a doctoral dissertation at the University of the West Indies entitled "Rex Nettleford: Choreographer as Cultural Philosopher in Three Classic Works – *Pocomania*, *Kumina* and *Gerrehbenta*".

Monika Lawrence, leader of the Stella Maris (Young Adult) Dance Ensemble

It was while at the Jamaica School of Dance that Lawrence was invited to join the NDTC. By that time she was leader of the Stella Maris Dance Ensemble, which she established along with the head of the Stella Maris Preparatory School, Sister Mary Joseph, in 1986. What started out as a creative outlet for preparatory school students in dance had by 1994 become the Stella Maris Dance Ensemble of some thirty dancers, with boys recruited from St George's College and Calabar High School, and girls mostly from the Stella Maris school. Since the Ensemble's 1997 Season, the troupe has undergone several important changes, the most notable being an addition to its name, which now sees the group being called the Stella Maris (Young Adult) Dance Ensemble, and a further reduction in the size of the troupe to approximately twenty-five top dancers. The emphasis has always been on education and dance. The troupe boasts former members who are now graduates in medicine, law and other professions and disciplines. The organizers have from time to time obtained funding to assist with the education of the less economically privileged members.

This ensemble furthered the quest for a truly indigenous mode of expression by giving young people a sense of pride in their own heritage. The premiere offering in 1994 reflected this goal: they mounted a full-length dance drama called *Children of*

Outburst, choreographed by Jackie Guy, danced by the Stella Maris Dance Ensemble (1997). *Photo by Monica DaSilva.*

Sisyphus, based on the acclaimed book of that title by Orlando Patterson. For 1995, their offering was the *Seventh Day*, another full-length dance drama which, while acknowledging the reverence that should be given the day of worship, also puts the Sabbath day within the wider societal context. Between 1996 and 1999, the Ensemble presented a series of thematic dance concerts that further underscored their artistic flexibility. For 2000, their offering included a full-length ballet called *Brown Sugar*, a work by five choreographers who explored the various cultural influences that have been brought to bear on the Caribbean region as a whole, and the distinct style that has evolved from this in each member country.

The Stella Maris Dance Ensemble has each year impressed judges and audiences at the JCDC's Festival Dance Competition, and in 1989 they became the first group ever to win both the junior and the intermediate categories. Their consistently high achievement in the Festival dance competition also resulted in their being awarded gold medals for all eleven dances entered in 1993. After a break of four years, the senior members of the ensemble entered the JCDC Festival Dance Competition in 1997 and, in addition to winning several gold medals for individual dances, topped the competition by winning the Ivy Baxter Trophy for the best overall group. They won that trophy again in 1998 to take a second consecutive, and third overall, hold on the trophy. In all they have won eighty-five gold medals.

The ensemble also targets festivals overseas, as it seems to them easier to attract audiences in a country without any Jamaican communities. They have come to realize that they need to have a knowledge of their own country, as foreign audiences want to know about Jamaica. That, in itself, gives the troupe a sense of pride, since they can tell their own stories better than other people can. It also helps them to develop greater self-assurance.

In 1986, the Stella Maris (Young Adult) Dance Ensemble became the youngest group to represent Jamaica overseas when they toured the Cayman Islands with *Stella's Tale*, a Christmas pantomime produced by the school. Between 2 and 5 July 1994, the dancers also represented Jamaica at the fourteenth annual Caribbean Cultural Festival of Art held in Santiago de Cuba. In April 2001 they again represented Jamaica, this time at the World Folk Dance Festival held in Spain. They have also performed in England, where they also conducted a workshop. In September 2002 the ensemble represented their nation at the inaugural Caribbean Music Festival, which was intended to forge closer cultural and economic ties between Caribbean Community (CARICOM) countries and Japan. They were invited to perform in Sakai, Japan, in 2002. It was the first time that a Jamaican dance troupe had performed in Japan, and the response to their performance was overwhelmingly positive. In 2004 and 2005 the ensemble again represented Jamaica in the eleven-month-long twenty-seventh season of the Black Academy of Arts and Letters (TBAAL), the Dallas-based organization that has been one of the leading multi-disciplinary arts organizations in the United States for more than twenty-five years. The ensemble received standing ovations for their performances during the season. They have also performed and conducted workshops in Los Angeles. In 2007 they toured Dallas and went to Los Angeles after the October season.

Monika Lawrence, artistic director of the group, says that the Stella Maris Dancers have always remained true to their motto, "Success through Hard Work", and are dedicated in their pursuit of excellence. The ensemble continues to impress at every level of national life, in which it sustains a unique identity as a group of innovative artists who stretch creative borders to achieve excellence in dance. The repertoire of the ensemble reflects the cross-fertilization of the various national themes which Lawrence has fused to create a Caribbean dance vocabulary and aesthetic. Certainly, there are further syntheses that will be achieved in the fullness of time.

ACT IV

MAJOR PRODUCTIONS, TRAINING, MUSICAL ACHIEVEMENTS

15

Jamaica Festival and Other Landmark Productions

The festival movement in Jamaica combines and assimilates features of festivals of ancient Greece and Rome that had by the Middle Ages already begun to spread to other countries of Europe. The Jamaican Festival also exhibits traits of the Royal National Eisteddfod of Wales and the Edinburgh Festival of Scotland. These have, of course, been fused with Asian and African survivals in Jamaican society.

According to Aristotle, that type of pre-dramatic ceremony grew out of the improvisations of the leaders of phallic songs. It often included a procession with a chorus which sang and danced as its members carried large phallic symbols aloft on poles. Some of these ceremonies also provided opportunity for considerable byplay and mockery between participants and spectators. Probably the most noteworthy characteristic of the Aristophanic comedies which survive is their commentary on contemporary society, politics, literature and the Peloponnesian War (raging at that time).[1] These were the times when, "In addition to fantasy, farcical situations [were] typical and considerable emphasis placed on the pleasures of eating, drinking, sex, wealth and leisure. Coupled with the comic elements [were] some of the most beautiful lyrics and some of the most obscene passages in Greek Literature."[2] These plays and their reception are not far removed from what is experienced today by those who attend the Jamaican "roots" or comedic plays.

Since Jamaica's first independence celebrations in 1962, the all-embracing nature of the festivities has also tended to take on a style resembling aspects of the Roman theatre during the time of Plautus and Terence. Terence's play *Mother-in-law*, for example, apparently cut too close to the bone and had to be withdrawn, as it generated critical abuse and opposition from the public at large during its performance. In Jamaican society, a remarkable parallel can be found in Jambiz productions at Center Stage in Kingston, or in the sexually explicit lyrics used by modern dancehall performers. Regarding the latter topic, on 7 March 1990, at the Creative Arts Centre,

Opposite: Pitchy-Patchy. *Courtesy of JCDC.*

University of the West Indies, Professor Carolyn Cooper and performer David Lovindeer gave presentations on "Erotic Play in the Dancehall" as part of a panel discussion on women in dancehall organized by the Women and Development Studies group for the celebration of International Women's Week. Dr Cooper's presentation explored the use of explicit lyrics in terms of a marked "slackness hiding from culture", while other presentations dealt with "Ambitious Woman – Commodified Man", "Heart of Slackness", "Slackness Feminized and Censured", "Diminished Masculinity", "Non-sexual Social Commentary" – all treated within the discreet intellectual space provided by the occasion.

Traditions Behind the Jamaican Festival Movement

No one can say when a festival in any sense of the word was first organized in Jamaica. The Spaniards had their Corpus Christi festival, and the Tainos before them marked the coming of spring in festivities which eulogized their *zemis* and departed chiefs. Once a year the villagers turned out in procession:

> They went on their way wearing ornaments, carrying baskets of cassava bread, and singing songs about their *zemis* (idols of worship). The chief sat at the entrance to the temple, beating a drum while the priests entered and dressed the *zemi*. After that there was merrymaking in which the villagers danced, sang and drank the intoxicating fermented cassava juice, offered prayers for protection and prosperity of the village and at the end of the day took home pieces of cassava bread, to protect them from accidents throughout the year.[3]

The performing arts in Jamaica, with their long and respected tradition of competitive and non-competitive events dating back at least to the nineteenth century, form the foundation of the Jamaica festival movement. Starting in 1897, as one of the events to mark Queen Victoria's sixtieth birthday, the Institute of Jamaica organized a festival along the lines of the Welsh eisteddfod. After this, schools and community groups would plan competitions along similar lines as a kind of "speech" or "open day" activity. The institute continued these eisteddfodau for the next nine years, when the trend was interrupted by the earthquake which destroyed much of the city of Kingston and other parts of the island in 1907.

Elocution contests seem to have been revived earlier than other competitions, and among the first organizers was T.S. Phillips of the *Jamaica Times*, who conducted the contests in 1910. The Jesuit fathers set a fine example at St George's College, where they staged a wide range of productions over the years. Beginning with the opening of the new school building in 1914, they brought a new enthusiasm to the school, and in addition to scholarship, they developed the talents and skills of their students in music, elocution, drama. In so doing they produced some of the finest artists in Jamaica during the early and middle years of the twentieth century, with Monsignor Richard Ho Lung currently one of their most distinguished producers of religious plays.

The Literary and Debating Society, which was later renamed the Arts Society of Jamaica, also staged mock trials, a practice obviously copied from England. Mock trials exploited Jamaicans' penchant for litigation, and provided an important aspect of the island's theatrical fare during the 1920s and the decades following. They may still be seen in roots productions by Ed "Bim" Lewis and Harold Holness, on television and on the Internet, produced by the Creative Production and Training Centre with such star-quality players as Lois Kelly (Barrow) Miller, Alma Mock Yen, Leonie Forbes, Barry Johnson and Oliver Samuels.

Ed "Bim" Lewis, comedian, theatre producer

The Literary and Debating Society was comprised of men and women who were influential in the literary, journalistic, educational, judicial, cultural, theatrical and artistic life of the island. They elected as first president C.G.X. Henriques, distinguished barrister-at-law and gold medallist in elocution at London University. Among the finest players and elocutionists to walk the boards were Philip N. Blake; E.M. Cupidon and his sister, Icema; H.A. "Tony" Ableton; Eric Coverley and his two sisters, Edna and Ivy; A.E.T. Henry; the Hill brothers, Stephen, Kenneth and Frank; Jimmy Fyffe; and Leacroft Robinson. The society encouraged the establishment of debating societies and the holding of debating competitions in villages and towns, and broadened the scope of their operations to include theatre and the fine arts. By 1950, however, interest had begun to wane, and when the National Festival of Arts was established in 1955 as part of the island's tercentenary celebrations, the Literary and Debating Society merged with that organization.

After Marcus Garvey's return from the United States at the end of 1927, he revived the Universal Negro Improvement Association (UNIA), and introduced a variety of cultural programmes under its auspices, as J.J. Mills records:

> In the early thirties, Marcus Garvey, wishing to expose his followers and the general public to High-class musical competition, organized a singing festival at Edelweiss Park [which the UNIA had purchased in 1929]. Over 2,000 listeners were packed on the ground floor and in the galleries. Microphones were not in use in Jamaica at the time. Contestants were classified into solos, duets, quartets and choral ensembles. All the items offered were serious, rather than popular music. They included selections from Haydn, Tchaikovsky, Arditi, Eli, Handel; offerings which ordinarily would hardly appeal to the musically unsophisticated. At the beginning Garvey described how polite society here and abroad behaved at concerts, and asked the listeners to show the same polite and encouraging behaviour to the contestants.
>
> Throughout the long programme of over twenty pieces interspersed with judges' awards and criticisms there was a polite, considerate and appreciative reception by the large mixed audience. Similar reception was given at the contests and other musical events subsequently given at Edelweiss Park.[4]

Recollections of such activities as Garvey's singing festival are corroborated by some of Jamaica's outstanding artists, including poet, playwright and broadcaster Archie Lindo, folklorists and comedians Ranny Williams and Lee Gordon, who learned their craft under Professor Gerardo Leon at Edelweiss Park.

For a short time in his youth, Garvey attended a private school run by two Fowler sisters, spinster aunts of Henry Fowler (the educator and theatre personality), at Shawbery, on the outskirts of St Ann's Bay. Garvey never forgot the sisters and, on his return to Jamaica from the United States, he felt the need to reconnect with them, even in their old age, and sought them out in their retirement at Rio Magno.[5] They had mentored him in the values of self-reliance and respect for other human beings, and helped him to develop an abiding appreciation of classical music and some of the finer things in life.

Jamaica Welfare Limited, started provisionally in 1936 by Norman Washington Manley and established by law in 1937,[6] was founded with the goal of fostering the growth of self-reliance among villagers. It was headed by Eddie Burke, who, at the beginning of radio broadcasts in 1939, used the medium of radio as one way to convey his messages. He also published a series of short stories under the general heading *Newsy Wapps*, and these "gave delightfully typical glimpses of youth of Jamaica life".[7] He was supported by Louise Bennett (later Coverley), who formed drama groups and taught the villagers to compose and perform their own plays, and Ivy Baxter, who also facilitated the advancement of the Festival movement, although such efforts remained primarily small, localized affairs.

Primary schools with children under fifteen years of age were the first groups to have drama festivals. The Little Theatre Movement (LTM) organized the first two in 1943 and 1945 in connection with the promotional work of the Bureau of Health Education. The intention was to make an indelible impression upon the minds of the young as they studied the plays and dramatized health issues.

Stephen O.D. Hill staged the first Adult Drama Festival at the Ward Theatre in 1944, but this consisted of three plays only – *Hamlet*, *Elizabeth Barrett Browning* and *The Late Christopher Bean* – and was primarily a Kingston affair. Then, in 1950, the British Council and the LTM inaugurated the Jamaica Secondary Schools' Drama Festival, a truly all-island competition for performers up to eighteen or nineteen years of age.

It was, however, the parish of Portland that led the way with an enthusiastic programme, later to be copied by all the other parishes. In 1946 a group of volunteers under the chairmanship of R.L.C. Aarons, collector of taxes, and accomplished short-story writer and novelist, with the energetic support of organizing secretaries Rex Shelton of the Port Antonio Collectorate and Clinton Cresser of Jamaica Welfare Limited, along with Bill Sikes and others, started a movement that embraced the teaching profession, the constabulary force, the churches, other community groups and individuals of goodwill. They absorbed the earlier Parish Elocution Contest of the 1930s into their Portland Festival of Music and Drama. Interest was high among persons like the Honourable F.V. Grossett, custos of the parish, who became patron of the festival; Howard Cooke, headmaster of Belle Castle Primary School, and a musician of quality; and Sergeant Fullerton of the constabulary, whose pugilistic style of conducting his Buff Bay Adult Choir provided a great deal of fun and excitement for the parishioners.

Teacher Howard Cooke later carried the Portland zeal to his home parish of St James during the Jamaica 300 celebrations in 1955. He was appointed chairman of the Cultural Development Commission, which was established to give permanence to the festival movement as Jamaica approached independence in 1962, and he retained his great interest in cultural celebrations when he became minister of education and later governor general of Jamaica.

The Portland Festival pioneered the comprehensive festival of arts on the island on a parish-wide level. It was a week-long extravaganza with eliminations held in some rural communities. Events came to a climax on Saturday, with the judging of the finalists at Titchfield High School in Port Antonio. Cultural organizations, including the Institute of Jamaica, the British Council, Jamaica Welfare Limited, the Poetry League of Jamaica and the Musical Society of Jamaica, provided the adjudicators. Prizes were donated by local firms and individuals. It was a completely spontaneous effort.

Jamaica 300 and After

From Portland, the festival movement spread to St Catherine (1949), St Ann (1951) and Manchester (1954). The opportunity to establish a *de facto* island-wide festival came in 1954 with Jamaica 300, a celebration of the tercentenary of the association between Jamaica and Britain. Jamaica 300 would take the festival idea to the remaining eight parishes of the island. Thus 1955 saw the birth of the first island-wide, year-long festival that embraced both child and adult Jamaicans. This was the first Jamaica National Festival of the Arts, designed to accompany the Jamaica 300 celebrations. It was as part of this festival that the first island-wide Adult Drama Festival was launched.

Jamaica 300 was spearheaded by parliamentarian and minister of finance Donald Sangster, who had been impressed by the centenary celebrations he had witnessed in New Zealand in 1954 as the representative of the Government of Jamaica. He envisaged a similar event in his own country to mark Jamaica's three hundredth year as a part of the British Empire. Looking back now, it seems clear that, for strategic purposes, it was decided at the time to overlook the harsh realities of three centuries of colonialism and slavery.

Band Wagon with Bob Verity (*standing right*), Sir Hugh Foot (*seated*) and Doris Duperley, behind Sir Hugh Foot, with the cast during the tercentenary celebrations

The Travelling Theatre: Scence from *The Two Brothers* directed by Father Francis Shea. *Left to right:* ? Murdock, Ronald Thwaites, Patrick Terrelongue, Carol Alberga, Lorna Ainsworth, Peter Symonds and *(above)* Valerie Cashman and Dwight Taaffe

Wycliffe Bennett, secretary of the Poetry League of Jamaica, and the person responsible for organizing the league's elocution contests since 1943, was invited to organize and coordinate the activities of the Jamaica 300 office. At the first meeting of the Tercentenary Committee that he convened, the governor, Sir Hugh Foot, who presided, said that the National Festival of the Arts should be a major component of the celebrations, a suggestion which was warmly supported by Donald Sangster. Bennett approached Sydney Hockey, director of the Jamaica Library Service, who unhesitatingly accepted the idea, which he saw as an opportunity to help his then-fledgling organization establish roots in the deep rural areas. He was supported by his deputy, W.F. Chape, and librarian-in-training Hazel Gray, who was being groomed to act as director on Hockey's departure (in early 1955) until the return of Joyce Lawson from study leave in England.

Bennett travelled throughout the island urging the existing Parish Festival Committees and social organizations to cooperate with the national arts festival, and, backed by the Jamaica Library Service, set up committees in the other eight parishes which had not previously held festivals. The response was enthusiastic and many influential persons gave their full support. It was the Jamaica Library Service that acted as the glue that bonded the loose parish organizations together. The Jamaica

300 committee had no resources to set up parish offices, so parish libraries provided a leadership role and a home for the parish festival activities in the cramped, makeshift quarters they occupied. In most instances, parish librarians, such as Norma Segre in St Ann and Leila Thomas in St Catherine (later in Manchester), served as voluntary secretaries of the festival committees. The parish libraries supplied additional secretarial staff, where possible, and provided stationery and free postage; often the chairmen and members of parish library committees doubled as chairmen and organizing members for the festival. The festival work was completely voluntary. The only paid officer was the general organizer, Bennett.

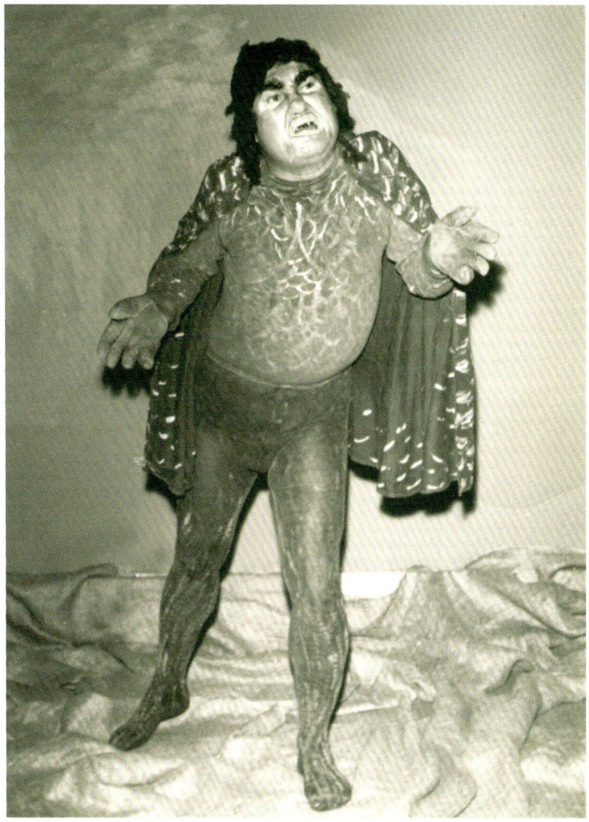

Ronald Harrison as Caliban in *The Tempest*, co-directed by Errol Hill and Hugh Morrison

The National Festival covered a wide range of subjects. It included speech and drama; instrumental and vocal music; and African ritual dance survivals like Jonkonnu, bruckins (from Portland), kumina and congo (from St Thomas), and etu (from Trelawny), along with such vestiges of European dance as the ballet, quadrille and schottische. The competitions were interspersed with non-competitive events, such as drama, modern dance and ballet presentations. Father Francis Shea of St George's College built a stage onto a truck, combined students of St George's College (boys) and Alpha Academy (girls) into a team, and toured the island giving open-air productions of *Everyman* and his own Jamaican version of the *Twin Brothers* of Plautus. There was a theatrical production of *The Tempest*, co-directed by Errol Hill and Hugh Morrison in Kingston; a religious service at the Spanish Town Cathedral; a ballet performance of *The Legend of Old Port Royal*, staged by the Madame Soohih School of Dance at the Ward Theatre; a photographic competition; and a national exhibition of art and craft, organized by Burnett Webster and Edna Manley at the old Victoria Market on Kingston's waterfront.

It was English playwright Noel Coward, a sometime resident of the island, who suggested to Sir Hugh Foot that there should be a Jamaica 300 bandwagon in the manner of the pageant carts of the English medieval morality plays. Robert Verity of the Institute of Jamaica was invited to take charge of this undertaking, which showcased a three-hour variety show of song, dance, drumming and drama, using a specially constructed moveable stage carried on a lorry. Local groups participated at each stop and the whole event met with enthusiastic responses as it moved across Jamaica from one parish capital to the next; Sir Hugh Foot attended every parish performance. To climax the year's festivities, a mammoth float parade organized by Eric Coverley, with entries representing different aspects of national life, wound its way through the streets of Kingston, from Cross Roads to the saluting base between the public buildings on King Street, to the great delight of the massive crowds of spectators lining the route.

Eric Coverley, float designer and builder, artist and impresario

The parade included floats highlighting agriculture, education, mining, shipping, the Jamaica Library Service, costume queens and beauty queens. Representatives from the army, the constabulary, the Boy Scouts, the Boys' Brigade and the Girl Guides paraded on foot. Some young men bore aloft effigies of nation builders created by artist Gordon Simpson. After a year of celebrations, all sections of society voted Jamaica 300 a mighty success, in that it created a feeling of goodwill and wholesomeness in the country. Just as significant was the unearthing and nurturing of artistic talent, distributed randomly across all classes and conditions of the society. It came at the right time to stimulate an appreciation of ideal beauty and deepen national consciousness.

While in no way interfering with the domestic operations of the constituent groups, the Jamaica Drama League (JDL), as an association of theatrical societies, developed much enthusiasm among theatre lovers, and commanded respect and support both at home and abroad. In 1956, encouraged by the tercentenary festival and in an effort to save the festival movement, theatrical groups came together voluntarily to establish the Adult Drama Festival as an annual feature of the island's cultural and artistic life. Their great assets were the goodwill of the country at large, their enthusiasm and their will to succeed. The foundation of the Adult Drama Festival not only increased activity among practising drama groups but also encouraged the formation of drama societies in different parts of the country.

The diversity of group representatives democratically elected to serve on the 1956 JDL committee consisted of chairman Wycliffe Bennett (Caribbean Thespians, Manchester Players and LTM); vice-chairman Tony Lopez (the Dramateurs); honorary secretary Mitzie Townsend (Caribbean Thespians); and honorary treasurer Enid Chevannes (Ivory Club). Other group representatives were Doris Duperley (Theatre Arts Club), Louise Bennett Coverley (University Extra-Mural Department) and Orville Cox (St Ann Dramatic Society). Production personnel for the 1956 festival also included George Carter, Maurice Harty, Peter Gert, Slade Hopkinson, Celia Carter and Maisie Van Courtland.

George Carter, veteran lighting designer and theatre manager

The Adult Drama Festival encouraged and fostered the organization and development of drama groups in different parts of the island, trained in all departments of the theatre, encouraged the establishment of a school of speech and drama (now a reality at the Edna Manley College), and organized an adult drama festival and a season of plays. The league was at one time affiliated with the British Drama League in London, and for a number of years received a small subvention from the Kingston and St Andrew Corporation. This was when groups like the Caribbean Thespians, headed by Tony Finn; the Repertory Company, headed by Orford St John; the Ivory Club, headed by Enid Chevannes; the St Michael's Players, headed by Kathleen Clarke (mother of Yvonne Brewster) and Evelyn Chin; Enid Wynter and the Coke Drama Group; Doreen Bramwell and Noel Dexter of the Port Antonio Drama Group; and Joan Swaby and the Manchester Players came into their own and achieved their best performances.

The University College of the West Indies Dramatic Society had been very active in the national festivals and was now fully organized with outstanding student actors from other Caribbean islands. The Theatre Arts Club, a group of mostly expatriates, created productions of high quality. While they could have assisted in the training workshops, they elected to remain outside of the mainstream movement. But, according to Ronald Harrison, "in fairness to them, they gave the Jamaican public the opportunity of seeing some fine English plays they would not have been able to see otherwise. They did, however, participate in some of the Adult Drama Festivals for a time and some of their individual members sat on the Organizing Committee."[8] In Harrison's words,

> There is no doubt in my mind that the above mentioned committee members, group representatives and production personnel gave no thought at the time that they were on the threshold of theatrical history in Jamaica, and that the Movement would create a revolution in uplifting drama to the heights it has attained today. There is also no doubt in my mind that all this was able to come about because of the courage and inspiration of the man who started a Drama Workshop Movement in 1946: The name of the man, Anthony Finn; and the name of the group, the Caribbean Thespians Dramatic Society.[9]

Orford St John, an Englishman, remained one of the few producers and directors in Jamaica in the 1950s who were fully aware of the revolution that had overtaken the British Theatre. He saw social mobility in the Jamaican context as an opportunity for interracialism in the theatre. He founded the Repertory Players in 1957 with interracialism as the stated objective. His group also demonstrated greater catholicity in its choice of plays than any other company until Theatre 77 in 1966.

The interest generated by these early efforts was such that upwards of a thousand performances of one-act and full-length plays were staged between 1955 and 1972. Some thirty full-length plays were performed in Kingston alone in 1974. Not surprisingly, these have been dubbed the "vintage years" of the Jamaican theatre.

A second festival of arts was organized in 1960. The Honourable Glendon Logan, who was the minister of housing and social welfare, accepted the recommendation of his arts committee that a retreat be conducted by the general organizer, Wycliffe Bennett, and his organizing associates. They met at the Falcondip Hotel on the North Coast, to study the impact of the festival movement to date and to submit proposals

David Williams (*left*) and Orford St John, in *A Flight of Sparrows*, directed by Orford St John

for placing it on a permanent footing. That committee recommended that a permanent committee with responsibility to provide a platform for talented groups and individuals be set up by the government. This committee, they recommended, should assist in improving the talents exhibited, with support from the Ministry of Education and the parish committees. Workshops and training seminars for teachers of the performing arts, community workers and participants should also be included, and support from the private sector should be sought and factored in. The minister took this proposal to Cabinet, which gave its support.

The Honourable Edward Seaga, as minister of development and welfare at the time, gave his full support, with government backing

A third arts celebration to mark Jamaica's political independence was organized in 1962. This was followed in 1963 by the first National Festival of the Arts of an independent Jamaica. This was the movement to which the Honourable Edward Seaga, as minister of development and welfare at the time, gave his full support, with government backing. Seaga saw the festivals which would follow as an "annual report to the nation". The Jamaica festival, which has continued since then, encourages the development of Jamaican literary, artistic and creative talents.

The drama competition at this festival incorporated the efforts of the LTM and the JDL, which had for years staged the Schools' and Adult Drama Festivals. Groups were encouraged to write and perform their own plays. Fifty years on, there is a marked improvement in the quality of the writing and performance.

According to the twenty-fifth anniversary report of the Jamaica Cultural Development Commission (JCDC), dance has maintained an extremely high profile and has kept its place as the most popular aspect of festival unchallenged.[10] This is because Jamaicans have a natural penchant for rhythm and movement. Dance competitions embrace all aspects of that art, from classical ballet to modern folk and the latest pop movements. It is the traditional dance forms, however, which express the African retentions that have, over time, superseded the European survivals. Classical ballet has been gradually fading from the festival scene, partly because the ballet examinations clash with the judging of festival dances, but also because Jamaican interest in this art form has diminished.

Festival has created the opportunity for musicians to develop and display their skills, and through the years has promoted original local music forms, like ska, rocksteady and reggae, with their accompanying dance movements. There have been years when adjudicators have been overburdened by the sheer volume of entries. The JCDC's twenty-fifth anniversary report describes the Festival Song Competition as follows:

> One competition of which every single Jamaican is undoubtedly aware is the Festival Song Competition. A distinction must be made between the Festival Song Competition and the Pop Song Competition. The former is mounted specifically for amateurs, and its main aim is to discover talent in the writing of lyrics and music and performance, while the Pop Song Competition is restricted to professional recording artistes. Entries are vetted by the Jamaican Federation of Musicians to ensure that non-professionals are not included. Professionals are taken to mean artistes whose records have been aired on the electronic media.[11]

Once the six or seven songs are selected, records are cut for play on the radio, and videos are made for television showing. Wide exposure is given to the songs and con-

Festival scenes. *Courtesy of JCDC.*

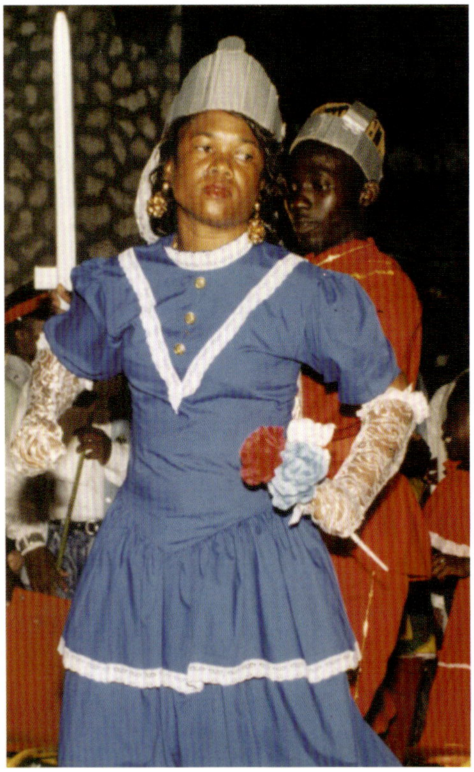

Dainty Browning Stewart dances the Blue Queen in *Bruckins*. She has been dancing the character for more than twenty-five years. *Courtesy of JCDC.*

testants through live parish performances. Selection of the pieces also involves the general public, which votes during performances.

Fine arts competitions are organized at parish and national levels. At the national level, recognized artists are invited to exhibit, the aim being to enable less experienced individuals to view their work in juxtaposition with that of their peers and the accomplishments of more established artists. There are some fifteen or more speech categories, including four choir classes – for professionals, impromptu speaking, dialect and storytelling. Of all the categories, dialect is among the most popular, although it is one of the weaker areas of presentation. According to adjudicators, the candidates tend to substitute aggression for timing and humour.

The Jamaica Festival has continued annually, partly from voluntary contributions and partly from government subsidy. While enthusiasm and cultural awareness are strong, local communities cannot fund the activities without help, as it involves formidable costs for advertising and promotion, costuming, meals and transportation, both within the parishes and counties and to the finals in Kingston. Government financial support, which has never been adequate, has dwindled proportionately over the years, and every year the Festival Commission must call upon private organizations to lend their support to this most significant aspect of nation building. Without the contribution of these public-spirited sponsors, the awarding of prizes and scholarships, as well as the participation of groups at the various levels, would prove impossible.

Over the years, with changing emphasis on cultural life, the activities of the Drama League have been incorporated into the National Festival, as was intended by the league's founders. Professional groups have developed on their own, independent of the festival movement, with paid directors, production staffs and casts. They have, by and large, proven to be financially viable, but the need for still greater cooperation prompted the formation of the Jamaica Association of Dramatic Artists in November 2001. Here again, the level of cooperation is not as was expected, and finances continue to be a major problem.

The annual National Festival of the Arts, organized by the JCDC, continues to discover and display artistic talent and to involve as many persons as possible in the creative process. Each year, seminars to deepen knowledge and improve artistic presentation take place in villages, in schools and among community groups, where offerings are critiqued and guidance in technique, choreography, costuming, and other important aspects of production offered. Increasing emphasis is placed on improving the quality of performances through training and professional adjudication. The most successful offerings are chosen for presentation in the major parish towns, as well as at the independence celebrations in Kingston during the first week of August of each year. These activities continue to give individuals the opportunity to improve their creative and artistic talents, and provide a window to display their achievements.

Not all items presented during independence week are competitive, as excerpts from the latest pantomime or production of a local play or dance, as well as recitals and performances by established groups and individuals, may be highlighted. Largely as a result of this tradition, the quality of choral speaking and singing has improved markedly. One of the local television stations, TVJ, sponsors an annual competition for school choirs outside of the festival season. A cellular telephone company, Digicel, also sponsors the Rising Stars competition, in which individuals make presentations over several weeks. Both sets of competitors receive critique, voice training and grooming. The end result is pleasantly impressive and a source of education and entertainment to the audiences, whose responses are encouraging. The significant financial awards continue to attract increasing numbers of entries, with a noticeable improvement in the quality of offerings. The programme also forms part of "Entertainment Report", a programme that has been one of the flagship offerings of Television Jamaica (TVJ) from the days when the station was known as the Jamaica Broadcasting Corporation.

In the past, a number of schools presented outstanding productions of Greek and other choral drama. Sophocles' *Oedipus Rex* was staged by Wolmer's Boys' School in 1960 and by St George's College in 1963. In 1962 St Hugh's High School presented Euripides' *Trojan Women* and provided thirty-three "Women of Canterbury" for the Greek chorus in T.S. Eliot's *Murder in the Cathedral*. Choruses, especially in the pantomime musical and in the productions of the Jamaica Amateur Operatic Society (renamed the Jamaica Musical Theatre Company, or JMTC), sometimes number up to fifty members. Poems have also been spoken to dance accompaniment, in the past by the Ivy Baxter Dance Group, and in more recent times by the National Dance Theatre Company. Because a tradition of choral performance has been established over the years, Greek and other choral drama can now be successfully produced. Participants get the opportunity to improve their creative talents, and on occasion some items have been published by the Festival Commission in print, audio, video or on the Internet in collaboration with private organizations.

Jamaica's independence from Britain in 1962 provided yet another opportunity for Jamaicans to organize a series of events over the several months leading up to Independence Day, designated as the first Monday in August (6 August in 1962). Each year educational institutions and scores of adult groups participate in a series of celebrations over the independence weekend. These events include street parades and costume queen parades which glamorize Jamaican life; street dancing; the best of folk and pop music; dialect verse; creative writing; arts and crafts; and culinary creations. Significant aspects of these activities afford massive numbers of people the opportunity to come together in villages and towns, to entertain and be entertained by each other. But perhaps the more lasting values of these activities lie in the training provided at the village and parish levels, and the development of artistic forms that continue to enrich the lives of thousands who otherwise would not have had the opportunity to showcase their talents and focus on the concept of nationhood.

Two events that attract special attention each year in Kingston are the "Mello Go Roun'", held either in the National Arena or at the Ranny Williams Centre for the Performing Arts, and the "Grand Gala", staged at the National Stadium. "Mello Go Roun'", at the beginning of the week leading up to Independence Day, highlights gold, silver and bronze medal-winning performances from around the island. There is no better way to describe these events than to quote one youngster conversing with his friend who did not make it into the National Stadium: "And it was perfect. I see everything. I ca'an explain, yuh have to come next year, den you will understand."[12]

Between Jamaica 300 in 1955, and 1976, when the second Caribbean Festival of the Arts (Carifesta '76) was organized, several events were mounted in the National

Stadium to mark special occasions, including the "Kingston 100 Grand Spectacular" (1972), a pageant with a cast of ten thousand to celebrate the centenary of the city of Kingston as the island's capital. Another grand pageant, titled "Jamaica Tribute" (1974), honoured Jamaica's national heroes in effigy, with a cast of fifteen thousand performers. This was originally prepared to honour President Julius Nyrere of Tanzania on his official visit to Jamaica in August, but was washed out by rain and later staged at the National Stadium on National Heroes' Day, 21 October 1974.

Hazel Bennett and participants in Kingston 100 making their props

Kingston 100 Grand Spectacular

Kingston 100: Grand Spectacular

Profile of a Production, 22 October 1972

MARINA MAXWELL

Kingston Born: four pools of light (North, South, East and West) discover children in flesh-coloured tights and leotards lying in foetal position. They move, yawn, stretch, get stronger and dance, symbolizing the birth of the City of Kingston. The four groups are connected by a large rope suggesting a massive umbilical cord which links them to the sea (choreographed by Alma Mock Yen).

"A plastic use of time and space is what I'm after", says producer and director Wycliffe Bennett, sitting in his office on the top floor at the National Stadium, surrounded by people coming and going, voices, telephones, walkie-talkies all abuzz . . . With the calmness of a born organizer and a dash of the mad magician mixing potions, he directs, with a sure sense of theatre; advises here, and with a quick eye overviews every detail happening. And still he has time to talk of the birth of what promises to be one hell of a show – the biggest event ever since 1937, when Father Daniel Lord staged Jamaica Triumphant at Winchester Park with four hundred performers. Here Kingston Spectacular presents ten thousand performers.

"There are several concepts I am attempting to synthesize in production," he says. "First is the Greek concept of Apollonian figures with Dionysiac support – the idea of heroes and followers, leading major characters and chorus. The superheroes are god-like, spiritual leaders here represented by the effigies of our National Heroes and Leaders of the Nation who appear in the proceedings. They include the five National Heroes (at the time) – George William Gordon, Paul Bogle, Marcus Garvey, Norman Washington Manley and Sir Alexander Bustamante – and current civic and political leaders: the governor general, Sir Clifford Campbell; the prime minister, the Honourable Michael Manley; leader of the opposition, the Right Honourable Hugh Shearer; and the mayor of the City of Kingston, Councillor Eli Matalon. The effigies are sculpted by Alvin Marriott, finished [in papier mache and painted] by Gordon Simpson. They are bigger-than-life figures in every sense as the leaders of the nation, and they are attended upon by the Chorus, one hundred strong, who enlarge the act orally by choral-speaking, music and mime . . . Secondly is the concept of the Roman Spectacular – the setting in the vast stadium lends itself to this – the Roman amphitheatre, arena-style."

"Mr Bennett," Fitz Weir's voice comes through the open office door, "These performers just arrived . . . but their rehearsal slot is for six o'clock this afternoon." Mr Weir is right-hand and left-hand man on loan from the Festival Office, a trooper in theatre and of pantomime fame who works mainly with the adult folk groups in the Spectacular. And a missing music-man follows Mr Weir. Wycliffe Bennett responds, "Master, would you please report here at eight o'clock? Arrange a room for him, so he doesn't have to leave here, somebody." (General laughter) . . . And then he continues on the Roman concept embodied in the Spectacular, having jollied along all the workers around to get on with business, pushing along thousands of people daily with the deft sense of humour, happy ponderosities and a dash of sarcasm which usually gets a laugh. "I want this done like yesterday" is his theme song.

"There is also the African concept of staging," he says. "According to the African way of staging, especially in dance theatre, a clearing out in the open is required – the open air stadium is perfect for this. I can use all levels of space not tied down in any way . . . so groups and figures can appear over there or here, or there or anywhere or come down from above or whatever is needed for dramatic spectacle. The show is conceived as a fast-moving spectacular which pays

*The text is taken from an unpublished press release prepared by Marina Maxwell for the Kingston 100 office. It conveys the amount of preparation, coordination and management required for this and other shows of its kind.

Kingston 100: Grand Spectacular (*cont'd*)

tribute [to] all the arts. Centrally, it is to give Jamaica and Kingston a sense of history and participation. It is a pageant of epic dimensions, evocative of the city's past and designed to stimulate pride and participation exemplified in the section 'Out of many, one people'" . . .

The "third group" (two hundred strong) in tribal robes (supported by forty musicians) represents an African element, and is being produced by John Akar, of Sierra Leone. Drummers, drummers, drummers in a tight circle at the LTM's rehearsal room. Black, green, gold and red, our Rastafari brethren, head-tied women backing them with beaded rattles, a crowd of downtowners in attendance, swaying to the sounds, one hundred dancers masked on stage. And at the centre of it all is Akar, moulding the item with his tensile hands and the lilt of Africa in his speech. Orchestrating the drums, he says: "We want to build, build, to slowly build . . . altogether it is just noise . . . so the big drums start first . . . dong . . . altogether here . . . then the Nyas follow . . . and you are the aristocrats of the drums . . . so you chat together, smile, nod, exchange . . . do you see? And the chac-chac . . ." He turns to the girl standing behind the drummers: "I want sh-shish, shish, shish, shish, not just shish, shish . . . you must vary the rhythms, see, but stay with the Nyas, stay with the Nya beat . . . OK? Now let's try again . . . Together the big drums . . . together . . . and smile, be joyful. In Africa we smile . . ."

And as the drums start, a film of the Sierra Leonese dancers (who used to be managed by Akar) comes up on a screen at stage left. Having worked from a tape of drumming before, Akar now synchronizes the various rhythms of the live drums and the film. And then the dancers come on, . . . knees bent, legs wide, arms up, head back and leap . . . leap . . . leap . . . forward . . .

Pulling a production together in the vastness of the stadium is no easy job. As Bennett points out, there will be twenty-four assistant stage managers. These will be in touch with each other by thirty-six two-way radios and with thirty-six army marshals for control and precision. The army under Lt Col Ken Barnes is providing an immense amount of help of all sorts. Apart from appearing in the show itself, the army will provide the guard of honour and are also giving invaluable aid during rehearsals.

Carter, the Caribbean's lighting expert and "magic-man", will create five performing areas with lights from ten towers, twelve to fifteen feet high, which from the office window seem to be growing out of the wide green.

"Magic is the aim," says Carter. Then again, magic is always Carter's aim, and he gets it every time. He has lighted every major show in Jamaica and down the Caribbean, and has been taking shows from Jamaica too, for longer than he wants to remember.

And the work goes on . . . Bennett adds: "Saturday the Set Girls (one hundred of them) rehearse; the Reds and the Blues costumed in detail according to Belisario's old Jamaica prints . . . Rehearsal at 4:00 pm today . . . Tivoli Gardens Drum Corps." And Sir Herbert Macdonald, former chairman of National Sports Limited, which controls the stadium, puts his head through the door and makes one of his characteristically humorous cracks. "As Comptroller of Kingston 100 he is a tower of strength," says Bennett. "The raising of money and the controlling of finances are his responsibility . . . As for Madge Parkin, the production secretary, I don't know how much sleep she gets. She is an admirable backstop to Sir Herbert and myself. Miss Lee Binns of the Festival Office helps to liaise with the various groups and to see that their costuming is under control . . ."

And Hazel Bennett is there, right-hand and left-hand woman, voluntarily helping however she can. "I'm just dog's body," she smiles, "fetch and carry and buy anything needed." But she's a lot more than that, really. The former deputy director of the Jamaica Library Service and librarian-in-charge of the School of Education Documentation Centre, University of the West Indies, she is now lecturer in the Department of Library Studies, which takes librarians to degree courses, and she had just brought in a complete piece of research she had just done on the history of theatre for an article to be written by Harry Milner for the Kingston 100 Celebration. Five minutes later she was off to check on the fire brigade, due in at six o'clock, and to pick up the paint needed, to see Harry Milner and to find a recording of Pomps and Pride . . . And there is Barry Davies with the blue-green Sunday morning hills behind him conducting a rehearsal of the 600-voice Kingston Centenary Choir.

Kingston 100: Grand Spectacular (*cont'd*)

"Alle, alle, alle . . ." the voices rise in the Negro spiritual which comes after the massed bands, the guard of honour and the floats depart . . . and the single spot pilots them. (Blackout!)

Then will come two hundred Excelsior school children making arabesques of light. This is being choreographed with supporting music and singing as a school project by Excelsior, and church bells will ring out . . .

"Mr Bennett, tell me about the high points of the show."

Mr Bennett: "It is difficult to talk of the high points of the show since there are no low points!" [Laughter] And the work goes on.

"It is a richly tapestried show," he says. "[The] culmination will be 'Let Kingston Dance' and 'City Life', including a Mock Trial, which has been a feature of Jamaican cultural life, particularly in the twenties, thirties and forties. Nine Night, Go-Go Girls, you name it." City Life! Coconut Carts, Candy Ladies, Marble Playing, Peanut Vendors, Stilt Walkers, Old Tramcar, Jonkonnu, Ring Games, Revival Meetings, Political Meetings, Buggy, Snowball Carts, Effigies of the National Heroes and Leaders: a telescopic picture of Kingston over the last one hundred years.

And finally there are the floats in the expert hands of Eric Coverley, who is busy at the National Stadium constructing, advising and helping to create the rich pageantry of a century. Fireworks will lift the production to the night sky and to the blue-black evening mountains. Kingston 100 Spectacular promises to be spectacular indeed.

Carifesta '76

The second Caribbean Festival of the Arts was hosted by Jamaica from 23 July to 1 August 1976. Its aims and objectives were several: to expose peoples of the Caribbean region to each other's culture through creative activity, thus deepening their understanding of the native aspirations of the region; to forge closer relations in the region through cultural participation; to demonstrate the importance of the arts as a unifying force in building a wholesome society; and to develop the content of our regional culture as well as its aesthetic forms. It embraced the fine and plastic arts, literature, crafts, photography, and culinary events, and ultimately boosted the festival movement by exposing participants and the general public to the cream of artistic endeavour from various parts of the region.

Carifesta was originally perceived as a mobile, cultural, regional exposition, taking place every three years in a different English-, Spanish-, French- or Dutch-speaking territory. The twenty-eight countries which had participated in the festival in Guyana in 1972 included the twelve English-speaking islands and Guyana, the Bahamas, the French Islands, the Netherlands Antilles, Cuba, Haiti, the Dominican Republic, Puerto Rico and the US Virgin Islands, as well as a number of mainland territories, including Brazil. To regularize participation, Carifesta '76 sought, in proper geographical terms, to embrace all the islands of the great archipelago from the Bahamas down to Trinidad and Tobago, and from Miami right down to Brazil and all the coastal states of the two continents washed by the waters of the Caribbean and its extension, the Gulf of Mexico.

Cover of the souvenir programme, Carifesta '76

Brazil had sent some Yoruba items from northern Brazil to Guyana in 1972 but the government of the day did not encourage the local Carifesta office to follow up. Overtures were made to New Orleans in the US state of Louisiana, because of the strong historical ties that city has had with some Caribbean territories (especially Haiti), and also to El Salvador, although that Central American country does not have a Caribbean shore.

Preparation for Carifesta '76 began in the knowledge that one such festival had already been held in 1972, and that the Commonwealth Heads of Government had decided to institutionalize Carifesta as an ongoing mobile, cultural exposition. It still remained necessary, however, to find something that would help give the movement resonance, especially in the non-English-speaking countries, and help mobilize artists and politicians, whose enthusiasm and support would prove indispensable. The organizers of Carifesta '76 could, of course, rely on Guyana, Trinidad and Barbados, among those lands united by the English language, but felt that the Carifesta Organization would be lacking credibility, if across the region they could not count on support from Mexico, Venezuela, Cuba and Haiti. Relying on the universal origins of festival and of the theatre, they appealed to each nation's sense of hero worship and decided that Carifesta '76 would honour five national heroes: Toussaint L'Ouverture of Haiti, Simón Bolívar of Venezuela, Benito Juárez of Mexico, José Martí of Cuba and Marcus Garvey of Jamaica. It proved virtually impossible for any country whose national hero was being honoured to refuse to participate. But there were some problems, and one brief story here should illuminate the point.

The Jamaican ambassador and the director general of Carifesta had been having intensive discussions with the secretary of state for tourism and culture on possible Mexican participation, but neither of them could get the secretary to make a commitment. On a second visit, the director general was accompanied by his wife, who, after listening to the conversation for about ten minutes, interrupted: "Sir, I find it strange that we in Jamaica should be organizing a festival in honour of your National Hero Benito Juárez, while Mexico remains indifferent." The secretary quickly took the point and, by the time Bennett had returned to his hotel, the secretary was on the phone to say that he had spoken to the president, and that Mexico would participate with a large contingent. Such is one instance of the power of hero worship.

An *ad hoc* organization was set up within the Office of the Prime Minister, which was responsible for art and culture. This special core organization was to tackle the undertaking within the incredibly short period of eighteen months and, to this end, liaise and interface, for example, with the Jamaica Festival Commission, the Jamaica Tourist Board, the Agency for Public Information, the Jamaica Defence Force, the Jamaica Constabulary Force, the Ministry of External Affairs and other government and non-government agencies, where appropriate. The core organization had a dual structure, consisting of the advisory/steering committee and the Carifesta Organization.

As chairman and director general, Bennett presided over the advisory/steering committee and headed the Carifesta Organization. The committee was advisory to the prime minister and his parliamentary secretary. It consisted, firstly, of a panel of chairmen for the several subject areas. These chairmen then selected and assembled their

HIGHLIGHTS OF CARIFESTA '76 GRAND GALA

HIGHLIGHTS OF CARIFESTA '76 GRAND GALA

Carifesta '76 photographs courtesy of Catherine Gray-Sosa

own panel members. When the organization was fully developed, there were some twelve full- and part-time directors who were responsible for specific subjects and reported to the chairman and director general, who was in turn responsible to the prime minister. Directors and other senior staffers of the Carifesta Organization became part of a two-tiered directorate: they served as resource members of the committee and as executives on a parallel management team, which coordinated the activities of the Carifesta Organization.

The committee was broadly based. Membership drew upon government ministries and agencies as well as upon individuals who had given outstanding service in relevant fields. Of strategic importance was the fact that the organization was located in the Office of the Prime Minister. Such a position provided the necessary leverage, and the required clout, which was always there but lightly used.

There were sundry other persons recruited on a more or less *ad hoc* basis. Even so, to give only the names of the advisory/steering committee and the Carifesta Organization is to tell but half the story. There were some thirty-four Carifesta sites across the nation, which required varying degrees of preparation: some had to be created; all had to be manned. They required front-of-house and stage management, as well as scene, lighting and sound technicians. The Jamaica Festival Commission built a number of new open-air stages in the parishes and shared responsibility for the operations out of Kingston, but additional trained production personnel still had to be found. Fortunately, the problem was anticipated in good time, and a rigorous training programme was introduced before the festival began. Over two hundred young men and women underwent training over a short period of time, culminating in a final six-week stint leading up to the opening of Carifesta.

Oswald Williams, "Count Ossie", drummer at Carifesta '76.
Courtesy of Catherine Gray-Sosa.

The internal liaison machinery operated through the subject area panels of the committee, on which served sufficiently senior officers who could speak for their respective ministries or agencies. It was of critical importance, therefore, that all the relevant agencies be involved from the very beginning, and be enabled to make their particular inputs from the planning stage.

Also, pre-emptive steps had to be taken to ensure that adequate accommodation would be available for overseas participants at places like the University of the West Indies, Mona campus, and at the Mico Teachers' College and elsewhere, which are often used for sundry other purposes during the summer vacation. Events like the Carifesta gala, which were based on mass participation, were protected by having the ministries of education and youth alert schools, clubs and parents, in good time, about the programme for the summer holidays. The Jamaica Tourist Board incorporated Carifesta '76 into its overseas advertising.

Contact with the countries of the region was established at a number of levels and in a number of ways. First, an official communication went out to all eligible countries. The letter went through ambassadors – high commissioners and consuls-general, where appropriate, but otherwise directly to the ministers or other officials responsible for culture. In addition to advising the various national governments of Jamaica's plans, the letter served as official notification that suitable representatives from their respective countries would be invited to take part in the Jamaica programme. In accordance with international practice, Jamaica would assume responsibility for accommodation, meals and transportation within the island, for the purposes of the programme and its presentation. Expenses for transportation to and from Jamaica would be borne by participating countries.

The chairman and director general made a special effort to visit what he regarded as the core countries – Guyana, Barbados and Trinidad, among the English-speaking lands – and the countries of the four non-Jamaican heroes: Mexico, Venezuela, Cuba and Haiti. He also went to Suriname, Curaçao and Panama, but because of financial constraints neither he nor any other Carifesta officials toured the remaining countries of Central America.

Four other officials completed the other tours that had to be undertaken. Ancile Gloudon, director of the Carifesta Grand Market went to nearly all the remaining English-, French-, Spanish- and Dutch-speaking islands, and to Colombia. He promoted the entire programme, but paid special attention to the needs of the Carifesta Grand Market. Yvonne Brewster went to assess the quality of the theatrical offerings being prepared by some countries, and to determine what was the most suitable Jamaican setting available for each of those productions. The late Neville Dawes attended a meeting in Guyana with poet and publisher A.J. Seymour to discuss the Carifesta publications. Frank Pilgrim, whose expenses were subsidized by UNESCO, visited CARICOM countries, especially the less-developed nations. His mission, like Ancile Gloudon's, was to urge them to participate, and to advise them of possible funding from UNESCO to assist them in coming to Jamaica.

Yvonne Brewster

Thus, in a real sense, Carifesta '76 became a regional showcase, providing a vehicle for the expression of regional identity, ethnic heritage and native aspirations. The hosts could not interfere artistically with contributions submitted for the programme, but could, and did, diplomatically decline acceptance on grounds of poor quality, programme requirements, etc. when necessary. Submissions in the field of theatre arts, in most cases, had to be seen, appraised and specifically invited. For Carifesta officials, it was important that participating countries recognize that international festivals were organized in this way, that international standards had to be achieved and maintained, and, moreover, that each sponsoring country would in turn exercise similar privileges and responsibilities.

Officials also emphasized that, since Carifesta was a regional festival, all entries had to be of regional origin; that is, there could be no Shakespeare, no Lope de Vega, no Beethoven, no Mozart, however wonderful the works of such artists were. A newspaper in Port of Spain front-paged the story "Carifesta Chief Bans Shakespeare", but, despite the high-profile headline, no one in that country or elsewhere seemed bothered by such omissions from the fare.

The Carifesta programme consisted of different amalgams of native Jamaican offerings and contributions from other Caribbean nations overseas. The official opening at the National Stadium in Kingston commenced with the national anthems of Guyana (host of the previous Carifesta) and Jamaica, followed by the unfurling of flags of participating countries and a salute in song to the five Caribbean heroes by eight thousand boys and girls, accompanied by massed bands. The presentation of the leaders of the delegations from the participating countries, and a welcome of visitors to Jamaica, also followed. The following day, the prime minister of Jamaica and several ambassadors of other countries addressed a mass rally under the theme "Culture for the Liberation of Our Peoples".

The Carifesta Grand Market was, in the first place, a market, in which participating countries offered representative items from their respective countries for sale, such as toys, keepsakes, fabric, silver artefacts, paintings, carvings and other craft ware. Inside the arena the Market was surrounded by a theatrical area with a stage and seating. Three shows were presented daily, consisting of feature-length programmes from specific countries or a miscellany of music, folklore, storytelling and folk dances from one country or several. Two large tents outside the National Arena featured the culinary arts of the Caribbean.

A film festival held at the State Theatre aimed at illustrating the development of cinematic art in the Caribbean and Latin American region under the theme "The Human Condition". On Sunday, 1 August, the Carifesta Song Festival featured popular singers of the region competing in new musical selections in English, Spanish, French and Dutch. Fine arts exhibitions showcased paintings, sculpture, graphics and ceramics of the region, as well as a comprehensive collection from Guyana. Music, folk, traditional and modern dance and theatrical presentations were held throughout the week at several venues in Kingston, May Pen and Montego Bay.

Seminars, symposia and workshops on the state of the arts, literature, film and the like in the region were organized. Float parades opened and closed the festival. The floats featured events in Caribbean and Latin American history, and the flora and fauna of the region. The grand finale, dubbed the Carifesta Gala, brought the week-long event to a close.

The Legacy of Carifesta '76

No one will ever be able to pay sufficient tribute to, or assess the contributions of, the vast army of volunteer workers – performers and organizers alike – who gave of their time and energies in the service of the arts for Carifesta '76. They ranged from the dozens of persons who made up the panels of the advisory/steering committee, the Jamaica Festival Commission and the parish festival committees; to the panels of the other subject groups and the teachers and social welfare officers island-wide; to the thousands of Jamaicans of all ages who participated in the Jamaica Festival and in other local events; and to the twenty-five thousand more who performed in the Carifesta gala. It was these people who, in their special ways, became surrogates and hosted Carifesta '76 on behalf of the government and people of Jamaica.

Every child who spoke a poem, everyone who sang or took part in a play, hosted Carifesta. In a word, the whole country had been mobilized. Thirty-two years later, the magic of Carifesta still resonates throughout Jamaican society. There is no part of the island where Wycliffe Bennett has travelled in which one or more persons do not come forward to greet him and declare that they took part in Carifesta. The latest occasion was on 14 February 2008, when Bennett, on his way to the bank, was stopped by a woman who proudly announced that she had not seen him in a very long time. On further enquiry, she explained that she had taken part in Carifesta as a child. After thirty-two years, that special bond still existed. Even today, the enduring legacy of Carifesta '76 is evident, as the following extracts from local authors' accounts of the celebrations show.

People of the Sun in All Their Glory

The Carifesta Grand Gala

JEAN LOWRIE-CHIN

Wycliffe Bennett captured the theme of Carifesta '76 in his Carifesta gala, a heart-stirring presentation of music, dance and movement on the field of the National Stadium, featuring twenty-five thousand participants. In a meeting held to discuss the event, as Wycliffe Bennett described his ambitious plan, someone commented that it could not be done. Mr B. turned to her and said, "My dear, you will always be a bystander at life's passing parade." He then proceeded, meticulous in every detail, brilliantly matching talent to task and harmonizing the whole with his unique blend of charm and tenacity.

Rehearsals at the National Stadium were near magical. How else could one explain twenty-five thousand school children of all ages, along with adults, pouring energetically through the tunnels and other specially created entrances onto the field, and then finding their places on that vast expanse of green within minutes? Then, to the beat of Mortimo Plano's Rastafarian drummers, they grouped themselves to represent the ethnic origins and historical milestones of the Caribbean, against the majestic backdrop of the mountains, performing brilliant dances and rousing songs directed by choreographers and musicians on the field. The costumes on the backs of the participants provided the setting, and each performer was his own prop, enriching the scenery.

Described as "a charming bully", Wycliffe Bennett's voice boomed from the stands during rehearsals and echoed back to [the performers] from the Beverly Hills range rising in the background. And so, while the drums beat and the participants danced and sang, the mountains echoed, "You are beautiful . . . beautiful . . . beautiful! I love you . . . love you . . . love you!"

Lush productions like this, his television production of Macbeth and several others led his admirers to describe him as "the Cecil B. de Mille of the Caribbean". Like the Hollywood director, he brought a richness and glamour to the field of the National Stadium which had never before been witnessed in the history of our cultural offerings. I can remember the twinkle in Prime Minister Michael Manley's eyes as Mr B. enthused at a Jamaica House meeting, "Mr Prime Minister, the stadium will be an amphitheatre embraced by the mountains, as if placed there by a prescient deity, under the canopy of the open sky."

His vision inspired and energized his overworked team, [who strove] to pack what should have been months of planning and rehearsals into weeks. One evening, the Aztec group arrived at about 2:00 p.m. but were encouraged to wait, because rehearsal was taking longer than expected. It was not until 10:00 p.m. that the group of one thousand strong were called onto the field, and every single one had remained; such was the level of their enthusiasm.

On the two days of the Carifesta Grand Gala, a panoply of dancers, singers and musicians movingly told the story of the Caribbean. One group brought to life a sugar plantation, another the Caribbean Sea, yet another the conquistadors arriving from Spain, oil workers with rigs and mobile books with names of such famous Caribbean authors as Sir Philip Sherlock, Claude McKay, Derek Walcott, George Lamming and Nicolas Guillén.

For the gala, heroes of the region were identified and honoured in a marching song, "Forward, Forever United", in English, Spanish and French. The strong voices of our children recounted the exploits of Haitian liberator Toussaint L'Ouverture, Venezuelan hero Simón Bolívar, Mexican hero Benito Juárez, Cuban poet and philosopher José Martí, and Jamaica's own Marcus Mosiah Garvey. As Wycliffe Bennett

---

Jean Lowrie-Chin was a member of the Carifesta '76 organization. This is her account of the rehearsal and performance of *People of the Sun in All Their Glory* at the Carifesta Grand Gala.

People of the Sun in All Their Glory (*cont'd*)

Wycliffe Bennett standing at podium directing the Carifesta '76 Grand Gala

explained, "These five men fought for freedom of the peoples of the region . . . they taught us to look to ourselves and not to external forces for strength and direction. They taught us to be proud of our heritage and to develop our indigenous art and culture."

It would have been enough of an achievement to stage a show like this once, but the Carifesta gala was held on two consecutive days, culminating on the day celebrating Jamaica's independence, 2 August 1976.

Choreographers led by Eddy Thomas, Joyce Campbell, and Dorothy Fraser; designers including Richard and Sally Montgomery; architect Pat Stanigar, who designed the ten thousand Aztec costumes; [and] Judith Salmon, Emma Crooks and Lee Binns, a technical team directed by George Carter, synergized their skills for a polished production.

Musical director Ouida Hilton-Tomlinson (now Dunphy), [and] musicians Olive Lewin and Lloyd Hall made their unique mark. The voice of popular Cuban singer Farah Maria rang out in the National Stadium, singing the original version of "Guantanamera" by a national hero of her country, José Martí.

The Jamaican media were on hand to cover this exciting event, taking live broadcasts to the entire nation, resulting in rave reviews from a dazzled and appreciative public. Once again Wycliffe Bennett had demonstrated his flair and genius for the grandest of theatrical presentations. In the thirty-two years since, Jamaica has not seen any production of this proportion and excellence, and those of us who were privileged to play a part still hear Wycliffe Bennett's voice echoing from the mountains, "Beautiful . . . beautiful . . . beautiful." Indeed it was.

Wycliffe Bennett and the Carifesta Grand Gala

YVONNE BREWSTER

Wycliffe Bennett, chairman of Carifesta '76, suggested Yvonne help him with the drama programme, which included the ambitious Gala. Better say what Carifesta is. In 1972 when Forbes Burnham was the all-powerful prime minister in Guyana he instigated the first Carifesta. Simply, it was an opportunity for the people of the West Indies to learn more about each other by coming together to share their art. Great Idea. She's often in the right place at the right time, my daughter, as this job turned out to be a delicious adventure.

First of all, she was to travel around the West Indies evaluating the various plays up for inclusion in the festival. This meant visiting many of the participating twenty-three nation states. What an opportunity to see the countries of the Caribbean, not only the British West Indies but the Dutch, the American, the French and the Spanish as well. I encouraged her like mad not to miss this opportunity. Often Jamaicans prefer to go to desultory Miami rather than explore other Caribbean islands. Talk about "Great Britain" mentality – this is the itsy bitsy Island mentality.

She came back with so many tales we called her Dr Livingstone for a while. Some stand the test of time. For instance, in Trinidad after being kept waiting in a dusty, hot room in an even dustier museum, when he finally showed up a Mr Alladin told her that, "Yes. The Republic of Trinidad and Tobago will be sending something, but what right do you, a nonentity from Jamaica, have to stand in judgement on work from Trinidad, the centre of all Caribbean creativity?"

Island pride has been handed down to us. This myopia is responsible for the continuing economic stagnation of the Caribbean. It aborted the Confederation of the West Indies and will continue to keep it fractured. Sensing the need for diplomacy, she played the "I am very honoured to be insulted by you" card . . . She was at least then told what play they intended to take to the Festival, which, as it happens, was (St Lucian) Derek Walcott's *O Babylon!*

"Isn't that about Jamaican Rastafarians?" [Yvonne asked.]

"Yes. So?"

"Do you think this might prove difficult in Jamaica?"

"No."

"Rastas with Trinidad accents is very creative and forward-looking, but I suspect the audience may not be quite ready for that yet."

"Too bad! Good day."

It was too bad. The whole exercise was doomed from the outset. The cast and crew of Trinnies arrived with Derek Walcott in his playwright mode . . . After her first-ever encounter with the great man she was devastated . . .

The play itself was wonderful. However, as had been feared, the audience regarded Rastas with Trinidad accents as travesties and there was no way round their often quite vocal opposition to what they regarded as ridiculous. The more sophisticated among you might pooh pooh this as backward and insular. I know in England nowadays it doesn't matter what you look like, you can play most parts, but I believe even there you are expected to sound right. Here in Jamaica in 1976 there was a lot of nationalistic angst, and not too many people showed up. Derek Walcott was absolutely furious and let it be known. However, apart from kidnapping people off the street there was nothing to be done.

The highlight of Carifesta for me was the Carifesta Gala. This man called Wycliffe Bennett I had always found a little pompous and patronizing, but after his success with managing Carifesta as a whole and the gala in particular I can forgive him for anything. It was his larger-than-life approach to life which allowed his special brand of creativity to flourish in this arena. He had a plan which lesser men could not

*Excerpted from Yvonne Brewster, *The Undertaker's Daughter* (London: Black Amber Books, 2004)

Wycliffe Bennett and the Carifesta Grand Gala (*cont'd*)

even imagine, much less deliver. Many of these timid souls thought the idea of staging a pageant with thirty thousand people in the large National Stadium was "foolishness, you know, one of Wycliffe's over the top grandiose ideas. No way that can work, man."

They were wrong. The Gala was dedicated to the Heroes of the Caribbean. I remember noting at the time that they were all men, but that was par for the course then. Bit better now. Enormous papier-mâché effigies of Toussaint L'Ouverture, Simón Bolívar, Benito Juárez, José Julián Martí and Marcus Mosiah Garvey paraded round the Stadium to excited cheers. The ranks of police, soldiers, school children, cadets, nurses, voluntary organization workers, dancers, singers, athletes and flag wavers, all 25,000 of them singing, parading, performing to an overflowing audience including numerous Heads of State, were disciplined and entertaining.

A particularly high point was the phalanx of [200] Rastafarian drummers who entered the stadium and silenced the tongue so the heart could feel. Good. And of course the sight of beloved Jimmy Cliff as a lone figure dressed in white singing "Many Rivers to Cross" brought tears even to my cynical eye. Whew. Never seen anything of this sort in Jamaica before or since! We couldn't do it now.

Yvonne was enjoying her job in charge of Theatre for Carifesta but she really grew in confidence as Wycliffe's assistant for the Gala. This meant her assisting him with the non-stop rehearsals in the broiling sun. "All you have to do is follow my lead and love the participants." Wycliffe had a phrase which he used to calm the ruffled feathers when the sun was too hot or the standing too long: "*Cool breeze.* Let me hear you all say *Cooooool breeeeeez[e].* It worked every time."

On the day of the Gala when the dignitaries all showed up in force Wycliffe turned to Yvonne in the control box and said, "There's Michael Manley, I must go and meet him. It's all yours." She was on her own to "call" this mammoth show with over [25,000] participants and a similar number of spectators. But she had been well trained by Wycliffe and the affair went off without a hitch. *Cool breeze.* Simply wonderful to see so many Jamaicans in one place without rancour, without gun shot, with talent, with love, just existing for a couple of hours of excellence.

The Carifesta Grand Gala

"The Greatest Show Ever Staged in the Caribbean"

LORNA GOODISON

"*Cool breeze*", he'd say and those words would waft across the field of the National Stadium to be sung back to him by the thousands of school children and adults rehearsing for what was going to be the greatest show, if not on earth, certainly the greatest show ever staged in the Caribbean.

For those of us who had signed up to help him produce Carifesta '76, working with Wycliffe Bennett was an experience we would never forget. The man was indefatigable. He thrived on long, intense working hours, and far from being exhausted at the end of the day he would move into high gear at night, chairing long, complicated planning meetings for the highlight of the entire festival, the Carifesta Gala. He chaired these gala meetings with much style and panache, and complete disregard for our lack of vision.

So he'd say to George Carter, Merrick Needham and Jean Lowrie-Chin, his tireless directors, "What we will have are many mass choirs, orchestras, marching bands, mento bands, Jonkonnu bands and thousands and thousands of school children and community groups, effigies, floats, parades by the police and the military, helicopters and fleets of cars, dancers, fireworks . . . " [T]he list is endless.

Try as they might to suggest to him that some things were really impossible to purchase (no foreign exchange), to find (did not exist), to assemble (would require manual labour), to transport to the national stadium (too high to pass through the Marathon Tunnel) he would just smile, light a cigarette and say, "*Cool breeze*". After a while it became clear that it was pointless to say no to Wycliffe Bennett. No matter what anyone said, he was going to stage the greatest show on earth . . .

As a member of the Carifesta team, I came to the conclusion that Wycliffe somehow managed to combine the skills of a powerful military leader and a kindly traffic policeman during those rehearsals. He employed a combination of hard-nosed discipline and wry humour as he marshalled his troop of performers.

Finally the great day arrived; and in the intervening years I have heard many Jamaicans say that on that Saturday afternoon in August 1976 they were proud to be part of what was perhaps the single most heart-stirring event ever seen in Jamaica. Wycliffe's greatest show was just that.

From the opening moments, when the Taino people and the Native peoples from all over the region filled the stadium, . . . our history began to unfold: Columbus and the Spaniards came, the English landed and Mortimo Plano in Royal robes led a band of Africans down the Marathon Tunnel and by then some people were openly weeping. And the Chinese danced a brilliant dragon dance and the East Indians their Hosay, and for the first time in our lives many of us could see that maybe our national motto, "Out of many, one people" was really true. The mass choirs and the bands made joyous music, and the artists, dancers, actors, singers and players of instruments were all there – *The People of the Sun in All Their Glory*, flawlessly directed by Wycliffe.

For those magical hours, every one of us wondered again and again how we could ever have doubted that he could have pulled this off, this stunning, brilliant, uplifting, successful grand gala. Truly, the greatest show ever seen by us: a show that would have made even Cecil B. de Mille proud. "*Cool breeze*", said Wycliffe.

16

Voice and Speech and the Jamaican Scene

The spread of speech training helped considerably to cement the British connection in Jamaica. The British theatre is based primarily upon an aural tradition, but the Jamaican pioneers did not necessarily have the theatre in mind. They saw their task as mainly concerned with removing social and economic barriers, and felt that the practice of "good" (standard) speech was one of the tools for raising social status within the society.

Fortunately, there were models whom the masses accepted without any feeling of inferiority, as, for example, the brilliant polemicist and debater, Dr Robert Love, a black medical doctor originally from the Bahamas who had been elected to the Legislative Council over a white colonial in 1906. There was also Marcus Garvey, who gained popularity through his rhetoric and elocution contests.

During the first decades of the twentieth century, debating societies were organized in villages and towns across the island and debating competitions were a regular feature of community life in places like Port Antonio, Buff Bay, Hope Bay, Swift River in Portland and Port Maria in St Mary. The Jesuit fathers stimulated an interest in debating, elocution and dramatics by their exemplary work at St George's College, a boys' school in Kingston, and the school's annual elocution contests and productions received enthusiastic support from the general public.

Marcus Garvey

J.J. Mills gives us this interesting anecdote about Marcus Garvey the elocutionist:

> I first saw Marcus Garvey in 1910 at an all-island Elocution Contest organized by Mr T.S. Phillips of the *Jamaica Times* [newspaper] and held at the Collegiate Hall in Church Street, Kingston.
>
> Each parish was represented by one reciter [*sic*], who had to give two selections of his own choice. Garvey then lived in St Ann where he was an apprentice printer. He

> seemed then, in [his] late teens or early manhood. His voice, highly pitched, had a complaining ring, but also commanded a wide speaking range. His gait was a little simple.
>
> Garvey chose a poem of vigour and action for his first "number". The audience learnt later that he had been placed first in that effort. His second rendition was the well-known extract from Lord Chatham's speech in the House of Lords, thundering against the evils of the War of Independence. Garvey's rendition, though convincing, provoked smiles and tittering, because of his sometimes squeaking voice. At last, a member of the audience sitting near the front interrupted loudly with a humorous remark. This caused loud laughter, which noticeably affected Garvey's performance, for he was eventually placed third. An echo of this was heard weeks later in the Law Courts.
>
> The man who so rudely interrupted was tried and found guilty of maliciously contriving to deprive Garvey of his chances of winning total championship of the Contest.[1]

Marcus Garvey

Garvey could personally attest to the benefits he had derived from an early interest in elocution. The log at the Ward Theatre records that he organized an "Elocution and Literary Evening" there in 1912. Soon after that, he founded the Universal Negro Improvement Association (UNIA), whose programmes included literature, elocution, drama and music among its cultural activities.

Garvey left the island in 1916 and had a phenomenal though turbulent career in Central America and the United States. By 1919 Garvey claimed that he had two million members in his UNIA, whose declared purpose was to unite "all the Negro peoples of the world into one great body; to establish a country and government absolutely their own". Garvey ran afoul of the American Government, was eventually charged with mail fraud and, after serving a prison term, was deported back to his native Jamaica in 1927.

He did not return in disgrace, however. He was widely acclaimed as the prophet of black redemption. He was primarily a social worker, politician and reformer cast in a messianic mould, but his efforts to take the arts to the masses are significant. He went on to achieve international renown as an orator, so much so that when England declared war on Germany in 1939, and Hitler addressed the German people, a section of the British press reported that the Führer had made a speech that only Marcus Garvey could have rivalled in impact and power.

Archie Lindo, poet, playwright and broadcaster

In 1929 Edelweiss Park, in Kingston, was purchased and became the headquarters of Garvey's world movement, the UNIA. Garvey himself went on to found the People's Political Party to contest seats in the Jamaican Legislature to ensure that the masses were represented. Although his party was defeated, two of the fourteen planks of the UNIA Manifesto (1929) deserve mention: to establish a Jamaican university and polytechnic, and a national opera house.

Mills's account of Garvey's conduct of affairs at Edelweiss Park is substantiated by several persons who performed there. Archie Lindo, poet, playwright and broadcaster, recalls competing in elocution contests with E.M. Cupidon and Una Marson. Ranny Williams and Lee Gordon, folklorists, scenario writers and two of Jamaica's foremost comedians, have spoken and written of the opportunities these contests provided them. During the early 1930s, Edelweiss Park became a veritable nursery for talent in the performing arts. Between 1929 and 1932, Garvey himself wrote, directed and produced a number of didactic dramas, including: *Roaming Around*, *Slavery:*

From Hut to Mansion, *The Coronation of an African King*, and *Wine, Women and War*.

During the early 1920s and after, annual elocution contests and plays organized by the Jesuits at St George's College received enthusiastic and sometimes controversial support from the general public. In commenting on a controversy in the press some forty years later, Vere Johns, who did not attend St George's, said that he was not really dipping into the argument as to the value of the annual speech festival, but noted that, in his day, those kinds of competitions were called elocution contests, and that he had "organized and won the first one held in Jamaica way back in the respectable Twenties – won it too with *Edinburgh after Flodden*". His contemporaries – Harold Brownlow, Eustace Bird, Una Marson and Douglas Judah – were all distinguished elocutionists. The contests referred to by Johns were sponsored by the Poetry League of Jamaica in 1927 and 1928.

Vere Johns, actor, elocutionist, journalist

Elocution and Musical Contests of the 1920s and 1930s

The 1920s witnessed further competitions in the performing arts after the founding of three other organizations: the Poetry League, in 1923 by J.E. Clare McFarlane; the Musical Society of Jamaica, by Grace Isaacs in 1926; and the Kingston and St Andrew Literary and Debating Society in 1929, with J.E. Clare McFarlane also as chairman. In collaboration with the Poetry League, the Kingston and St Andrew Literary and Debating Society continued to promote elocution contests. Vere Johns and Una Marson, also members of the Poetry League, had organized the two elocution contests for adults in 1927 and 1928. Then, in 1934, Philip N. Blake introduced a more broadly based contest when he staged the first championships in which both children and adults could participate. He set up four divisions: one for elementary schools, one for secondary schools, one for men and one for women.

Both the elocution and musical competitions demanded high standards of contestants and adjudicators alike. In the case of music, adjudicators were brought from England for the judging of finalists. In spite of their claims at being all-island, these contests were largely confined to Kingston, with the exception of a few brave souls from some rural communities who dared to enter the competitions in the city.

J.E. Clare McFarlane set forth as one of the Jamaica Poetry League's aims the creation of a conscience for ideal beauty in the community. The league tried to give practical expression to this ideal in a number of ways by organizing lectures, literary competitions and radio programmes. At poetry evenings and outings, authors and popular elocutionists like Una Marson, Archie Lindo and Catherine McNair would either read or recite poetry; and, largely spearheaded by Vere Johns and Una Marson, the league promoted elocution contests for adults with a view to developing the art of public speaking.

A black Jamaican, Philip N. Blake was himself an excellent speaker. Wycliffe Bennett recalls his own student days during the early 1930s at Central Branch Elementary, when Blake would visit his school, recite poems and dramatic selections, and urge students to take part in the contests. In 1929 the Musical Society of Jamaica inaugurated the Musical Competition Festival of Jamaica, which was held at approximately biennial intervals; and, for the very good reason that the voice is the oldest musical instrument, the organizers established a section for verse speaking.

When Blake moved over to the Poetry League in 1935, A.E.T. Henry became general secretary of the Literary and Debating Society, and G.S.A. Smith assumed responsibility for the contest. The Literary and Debating Society also staged mock trials, which may have been an unconscious importation from England that had taken root in the Jamaican society. Mock trials exploited Jamaicans' penchant for litigation and provided an important part of the island's theatrical fare during the late 1920s and subsequently. Some of the participants were among the finest players ever to have stepped onto our boards, and most of them were outstanding elocutionists.

H.A. Val Cotterel, a well-known debater and exponent of the mock trial, became president of the Literary and Debating Society in 1936. Two years later, the society was reorganized to include theatre, for which George Bowen became the officer mainly responsible, and the fine arts, of which Theodore Sealy was the prime mover. At the same time, the society was renamed the Jamaica Arts Society, and C.G.X. Henriques (later Sir Cyril) was elected president.

Henriques was born in 1908. After graduating from St George's College, he attended London University and went on to qualify as a barrister-at-law. He became a member of the London University Dramatic Society and played many Shakespearean roles. In 1934 he won an open scholarship in elocution to study at the London School of Dramatic Art.

As president of the Jamaica Arts society, Henriques headed an executive committee consisting of men who were to become very influential in the literary, journalistic, educational, cultural, theatrical and artistic life of the island. Thus, in addition to the biennial operations of the music festival, by the late 1930s there were two separate bodies, each sponsoring an annual all-Jamaica elocution contest. One was the Poetry League of Jamaica and the other the Jamaica Arts Society. Stephen O.D. Hill, who was to distinguish himself as Hamlet in 1944, won both championships in 1935.

In addition to the retired champions, the adjudicators included several outstanding Jamaicans: N.W. Manley, a brilliant advocate who later became premier of Jamaica and a national hero; Canon P.W. Gibson, founder and headmaster of Kingston College, later Lord Bishop of Jamaica; Philip Sherlock, secretary of the Institute of Jamaica, later Sir Philip Sherlock and vice-chancellor of the University of the West Indies; and J.J. Mills, vice-principal of the Mico Training College for Teachers.

Five ladies highly trained in speech and drama – one Jamaican, three British and one American – exercised a salutary influence upon developments. In 1935, Ena Marshalleck returned home from London with a teacher's diploma in speech and dramatic art from the Royal Academy of Music, and, for the next thirty-six years, taught, adjudicated, acted, and poured her heart and her energies into giving recitals in verse and dramatic selections. During the War years (1939–45), Joan Grant, Elinor Lithgow and Molly Ward Johnson, all from England, settled in Jamaica. Professionally trained, they were highly productive during their sojourn on the island. By 1951 they had all returned to England but they left significant skills with the persons they had trained. They were to become leading lights in the march forward in training and production in voice, speech and drama.

The American Doris Mitchell, of the New York stage, also made an invaluable contribution by helping to raise the level of production among drama groups such as the Caribbean Thespians and the Repertory Players in Kingston. Her work as a producer and director for radio and stage had exemplary professional polish. She directed for the ZQI Players and the Theatre Arts Club, and served as an adjudicator for the Adult Drama Festival. She married a Jamaican, Howard Hastings, and died in Jamaica in 1962.

The Poetry League

The outbreak of the Second World War brought cultural activities to a grinding halt, but people eventually began to pull their lives together, and in 1942 a number of organizations pooled efforts to revive the annual All-Island Elocution Contest. The revival was spearheaded by the Central Branch Old Students' Association, along with the Poetry League of Jamaica and the Jamaica Arts Society. By 1950 the movement had become known as the All-Island Speech Festival, and since neither the Arts Society nor the Central Branch Old Students' Association was still active, the Poetry League became the sole sponsor of the speech festival. Wycliffe Bennett became secretary in 1943 and succeeded to the chairmanship of a greatly expanded organization in 1959, with Dorothy Blondel Francis as vice-chairperson and Greta Lyons as another very active member of the committee. Bennett remained chairman until 1963 when he left the island to further his studies at Yale University. Once the National Festival was firmly established in 1963, however, the speech festival activities were handed over to this new organization. Twenty years provided these key figures with ample opportunity to develop the philosophical basis of the movement, and to put it on a proper island-wide footing, but the foundations had already been well and truly laid before the Second World War.

C.G.X. Henriques, Joan Grant and Douglas Judah were the three judges at the championships organized by the Poetry League in 1937. They delivered a report entitled "Standards of Elocution in Jamaica", which remains a seminal document. They combined the best English, American and Jamaican expertise available, and clearly indicated the directions the movement should take. In their statement they said:

> In summing up our impressions of this year's contest we offer the following notes on the standards to be aimed at and the faults most in evidence, not in an over critical spirit, or because we want to stress the candidates' shortcomings to the exclusion of their good points, but because we feel such details will serve as a guide to future study and improvement and will give the teachers in the schools a clearer idea of the aims of this competition.[2]

They commented on the general lack of literary merit in the pieces chosen, and their unsuitability to the age and powers of the children speaking them. They continued:

> The object of elocution in schools should not be to attempt to give the children the equipment of a dramatic performer, or even of a drawing-room entertainment but should be used as the valuable aid it is towards the better appreciation and more detailed realization of the finer points of good literature, whether it be lyric poetry, drama or

> prose. At the same time some of the necessary training in the correct use and control of speech, voice and body must be given, in order to enable the public to respond to the inspiration of the words in an active manner . . . Thus a dual educational purpose is achieved, a literary and a more practical one; the exercise of mind and imagination involved in studying a poem or other extract with the object of interpreting it aurally for one's listener which is obviously of great cultural value; and the cultivation of pure, clear speech, a pleasant-toned, carrying voice together with a well-poised body, free from self-conscious mannerisms, that will prove assets to the possessor at all times and in all walks of life . . .[3]

On the speaking of lyric poetry the report said:

> The speaking of lyric poetry demands a delicate and vivid imagination, a sense of music and rhythm, and a simplicity and sincerity of feeling, all of which are often innate in the very young and can be so easily brought out and fostered by careful and sympathetic teaching.
>
> Voice Production requires breath, supply and control – placing and projection of the voice – quality and fullness of tone – variation of tone and pitch – freedom from throatiness, nasal intonation . . .[4]

In critiquing the men's class, the report referred to a prevailing lack of control which often "resulted in a monotonous 'booming', though on the whole the voices were exceptionally fine, full in tone and potentially powerful and carrying." The critique continued: "The foundation of voice production is adequate breath supply and control and that this was often absent was proved by frequent 'dropping' or fading out of the voice at the end of phrases, and the breaking up of sentences and phrases, when according to sense and rhythm a well sustained flow of voice should have been maintained. Sometimes even a definite 'gasp' for breath was heard."[5] Regarding the women's class, reference was made to the weak carrying power of some of the voices, although they were sometimes pleasant in quality. The report stated: "Under this heading it may be noted by all candidates that the practice of inhaling and exhaling fully and steadily for a short time just before making a public appearance is a good cure for nervousness in general and as affecting the voice in particular."[6]

The judges went on to explain that the aim of this particular contest was to encourage the interpretation of good literature, rather than to provide mere dramatic entertainment. They continued:

> The high standard maintained by the men's class was most praiseworthy, and this coupled with the wide range of selections offered, made judging in this class very difficult. It should be noted however that decisions were reached by the detailed system of marking outlined in this report. It has been suggested that the judges should explain or justify their reasons for not making any or higher awards to certain competitors. It is felt that such a course would be undesirable. Disappointed competitors should, by a conscientious consideration of this report, be able to decide upon their shortcomings for themselves.[7]

By the 1940s a strong aural tradition had developed, to which not only the performers and their teachers, but also the general public subscribed. There came into being a healthy respect for the spoken word, how it was produced and what it could do, and its uses and possibilities in the solo and group presentation of poetry. It was primarily the existence of such a norm that has made possible the successful presentation of the classics. Thousands of children and adults have taken part since the speech festival started, and it is on the cumulative testimony of these people that the movement has continued and developed.

The aims and objectives of the speech competition, included in the annual Festival handbook, are as follows: (1) to encourage a scientific study and use of the spoken word (a linguistic as well as a literary approach is required); (2) to encourage the development and use of an expressive, pleasing and intelligible type of speech in Jamaica, and, based on the criterion of educated opinion, to set the foundation for such development in the primary and secondary schools; (3) to encourage an interest in the art of verse-speaking and the presentation of prose and dramatic selections; (4) to foster the development of choral speaking as an art form in Jamaica; (5) to preserve an active interest in Jamaican dialect; (6) to develop a healthy social atmosphere in which performers from different schools and areas, by competing with each other, help to improve their own standards; and (7) by the foregoing means, to assist in the development of a fully integrated Jamaican personality.

The end product is intended to be the development and use of a norm of received pronunciation, in which the child and adult Jamaican will feel at home wherever good modern English is spoken – a norm in which his competence as a speaker and his knowledge of the spoken word will free him from any feeling of linguistic inferiority; a norm of speech which, while recognizably Jamaican, is internationally understandable.

Since 1950, as part of the annual Festival of Arts activities, the organizing committee issues a special anthology in support of its training programmes and symposia. No attempt is made to impose what may be called a "refined" accent upon participants. The organizers recognize that *accent* is the mode of utterance peculiar to an individual, a locality or a nation, and that each individual will have his own accent within a locality and each locality its own accent within a nation.

The scientific basis of this work is not new. It follows on lines developed in the United Kingdom and practised also in other countries in which an academic distinction is made between voice and speech – voice being simply the making of vowels and speech the making of consonants. To be more specific, this work is in accordance with modern teaching of voice in the United Kingdom and derives from Dr W.A. Aikin's great work, *The Voice: Its Physiology and Cultivation*, which was first published in London in 1900, and subsequently revised as *The Voice: An Introduction to Practical Phonology*.[8]

Voice and Speech Training

Since 1968, when Wycliffe Bennett took up his appointment as general manager of the Jamaica Broadcasting Corporation (JBC), he has been teaching voice and speech in accordance with a method he developed under the tutorship of Professor Greta Colson of the Royal Academy of Music. He has made phonetics, using the International Phonetic Association's chart, an important thrust of his teaching. The emphasis

Rappin' presenters (*from left*) Simone Clarke, Yvonne Chin, Paula Ann Porter and Lisa Hanna. *Courtesy of CPTC.*

is to get his students to know how speech sounds are made, and to do so with accuracy and confidence, thus reinforcing their individuality and feeling of authority and their sense of freedom. Unless the student is required to produce a foreign accent for a specific role, there has never been any attempt at imposing a foreign accent upon his or her speech. After all, a man's speech is like his shadow, inseparable from his personality. Individually, their accents had to remain inevitably their own. This was to ensure that none of them would sound like their tutors. They were to achieve a neutrality that would be intelligible and receivable anywhere in the English-speaking world.

Bennett worked closely with staff at the JBC, and took a similar approach at the Creative Production and Training Centre (CPTC) when he went there as chairman and chief executive officer in 1989. He developed a core of young presenters based on the programme entitled *Rappin'*, which drew upon students in high schools and tertiary institutions to manage and present live discussion under his supervision. These former students now hold very responsible positions and are taking the training further in formal classes which the CPTC offers as part of its training programme. The core of this group included the following persons: Denzie Stephenson, now programme manager of TVJ (formerly JBC); Simone Clarke Cooper, now senior presenter, TVJ; Yvonne Chin, currently director of public relations, Commonwealth Secretariat (London); O'Neil Miller, technical director/consultant, TVJ (at the time of writing, on contract to the Commonwealth Secretariat); Paula Ann Porter, senior presenter, TVJ; Lisa Hanna, member of parliament and Miss World 1975; and Livingston White, who, under Bennett's mentorship, is developing a distinguished academic career and is pursuing a PhD in communication studies, with the aim of expanding upon the work started by Wycliffe Bennett. Upon leaving high school in

1993, White went to the CPTC, where he began training in voice and speech for radio, television and stage. He was eventually invited to be one of the hosts of the teenage television talk show *Rappin'*. He spent the next three years as part of the *Rappin'* presentation team, visiting over thirty high schools across Jamaica and participating in live interchanges with students on a number of important issues, which were then broadcast to the nation. The time spent at CPTC proved the most influential in White's career path, and provided a strong foundation for the work he would eventually undertake in television, theatre and teaching.

Rappin' presenter Livingston White, addressing students

In 1994 White began studies at the Caribbean Institute of Media and Communication (CARIMAC) at the University of the West Indies, where he read for a bachelor's degree in mass communication with a minor in linguistics. At this time he began assisting Wycliffe Bennett with teaching voice and speech at the CPTC – a task he continued with Paula Ann Porter and Simone Clarke (Cooper) after Mr Bennett's retirement from the CPTC.

From 1997 to 1998, with his experience as a *Rappin'* presenter from CPTC, and a graduate of CARIMAC, Livingston worked as a freelance broadcaster, providing live coverage for festivals, church services, carnival parades and other events of national significance at what was then the JBC, before it was privatized. He also did a short stint on the morning show *Morning Time*, produced by Patrick Prendergast, working with Fae Ellington and Simone Clarke on live outdoor broadcasts from various locations across Jamaica.

Wycliffe Bennett (*centre*) in a training session with *Rappin'* presenters. *Courtesy of CPTC.*

Livingston's interest in theatre began when he was twelve years old, when his sister took him to see a matinee performance of the national pantomime *King Roots* at the Ward Theatre. Until then he could not muster up enough courage to enter the darkened theatre halls because he was afraid of the dark. Of course, when the overture began, the lights dimmed and the curtains went up, it was love at first sight for Livingston. He still remembers the opening scene of *King Roots*, which had a storm occurring through the night, the houses swaying in the wind, lightning and thunder, and the villagers waking in the morning, singing about the night storm. According to Livingston, he experienced the magic of theatre at that moment in his life. With the lighting from the stage, Livingston had no fear of the darkness anymore. Instead, he was mesmerized by the colourful costumes, the setting, the lighting effects and the energetic performances, not only from Volier Johnson and Dorothy Cunningham, who played lead roles, but also from the entire cast of performers.

Dorothy Cunningham, actress

And so he became an active member of his high school's drama club under the guidance of his drama teacher, Helen Daley. During his time at Wolmer's (1986–91), he participated in the school's annual inter-house arts competition, not only performing in but also helping to produce, write and stage small skits. By fourth form he was instrumental in Wolmer's entry in the Secondary Schools' Drama Festival, held at the Little Theatre, and helped to build props and paint sets for *The King's Warrant*. Within a year he wrote and produced the play that was to be the school's next entry in the drama festival, *Not Just a Nightmare*, a play about environmental degradation. He also assisted in producing Wilfred Redhead's *Goose and Gander* for a final-year drama student at Edna Manley College who had to present a dramatic production for her final exams.

Wolmer's drama club offered Livingston an outlet for his love of the theatre, but it was not enough. In 1990, before graduating from Wolmer's, he joined Cathi Levy's Little People and Teen Players Club. He was actively involved with this youth theatre group from 1990 to 1993. He can best be remembered for his role as Uncontrollable Urge in the production *Vibes in a World of Sexuality*, which was designed to educate young people about safer sexual practices. He was a member of the original cast, which toured Toronto, Canada, as well as many high schools in Jamaica, and also performed in the video production of the same play. Another memorable role while with Little People was "Actor Boy", the Jonkonnu character of Jamaican folklore, who leads the narration with other Jonkonnu characters for the show *Applause for the Performing Arts*. This 1992 production of the Little People Club celebrated various aspects of the performing arts and their development through time. This performance gave Livingston the chance to perform on the stage of the Ward Theatre, the same place where he had first fallen in love with theatre at the age of twelve. The time spent with the Little People strengthened him as a performer. He worked and trained with Cathi Levy, the group's artistic director; Paulette Bellamy, the group's musical director; and Joseph Robinson, the choreographer. It was this great interest in the theatre which led him in the first place to CPTC, and to a career in linguistics.

17

Music

Classical and Traditional

When the first National Festival of the Arts was organized in 1955 to mark the tercentenary of Jamaica's association with the United Kingdom, it brought together some three thousand choirs in competition from primary and secondary schools and colleges, as well as from churches and other community groups. This should not be surprising. The tradition of choral music has been part of Jamaica's cultural heritage since it was first brought to the island by colonizers from Europe. Choral music's long history in Jamaica accounts for its pre-eminence in the first instance, and explains why its practice remained predominant until recently. This music is distinct from the music brought by slaves and subsequent immigrants from Africa, whose offspring today, after four hundred years, make up some 95 per cent of the population.

In the past, European music was used formally in churches by choirs and congregations, and in the homes of those aspiring to perfect their knowledge and practice of European culture. Thus European classical and folk as well as vocal and instrumental forms were given a treasured place in the psyche of the Jamaican middle classes of all colours and shades. One of the most outstanding of such groups was the Kingston Choral Union, established by Thomas Ellis Jackson in 1882 and, for almost forty years, one of the leading choral groups on the island. This choir won the first Island Choral Competition in 1895 and toured the United Kingdom between 1906 and 1908. Somewhere in that period the group changed its name to the Jamaica Choir. Its members incorporated selections from Shakespeare and dialect verses into their performances and broke new ground when they performed dialect pieces on the London stage. After the deaths of lead singers Carlton Bryan and Connie Coverley in 1917, however, the choir gradually faded out of existence.

A Touch of Elegance: Jon Williams (violin), Paulette Bellamy and Maurice Gordon

The Cudjoe Minstrels

Even among blacks and browns, folk and traditional music of African origin was looked down upon and for generations prohibited in the homes of all but the humblest folk. It took foreigners from England and the United States to be among the first to recognize the importance of this rich African heritage, and to initiate its proper research and study. In 1935 a group of white Jamaicans under the leadership of Linda Stockhausen of St Andrew High School came together to form an entertainment group which they called "The Cudjoe Minstrels". This was about the time when Southern white Americans were putting on "black face" and mounting burlesque shows by singing Negro spirituals. The Jamaican group, in the words of its founder, was never intended to ridicule black folk. According to her, it was a genuine effort to preserve the folksongs and folk tales she had heard as a child growing up in Stewart Town, Trelawny. To achieve authenticity they used burnt chalk to "blacken" their faces.

The first performance of the Cudjoe Minstrels was hurriedly arranged for a fair and concert at St Andrew High School in aid of the tuberculosis hospital. This was followed shortly after at a concert for scouts put on by "the late Mrs Cargill". It took the group two years, however, to collect folk music, clean up some of the language (some expressions were considered vulgar by the more conservative) and put a show together.[1] This show was at a church in the Cross Roads area in Kingston in 1937. The minstrels had the encouragement of Philip Sherlock, an active social worker and educator, who was then secretary of the Institute of Jamaica. A member of the group, he served as their presenter at public events and used them in the Jamaica segment of his *Pepperpot* shows. He also invited them to illustrate his lectures on Jamaican folklore.

Astley Clerk, then-owner of Cowen's Music Room, was himself deeply interested in preserving Jamaican culture. He arranged for the group to give a private concert for Arthur Benjamin, the English composer and concert pianist who was at the time adjudicating the 1937 biennial Musical Society Festival. Benjamin was obviously impressed with what he heard and he later composed his now-famous *Jamaica Rhumba* set to the music of the folk song *Mango Walk*.

On 2 February 1938, Sherlock staged his show, *Pepperpot*, at the Ormsby Memorial Hall, and shortly afterwards at St George's Hall. This show presented two groups of Negro spirituals in an otherwise exclusively Jamaican programme that included ring games, Anancy stories and Jonkonnu dances to the sound of drums. Eric Coverley, well-known comedian of the day, danced the part of Horse Head. There were also items by two comedians, Slim and Sam, and two sets of folk songs by the Cudjoe Minstrels. A reviewer of the show, speaking of the dance segment, noted that the drummers deserved special praise for their skill, "for they proved that drums could make music". It was obvious that, until then, the reviewer had never paid much attention to the sound of the drum. In middle-class society in colonial times the drum was seen as a subversive instrument, an omen of trouble brewing.

The Cudjoe Minstrels were soon performing to full houses at the Ward Theatre, at the Strand Theatre in Montego Bay, at social gatherings and at church functions.

To show how involved they were, the Minstrels had their own authentic cow skull that they used in the Jonkonnu dance. Linda Stockhausen and her team developed a loose story line, "Manda Goes to Town", along which the action moved. In this story, Manda is a young country girl who leaves her village for the bright lights of Kingston, but she meets with disappointment and decides to return home, only to find that her sweetheart is about to marry someone else. Manda's exploits, sometimes narrated by Philip Sherlock, were strung together with folk or Revival songs, a "duppy" story or two, an Anancy story, a Jonkonnu dance or some other activity typical of rural life. The finale was always the same – the marriage scene with loquacious speechmaking, eating and drinking.

In 1938 the actress Doris Hastings attended one of these shows; afterwards, she taught the cast proper make-up and some stagecraft. The group at one time numbered about twenty and included two gardeners who played the guitar. For various reasons, the Minstrels did not last for more than about three years. By 1940 the group had faded out. In 1953, however, it was revived for a royal performance at King's House in honour of Queen Elizabeth II.

Edward Seaga, Olive Lewin and the Search for Jamaica's Folk Roots

During the years of unrest which came to a head in the riots of 1938, there was rapid growth of national consciousness, releasing the urge for Jamaicans to seek out and document their folk tunes and traditional dances. In the early 1950s, Ivy Baxter was among the first to identify some African dance steps which had survived in different parts of rural Jamaica, and to begin to incorporate them into a modern dance idiom. During that same period, Edward Seaga, scholar, researcher, innovator and administrator, began his two-year period of research into the folk culture of the island. He studied the religious and spirit cults and the music associated with these and other folk cultures – Revival choruses, ceremonial cult rites, secular music comprising "digging" songs and "ring play" tunes in one section of Jamaica. Some of this work is documented in *Folk Music of Jamaica*, published by Folkways Records in 1956.

Perhaps one of Seaga's most abiding legacies, in addition to his own folk research, was the necessary institutions and infrastructure he put in place, as minister of culture in the 1960s and as prime minister from 1980 to 1989, to continue research into Jamaica's folk culture, and to preserve and make this research accessible to the people of the country. He established the Folk Music Research Unit at the Jamaica School of Music in 1966, and had musicologist Olive Lewin appointed as folk research officer. This post enabled her to continue the collection, transcription and publication of Jamaican folk songs. She also assembled the now-famous Jamaica Folk Singers, which went on to perform Jamaican folk songs around the world. Olive Lewin's monumental work has influenced greatly the National Festival organized annually by the JCDC, and each year young people enthusiastically enter items in the folk music and folk dance categories, which highlight the centrality of the drum and the accompanying music and dance.

George Goode and Church Music

George Goode, organist. *Courtesy of NLJ.*

George Davis Goode was born at Port Royal in 1882, and from an early age demonstrated a keen interest in music and musical instruments. At nine years of age he began training under Charles Goldson, an organist in Kingston who journeyed to Port Royal weekly to give him lessons. Young Goode first played the harmonium at St Peter's Church in Port Royal for weekday services and was appointed organist at age fifteen, when the church acquired a new organ.

Goode accompanied the Garrison Choral Society from Up Park Camp when they performed the cantata *The Holy City* (by Alfred Gaul) at the Kingston Parish Church in 1905. So creditable was his accompaniment that he was invited by Archdeacon Downer to serve as organist for the Kingston Parish Church the following year. He played there for three years, then moved on to the newly restored St Michael's and All Angels Church, where he remained until 1961, when ill health forced him to retire. In 1948 Goode also accepted the position of organist to the United Congregation of Israelites at their synagogue on Duke Street, which position he held until 1960.

When the first examinations of the Associated Board of the Royal Academy of Music and the Royal College of Music were offered in Jamaica in 1908, there were two organ candidates, George Goode, then organist of St Peter's Church in Port Royal, and Samuel Kitchin, organist of the East Queen Street Baptist Church. Both passed the higher division examinations. Over the years they worked closely together in the cause of musical development. For some time, Goode took lessons via correspondence course from Arthur Eaglefield, founder of the Huddersfield College of Music. One of the exercises Goode submitted was so outstanding that Dr Eaglefield sought his permission to include it in a collection of works for students.

While Goode was first and foremost a musician, he had other equally important skills. He completed the diploma in agriculture at the Agricultural School, Hope, in one year instead of three years. With his training in chemistry, he was appointed assistant chemist at the government laboratory in Hope in 1906, and in 1910 was appointed a master at the newly established Farm School. Teaching agriculture was not much to his liking, and two years later he transferred to the administrative section of the Department of Agriculture, where he served for thirty-one years, acting as assistant director of agriculture for three years, from 1920 to 1923. This was a rare achievement as it was not the norm to appoint coloured colonials to such posts.

In his spare time, Goode continued to teach physics and chemistry at teacher training colleges, and music at several well-known high schools, including Jamaica College (school and chapel choirs), 1943–50; Kingston College (school and chapel choirs), 1945–49; Excelsior School, 1947–52; Camperdown School, 1944–49; and Merle Grove High School, 1947–49. He took early retirement from the civil service in 1942 in order to spend more time on his musical career.

In 1905 the Westminster Glee Singers, an a cappella group from England, visited Jamaica and Goode was so thrilled with their singing that he determined to establish a similar group in Jamaica. Four years later, in 1909, he formed the Kingston Glee Singers' Society, whose objective was "the study of unaccompanied vocal partsinging".[2] He became its permanent conductor. That same year, he married Hilda

Dawkins, an accomplished singer trained in the *bel canto* (beautiful song) school, the lyrical style in which beauty of tone creates all musical effects, in contrast to the more declamatory style of the nineteenth century.[3] They soon became a well-known musical pair.

Goode organized the Coleridge-Taylor Commemoration Festival in September 1913, partly to honour the recently deceased poet and partly to raise funds for the building of the St Michael's Church hall. The festival was described as a "distinct triumph".[4] Miss Ethel Marson, a personal friend of Goode's, described the production of the commemoration festival as follows:

> The entire programme was drawn from the works of the distinguished composer [Coleridge-Taylor] and included the famous cantata "Hiawatha's Wedding Feast". For this festival Goode organized a choir of one hundred voices and an orchestra of over thirty performers from Kingston and the neighbouring parishes. This was the largest choral and orchestral body ever organised in Jamaica, and this fact contributed to making the performances of more than usual interest.
>
> The theatre was comfortably filled on the first night, and His Excellency the Governor attended. The attendance on the second night was not as good. The music loving public of Jamaica was not sufficient to fill the theatre on two consecutive evenings. But the performances were a splendid success and the audiences were "delighted as they were kept entranced with the magnificent music of Coleridge-Taylor".[5]

George Goode at his Organist's piano. *Courtesy of NLJ.*

The *Daily Gleaner* and the *Jamaica Times* wrote glowingly about the *Hiawatha* presentation and congratulated Mr Goode and the members of the choir. The *Gleaner* reported:

> To have got together one hundred and thirty persons, all workers who have to attend to other things besides music; to have trained them to take part in the production of a musical masterpiece; to have succeeded so signally, and to have won appreciation in a city which is not accustomed to very good music and is not very keen upon appreciating local musical talent – this is no ordinary achievement . . . The production of *Hiawatha's Wedding* was in every way meritorious and praiseworthy, and the orchestra which rendered some of Coleridge-Taylor's music was a credit to Kingston.[6]

The *Gleaner* also praised Goode for his patience, energy and talent in training such an immense choir, and for organizing such high-class entertainment. An author for the *Jamaica Times* wrote:

> The rendering of selections from the music of Coleridge-Taylor, particularly from his *Hiawatha*[,] at the Ward Theatre was an artistic triumph of which Jamaica may feel proud. It was also a personal triumph for a young Jamaican with whose ability and high gifts of character and musical ability readers of the *Jamaica Times* have for some years now been familiar. The happy season has come now when this ability and this fine personality is winning the appreciation of others.[7]

Years later, when Hazel Johnston produced the ballet version of *Hiawatha*, George Goode was among the first to applaud the production.

Goode seized every opportunity for self-improvement. He used gramophone records to study and familiarize himself with the works of the great composers, and lined the walls of his study with books, which included all the standard works on the branches of music in which he was interested – voice production, singing, organ-playing, choral music, church music, conducting. He was constantly on the lookout for the latest books on these subjects, which he promptly imported.[8] He owned a special instrument, which he imported in 1912 from the makers, Messrs George Rogers and Sons of London. This instrument has two manuals and pedals like an Organ, but is also capable of being played as an ordinary piano when required. Thus he was able to practise his organ technique at home. His organ pupils also had their first lessons on this instrument.[9]

When the Anglican Church decided to commemorate the hundredth anniversary of the founding of its bishopric in Jamaica in 1924 (the Anglican Church having been the state church since Jamaica became a British colony in the seventeenth century), George Goode was asked to organize this grand musical festival. A choir and orchestra of some two hundred persons were formed, with George Goode as conductor. The performance took place at the Ward Theatre on 19 December 1924, and, according to an article in the *Cosmopolitan* magazine,

> Jamaica for the first time had the opportunity of becoming acquainted with some of the most beautiful Choral Works ever written, among them Parry's *Blest Pair of Sirens*; Mendelssohn's *95th Psalm*; Wesley's *Motet* (unaccompanied); *When Israel came out of Egypt*; Sullivan's *Te Deum* . . . So great was the success of this effort that it was decided to form the Choir into a permanent Organization to be known as the Diocesan Festival Choir, to function under the auspices of the Diocese of Jamaica and to give biennial performances of a similar kind to that given in December 1924.[10]

Members of the Kingston Glee Singers' Society became the foundation members of the Diocesan Festival Choir. Two years later, in December 1926, the choir gave its first performance at the Ward Theatre, and, after more than eighty years and many distinguished conductors, it still performs and is renowned for the excellence of its presentations. Goode stayed with the choir until 1947, when he became organist at the Jewish Synagogue. Starting without any knowledge of Hebrew, he schooled himself in ritual and music, and learned all the dates of the Jewish holy days.[11] Goode may not have given as many recitals as his friends Sibthorpe Beckett and B.C. O'Brien Nation, but he was regarded as an authority on the *fugue* and on the proper technique of organ pedalling. He served as technical adviser to many groups when they sought to acquire a new organ or to remodel their old instruments. After suffering for some time from failing health, Goode died in 1961 at the age of seventy-eight years. His greatest contribution to music in Jamaica was as

> a pioneer in the development of choral singing in the community at a time when this form of cultural activity by Jamaicans was almost non-existent. Such activity as did exist was confined principally to visiting artists and resident foreigners. The going was hard but he met the challenge with determination and perseverance. As a result chiefly

of his missionary work, there is today throughout Jamaica a genuine interest in choral music and a high standard of attainment in this art.[12]

Today, Organizations such as Television Jamaica (TVJ) continue the tradition started by George Goode, by sponsoring annual competitions for school choirs while at the same time offering voice training and appropriate selection of musical items for different occasions, as well as criticism, grooming and a handsome reward for the winning choirs. In George Goode's footsteps have come a host of organists and conductors, such as J.J. Williams, Hazel Lawson Street, Olive Lewin, Lloyd Hall and Noel Dexter, who have continued the high quality of musical presentations, and shared their expertise with adult and junior choirs in towns and villages across the country.

Sibthorpe Beckett and the Jamaica Philharmonic Symphony Orchestra

Sibthorpe Beckett, musician, conductor and choirmaster. *Courtesy of Handel Beckett.*

Sibthorpe Beckett, musician, conductor and choirmaster, founded the Jamaica Philharmonic Symphony Orchestra and the "Y" Choral Group (Young Men's Christian Association). He was born in Kingston, on 16 December 1920, to Joshua Uberto Beckett, superintendent of police, and his wife, Rebecca. He attended Calabar Primary School and Kingston College, and then pursued commercial studies at Kingston Commercial College. He joined the Jamaica Civil Service, where he was assigned to the Supreme Court because of his interest in law. He later served in various capacities as trust officer in the Department of the Administrator General, and finally as assistant trustee in bankruptcy.

It was as a member of the St Michael's and All Angels church choir that he first came under the influence of George Goode, who taught him voice and organ construction. He became entranced with the music of the great masters, and in 1940, at the age of twenty, he formed the Surrey Philharmonic Symphony Orchestra with fourteen other young musicians then living on Central Avenue in Kingston Gardens. (The name was later changed to the Jamaica Philharmonic Symphony Orchestra.) Three years later, in 1943, Beckett formed the "Y" Choral Group as an offshoot of the Young Men's Christian Association, where he became conductor and director of music. For more than fifty years under his baton, the Jamaica Philharmonic Symphony Orchestra and "Y" Choral Group arranged concerts, sometimes performing in church halls, in hotel ballrooms, at the University of the West Indies chapel, in cinemas and in any other available place that would accommodate them.

He took the orchestra from the capital city to Montego Bay, Mandeville, St Ann's Bay and Ocho Rios, often playing to somewhat small audiences who were nevertheless appreciative lovers of classical music. It was under such circumstances that people in rural areas across the island became exposed to a feast of classical music for a sustained period of more than fifty years. Beckett and his orchestra also reinforced their contribution to the development of music in Jamaica by awarding scholarships to talented young Jamaicans.

After the island became independent in 1962, the government of Jamaica felt the need to strengthen the preservation of peace through a cultural exchange programme. This was officially launched by the Honourable Edward Seaga, then minister of development and welfare, in April 1963. On that occasion the initiative was with Canada, and the Orillia District Collegiate Concert Band visited Jamaica on a nine-day goodwill tour, promoted under the name "Operation Hannibal". It gave concerts in Kingston and in other parts of the island, and Sibthorpe Beckett was chairman of the planning committee. The following year, Jamaica sent representatives to Canada as a return gesture. The NDTC performed at Stratford, Ontario, the Frats Quintet performed at the Mariposa Festival in Toronto, and Sibthorpe Beckett was invited as guest conductor for Victoria Day celebrations at Aqua Theatre, Couchiching Park, Ontario.

This exchange programme continued for several years, alternating with Canada and the United States. During that period, Jamaica, through the Philharmonic Symphony Orchestra, hosted over seventy guest artists from the University of Toronto, the University of Western Ontario's Faculty of Music, the Manhattan School of Music, the Boston Conservatory of Music (which visited several times over the years), and Tübingen University, West Germany (1981).

Copies of the programmes show not only the major works of Haydn, Mozart, Handel, Bach, Beethoven, Chopin and other classical composers, but also Jamaican folk music and Negro spirituals. Always, the "Y" Choral Group took part in the concerts. Beckett conducted the world premiere of Patrick Samuels's *Symphonic Impression of Jamaica*, as well as a host of other pieces such as Dvorak's *New World Symphony*, Dettingen's *Te Deum*, Mendelssohn's *Elijah*, Brahms's *German Requiem* and selections from more popular musicals, including Gershwin's *Porgy and Bess*, with local soloists Beverly Dexter, David Reid and Barry Bellamy participating. The Negro spirituals included *Mighty Lak a Rose*, *Let Us Break Bread Together*, *Ain't Got Time to Die*, *Scandalise My Name*, *Ride On, King Jesus*, and many more.

Members of the Frats Quintet

The Frats Quintet

CHERYL RYMAN

The night was 1 November 1954. The applause died slowly. The first half of the programme had ended on a high note. The new group of five male singers had lived up to the reputation of the East Queen Street Baptist Young Men's Fraternal, the larger group from which they had been formed three years before. This was their first formal recital and they had so far pleased the large audience, but now an air of anticipation hung over the Ward Theatre. What had been billed as the "Jamaica Folklore: Special Feature" section of the programme was about to begin. For the Jamaican audience it was to be a rare experience – to hear Jamaican folk songs not only brought on to a concert stage but presented as the main item in a recital.

The change was heralded by the bright bandana jackets worn by the five men as they walked back on to the stage. They went on to perform with the consummate style which was to become the hallmark of the Frats Quintet. The stunned silence which greeted the end of their recital reflected myriad reactions ranging from rejection and shock to pleasure and reconnection. It was the colonial governor, Sir Hugh Foot, patron of the concert, who rose to his feet and shattered the silence of cultural insecurity and ambivalence. His purposeful and insistent clap galvanized the rest of the audience into loud applause.

For the next seventeen years or so, the Frats Quintet would represent Jamaica on the concert stages of the world and sing their way into the hearts of their fellow Jamaicans. When the lead tenor, Granville Lindo, left the island in 1968 he was not replaced, and the remaining four members of the group continued as the Frats Quartet.

In their time, the Frats Quintet made a significant contribution to the awakening of Jamaicans to their cultural heritage. Their brilliant harmonization revealed the full purity, wit and brilliance of the music. They were pioneers in making Jamaican folk music "respectable", the forerunners of groups such as the Jamaican Folk Singers, the NDTC [National Dance Theatre Company] Singers, and the University Singers who have brought folk music to such a high art form in Jamaica today.

The Frats were not the first to collect and perform Jamaican folk songs. There was, of course Walter Jekyll's pioneering work *Jamaican Song and Story* (1907) and the work of researchers such as the American Martha Warren Beckwith. And there were the efforts of people such as Astley Clerk [who composed beautiful school songs highlighting Jamaica's landscape and flora]. The singing duo Slim and Sam in the late thirties and forties had gained renown for the witty topical songs that they wrote themselves, and Philip Sherlock had daringly included them on a concert programme at the Institute of Jamaica. But folk songs were mostly relegated to the more "popular" stage shows, and were not considered fit for the respectable concert stage. . .

The educator J.J. Mills, who had a great deal of interest in Jamaican music and culture, summed up the attitude to folk music in his day when he wrote in his autobiography:

> Folk songs were plentiful in St Ann when I was a boy. The peasantry and "meeting" people sang and danced them. But they were largely tabooed by the churches and schools because they often had vulgar themes and exclusively used patois which was considered a great enemy to good taste and learning of good English. At picnics for Sunday Schools, day schools and the Christian Endeavour, some caution had to be used in the selection of ring-songs lest the "Jamma" songs [jammasing] should drag down the day's function to a coarse and immoral level.

Even after the Musical Society was formed in 1923 and the All-Island Musical Competitions began to be staged in the late 1920s, it was extremely difficult to get entries in folk songs for the festivals.

---

*Adapted from Cheryl Ryman, "The Frats Quintet", *Jamaica Journal* 22, no. 1 (1989): 2–10.

The Frats Quintet (*cont'd*)

The Frats Quintet were the first to treat Jamaican folk songs as a genuine art form, which could stand on its own as concert material for all types of audiences. They performed without any stage effects, movement or accompaniment. The music, the purity and blend of their voices, was the thing. The undeniable technical excellence of the Quintet married to the equally excellent transformation and arrangements of the songs established a standard in authentic folk music renditions for theatre. The Frats lifted a "lowly" art of the people from the "yard" to the concert stage; rescued it from obscurity and denial to acceptance by and respectability among Jamaicans of all classes and artistic persuasions, and presented it with authority to audiences at home and abroad. It won them acclaim as "the undisputed masters of the choral renditions of Jamaican folk songs" . . .

It was not easy. Although nationalism was in the air in the decade before independence, although Louise Bennett had collaborated with [the Scot], Tom Murray, to produce a new book of Jamaican folk songs and music, which came out in 1951, strong resistance still prevailed in certain sections of the society, particularly in the world of music. The *Gleaner* reviewer Peter Dawson [Pamela O'Gorman] noted their contribution as follows:

> Among our musicians and musical bodies . . . [the Frats Quintet is] unique – ironically enough unique only in being unmistakably and unselfconsciously Jamaican. Who else suggests the capability of being equally acceptable to an audience at King's House and one in West Kingston? Who else has taken similar time and trouble to seek out our own folk song and spend such devoted care in its presentation as to draw equal response from native and foreigner alike?

To trace the history of the Frats Quintet and their impact on Jamaican music, we must go back to their parent body, the East Queen Street Baptist Young Men's Fraternal . . . [which] was more than a singing group. It was also a social club and it played a central part in moulding the characters and developing the national and patriotic sensibilities of the young men who flocked to it . . .

Although affiliated with a church, the group sang not only sacred music. Their repertoire included light classics and some folk songs (international and Jamaican) . . . In 1934 some of these singers came together and featured in Una Marson's *Pocomania* – a milestone in theatre, then as now regarded as the first all-Jamaican play. *Pocomania* fortuitously brought together these restless members of the Fraternal and young Winston White, originally from Trelawny but now totally in love with the sights and sounds of the capital city to which he had moved. This meeting was to be the catalyst in the formation of the Frats Quintet. White loved especially the traditional music which he could hear thumping from Kingston's streets and yards. He found the music of the Revival cult Pukumina [*sic*], particularly exhilarating and used to frequent famous "Poco" yards such as that of Mother Surr, Brother Samuel's balm yard in Jones Town and that of Shepherd Levi . . .

It was these experiences that drew him like a magnet into the Ward Theatre one night in 1934 when he heard the familiar "poco" sounds. What he found was Una Marson's play in rehearsal. White remembers simply "crashing" the rehearsal and finding himself on stage with members of the Fraternal – sometimes even leading the songs. Una Marson heard this new authoritative voice before she saw the owner, talked to him and succumbed to the beguiling charm of Winston White. He was invited to join the production. After that, as he recalls, "Music started oozing out of me."

In 1937 he joined the Fraternal. White, a born leader, proved an ideal partner for J.J. Williams [the leader of the Fraternal]. In time, the work of running the Fraternal was harmoniously distributed between them. White acted as choirmaster and as president, and shared some of the responsibilities for the wide-ranging social programmes that were offered outside the choir.

White, like Williams, was one of those anxious to perform folk music. In 1941 he was, with others of the Fraternal, among the featured singers of the cast of the pantomime *Jack and the Beanstalk*. They and Ethlyn Rhodd, who played the Witch, were the only black members of the cast, the first dark-skinned Jamaicans to appear in [the first LTM] pantomime . . .

The suggestion for a quintet rather than a quartet came from White, who pointed to the greater effectiveness of a well harmonized sound punctuated by a lead solo voice – the fifth voice. Granville Lindo possessed such a voice.

The Frats Quintet (*cont'd*)

It is not an exaggeration to say that the Frats Quintet "sound" was dominated by his readily identifiable and inimitable tenor cry. Lindo's "Chi-chi Bud O!" still resounds for those who had the privilege of hearing them perform or of "growing up" with the Frats . . .

It was the rare combination of high technical skill and commitment to an enjoyment of Jamaican folk songs that helped the Quintet to achieve and maintain the levels of excellence which became their hallmark. It was a marriage of well-prepared arrangements and joyous spontaneity in performance together with the exceptional ability to maintain an almost perfect pitch individually and collectively.

Pamela O'Gorman notes:

> The disposition of parts was also noteworthy. The frequent use of the top voice in a soft falsetto register adding an obligato to the melody line rather than to stating it (a function that was left to the lower voices) was redolent of barbershop quartet techniques; but the harmonic flavour was unmistakably Jamaican.
>
> The rhythmic attack and the often brilliant contrapuntal movement of the lower voices to "fill in" melodic space gave the music a forward momentum that was irresistible.
>
> Although they eschewed body movement, the rhythmic thrust that was contained in the unaccompanied voices – a thrust that owed as much to the use of silence as of sounds – kept audiences riveted.

Although the Frats were able to draw on the ready-made repertoire of sacred songs, light classics and Negro spirituals for at least the first half of their formal song recitals, a great deal of work still had to be put into the development of their folk repertoire. They willingly accepted the challenge "to dig up, resurrect, study and perform the old Jamaican songs which are fading out". They did much more than this, of course. They transformed for stage, popularized and preserved many of these songs for generations to come. They also inspired the formation of other groups which were to carry on the work.

Pamela O'Gorman continues:

> Their repertoire was extensive. The sample which follows could well be used as a test of the reader's knowledge of contemporary Jamaican folk repertory: Hosanna, Run Mongoose, Day Oh, Mattie No Drownded, Linstead Market, Rocky Road, Chi Chi Bud, Nobody's Business, Los' Cyan Find, Jackass Wid im Long Tail, Matilda, Brown Skin Gal, Fan me soja man, Rain, Coverley, Come We Go Down a Unity, Angelina, Emmanuel Road, Mattie Rag, Colon Man . . .

A list like this makes us realize the tremendous debt that the country owes to the Frats Quintet. It is instructive, also to recall how many of these songs are in the repertoires of today's folk groups and to observe how frequently the Frat's original arrangements and interpretations have been imitated by others.

There are a number of songs that the Frats made definitively their own: "Parakeet in the Garden", "Chi Chi Bud", "O ZuZu-Wa", "Dog War a Matches Lane", and the unforgettable "Mrs Flannagan".

Winston White was not only leader, but also conductor and folk-song researcher for the group. White was well positioned both by inclination and background to be the primary collector of songs. Kingston, and in particular Camp Road, which was under extensive reconstruction, provided a plethora of Revival and digging songs for inclusion. These, in addition to those collected when the group toured all over Jamaica constituted the raw material of their folk song repertoire.

But aside from learning the words, melody and rhythm, the group had other work to do before these songs could be considered ready for presentation to "respectable" audiences. The Frats Quintet, like groups before – and after – had to "clean up" the lyrics of many of the traditional songs . . .

In emphasizing a folk repertoire in their very first concert on ZQI in 1951, the Frats placed themselves at the vanguard of cultural assertiveness in music. By 1954 when they gave their first formal song recital at the Ward Theatre, they had established pride of place for traditional and folk material. Later they became almost exclusively associated with the presentation of Jamaican folk songs. They also established a tradition for folk singers to be associated with Jamaican Dance Theatre groups, a tradition which began with Ivy Baxter in the 1950s.

The Frats Quintet (*cont'd*)

Their excellence, combined with the fact that the society was beginning to accept what the Frats had to offer, was attested to by the fact that they were frequently chosen to represent their island in preference to many other excellent choirs in Jamaica at the time. They were the only choir selected to perform before the youthful Queen Elizabeth II and the Duke of Edinburgh when they visited Jamaica in 1953. They were the only male choral group included in the 1955 Tercentenary Bandwagon Show which toured the fourteen parishes of the island . . .

Their fame also spread abroad as they were often called on to represent Jamaica overseas. In 1955 they were selected to participate in the predominantly Latin American Miami Music Festival. In 1961 they became the first Jamaican group to participate in the Mariposa International Music Festival in Orillia, Canada. Later, they also performed (with the National Dance Theatre Company) at the famous Canadian Stratford Festival.

Closer to home, they received acclaim for their performance at the 1958 Festival of Arts staged to celebrate the opening of the federal parliament in Trinidad. They were the only choral group and, according to the *Trinidad Guardian* headline, received "a million rose gardens" from the Caribbean audience.

But their greatest achievement was probably their participation as the Caribbean/Jamaican group entry in the 12th International Music Eisteddfod held in [Llangollen] Wales in 1958, where twenty-five countries competed. Wycliffe Bennett, who initiated their invitation [and managed their tour] to Llangollen, said that the Frats were probably one of the most popular groups and one of only three groups which gained a perfect score of 94 for any entry. They placed third in the competition with 185 points; the first and second place winners scored 187 and 186.

They again made history on 10 December 1964, when they became the first Jamaican group to perform before the United Nations Council on the occasion of the 16th anniversary of the Declaration of Human Rights . . . in the presence of such renowned fellow performers as the soprano Eileen Farrell, violin virtuoso of Bolivia, Jaime Loredo, and British actor Sir John Gielgud who narrated the preamble to the Universal Declaration of Human Rights . . .

The next year, the Frats had another triumphant overseas tour, this time to the Commonwealth Arts Festival in Cardiff, Wales, and to Brixton and London.

Parallel to the highly successful independent career of the Quintet was their continued association not only with the East Queen Street Young Men's Fraternal but also with the National Dance Theatre Company, which was founded in 1962. They performed as featured singers with the NDTC from its inception until 1967. By then, the NDTC had formed its own choral group, under the leadership of Joyce Lalor . . .

After 1968, when Granville Lindo, the unique lead tenor, migrated to the United States, the group performed less and less. Although replacements had been found for other members in the past, it seems that Lindo was irreplaceable. The remaining four members of the group nevertheless continued to sing together as a quartet . . .

The Frats Quintet must be credited with inspiring the formation of most of the pure folk or folk-oriented groups in existence today; groups such as the Jamaican Folk Singers, the NDTC Singers and the University Singers all acknowledge a debt to the Frats . . .

In 1986 Winston White received a bronze Musgrave Medal [from the Institute of Jamaica] in recognition of the Frats' contribution to Jamaican [Music]. Despite the accolades heaped on the group at home and abroad during their heyday, the greatest tributes have come from their peers. As Wycliffe Bennett, who has been associated with the arts in Jamaica for so long and who was closely associated with the Quintet, stated:

> The Frats Quintet sang for the sheer joy of singing and they sang with excellence and such splendid authority. There was nothing pretentious about them. They were willing and happy to sing anywhere and anytime. Whenever anything important was happening in Jamaica or wherever Jamaican representation was required abroad, the Frats Quintet were always invited. They gave some of the most satisfying performances of any performing arts group in Jamaica in the 1950s and 1960s.

The 1982 concert programme records: "As we approach our forty-second anniversary as pioneers in the field of orchestral interest and development, we face the challenge of our place in history. The value of our sacrifice and service may not be measured in material gain, but rather, we hope, in the well-tuned spirit of goodness, sincerity, truth and beauty." In paying tribute to the orchestra, Jamaica's ambassador to the United States at the time, Keith Johnson, noted: "Your organization has surely been serving to enrich the cultural experience of this nation long before Independence was achieved. This contribution has not diminished with the years. Its members have always sought to bring to the audience, in highly professional terms, the musical treasures of the masters. The Jamaica Philharmonic Symphony Orchestra has, through its music, helped the spirit of brotherhood and understanding among peoples."[13]

Beverly Dexter, soprano

Another of Beckett's contributions was keeping together, for more than half a century, individuals who had learned to play stringed instruments, and giving them purpose beyond the routines of their daily lives. In 1963, Beckett was awarded the Musgrave Silver Medal by the Institute of Jamaica in recognition of his sustained contribution to development in the field of music, and in 1973 he received the national honour, the Order of Distinction (OD). In his choir there were well-known names such as Beverly Dexter, soprano; Joyce Thompson, contralto; David Reid, choirmaster and tenor; and Douglas Bennett, tenor, of the Junior Music Theatre, and bass singer. Beckett himself died in 1998. His orchestra did not survive, but members of the "Y" Choral Group joined with the Jamaica Musical Theatre Company and still give concerts targeted at the elderly at the Alhambra Inn.

The Jamaica Musical Theatre Company

Within a span of forty-eight years (between 1960 and 2008) the Jamaica Musical Theatre Company (JMTC), founded originally by a group of musically inclined volunteers of Jamaican and expatriate derivation, staged one hundred thirty-six productions. Their original objective was to mount quality theatrical productions that had been popular on Broadway and London's West End, and most of their shows received high praise from local audiences. Professionally, the JMTC has received forty-six major awards from the local arm of the International Theatre Institute (the Actor Boy award) since that organization came into being in Jamaica in about 1988. Of this number, forty-one have been received in the last fifteen years; twenty-four have been awarded to the JMTC, and twenty-nine to the Jamaica Junior Theatre (JJT). The awards include best production, best musical, best actress in a lead role, best costumes, best set, best lighting, best movement and best children's theatre. The 2007 production of *Disco Inferno* also received the award for best musical at the 2008 Actor Boy Awards ceremony. In addition, the JMTC received the Gleaner Merit Award in the category of Arts and Culture for 2003. Consensus is that the ten top productions by the JMTC since its inception have been: *The Merry Widow* (1968), *The Sound of Music* (1982), *Fiddler on the Roof* (1984), *Cats* (1991, repeated 2008), *Phantom of the Opera* (1997), *Beauty and the Beast* (1998), *The Lion King* (1999), *Bubbling Brown Sugar* (2001), *Sarafina* (2002) and *The Wiz* (2005).

The Sound of Music, with Peter Haley and Dawn-Marie Virtue. *Photo by Monica DaSilvia.*

The JMTC started out as the Jamaica Amateur Operatic Association but, after twenty-two years of struggling to survive, they dropped the word "Amateur" and changed the name to the Jamaica Musical Theatre Company, to reflect more accurately the responses of Jamaican audiences. Their first performance, in 1960, staged at the Ward Theatre, was Gilbert and Sullivan's *The Pirates of Penzance*, the same show which had been chosen forty-eight years earlier, in 1912, to open the Ward. Since then, the JMTC has staged ten other Gilbert and Sullivan comic operas, four grand operas, twenty-five major musicals and many other operatic concerts and presentations.

In the early years, the group drew heavily on standard shows performed in England with mainly expatriate performers in the cast, but has since shifted to more popular musical forms from the London and New York stages, with an increasing number of local players. Since 1983, the association has sought to provide for its own sustainability by establishing a young people's section, the JJT. Beginning with *Alice in Wonderland* in 1984, this development has enabled some five hundred young people of talent to improve their musical and histrionic skills and become committed to the performing arts.

Proceeds from major presentations are distributed among charities such as the Young Men's Christian Association (YMCA), the Maxfield Park Children's Home, the Jamaica Cancer Society, Sophie's Place (for abandoned babies) and the Lister-Mair Gilby School for the Deaf. Over the years the JMTC has benefited from the presence of such professional performers as Peter Haley, David Reid, Cecil Cooper, Marilyn Bryce McDonald, Carole Reid, Willard White (now Sir Willard), Douglas Bennett, Lucille Cargill and others, all of whom have given unstintingly of their time, energy and talent to build the sterling reputation which the association enjoys today. These members are not paid despite the high professional quality of their efforts. Indeed, the constitution of the association requires that all such efforts be on a voluntary basis.

The JMTC has a schedule of concerts for five months each year. These concerts provide affordable entertainment for its patrons, many of whom are pensioners. At its concert in March 2008, the accompanist for the three-hour-long presentation was ninety-year-old musician Mrs Dorothy Degazon, a founding member of the group. In recent years these shows have taken place at the Alhambra Inn. Tea is provided at cost and is included in the audience's contribution, while the hotel makes accommodation available without further charge as its contribution to the musical society.

Douglas Bennett, tenor, of the Junior Music Theatre

Behind the organization are such stalwarts as Douglas Bennett, a businessman of Scottish origin, who came to Jamaica in 1964 and has resided on the island ever since. He has been chairman of the JMTC since 1981, and has concentrated mainly on the management aspects of the organization. He is not only a recognized baritone, but has completed his LRSM and FTCL diplomas in solo singing (1967–72) at the Jamaica School of Music under the tutelage of Marian Nowakowski and Robert Williams, and has shared solo singing competitions with Cecil Cooper and the world-famous Jamaican opera singer Sir Willard White. Bennett won twenty-one of the school's solo singing competitions for all five years, as well as the Roderick Jones trophy for outstanding male voice.

His operatic stage appearances have included Leporello in *Don Giovanni*, Mephistopheles in *Faust*, and Sarastro in the *Magic Flute*. He was selected, along with Jeanette Cross, as one of the soloists in the world premiere of Hermann Reutter's operatic scene *Adam and Eve*, and his oratorio repertoire includes *Messiah*, *Samson*, *Judas Maccabæus*, the *St Mark's Passion* and the *Christmas Oratorio*.[14]

Olive Lewin: Conductor, Musicologist

Dr Olive Lewin, was born in Vere, Clarendon, on 28 September 1927. She was educated at Hampton High School for girls, the Royal Academy of Music, London, and Queen's University, Belfast. She obtained licentiateships in piano and violin teaching; harmony, counterpoint and composition; piano performing; and solo singing, and with these skills has achieved an outstanding career as a social anthropologist, musicologist, pianist, violinist, singer, music teacher and researcher.

While in England, Olive Lewin gave recitals on BBC radio and television, at the Royal Festival Hall, London, and elsewhere. She also played the role of May in *Dragnet* on the London stage. Back in Jamaica, she taught at Hampton, then at Knox College, before returning to England to the Middlesex County Council school system, where she taught from 1959 to 1965. On her return to Jamaica, she lectured at the Mico Training College for Teachers for a year before taking up an appointment as folk music research officer at the Jamaica School of Music. Over the next twenty years, Olive Lewin made her greatest contribution to Jamaican music by collecting, transcribing, classifying and cataloguing Jamaican folk music.

She has hosted the programmes *Sunday Promenade* and *Folk Music from around the World* on local radio. She has been responsible for the dissemination of Jamaican folk music at two levels: in the scholastic field, with the presentation of papers, lectures and seminars, as well as on radio and in television programmes, both at home and abroad; and in the performance field, with her involvement in training and presenting the Jamaican Folk Singers, the group she formed in 1966, when she first started the collection of Jamaican music.

To her arrangements of Jamaican folk songs, she has brought superb craftsmanship; to their performance, an exemplary discipline; and to the presentation of the music, a deep love of Jamaica and the Jamaican people. The Folk Singers have travelled throughout Europe and the Americas, revealing to those countries unsuspected treasures of Jamaican folklore that have helped to give Jamaica the cultural prestige the country now enjoys internationally. She is also the founder of the Jamaica Orchestra for Youth (JOY), where she has taught violin to numerous youngsters, many of them from underprivileged communities in Kingston.

Lewin has not only helped to revive the traditional Jamaican spirit, but has contributed her talents, her teaching abilities and her infectious enthusiasm to many levels of society, including involvement in music therapy for persons in the tourism industry, and as director of art and culture in the Office of the Prime Minister. She has also worked with Grace, Kennedy and Company, who subsidized some of her youth programmes. Her published materials include numerous articles on Jamaican

The Jamaican Folk Singers

music for newspapers, magazines and scholarly publications; four volumes of transcriptions of Jamaican folk songs; and three recordings on videotape and discs of performances by the Jamaican Folk Singers. She has also composed and arranged a substantial amount of music based on Jamaican folklore (unpublished); contributed the article on mento to the *Grove Dictionary of Music and Musicians*; and published *Rock It Come Over: The Folk Music of Jamaica*, based on her doctoral dissertation, *Timeless Truths from Humblest Hearts*; and edited *Come Mek Me Hol' Yu Han': The Impact of Tourism on Traditional Music*, a set of essays by ethno-musicologists from around the world. She has received high awards, both local and foreign, including the Jamaican government's Order of Jamaica (OJ), the Institute of Jamaica's Gold Musgrave Medal, and Chevalier dans l'Ordre des Artes et Lettres from the French Ministry of Culture. She is also an initiated Maroon.

Lloyd Hall: Conductor and Music Educator

Lloyd Hall, composer, concert pianist, conductor of choirs and orchestras, and music educator, has devoted a lifetime to music in Jamaica. He is a Fellow of the Royal College of Music and a lifetime vice-president of the School Music Association of Great Britain. Born in Kingston on 10 May 1923, Hall received his early training in music from Sybil Foster (later Foster-Davis) for seven years, after which he was awarded the LRSM diploma and a scholarship from the Associated Board of the Royal Schools of Music to further his studies at the Royal College of Music (1945). He graduated from the Royal College with the GRSM, and gave recitals in London, Sweden, Finland, Belgium and Switzerland under the auspices of the International Friendship League. One of his more memorable performances was at the Ward Theatre in a duo piano recital with Arthur Benjamin, the famous British composer who had come to Jamaica to adjudicate the Royal College of Music examinations and the biennial music festival organized by the Jamaica Musical Society in 1965.

On returning to Jamaica in 1949 Hall taught music at the Shortwood and Mico teachers' colleges. From 1955 to 1956 he attended Darlington College, England, where he immersed himself in music at the primary-school level. In 1957 he was awarded a fellowship to Canada, where, among other things, he observed music education and school festivals, and earned the teacher's certificate from Dalhousie University. Hall also received other bursaries and scholarships to the United States and the Federal Republic of Germany.

In 1957 he joined the Ministry of Education as a music education officer, and served in that position for twenty-six years. He made a significant contribution to

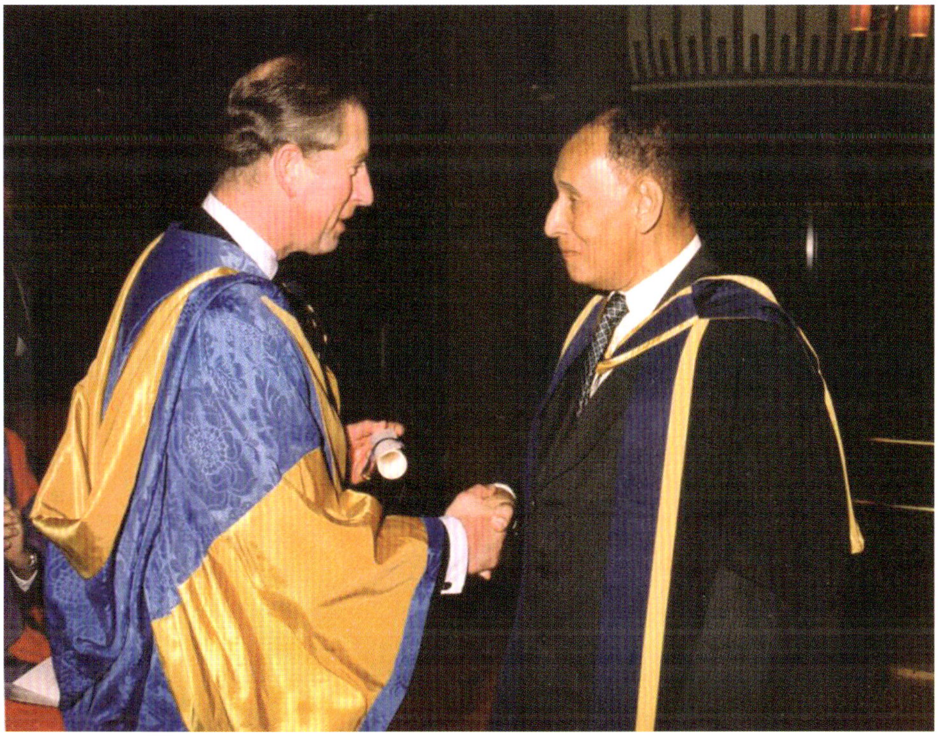

Lloyd Hall, choirmaster, music educator, concert pianist, being presented with the appointment of Fellow of the Royal College of Music by the Prince of Wales (1989)

the teaching of the basics of music and choral singing in schools. On his retirement from the ministry in 1983, he returned to Shortwood as head of the music department and taught there for the next twenty years.

He is recognized for his work with church, college and national choirs. He conducted the thousand-voice children's choir that performed for Queen Elizabeth II in 1966 at the National Stadium. He has also conducted, and continues to conduct, choirs while also serving as a church organist. He has written a manual, *Music Handbook for Teachers*, and compiled *Junior Songs for the Caribbean*, *Senior Songs for the Caribbean*, *Jamaica, Land We Love* (a collection of national and folk songs), and *Missa Brevis*, a short mass dedicated to the St Jude's Anglican Church for their Patronal Festival (1982). He set to music A.L. Hendricks's poem *Jamaica, Land of Beauty*, and also George Campbell's *Litany* ("I saw my land in the morning"), works which are known by almost every school child in Jamaica.

For more than fifty years Lloyd Hall has been organist at the St Andrew's Scots Kirk, where he has introduced three landmark events: the annual Festival of St Cecelia (since 1956), the annual Palm Sunday recital (since 1964) and the annual Christmas candlelight ceremony. When he invited the NDTC to perform two of their famous creations – *Ave Verum* by Mozart, and *Misa Criolla* by Ramirez – for a Good Friday recital at Scots Kirk, it was only the second occasion on which dance was performed in that kirk. The first was in *Murder in the Cathedral*, by T.S. Eliot, as part of the official programme of the independence celebrations in 1962.

In his early years at the Ministry of Education, Hall's educational radio broadcasts reached almost every primary and secondary school in Jamaica, two and three times per week, for a long time, and undoubtedly contributed to the improvement in the quality of choral singing in the country. For his work in music he was awarded the Commander of the Order of Distinction (CD) by the Government of Jamaica and the Silver Musgrave Medal and the Centenary Medal by the Institute of Jamaica. In 2007 he was especially invited to receive his appointment as a Fellow of the Royal College of Music (FRCM) from the hands of Prince Charles, who is president of the Board of Governors of the College.

Shirley Thompson: Composer, Conductor, Musicologist

Shirley Thompson, performer, composer, conductor, musicologist

Shirley Thompson has been described by Classic FM radio in the United Kingdom as "a leading voice in Contemporary Classical Music". She has been widely celebrated for her "pioneering, eclectic and original writing style", and is the first female in the last thirty years to compose and conduct a symphony in Europe. Growing up, Thompson played in youth symphony orchestras in London and sang with local choirs; through these activities she received a foundation in classical, orchestral and choral works. Later, she studied music at the University of Liverpool and composition at Goldsmith's College, London. She received her first major commission from the Greenwich International Festival (funded by the Arts Council of Great Britain) to compose a chamber work, *Visions* (1985), which was performed by the Greenwich Ensemble at the Eltham Palace in South London.

Her second composition, *Songs of Dawn* (1987), again commissioned by the Arts Council, attracted public attention. It was composed for a mixed instrumental ensemble, including alto sax, bass clarinet and a Latin American instrument, the marimba. Thompson declares that her inspiration was the glorious sunrise in the Caribbean. The persistent themes in her work include social justice, notions of identity, migration and reflections on London, because, to her, "London is a rich treasure trove of history, an exemplar of urbanization and cultural diversity in its many manifestations".

Although Shirley Thompson is a British national by birth, she is Jamaican by heritage and identifies closely with her ancestral homeland. Her ensemble – the Shirley Thompson Ensemble – has performed at the Ward Theatre in Kingston. She is the daughter of immigrants to Britain, who have now returned to Jamaica. Her West Indian heritage has markedly influenced her music, even in the choice of some of the instruments she incorporates into her ensemble – instruments which are not often to be found in traditional orchestras, like the marimba.

All her compositions are based on themes that reflect her social consciousness. *Visions* is based on the assassination of Grenada's prime minister, Maurice Bishop, in the 1980s. The "lyrical qualities and rhythmic intricacy of the work" attracted the attention of the BBC and led to her being commissioned to write the music score for the BBC drama series *South of the Border* in 1990. Thompson's score for this program has been selected as one of the top twenty BBC-TV themes. Her score for the film *Dreaming Rivers* earned her the Mannheim Film Festival prize in that same year.

Thompson is constantly experimenting. Her opera, *A Child of the Jago* (1997, funded by the Arts Council), employed singers from a wide range of musical backgrounds: "Trained opera singers mingled with singers from musicals and the popular music stage to create a unique synergy of voices that was remarkably effective."[15] *A Child of the Jago* is adapted from the novel by M. Belloc Downes, and narrates the life of a young man from the East End of London at the turn of the nineteenth century who gets caught up in tragic criminal activities as a result of growing up in the squalid conditions in that part of the city. Thompson has also collaborated with Professor Eleanor Earl (at time of writing, at the University of West Virginia, United States) to adapt a musical drama *Incidents in the Life of a Slave Girl* (2001):

> The music offers a seamless transition between songs composed in the traditional musical song form and atmospheric, lyrically polyphonic instrumental interludes. The drama aims to create a balance between spoken passages, song and instrumental sections. *Incidents in the Life of a Slave Girl* offers a contemporary interpretation of an early nineteenth century slave narrative, and explores the stylistic balance between representing the American South in the eighteenth century while retaining Thompson's original compositional style.[16]

Thompson continues to write for the symphony, the opera, the ballet (*PUSH*, performed by London's Sadler's Wells Theatre, was, at the time of writing, touring worldwide), for the stage (*The Lodger*) and for film. Her instrumental works experiment with improvisations which require the skills of versatile musicians that can glide effortlessly between contemporary classical and diverse popular music styles.

The Shirley Thompson Ensemble is constantly experimenting and combining conventional and unconventional elements, in both vocal and dance performances; for example, in juxtaposing a rap artist against a classically trained vocalist, or a classical ballet dancer with an instrumental ensemble. "The aim of these compositional devices", she says, "was to present a gritty, dynamic and colourful tapestry that comments on the state of living in London, a culturally diverse, urban melting pot where all kinds of cultural experiences are possible."[17]

Her latest orchestral work, *New Nation Rising: A Twenty-First-Century Symphony*, has been recorded by the Royal Philharmonic Orchestra. It required the Philharmonic to utilize two choirs, solo singers, a rapper and dhol drummers in an epic musical story celebrating London's thousand-year history. At time of writing, Thompson had been short-listed to write the music for the 2012 Olympics, set to take place in Britain.

Sir Willard White: Bass Baritone

Sir Willard White, baritone, actor

In May 1995, the Institute of Jamaica awarded the acclaimed bass baritone Willard White the Musgrave Gold Medal "for distinguished eminence in the field of music . . . for continued success and the consistent level of excellence which he has displayed during his career".[18] Born in Ewarton, St Catherine, on 10 October 1946, White attended Excelsior High School, where he was taught by the soprano Roma D'Oyen Fitchett (formerly Roma Presano) of the Glynebourne Theatre, England. Later, at the Jamaica School of Music, he received training from Marian Nowakowski, a former leading bass of the Royal Opera, Covent Garden. During the 1960s he appeared in productions by the Jamaica Operatic Society (now the Jamaica Musical Theatre Company) and the Jamaica Folk Singers, directed by Olive Lewin, and won prizes in the Jamaica Festival Commission's annual events.

White also played a minor role as the young chief in *Anancy and Pandora* (1967) and received mention from a *Daily Gleaner* critic who complained that the band was so loud it had "drowned out Willard White's strong voice". In 1968, after leaving the Jamaica School of Music, White entered the Julliard School of Music on full scholarship. It was while in New York, as a member of the New York City Opera, that he made his debut at the Lincoln Centre in the role of Colline in Puccini's *La Boheme*.

From New York, White moved to England, where he continued to build his career, performing with the Welsh National and the English National Operas. He performed in Verdi's *Requiem* with the Birmingham Symphony Orchestra, with the Royal Liverpool Philharmonic Orchestra in *Messiah* at the Royal Festival Hall, London, and in the role of Porgy in Gershwin's *Porgy and Bess* at the Glynebourne Theatre, England. Since those days, White's progress has been meteoric. He has sung in some of the greatest opera houses of the world and has performed with many of the world's most celebrated symphonies in the United States, France, the former Czechoslovakia, Spain, Norway, Canada, Austria, Israel, Germany, Italy, Japan and in his native Jamaica, among other places. His repertoire extends from the classics to Jamaican and American folk songs. In 2000 Willard White was awarded the Order of Merit (OM), Jamaica's highest honour to a native son, "for international distinction in the performing arts". He was knighted by Queen Elizabeth II on 24 November 2004.

18

Popular Music

Since Jamaica's independence, a number of dance and music forms have emerged. Mento, ska, rocksteady, reggae and dancehall have a special place in the world of entertainment. Practitioners have elicited ways in which they view their own special contributions to the growth and development of music in Jamaica. Even when they have achieved international acclaim, it is their Jamaican individuality that gives them a special place in the world of entertainment.

Of the five popular Jamaican music forms, reggae is the most known internationally. Reggae gradually became the music of the nation "as one by one institutions such as the University of the West Indies and the School of Music, which had previously disdained local popular music as an unfortunate subculture, and had recognized only music of the European tradition" became its latest patrons.[1] Devotees gather in groups at concerts, at deejay sessions, at house-parties and in basements, to dance and to listen. The same thing happens around the world, where the performances of the early masters (like Bob Marley and his original band of Wailers), as well as younger and more recent reggae stars (like Marley's son, Damian) and a host of other talented Jamaicans, have inspired imitators and academic researchers in Europe, Japan, Africa and the Americas. In the words of Dermot Hussey, "A century gone, another underway, and the accolades continue to come", although Marley has been dead since May 1981.

"One Love" closed as the BBC's "Millennium Song", and *Time* magazine's "Album of the Century" (2000) was *Exodus*. The *Guardian* newspaper described Marley as the most eloquent ambassador of reggae – one of the most powerful and conscientious voices of the century, for his conviction, his integrity and his commitment to his faith – and said that he would be missed as much for the timeless splendour of the music he produced.

Popular interest in Jamaican music overseas began with the advent of ska in the late 1950s and, since independence in 1962, Jamaican pop music has been producing an increasing number of international hits. In addition, several home-grown stars and their aggregations have taken the Jamaican product abroad in live performances. These Jamaican ambassadors have included Byron Lee and the Dragonnaires, Toots

Sonny Bradshaw Seven

Jimmy Cliff

Alton Ellis

and the Maytals, the Sonny Bradshaw Seven, Count Ossie and the Mystic Revelations of Rastafari, Bob Marley and the Wailers, Third World, Peter Tosh, Dennis Brown, Jimmy Cliff, Desmond Dekker, the Mighty Diamonds, Zap Pow, Burning Spear, Ras Michael and the Sons of Negus, Culture, Alton Ellis, Sugar Minott, Papa Michigan and General Smiley, Roy Sibles, Black Uhuru, the Revolutionaries, Lloyd Parkes and We the People Band, Yellowman, and all four of Bob Marley's sons. Bob Marley and some of his peers have passed on, but there is no lack of younger deejays taking their place and making a name for themselves internationally.

A number of articles, monographs and books have been written by Jamaican and other specialists to explain this phenomenon. Not incorrectly, most writers have emphasized the ghetto origin of reggae and the fact that it draws heavily upon Rastafarian culture; but these are only two aspects of its lineage. Reggae has an eclectic musical form. It shares ancestry with black American and Latin American cultures. Its lyrics are freighted with the contentions of contemporary life, but its roots, both musical and psychological, go deep into Jamaica's past.

There are many types of traditional music in Jamaica, including music from Africa, Europe and Asia, as well as from the United States. Fragments of sea shanties that go back to the seventeenth century can still be heard, And the quadrille, the maypole and other set dances still enjoy great popularity at folk festivals and celebrations. Pockets of resistance have been preserved among the blacks, who make up some 95 per cent of the population, remnants of West African cultures which have survived both the Middle Passage and the conditions of slavery.

Leading up to and since independence in 1962, Jamaica's creative artists have been making use of these cultural retentions in creating their music; they have used, for example, elements of kumina, which came from the Congo, of the etu of the Yoruba tribe of Nigeria, and aspects of the Akan culture of Ghana. The influx of slaves during the American War of Independence brought to Jamaica a rich treasury of Negro spirituals; and, since around the middle of the nineteenth century, migration to Central American countries in search of employment, together with the cluster of radio stations that broadcast from those countries, have given Jamaicans a taste for Latin American rhythms.

Ras Michael

The first indigenous Jamaican dance music, however, was the mento, which has a song-dance style. The music is syncopated, and characterized by accentuation on the last of four beats in the bar. The mento betrays Latin American influences. Better known examples include *Solas Market*, *Brown Skin Gal*, and *Fan Me Soja Man*. In the hands of masterful Carlos Malcolm, *Rucumbine*, which has become a classic, has a distinctly Latin texture. The dance consists of a series of sideways and backwards steps, then two-step turns, while the hips move in a circular motion in an almost gyrating fashion, reminiscent, some believe, of the fertility rites associated with the early Jonkonnu movement. The lyrics often deal with topical events, carry social commentary, and are sometimes satirical. The mento came into existence some time after the middle of the nineteenth century, and enjoyed waves of popularity up to the 1940s and 1950s. Just prior to the outbreak of the Second World War, however, the big "swing" bands were becoming the vogue, and they superseded the mento bands in the urban areas, playing at night clubs, dance halls, fairs and occasionally in private homes.

Jamaica's recording industry began with the recording of popular songs that focused on the economic deprivation of and social injustices against the people, recounting both the personal and collective elements in the life of the poor, but also the hopes that independence would solve. There were the popular performances of mento songs by Lord Fly, Lord Flea, Hubert Porter and Count Lasha, but it was the "sound system" man and the 45rpm record that gave the popular song its biggest boost. Rhythm and blues accentuates the second and fourth beats of the musical measure – the afterbeat – in the manner of mento, and by the time the transition from ska through to rocksteady was complete, mento rhythm had become dominant.

During the war years, hundreds of workers left Jamaica from all parts of the island to work on American farms. They were exposed to sound systems and black American music, and, on their return home, some of them brought back equipment and examples of soul, boogie-woogie, rhythm and blues, and early rock and roll music by such exponents as Fats Domino, Wyonnie Harris, Johnny Ace, Louis Jordan and Bill Doggett. These Americans were the exemplars of the early Jamaican recording artists, including Laurel Aitken, Derrick Morgan, Owen Gray and Jackie Edwards. At the same time, an increasing number of radio sets on the island also enabled Jamaicans to listen to these types of music from radio stations in New Orleans and Miami. Soon the island became dotted with sound systems, juke boxes, and the big swing bands went into eclipse.

Clement Dodd (Sir Coxone)

The two greatest "system" men were Duke Reid and Clement Dodd, the latter of whom disc-jockeyed as Sir Coxone. They would truck their over-sized speakers and powerful amplifiers from one end of the island to another. Their success created rivals. The existence of a number of talented musicians, many of whom had been trained at the Alpha Boys' School, and who had been performing with success in the swing bands, encouraged Reid and Coxone and another system man, Prince Buster, to

Prince Buster

become producers. With the emergence of such entrepreneurs in the field, a new era in Jamaican pop music began.

In addition, the Jamaica Broadcasting Corporation, founded in 1959, established a resident band, and gave considerable encouragement to local music-making. The JBC also produced a number of the early ska records. Ernie Ranglin claims to have been the first person to do ska, and he did it at the JBC for Sir Coxone. The band consisted of Roland Alphonso, Cluet Johnson on bass and Rico Rodriquez on trombone, while Theophilus Beckford played a steady boogie-woogie riff on his piano. Beckford's seminal "Easy Snappin'" is commonly regarded as marking the transition from boogie-woogie/rhythm and blues into ska. Beckford and Ranglin, it would seem, officiated at the birth of ska.

Another element came from the Rastafarian movement, at first musically and ideologically. Count Ossie, an ardent Rastafarian, had developed a new style of drumming, which he had derived from the rhythms of the "burru", itself a cousin or offshoot of kumina.[2] Count Ossie, supported by four other drummers, can be heard in that 1959 Folks Brothers' hit, "Oh Carolina". But it was trombonist Don Drummond who dominated the era of ska. Regarded as one of the world's great trombonists of his day, he developed a highly personal instrumental style. He murdered his sweetheart and died in a mental asylum in 1959. He is survived by some unique musical compositions, which reflect a melancholy mood, a consuming passion and a deteriorating mental state.

Ska was played primarily for dances characterized by fast-paced movements, such as the "shuffle and split". Some stylized versions of these dances featured hands moving upward and downward, or sideways and back and forth, as in the "wash-wash". This dance simulates the movements of people washing clothes, so that the fists are kept closed and rubbed together. Another variation is the "press along", in which the dancer thumps out the rhythm with his arms at shoulder level. Yet another movement consists of spiralling down to floor level and back up. Ska achieved great popularity, with the efforts of bands like the Skatalites, which broke up after the death of Don Drummond, and Byron Lee and the Dragonnaires, which has remained Jamaica's most popular big band over the last twenty-five years.

Ernie Ranglin

Towards the end of the 1960s, ska was superseded by rocksteady. Soul was to rocksteady what rhythm and blues was to ska. With a tempo slower than that of ska, rocksteady places more emphasis on syncopation. The bass is given greater autonomy and achieves a melodic function. The drum pattern harks back to the rhythmic structure of mento, and the strum of the guitar is also similar to that of mento. From a dancing point of view, the main difference between rocksteady and ska lies in the tempo of the music. In rocksteady, dancers keep their feet fairly steady and slowly shift their weight from one foot to the other. At the same time, each dancer shakes the shoulders and moves the arms and hands to the beat of the music, as the rest of the body rocks or sways. On the dance floor, dancers rocked to Delroy Wilson's "Dancing Mood" and to Alton Ellis's "Rock Steady" as if glued to one spot; this move became known as "renting a tile".

As the earlier music had been one manifestation of changing conditions in Jamaican society, so had changes in the middle of the 1960s begun to be reflected in the lyrics and style of local musical productions. Unlike ska, which, with its deep mento roots, had always possessed a joyful, collective side, rocksteady was slow, painful and almost sinister. Hopeton Lewis's "Sounds and Pressure" and "Cool, Cool, Coolie", with their slow, "stepping" rhythm as opposed to the fast, "running" ska beat, are good examples of songs from the new period, in which "the rude boy" became a significant social character. Armed with his ratchet knife, razor and occasional gun, "the rude boy" was the product of a society that had not been able to satisfy the material needs of the mass of the people. Among the tunes which highlighted this social phenomenon were Desmond Dekker's "007", Prince Buster's "Judge Dread", and the Wailers' "Rude Boy". The "rude" boy's outlook on life was perhaps best captured in the Wailers' "Steppin' Razor", a little-known number which, nevertheless, speaks for itself. The Wailers, more than anyone else, could touch the pulse of the people.

By the late 1960s, social unrest again affected the content and form of Jamaican music. Unemployment, by this time, had struck 25 per cent of the working population. Strikes for higher wages and better working conditions, as well as other social disruptions, were reflected in new songs like "Me a Sufferer", written by the Kingstonians, "Starvation" by Boston Jack and the Soulites, and "Everything Crash" by the Ethiopians. The singers of the National Dance Theatre Company of Jamaica have revived many of the songs of the 1960s with successful performances in different parts of the world.

Rocksteady had a short lifespan. Even as it was coming into vogue it was being overtaken by reggae. Rocksteady, which had featured a tempo slower than that of ska, and had popularized the "one drop" drum rhythm, joined with elements from earlier traditional forms to help create the new sound. Two key contributions were those of the Rastafarian movement and the black music of North America. The Rastafari had a significant influence, since they were the exponents of the "heart throb" drum beat, which is so much a characteristic of the "dread mood" of reggae. The Rastafarian philosophy is also strongly projected in the lyrics of reggae songs.

The dances which emerged alongside reggae incorporated many of the moves that had evolved out of previous styles, and were such faithful enactments of various events in Jamaican history and culture that they could well be regarded as social chronicles of the times. Because most of these dances originated in the groups which followed the sound systems, they projected easily identifiable ghetto styles. Among the more notable new steps were the "S90 Skank" and the "Moon-Walk", inspired by man's first landing on the moon.

Among performers of reggae, Toots Hibbert claims to have invented the genre with his early song "Do de Reggae". To him, "reggae" means coming from the people of the ghetto, and it symbolizes poverty, suffering and Rastafari. It is a form of protest music. Toots has the "open-throat" style of the Jamaican Revival singer, and has reminded American writers of Ray Charles and Otis Redding. His trio, Toots and the Maytals, produced *Six and Seven Books* in 1963, followed by *Pain in My Belly*. Then, after

Desmond Dekker (*centre*) and the Aces, 1967

Bob Marley

Rita Marley

Marcia Griffiths

serving a prison term in 1966 on charges of dealing in ganja (marijuana), Toots wrote "54-46 That's My Number", followed by another classic, "Pressure Drop".

Depictions of the Kingston slums, often referred to as "Shanty Town", spawned popular reggae. The 1970 film *The Harder They Come*, by Perry Henzell and Trevor Rhone, helped to establish reggae on the international scene, with the casting of reggae singer Jimmy Cliff in the role of the anti-hero, Ivanhoe Martin. Off screen, Cliff has recorded such hits as "Many Rivers to Cross" and "Wonderful World, Beautiful People". He has a massive following in Africa, Brazil and the former Soviet Union.

In 1972 Delroy Wilson's "Better Mus' Come" became the electioneering theme of the People's National Party, and former prime minister Michael Manley himself was recorded making a political speech to the background of a reggae rhythm. Another folk poet, the Burning Spear, in his work "Marcus Garvey", suggested that conditions in Jamaican society reflected the period of the apocalypse that Garvey, as a Jamaican "national" hero, was supposed to have predicted.

Of course, the greatest international reggae star was Bob Marley, who, along with Peter Tosh, Bunny Livingston and Junior Braithwaite, began rehearsing in Trench Town in the mid 1960s. Initially they echoed the resentment of the "rude boys". In 1973 their first internationally acclaimed album, *Catch a Fire*, was produced by Chris Blackwell's Island Records of London. Critics in the United States and Great Britain hailed the production as a new wave in rock music. But the sweetness of the success soured. In 1975 Tosh and Livingston withdrew and launched independent careers.

Bob Marley, now on his own, acquired a new supporting group, the I Threes, which consisted of his wife, Rita, Marcia Griffiths and Judy Mowatt, outstanding singers in their own right. With their backing, Marley, as a performer, developed his own characteristic style of presentation: he danced, stomped, sang and shook his shaggy mane in electrifying performances. With the I Threes he produced *Natty Dread* in 1975. Other outstanding albums followed, including *Rastaman Vibrations*, *Exodus*, *Survival*, *Uprising* and *Confrontation*. Marley's songs are not only about social protest; he also had songs of love and, indeed, explored the whole of the human experience.

Michael Witter, lecturer at the University of the West Indies, Mona campus, sees Marley as part of a generation of remarkable young leaders who never lived past forty – John Lennon, Malcolm X and Che Guevara included – and he credits Marley's genius with taking the national liberation struggles that were then going on in the world beyond the political here-and-now into a people's identity and culture.[3] Marley is universally recognized as the reggae master *par excellence*. A folk poet, he understood the aspirations of his people and had a conviction and a force of logic that could be understood by people in every land. He had a very good group of supporting musicians. His music helped his lyrics to realize his message. In performance, Bob Marley himself, his music and his message were one and indivisible. Rastafarianism was at the heart of his message and his musical style. He died in May 1981. His passing was mourned internationally, and stimulated interest in reggae music.

APPENDIX

Profiles and Biodata

Most of the personalities cited below – whether they have contributed to drama or comedy, classical or popular music, or dance – have served with distinction and excellence. Their works may not have received full treatment in the main text, as it is impossible to include everything and everyone in a small volume. But their contribution to the performing arts in their own (or adopted) country as performers, directors, producers, vocalists, composers, conductors, dancers, actors, designers or technical personnel is of great significance and, if for no other reason, they deserve mention, however briefly, in this publication. Without their contribution, the history of the performing arts in Jamaica in the twentieth century would have been incomplete.

Stafford Ashani

Stafford Ashani (Stafford Harrison) is a Jamaican playwright and television producer. He was educated in Theatre Arts at the Tish School of the Arts, New York University, where he gained a BFA – a double major in theatre, film and television production. Ashani, a Rastafarian, has a strong sense of social injustice, accepts responsibility for himself and for his work, and possesses a creativity that has produced enduring work.

As a playwright and screenwriter he has written *Bar Jonah*; *Night Noises*; *Quickie* (1974), a full-length movie; *Maskarados* (1976); *Anancy and the Unsung Heroes* (1977); *Reggae* (1979–80); *Ma Ma Black Sheep* (1986); *Foreign Mind* (1987); *Bacchanal of Black Inventions*, a musical (1990); and *Redem'tion Day* (1990), which examines some of the choices that the majority of Jamaicans faced after slavery – to remain on their former masters' estate, to live in the "free villages" or to live in the hills like the Maroons – and the consequences of those choices.

As an actor Ashani has performed in *Entry Denied* for Banyan Films (1997), *Fools Paradise* (a US–Jamaican movie, 1996), *Klash* (a US–Jamaican movie, 1994), *Going* to *Extremes* (a Lorimar TV series), *Marked for Death* (a Hollywood production), *Just Like America* (a Hungarian–Israeli Film), *The Task* (a PSCSA production), *The Tempest* (UWI production), and *Macbeth*, directed by Wycliffe Bennett for television. He has played on Broadway and on ABC Television. As a television producer he has worked for clients such as Mercury and Loose Cannon Records, and has directed *Reggae Strong* as well as music videos for Jamaican artists such as Buju Banton, the Wailer's Band, Capleton and Tony Rebel, among other well-known international reggae personalities.

Jeanne Barnes

Jeanne Barnes, actress

Jeanne Barnes arrived at the Creative Production and Training Centre (CPTC) as managing director in 1987, having previously worked at the Jamaica Broadcasting Corporation (JBC), Radio Jamaica, Jamaica Information Service and in private organizations. Her major concern at the start was to shape the CPTC into an organization that could produce *ad hoc* quality features, as well as turn out Jamaican television programmes on a regular basis. She was also concerned that the staff of the CPTC should have some form of long-term commitment to the institution, so she set up insurance and pension benefits and a revolving loan fund to assist staff in financial problems.

JBC was the only television station at the time, and the CPTC entered into an arrangement with that organization so that CPTC productions could be aired. The CPTC's budget did not allow for much unrecoverable production expenditure, so sponsorship from the private sector had to be sourced. It was a tough job, because business houses had fallen into the cheap and easy habit of sponsoring packaged, pre-rated foreign programmes. They were usually unwilling to face the unknown hazards of home-grown productions.

Production skills had to be polished at the CPTC to satisfy the expectations of viewers and sponsors. The ability to meet regular deadlines had to be developed in order to keep commitments. There were several experiments, like the magazine programme *Today in JA*, hosted by Cathi Levy, and the *Tea Meeting* series, which featured a variety of well-known, talented Jamaican musicians, singers and actors, such as Olive Lewin and her Jamaica Folk Singers, Lois Kelly Barrow, Alma Mock Yen, Paulette Bellamy, John McFarlane, Leonie Forbes, Beverley Dexter, the University Singers and Charles Hyatt. Christmas features highlighted such people as athlete Grace Jackson, cricketer Jeffery Dujon and singers Curtis and Pauline Watson. A Mobile Broadcasting van was acquired to expand the range and scope of the CPTC's capabilities.

A breakthrough came when JBC, through a short-lived Public Broadcasting Unit, collaborated with the CPTC in establishing a programme series for young people, aimed primarily at high schools and entitled *Rappin'*, and another still-running series, *Hill an' Gully Ride*, which sought to reach into every corner of Jamaica. *Rappin'* ran for several years after Jean Barnes left the CPTC. The most spectacular of the CPTC's production achievements, however, were the dramatized feature on drug abuse, entitled *Fix*, funded by UNESCO, and the five-part series *Flashpoint '38*, sponsored by the National Commercial Bank, to commemorate the fiftieth anniversary of the 1938 upheavals in Jamaica.

Jeanne Barnes's next project was to establish the training component of the CPTC. This was perhaps just as difficult a task, since the whole question of market needs, entrance qualifications, officer training and achievement standards had to be painstakingly worked out. One of the first persons taken on was English-language expert Vivien Carrington, who was charged with upgrading writing skills and assisting generally in the training of scriptwriters, especially in the production of documentaries. The radio section of the CPTC also began to play a more functional role, and the studio began to be booked on a regular basis. CPTC soundmen, cameramen and directors were regularly part of national outside broadcast assignments for the coverage of sports, festivals and national events. Jeanne Barnes left the CPTC in 1990, after a hectic three years, having set many programmes in place.

Kirk Buchanan

For the last thirty years, Kirk Buchanan has been a production specialist, trainer and broadcast media manager of production houses that effectively compete in an increasingly global media landscape. His latest assignment is at the CPTC on Arnold Road in Kingston. He is experienced in broadcast media and production management, and in developing strategies and objectives for specific units, and has vast experience in developing funding proposals.

Kirk Buchanan, production specialist, trainer and broadcaster

He is highly skilled in conceptualizing and developing ideas for television productions, in the production of commercials, documentaries and multi-camera and outside broadcasts, as well as music videos. He has developed curricula for television and radio production training courses and in teaching television production. From 1985 to 1989 he was senior editor of the Jamaica Information Service's television department; from 1994 to 1998 he was production manager of CVM Television, of which he was general manager from 1998 to 1999.

Buchanan has planned, directed and produced radio and television coverage as well as the international broadcast for the World Netball Championships, held in Jamaica in July 2002 and broadcast on CVM-TV. That same year, he was executive producer in charge of planning and coordinating the coverage and worldwide broadcast of the World Junior Athletics, also in Jamaica. He developed and prepared the proposal and guidelines for the establishment and operation of the CPTC's cable channel, CTV. In 1994, he coordinated the television coverage of the visit of Queen Elizabeth II to Jamaica. He also produced, directed and edited the weekly television drama series *Dear Mama* for Jamaica Information Service television. A state-of-the-art operator, Buchanan is very much at home in the global landscape.

Glen Campbell

Glen Campbell, actor

As an actor, Glen Campbell has performed in Barbados, the Cayman Islands, the US Virgin Islands, Canada, the United States, Germany, India and Belize. He has been portrayed mainly as a comedian, but has also demonstrated his versatility by taking on a number of serious roles in straight dramatic pieces, including *I, Marcus Garvey*, *The Task*, *Beyond the Horizon*, *I Thought You Had Gone as Well*, *One of Our Sons Is Missing*, *State of Emergency* (a Jamaican adaptation of *Death and the Maiden*), *One More Time* (a Jamaican adaptation of Neil Simon's *They're Playing Our Song*) and – his favourite character to date – the role of Doggy in *Dirty Diana*, in which he carried his audience all the way from belly laughter to actual tears.

To date he has received nine Actor Boy nominations: Best Actor, *Smile Orange* (1993); Best Actor, *Run for Your Wife* (1995); Best Actor, *State of Emergency* (1996); Best Actor, *Oliver and Pinocchio* (1998); Best Actor in a supporting role, *Breadfruit Kingdom* (1999); Best Actor, *Dirty Diana* (2001); Best Actor, *Cindy Relisha and the DJ Prince* (2002); Best Actor in a supporting role, *Christopher Cum Buck Us* (2003); Best Actor, *Cutie and the Freak* (2006).

Born in London, England, on 24 August 1964, Glen Campbell has been actively involved in commercial theatre in Jamaica from 1981 and, since then, has played major roles in more than fifty stage productions. Campbell takes pride in having shared the same stage with the Honourable Louise Bennett Coverley in the special tribute concert "Miss Lou and Friends" in 1990, and in being invited to perform at the Black Theatre Festival in Durham, North Carolina, in 1996. He also had the opportunity to work in India for more than a month alongside a team of international theatre practitioners from India, Germany and Austria in the UNESCO-sponsored World Theatre Project in 1994.

In addition to performing, Campbell has directed the Belizean production of *Run for Your Wife*. He is the resident dramatic advisor and stage manager for the Stella Maris (Young Adult) Dance Ensemble, assists the University of Technology Drama Society from time to time, functions as talent liaison for Jambiz Productions, and works on various projects with the Center Stage Theatre Workshop. He is an adjudicator for the annual National Speech and Drama Festival sponsored by the Jamaica Cultural Development Commission (JCDC), and works in collaboration with the Jamaica Tourist Board's Educational Drama projects.

A graduate of Jamaica College, Campbell holds a certificate in public relations from the Institute of Management and Production, a certificate from the University of the West Indies Radio Unit and a diploma in public relations from the Jamaica Institute of Management. He recently completed a two-year course for which he received certificates in theatre studies from the University of Manchester, England, and the Rose Bruford College, London.

His role as Titus in the 1990 Jamaican television sitcom *Titus in Town* made him a household name among Jamaican audiences, both locally and overseas. He has since done more television and film work, playing leading roles in docudramas for the Jamaica Information Service and the National Family Planning Board, and has appeared in the movie *Hammerhead*, an episode of Lorimar's series *Going to Extremes* and the Jamaican short film *Entry Denied*.

Glen Campbell has recorded numerous commercials and music videos, including appearances in internationally distributed commercials for AT&T, Malibu Rums, Western Union and Red Stripe Beer. His last film appearance (at the time of writing) was a cameo role, as a security guard in the Jamaican film *Third World Cop*. He recently completed filming of a thirteen-episode sitcom entitled *Tiny's Place* alongside Claudette Pious. He continues to be seen regularly in local television commercials, including ones for Maxfield Bakery, Singer Company and Victoria Mutual Building Society, and can be heard regularly on radio commercials.

The Team of Reggie and Sheila Carter

Reggie Carter as Simon Bolivar

Reggie Carter, in his own special ways, was a Caribbean man, born 20 May 1936 in Panama City, to a German father who spoke fluent English and to a mother who was a ballet dancer. He lived in Antigua and Barbados before coming to Jamaica in 1940 at the age of four. He inherited his artistic leanings from his father, who took part in plays and read poetry on Jamaica's first radio station, ZQI; his gentle manner came from his mother.

While at Priory School under headmaster Henry Fowler, Reggie Carter participated in drama and took part in the Secondary Schools' Drama Festival, launched by the Little Theatre Movement (LTM) and the British Council in 1950. He came under the influence of Maurice Harty, then an outstanding young Jamaican producer and director, and was afterward brought into contact with Doris Hastings (*née* Mitchell) a former actress and producer from Broadway, who was at the time producing for the Theatre Arts Club and the ZQI Players, in addition to adjudicating for the Secondary Schools' Drama Festival. Carter's first major role was as Benjy in *The Harrowing of Benjy*, by Roderick Walcott of St Lucia. The role of Rasta Man earned him the award for outstanding actor in the 1957 Drama Festival.

Carter credits Doris Hastings with introducing him to the theatre, and Eric Rumsey for instructing him in stage management and lighting design. He honed these technical skills by assisting with technical production and by operating the follow spotlight for *Blythe Spirit* at the LTM's old Rainbow Theatre at Half Way Tree in 1951, and in the 1960s with George Carter at the Ward Theatre. He went on to perform in two pantomimes.

Reggie Carter was the product of a sound Jamaican secondary school education. It was this preparation, backed by tuition in voice and speech, drama and music from first-rate local practitioners, that he brought to his craft as actor, news-reader and presenter at the JBC when that station came on the air for the first time on 1 April 1959. His was the first voice to say over the air: "This is the Jamaica Broadcasting Corporation." And still, "Whether in broadcasting, advertising or in the theatre, or as talent or performer, Reggie Carter, by virtue of his use of the spoken word remains Jamaica's great exemplar."[1]

At JBC, Carter was hired as an actor for radio drama and played the title role in the medieval classic *Everyman*, which was chosen as one of the offerings to open the station. He later became production manager for radio, and in 1960 was sent to a radio training course at the BBC. Three years later he went on another BBC course, this time in television, as JBC was about to enter the television age.

In about 1966, Carter and Sheila Hill (who became his wife), along with Keith Sasso, Geoffrey Searle and a number of other persons, formed the Jamaica Playhouse. According to Sheila, "This was an expression of Reggie's love for the theatre, good theatre. Theatre that he was sure Jamaica deserved to see. Productions of works of merit, to a standard that belied the fact that members of the Jamaica Playhouse all had full-time jobs off the stage."[2] Reggie Carter, master craftsman, perfectionist, a true professional, worked no less than an artist – blocking, shaping, moulding – adding here and there, standing back with a smile, or the whole thing would be scrapped and he would start all over again.[3]

Members of the Jamaica Playhouse were a dynamic team. They learned to switch roles on stage, tackle technical tasks backstage and even to ad lib when the lights were late in coming up. The aim was to have two productions a year. For the tenth anniversary celebrations of the Playhouse, they had two productions opening simultaneously and revived ten past plays, among them *The Owl and the Pussycat*, followed six days later with *You Know I Can't Hear You When the Water's Running*, *Slow Dance on the Killing Ground*, *Tarshan Lace and Velvet*, and *Rogers, Hamlet & Co.*

Carter was technical director in *Butterflies Are Free*, co-director with Don Bucknor in *One Time Long Time*, with Keith Sasso in *Double Event*, with Bobby Ghisays in *Dat*, and with wife Sheila in what was to be their final production, *Double Take*, in 1977. In 1965 Carter left the JBC for the field of advertising, where he remained until his death on 2 September 1995 – all the while maintaining his deep involvement in the theatre.

Reggie Carter in *The Devil*, directed by Lloyd Reckord (1972). *Photo by Maria LaYacona.*

Shakespeare's *King Lear*, with Reggie Carter, in a 1966 production directed by Noel Vaz. *Photo by Maria LaYacona.*

Carter was a three-time winner of the best actor award, including two consecutive wins of the Drama Critic Award for performances of lead roles, for his work in Moliere's plays *The School for Wives* and *The Imaginary Invalid*. He acted in all forms of theatre and directed scores of productions. He played *Hamlet* in the show directed by Carroll Dawes and produced by Wycliffe Bennett, *Othello* under the direction of Sy Syna and *King Lear* under director Noel Vaz. He played Theseus opposite Tess Thomas in the title role in Racine's *Phædra*, directed by Wycliffe Bennett, and in other French classics, including Moliere's *The Miser* and *School for Wives*, in the American musical *Oklahoma*, and in seven revues in the *Eight O'Clock Jamaica Time* series produced by Tony Gambrill. He had small parts in three films: *Dr No* (1962), *The Lunatic* (1992) and *Sankofa* (1993). He had also established the lead role of Ted Blackburn in a local television series, *Royal Palm Estate*, produced and directed by Lennie Little-White, through which he became a household name before he died of a heart attack at the age of fifty-nine.

Sheila Carter was the other half of that rare husband-and-wife team in Jamaican theatre, skilled in all aspects of the craft – costuming, scenery, lighting and sound effects – as well as being a brilliant actress. Sheila (*née* Hill) was born in Kingston on 25 November 1939, and her interest in drama began at Coke Church when she was just eight years old. She later attended St Andrew High School and the University of the West Indies (UWI), where her interest in drama continued.

At St Andrew High School she came under the influence of Jean Watson, who helped to establish that school's theatrical tradition. She also acted small parts in Shakespearean plays directed for schools by Noel Vaz, and gained further experience by travelling the country with Louise Bennett Coverley's drama group, for which she did mainly backstage work.[4] She received speech training from Wycliffe Bennett and from Trevor Rhone, and in 1963 won the Sir Alexander Bustamante Cup for best actress in the Carey Robinson play *The Runaway*, in which she acted the part of the old witch. In 1964 she was invited to perform in the LTM's pantomime *Bredda Buck*.

Sheila Carter, actress, co-founder of Jamaica Playhouse with Reggie Carter

As a student at the UWI, Sheila became an active member of the Drama Society in the company of such thespians as Dennis Scott and Peter Maxwell. The group mounted several shows that toured the Caribbean Islands. She also made costumes for the UWI carnival celebrations, which, in those days, were a major feature of campus life, coinciding with the Trinidad Carnival that takes place every weekend before Ash Wednesday.

In 1966 Sheila joined Jamaica Playhouse, founded by Reggie Carter, and they were married three years later. She started the Romper Room series for young children at JBC-TV, and remained with the programme for four years. She was a full-time teacher of Spanish but her heart was in theatre. In Jamaica Playhouse, Sheila and Reggie were a formidable team, training, producing and creating performances of quality. Together they made a monumental contribution to the Jamaican theatre.

Aston Cooke

Aston Cooke, playwright

Aston Cooke began writing for the Secondary Schools' Drama Festival while he was a student at Wolmer's Boys' School in the 1970s. He read for a Bachelor of Arts degree in mass communications (1984), and was the recipient of the Canadian Commonwealth Scholarship in 1989 that enabled him to earn a Bachelor of Commerce in hospitality and tourism management (1993) at Ryerson Polytechnic University, Toronto. He then returned to Jamaica and completed the master's in communications studies (2001) at the UWI.

Cooke wrote the first episodes of the very popular comedic series *Oliver at Large* for Oliver Samuels. He has also written the LTM pantomime *River Mumma and the Golden Table* (1987) and a number of farces, including *Children-Children* (1985), *Jamaica Run Down* (1995), *Jamaica Pepperpot* (1996), *Country Duppy* (2000), *Single Entry* (2003), *Jamaica2Rahtid* (2005) and *Concubine* (2007) – most of which may be styled "roots" plays appealing to the sensual urges.

Cooke is artistic director of the Jamaica Youth Theatre, a group he founded in 2004, which serves as the performing arm of the Schools' Drama Festival of Jamaica. He continues to serve the annual Secondary Schools' Drama Festival of Jamaica as coordinator. In 2007, he was inducted into the Caribbean Hall of Fame for his contribution to Jamaican theatre.

Vivian Crawford

Vivian Crawford, organist

Vivian Crawford has been a management consultant since 1995. Besides being a graduate of the Mico Teachers' College, the UWI and Nova Southeastern University (United States), he has had extensive financial experience in the private sector. He has taken this expertise to his latest job as executive director of the Institute of Jamaica since 2000. Under his watch, the Institute has restored Liberty Hall, the legacy of Marcus Garvey, and has implemented the Sites of Memory programme, which commemorates outstanding records of Jamaica's history through the installation of plaques at such sites as the Old King's House, Spanish Town (where the Abolition of Slavery Act was read in 1834), the last house where Marcus Garvey lived, and the birthplace of Mary Seacole, perhaps Jamaica's most outstanding nurse of the nineteenth century.

Crawford served with distinction as chairman of the JCDC for ten years, and continues to serve on numerous other cultural and educational boards. In 2003 he was instrumental, with Dr Olive Lewin, in having UNESCO declare the music of the Moore Town Maroons as part of the Intangible Heritage of Mankind (one of only twenty-five such declarations to date). Crawford is himself a Moore Town Maroon. He is also a church organist and choirmaster. He has received many honours and awards, including the Order of Distinction from the Government of Jamaica, and the University of Technology's Distinguished Service Award.

Basil Dawkins

Dawkins entered the world of theatre as an actor at the UWI Inter-Hall Drama Festivals while reading for his degree in government in the 1970s. During his undergraduate years, he acted in over twenty productions, notably among them *Blues for Mr Charlie*, *Black Jacobins* and many experimental pieces. After graduating from the UWI, Dawkins became a member of the Caribbean Theatre Workshop (CTW) and was later inspired to write as a pastime in order to stay involved in theatre. To date he has written twenty plays, and has undoubtedly become one of Jamaica's foremost writers.

Basil Dawkins, playwright

Critics have consistently hailed Dawkins's comedies and dramas as being engaging and entertaining while, at the same time, being serious but not overbearing and pertinent to current Jamaican issues and with a universal resonance.

Dawkins's list of plays include *Flatmate*, *Parson and Mrs Jones*, *Couple*, *Champagne and Sky Juice*, *Same Song Different Tune*, *God Bless*, *Power Play*, *Toy Boy*, *Feminine Justice*, *What the Hell is Happening to Us, Dear?*, *No Dirty Money*, *A Gift for Mom*, *No Disrespect*, *Hot Spot*, *Uptown Bangarang*, *Uptown Bangarang 2*, and *Which Way Is Out?* It is not unusual for his plays to enjoy lengthy runs with packed houses in Jamaica, followed by successful tours to the United States, Canada, the United Kingdom, Bermuda and Grand Cayman.

Basil Dawkins has been the recipient of a number of awards for his work in theatre, in literary activities and at the national level. His success has not only been driven by well-written, award-winning scripts, but by the professional teams of actors and technical personnel which he selects. Dawkins ensures that, whenever possible, he exposes both new and old talents in theatre, giving them prominence and personal success while keeping theatre constantly refreshed. His dream is to see "theatre becoming a potent force to be integrated in the economic mainstream, contributing to economic growth and development".

Members of Basil Dawkins's theatre company

Over the years he has found time to serve in different capacities, contributing to the development and promotion of theatre and culture at the national level in such organizations as the Jamaica Association of Dramatic Artists (of which he is the founding president), the Government of Jamaica Entertainment Advisory Board, the CHASE Advisory Committee, and the Ward Theatre Foundation. His annual productions are supported by over eighty associations, non-governmental organizations, service clubs and charities, which buy out the houses and resell the tickets as a means of raising funds to support their various community development and outreach projects.

Noel Dexter

Noel Dexter, musican, composer

Noel Dexter was born at Red Hazsell in the parish of Portland on 21 December 1938. His first stage performance was at age six when, with his beautiful treble voice, he won the first prize of an ice cream cone in a church harvest supper talent competition. At age eight he played the lead role of the Prince in his elementary school's production of the operetta *Cinderella*. Around the same time, his family acquired a piano for his older brother and sister, who were taking piano lessons. Noel taught himself to play the instrument so that, two years later, when he had his first piano lesson he impressed his teacher by sight-reading a grade 4 piano piece. Soon after, he was playing solos and accompanying soloists at concerts in Port Antonio.

At age twelve Dexter was appointed assistant organist at the Methodist Church and was pianist for morning prayers at Titchfield Secondary School, which he attended from 1953 to 1958. He excelled in sports as well as in drama and dance. He choreographed his school's entries in the National Festival competitions and later for the Port Antonio Dance Troupe; he also acted in and directed a number of religious plays for his church's youth group and played the piano at a local club on weekends.

His dramatic talents began to shine when he played the lead role in *The Harrowing of Benjy*, and in *Square Peg*, his group's entry in the Adult Drama Festival in Kingston in 1960. When he moved to Kingston, he continued to play a number of minor roles in plays produced by Orford St John and Keith Parkin for the Repertory Players. It was for his role as Man Boy in a production of Sam Hilary's *Chippy* (1961), however, that he again received special recognition. He was named the best supporting actor in the Adult Drama Festival that year.

For two consecutive years, Dexter participated in the speech festival and was runner-up to the All-Island Champion in the adult class, despite the fact that he had never had a coach. He was invited by organizer Wycliffe Bennett to accompany him to rural parishes to participate in training workshops, but his love for music soon took over and he joined the then newly formed Jamaica Amateur Operatic Society. With this group, he performed in the chorus line of *Pirates of Penzance* and *Desert Song*, as well as in Derek Boughton's production of *The Boyfriend*.

Dexter was then a teacher of economics at Ardenne High School. He gradually became more involved in the school's music programme and eventually became music teacher. He had been attending the Jamaica School of Music for some time, and in

Man Boy in a production of Sam Hilary's *Chippy* (1961). *Wycliffe Bennett collection.*

1970 gained the LTCL in Class Music Teaching from Trinity College of Music. Under Dexter's direction the Ardenne High School Choir developed a reputation for excellence in the Jamaica Festival competitions, winning several gold medals over the years. Dexter also taught music part-time at Mico Teachers' College and at Mona Preparatory School, where he directed outstanding choirs. He founded the Youth Fellowship Singers from among young people in the Corporate Area congregations of the Church of God in Jamaica. The choir distinguished itself in the National Festivals and made tours overseas to the United States, Grand Cayman and the Bahamas. With this choir Dexter produced a long playing record, *Caribbean Church Music*, for the Caribbean Conference of Churches (CCC). The Youth Fellowship Singers Choir also led the music for the funeral service for the late premier (later national hero) Norman Washington Manley, and the service welcoming Bishop Desmond Tutu of South Africa to Jamaica.

In the 1970s Dexter served as the first coordinator of the Caribbean Church Music programme of the Caribbean Council of Churches. This position enabled him to travel throughout the English-speaking Caribbean islands, where he encouraged the creation of indigenous church music and compiled *Sing a New Song*, a collection of Caribbean religious hymns and songs used today in churches throughout the region.

In 1977 Dexter was appointed director of music on the Mona campus of the UWI and served in that capacity for twenty-seven years. He became musical director of the University Singers, and together they created musical arrangements and compositions. The University Singers is today one of the leading choral groups in the anglophone Caribbean and, under the guidance of artistic director Rex Nettleford, has become one of the leading exponents of what is called Caribbean choral music theatre. The choir performs regularly at important events on the Mona campus, at national and other events, and has toured locally and overseas on many occasions. They have produced a number of recordings that are recognized for their consistently high standard of performance. Dexter's wife, Beverley (Aarons), is an outstanding soprano.

Doris Duperley

Doris Duperley, a teacher by profession, came to Jamaica in 1933. She soon became involved with Henry Fowler and Greta Bourke (Fowler) in the cultural and theatrical activities of Kingston. When the LTM was formally organized in 1941 she was one of the early members. She took part in several plays and pantomimes, and eventually became secretary of the LTM. She was also a member of the Theatre Arts Club, where she was responsible for publicity and acted in four plays: *Arms and the Man*, *Still Life*, *Present Laughter* and *Gaslight*.

Always a keen actress, Duperley never sought the limelight but threw an increasing amount of her effort into theatre with a devotion and dedication that made her an example to all. She earned her living operating the Phoenix Bookshop (and Lunchroom) in Kingston for over twenty years. She raised bookselling from a trade to a conscious intellectual service and an exciting and challenging venture, and her bookshop became a meeting place for intellectuals. Duperley spent vast energies on the development of the Schools' Drama Festival, and finally dedicated herself wholeheartedly to working for the creation and maintenance of the Little Theatre as a service to the community. For her, the theatre became a way of life in which she completely immersed herself with unswerving dedication and energy. She was at all times indefatigable, unflappable and indispensable.

Her great energy, her enormous capacity for work (even if it was strenuous, dull and dusty), her great inventiveness as costumier and designer, her generosity of spirit and magnanimity of mind made her the pivot of the Little Theatre, which is, in large measure, a monument to the fixity of purpose and unceasing daily concentration with which she laboured year after year. Without her tenacity, her steady attention to routine, the Little Theatre might not have been built, nor would the theatre tradition in Jamaica have been so firmly established. The amazing theatrical renaissance of the 1950s and 1960s owes much to Doris Duperley. Many young actors in Pantomime, some now established stars of the theatre, regarded her as the solid rock on which the Jamaican theatre world depended. Her contribution has been immense. Doris Duperley died in 1975.

Fae Ellington

Fae Ellington, born in Clarendon on 28 May 1953, is a broadcast journalist, actor, lecturer, trainer and speaking coach, a sought-after master of ceremonies and motivational speaker. In school, she earned both a diploma in mass communication and a Master of Arts degree in communication studies from the Caribbean Institute of Media and Communication (CARIMAC), UWI. Her experience in the communications field spans more than thirty-five years: she has been certified by the BBC as a trainer in radio and television production since 1985; and she served from 1974 to 1999 at the JBC as a radio and television announcer, presenter and producer, excelling in such programmes as *Morning Time*, which she anchored for close to two decades. She has also worked as a news anchor on television, and has taught voice and speech, as well as radio and television production, at CARIMAC for more than twenty-one years.

Fae Ellington, actress

Ellington has played major roles in several leading plays and pantomimes, including *Music Boy* (1971) and *Trash* (1985). She also acted in *Servant of Two Masters* (1971); *Macbeth* for television (1974); Louis Marriott's *Pack of Jokers* (1978); *Playboy* (1981); *Bedward* (1984); Easton Lee's *The Rope and the Cross* (1972–82); *Smile Orange* (1981); Godfrey Sealy's *One of Our Sons Is Missing* (1983); Neil Simon's *Hotel Suite*, for which she received an Actor Boy award; and Patrick Brown's *Breadfruit Kingdom* (1999), for which she also received the Actor Boy award for best supporting actress. In addition, she has directed a successful one-woman show, *Who Will Sing for Lena* (2005), powerfully acted by Makeda Solomon.

Fae Ellington has developed a national reputation as a highly prized stage, radio and television personality, and is often invited to host national events and to report on royal occasions. Her work is characterized by deep study and preparation and an exemplary professional delivery. She has become a model for a younger generation to learn from.

Leonie Forbes

Leonie Forbes – actress, broadcaster, producer, lecturer – is a graduate of the Royal Academy of Dramatic Art (RADA), London. She has worked at the Jamaica Broadcasting Corporation (JBC), the Australian Broadcasting Corporation (ABC) and the British Broadcasting Corporation (BBC), as well as in Canada and the United States and on stage in several RADA and TALAWA theatre group productions in England.

Leonie Forbes, actress. *Photo by Monica DaSilva.*

Forbes is one of Jamaica's most talented actors in theatre, radio, film and television. She was first introduced to radio while a secretary in the Radio Education Unit of the UWI. She claimed that typing Barry Reckord's script of *Miss Unusual*, accompanying him to the Government Information Service and doing small parts in radio programmes triggered her first real involvement in theatre. She claims (tongue-in-cheek) that, after performing in only two pantomimes, *Busha Bluebeard* (1957) and *Quashie Lady* (1958), she was the first person to organize a "strike" in the Jamaican theatre (1957). Her complaint was that the cast was working long hours without even refreshments. For this she incurred the wrath of some of her fellow actors, who felt that they had just managed to get black people into the pantomime, and that her actions were jeopardizing these advances. The strike was a success as, according to Forbes, "We got lunch: a soft drink and a patty."

Forbes was part of director Lloyd Reckord's *Busha Bluebeard* cast, which went to Trinidad in May 1958 to represent Jamaica at the West Indies Festival. Because of a travel disruption, some of the props and the main attraction, Louise Bennett (Coverley), did not arrive on time, and Leonie was sent front-of-curtain to sing one of

Leonie Forbes as Mary in *The Rope and the Cross*. *Photo by Monica DaSilva.*

"Miss Lou's" favourites, which was well received. She began working at JBC Radio as a duty announcer in 1959 and was encouraged by Robin Midgely (at that time seconded from the BBC to establish the drama department of JBC Radio) to improve her training in broadcasting. With his help, she obtained a scholarship to RADA, where she spent six years (1960–66), finally graduating with a diploma in radio, television and stage. At the same time she worked on scripts in the BBC's Caribbean section. Forbes also appeared in several RADA productions, including the pantomime *Cinderella*. She played in *Days of the Lion* and *Anthony and Cleopatra*, and featured in a television drama series on BBC while she also worked in other independent television networks. Her first appearance in professional theatre was Reckord's production of the musical *Double Entry* (London, 1962), for which she received high praise from critic Kenneth Tynan.

On her return from Britain to Jamaica in 1966, Forbes worked at JBC for the next two years before leaving for Australia with her husband, who had received a Commonwealth veterinary science scholarship. In Australia she appeared in the *Merchant of Venice*, worked at the Australia Broadcasting Corporation in radio plays, taught drama at Brisbane schools and worked at other jobs.

On her return to Jamaica from Australia in 1970, she was employed at the JBC as producer and presenter for television. She spearheaded Radio Two, JBC's FM stereo service, and ran their television drama workshop. At the same time, she served as an adjudicator for the Jamaica Festival Commission. She was appointed director of broadcasting (1976–77) and joint head of their Department of Theatre, with Charles Hyatt, in 1978–79. She also played the character of Miss Aggy in Trevor Rhone's popular *Old Story Time* (1979). Out of the drama workshop came screen plays (*A Scent of Jasmine*, *What's Good for the Goose* and *Let's Say Grace*), which she wrote and produced for television and radio.

Leonie Forbes and Charles Hyatt in *Old Story Time*, by Trevor Rhone. *Photo by Monica DaSilva.*

In referring to the 1982 production of Trevor Rhone's *Two Can Play*, Forbes noted at the time that there was no actor's equity, no residuals. Work was offered and accepted without proper contractual arrangements, which made for ready exploitation from both local and overseas companies. Forbes has acted in some twenty films, including *Club Paradise*, *Milk and Honey*, *Children of Babylon* (1980), *Lord Have Mercy* (2003) and *Glory to Gloriana* (2006). Her latest film, *A Winter's Tale*, premiered in Toronto in December 2007, and opened the fifteenth annual African Diaspora Film Festival in New York.[5]

Forbes has acted in leading roles in twelve pantomimes in Jamaica. Some of her other stage roles include *Ask Your Mama* (Langston Hughes), *Moon on a Rainbow Shall* (Errol John), *Champagne and Sky Juice* (Patrick Brown), *The Rope and the Cross* (Easton Lee), *December* (Patrick Brown), *Arawak Gold* (Carmen Tipling) and *Toy Boy* (Basil Dawkins). Her television credits include *South of the Border*, *I Is a Long Memoried Woman*, *The Orchid House*, *Passion and Paradise*, *Born Free*, *Going to Extremes*, and *Miranda Hill*. Along with Alma Mock Yen, she co-authored *Re-Entry into Sound*, a work which has become a standard text for training broadcasters in the Caribbean. She has received the Centenary, the Bronze Musgrave and the Silver Musgrave Medals of the Institute of Jamaica, and a gold medal for craft (for crochet items) from the Jamaica Festival Commission.

She was awarded the Order of Distinction (OD) by the Government of Jamaica in 1980. In November 2007 she was recognized by the United States Congress and the Jamaican community in New York for her five decades of professional excellence in broadcasting, theatre and film. In paying tribute to her, Jamaica's acting consul general in New York presented her with a certificate of merit, and Congressman Ed Towns of Brooklyn, in his citation, stated that Leonie Forbes had blazed a trail of excellence and had paved the way for aspiring Jamaican and Caribbean actors and actresses.[6]

Henry Fowler

Henry Fowler, co-founder of the LTM

Shortly after Henry Fowler's death, an eloquent editorial was published in the *Gleaner*, praising his contribution to Jamaican national life, education for development and the Jamaican theatre:

> Another link with Jamaica of the past has been severed, with the passing of Henry Fowler, who died in Oxford, England, in the past week. Born when the last century was still relatively young (he saw the light of day May 1915), Fowler was a representative of a class of Jamaicans who were regarded as privileged by virtue of colour, and class. Yet he, like others of that ilk, did not hesitate to engage with the wider community and to embark on the journey towards the creation of a nation.
>
> He grew up in colonial times, when the Jamaican identity was associated with a culture rooted in a distant land. Even though, as a Rhodes Scholar, he was educated in "Mother England", he set his sights on helping to build a new Jamaica according to the vision of Norman Washington Manley, who was to become one of the iconic figures of Jamaica's quest for nationhood, and whom Fowler greatly admired.[7]

After graduating from Oxford, Fowler returned to Jamaica and became actively involved in the social revolution that was just then coming to the fore. He joined the People's National Party along with a band of social activists who were determined to lay the groundwork for a new Jamaica as they campaigned for self-government. At the same time, Fowler took on the role of editor of the *Public Opinion* newspaper, a vehicle purveying liberal views that were not necessarily in keeping with that of the colonial establishment. He also embraced the cause of education and founded the Priory School in 1944. He served as this school's headmaster from 1944 to 1973, as well as on many boards of the Ministry of Education. Considered an elitist institution at the time, Priory was one of a group of schools – Knox College in Manchester and Excelsior College in Kingston being the others – which were part of a new ethos "challenging the old definitions of education and setting new boundaries for the young . . . in their quest for a more relevant education system [appropriate] to the hopes and aspirations of a new generation".[8]

The establishment of the public library service in Jamaica in 1948 was a logical extension of Fowler's vision of education and lifelong learning, and he enthusiastically joined the board of the Kingston and St Andrew Parish Library Committee, of which he served as chairman for many years, helping to introduce the general public not only to books but also to the fine arts. For several years this library became a place where young unknown artists, like the intuitive Kapo (Mallica Reynolds), had their first exposure to public viewing, and aspiring young writers such as Vic Reid researched the settings for their chosen topics.

Apart from his involvement in Jamaica's library system, Henry Fowler served as a consultant in the Ministry of Education to successive Jamaican governments over a twenty-six-year period, and represented the country as Jamaica's minister consul to the United Nations Educational, Scientific and Cultural Organization (UNESCO) in Paris (1977–81), where he helped to place Jamaica on that organization's agenda through his interest and influence in education and the arts. He also represented the country at various conferences and missions in Australia and in several African countries.

In 1941 Henry Fowler co-founded the LTM, along with Greta Bourke, whom he later married. Under LTM auspices, the Fowlers later established the Jamaica Theatre School, which, by 1972, became known as the Jamaica School of Speech and Drama. This institution, in turn, was handed over to the government and became a component of the Cultural Training Centre, now the Edna Manley College for the Visual and Performing Arts. After the passing of Greta Fowler in 1979, Henry became president of the LTM and Barbara Gloudon succeeded him as chair.

Fowler was chairman of the provisional board set up by Premier Norman Manley in 1957 to explore the feasibility of, and then pilot the establishment of, a television station for Jamaica. When the JBC (TV) Board was officially established in 1959, Fowler was appointed to the board and served until 1963. He was also, successively, vice-chairman and chairman between 1973 and 1976. He was also the main inspiration behind the establishment of the Ward Theatre Foundation, whose main objective was to save the landmark building and preserve its heritage as a part of Kingston's cultural history. His was a lifelong interest in the LTM and the Ward, and he was a passionate advocate for maintaining these national symbols.

Ward Theatre Foundation chairpersons. *Left to right:* Wycliffe Bennett, Ruby Martin and Donald Banks (person to the right unidentified).

In his declining years, with his second wife, Beryl Chitty, a former deputy British high commissioner to Jamaica, Fowler relocated to Oxford, where he resided until his passing at the age of ninety-one. As long as he was able, he kept in touch with his beloved Jamaica through annual visits. He remained committed to this country and its advancement, believing to the very end in the possibility of a "new Jamaica".

In paying tribute to Henry Fowler, at the memorial in his honour on 26 March 2007 at the Little Theatre, Wycliffe Bennett recalled:

> As Eve had to be taken from Adam's ribs, so had the LTM from the Ward Theatre's. As Life Member of the LTM and Chairman Emeritus of the Ward, I therefore have a dual function here this afternoon to speak on behalf of the LTM and the Ward Theatre Foundation. They were both founded through the efforts of the late Henry Fowler, whose life and humanity we celebrate today. And I do so with gratitude and pride, because without Henry's intervention in my life I might not have been here standing before you in the capacity of Chairman of the Ward Theatre Foundation and Life Member of the LTM.
>
> I first met Henry in 1943, when I became Secretary of the Poetry League of Jamaica and began organizing Elocution Contests. I had gone to invite him to serve as one of the adjudicators and to get him to donate a prize for an outstanding candidate. This he did, and immediately afterwards I was invited by his close associate Greta Bourke, whom he later married, to become a member of the Little Theatre Movement. As you just heard from George Carter, they were always talent hunting, so they tried never to miss any local show, no matter where it was held.[9]

Here are Fowler's own words, when Bennett interviewed him in 1991, about the birth of the LTM and the first Jamaican pantomime:

> I vividly remember fifty years ago in 1941 sitting on Greta's veranda at 80 Hope Road, discussing the first Jamaican Pantomime, *Jack and the Beanstalk*, with a committee which included Lindsay Downer (the doyen of Jamaican producers), Ansell Hart, Neville (later Sir Neville) Ashenheim, Edna Manley and O.T. Fairclough. The budget which I had prepared showed the unprecedented and frighteningly large total of some £500 for five performances. Wise heads wagged warningly and the idea of a Jamaican Pantomime seemed doomed, when Greta suddenly excused herself from the meeting and returned two minutes later with the announcement: "My sister, Peggy Dougall, has offered to underwrite the Pantomime to the extent of £250". That was how the Jamaican National Pantomime tradition was born 50 years ago.[10]

Fowler was then tutor to the children of Sir Arthur Richards, governor of the island. Robert Henry Fowler, his nephew, remembers:

> Henry was a second-generation Fowler teacher, having himself been taught at an early age by his spinster aunts, who had a school at Shawbery on the outskirts of St Ann's Bay and then at Darliston in Westmoreland . . . Among other beneficiaries of my Great Aunts' tutelage there was also one Marcus Mosiah Garvey, who was so influenced by Henry's aunts that he sought them out in their retirement to visit with them on the Fowler property at Rio Magno.[11]

The important thing to remember is that, in 1943, the island was four years into the Second World War, which had brought several activities in Jamaica to a grinding halt. Such were the realities of the times that Bennett had to seek permission of the governor to organize the elocution contest. In reliance upon the emergency regulations, the governor had found it necessary, at least so he thought, to consign a number of individuals without trial to a concentration camp. Some of these detainees were Frank Hill, Arthur Henry, Richard Hart and W.A. Domingo. They were part of the progressive movement advocating self-government for Jamaica, and the governor thought that such activities, in a time of war, were dangerous and had to be silenced. Fowler was a progressive but, perhaps because of his close association with the governor's family, he escaped the dragnet.

These matters provided the LTM with grist for Jamaica's first locally produced pantomime, *Jack and the Beanstalk*. Wycliffe Bennett continued in his tribute:

> Henry reminded me of the matter fifty years afterwards, in 1991. It is sometimes thought that the Jamaica National Pantomime was originally a purely English transplant. Nothing is further from the truth. Greta was one of the true pioneers of the cultural revolution, which inspired the spirit of the New Jamaica from 1938. The very first pantomime, *Jack and the Beanstalk*, featured a brilliant satire in the figure of the Giant who sentenced his captives to prison without trial. The Giant was a recognizable caricature of the current Colonial Governor, who had just interned Jamaican political leaders, including Bustamante, without trial.[12]

Today, the names Greta and Henry Fowler are synonymous with that of the LTM. As regards the Ward Theatre, Fowler remained deeply conscious that, without the Ward, there would have been no Little Theatre. He saw the Little Theatre as a feeder for the Ward Theatre, and recognized that he needed the revenue from the pantomimes staged at the Ward to finance the operations of the LTM. For many years his was the sole voice fighting to preserve the Ward Theatre, a gift to the people of the city of Kingston by the Honourable Colonel Charles James Ward, custos of Kingston. Fowler formed a committee which eventually evolved into the Ward Theatre Trust, to lease the Ward Theatre for twenty years, to rescue it from being used as a cinema and to restore its rightful role as a home for theatre in the true meaning of the word. Two members of the Ward Theatre Foundation signed the lease – Edward Miller, permanent secretary in the Ministry of Local Government, and Wycliffe Bennett as honorary secretary-general of the Ward Theatre Foundation. It caused Fowler much pain when the pantomime had to be removed from the Ward to the Little Theatre in 2002.

Bobby Ghisays

Born in 1934 in Kingston of a Columbian father and Jamaican mother of Lebanese descent, playwright, actor and television director Bobby Ghisays began his acting career at fourteen years of age. From 1951 to 1955 he attended Holy Cross College, Massachusetts, where he earned a Bachelor of Arts degree; from 1955 to 1957 he attended the Royal Academy of Dramatic Art, where he acted in several shows open to the public, including *The Merchant of Venice* and *Electra*. In the 1960s he worked for three years as a correspondent for Reuters in Rome in the areas of film, television and theatre. After returning to Jamaica in 1970, he worked as a freelance presenter and producer in the news and public affairs department of the JBC, and also taught drama at Queen's and St Andrew High Schools.

Bobby Ghisays, playwright, actor

Between 1960 and 1980, Ghisays directed over twenty plays, both locally and abroad. Some of these include *Annie Get Your Gun*, *Come Blow Your Horn*, *Eight O'Clock Jamaica Time* (a review), *Come Home to Jamaica* and *The Dread Mikado*. He also co-authored and directed *Bathurst Street*, and directed *A Raisin in the Sun* (Hansberry) at the invitation of the Black Theatre in Canada. He later directed several more plays, including the pantomimes *Johnnie Reggae*, *Pirate Princess*, and *General B*, and in the 1980s he produced and presented the *Sunday Morning Classic* for JBC-TV, which brought film classics to the local scene. He also brought to television new movies not yet shown in local cinemas, until government injunction forced the discontinuation of the practice.

As a performer, Ghisays acted in more than a dozen plays, including Trevor Rhone's *Old Story Time* and in the revival of the pantomime *Queenie's Daughter*. He also acted in the BBC Television series *Fight against Slavery* (written by Jamaican Evan Jones) and played the governor in Perry Henzell's film *Garvey: The Musical* (1987). Ghisays had small roles in the following films: ABC's Armchair Theatre series (1957), *Club Paradise* (1986), *The Mighty Quinn* (1989), *Passion and Paradise* (1989) and *Popcorn* (1991). He also appeared in the following television presentations: *Macbeth* (1974), produced and directed by Wycliffe Bennett for JBC-TV; *Salomé*, directed by Donat Bucknor (1979); the soap opera *One Life to Live*; *Saturday Night Sit-In* (1970s); and the miniseries *The Orchid House* (1991), set in Dominica. Ghisays died in 1990.

Ancile Gloudon

Ancile Gloudon, actor and producer. *Courtesy of LTM.*

Ancile Gloudon was one of the early members of the University College of the West Indies Dramatic Society during the period 1952–57. He first appeared in Derek Walcott's landmark production *The Sea at Dauphin*, in the role of Augustin. He followed up this performance with parts in *King Lear*, *Henri Christophe*, *The Tempest*, *Othello* and *A Midsummer Night's Dream*, and played the lead role in Errol Hill's *Man Better Man*.

On graduating from the University of the West Indies, Gloudon joined the New Theatre group and appeared in the lead role of Stephen in *Murder Without Crime*. He directed Tom Theobald's adaptation of *Look Back in Anger*, and acted in Trevor Rhone's *The Gadget*, which later developed into *Old Story Time*. He appeared as Hector in *Tiger at the Gates*, produced and directed by Lloyd Reckord; as the King in *The King and I*; as Aatahualpa in *Royal Hunt of the Sun*; in *The Fantasticks*; and in *A Funny Thing Happened on the Way to the Forum*.

For Gloudon his most memorable performance was as one of the kings in *Three Kings Darkly*, which he produced after the show's initial run. He appeared as one of the main protagonists, a fisherman, in the film *Piranha 2: The Spawning* and as a sailor in two episodes of *Return to Treasure Island*, a serial depicting the life and times of an off-shore university on a tropical island. He also played the role of the priest in the Canadian film *Undue Influence* and appeared in a film about the death of Sir Harry Oaks, and as the butler in *Wide Sargasso Sea*, repeating the role in the BBC docudrama.

Anya Gloudon-Nelson

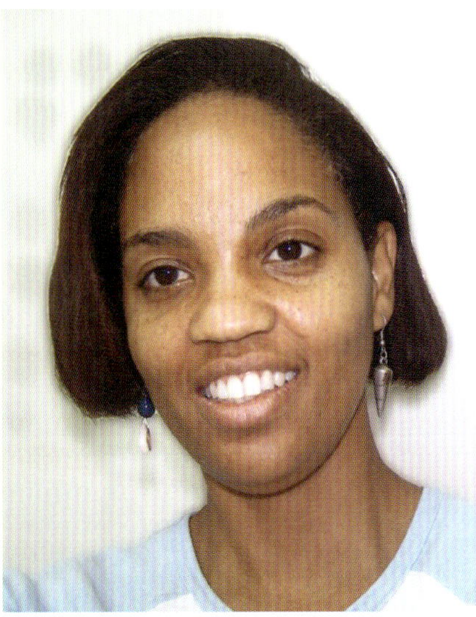

Anya Gloudon-Nelson, costumer designer for LTM. *Courtesy of LTM.*

Anya Gloudon-Nelson, a graduate of the Edna Manley School for the Visual and Performing Arts (now the Edna Manley College), is currently a freelance graphic artist producing print and web-based artwork for various organizations and companies, including the Jamaica Civil Service Association, Caribbean Food and Nutrition Institute, and the UWI School of Nursing.

Anya is a member of the LTM's Pantomime Company design team. Her first foray into costume design was the 1991–92 production *Man Deh Yah*. Since then she has worked on sixteen other pantomimes and has been recognized by the Actor Boy Awards with several nominations and an award for best costume design for the 2003–4 pantomime *Miss Annie*. Over the years, the various storylines have brought the challenges of creating costumes for everything from moon creatures to Tainos (Arawaks). Anya draws on Jamaican folk culture forms as well as on contemporary trends for inspiration. She serves as graphic artist to the LTM and is webmaster of the pantomime's website.

Olivia Atavia Grange

Olivia "Babsy" Grange, minister of information, culture, youth and sports since September 2007, has had a long, vibrant career as a politician, journalist, media specialist, entrepreneur and promoter of popular Jamaican music. As a parliamentarian she has served in the Senate and in the House of Representatives, and has worked on several parliamentary committees covering diverse issues – the Access to Information Act, the Offences against the Person Act, the Incest Act, the promotion of women's affairs, and legislation dealing with reparations. She is also committed to creating opportunities for youth in early childhood education, as well as creating better conditions for the elderly. She has served on the boards of Radio Jamaica and TVJ.

Olivia "Babsy" Grange, popular music promoter and presently minister of information, culture, youth and sports

Born in Kingston on 19 April 1946, Grange's formal education includes Gaynstead College (where she was head girl), Keele Vocational Training School (Canada), and Ryerson Polytechnic University (Toronto, Canada). During her stay in Canada (1969–71), she co-founded and was managing editor of *Contrast*, Canada's first black community newspaper, which offered black Canadians an avenue of expression and a chance to promote their culture through a medium which was both familiar and committed. At that time they had no outlet in the country's established newspapers.

For most of her life Babsy Grange has been an ardent supporter and promoter of Jamaican culture through her contribution to the development of popular Jamaican music, especially the reggae music industry in Jamaica, Canada and the United States. During the 1980s and 1990s, she was manager of a group of musicians who are now famous international artists: Shabba Ranks, Yellowman, Carlene Davis, Ken Boothe and Damian Marley (Junior Gong). She has been chief executive officer of an entertainment promotions company with a talent and flair for film, television and music production. Her record production label was Orange Productions.

Her involvement in Jamaican culture dates back to the early years of Jamaica's independence, when a young sociologist, Edward Seaga, who later became minister of finance and then prime minister, began to develop the inner-city slum "Back-o-Wall" in West Kingston into a modern housing community. Grange was involved in organizing cultural programmes for youth in the community, and was the first president of the Chocomo Lawn–based Victor's Youth Club, which produced many of the early popular stars of rocksteady and reggae, including the Techniques, Slim Smith and Pat Kelly.

She worked in West Kingston primarily as a social and cultural activist, but within an environment dominated by Edward Seaga as the member of parliament, and the Jamaica Labour Party (JLP) as the dominant political party in the area. From 1972 to 1977 she was an arts officer of the Institute of Jamaica and worked in community cultural development programmes in West Kingston. From 1981 to 1983 she served as entertainment arts director and director of cultural development at the JCDC, and in 1983 as executive director. She was responsible for one of the most successful periods in Jamaica's cultural development.

During Grange's tenure as at JCDC, the annual Festival Song Competition grew immensely in terms of the quality of the songs, interest in the competition and attendance at live shows, resulting in increased revenues to support the events. In addition, other areas of the festival movement also showed significant improvement during the period, benefiting immensely from the experience gathered by the director over the years in West Kingston, as well as her strong commitment to the development of Jamaica's arts and culture.

Babsy Grange has presided over one of the most significant periods in the development of Jamaican pop music, with the emergence of dancehall music in the mid-1980s as a new form of expression. Grange served as music director for the reggae film *Klash* (a romantic thriller set in Jamaica and featuring popular African-American actors Giancarlo Esposito and Jasmine Guy) and the Jamaican feature film *Another Kind of Music*. In television, she was co-conceptualizer of the very popular *Oliver at Large* series, featuring actor Oliver Samuels. She is also executive producer of the Edward Seaga *Vintage Jamaican Music* CD series.

In her political life, Grange has served as senator, parliamentary secretary for information and culture (1983–85), and minister of state in the Office of the Prime Minister (1985–89). She assisted in the development of the Jamaican Copyright Act (1995) and was a founding member of the Jamaica Association of Composers, Artists and Performers (JACAP), of which she is a director. Since 1997 she has been a lecturer at the Institute of Management, Kingston, on entertainment and music management. Grange was awarded the 1982 City TV Iris Award for production of Special Music Events in Toronto, Canada; and in 1997 she was nominated for Jamaica's Woman of the Year.

Peter Haley

Peter Haley, actor, director

Peter Haley, FAIA, FCIM, was born in England on 15 September 1934. He spent the first years of his theatrical life with the Oxford Society and the Bolley Players, participating in some six productions, including *The Mikado*, *Nude with Violin*, *The Room* and *Summer of the Seventeenth Doll*.

On his arrival in Jamaica in 1962, Haley joined the Jamaica Amateur Operatic Society (now the Jamaica Musical Theatre Company) and acted in no less than twenty-five productions, including *The Gondoliers*, *The Merry Widow*, *Orpheus*, *Carousel*, *Lock up Your Daughters*, *The King and I*, and *The Sound of Music*. He also directed four shows for the adult group – *Fiddler on the Roof*, *Jesus Christ Superstar*, *West Side Story* and *Bubbling Brown Sugar* – as well as nineteen for the Junior Theatre, including *Cinderella*, *Rockin' Romeo*, *Scheherazade's Tale*, *Aida*, *Cats* (twice), *Joseph and the Amazing Technicolor Dreamcoat* (twice), *Beauty and the Beast*, and *The Lion King*. Some of these shows have won local Actor Boy awards.

Haley was also a member of the Noel Vaz New Theatre Company and the Paul Methuen group, and took part in the annual pantomime *Morgan's Dream of Old Port Royal*. He acted in other shows such as *The Bald Soprano*, *The Cherry Orchard*, *Tiger at the Gates*, *Blythe Spirit* and seven Shakespearean plays: *As You Like It*, *Romeo and Juliet*, *Much Ado about Nothing*, *A Midsummer Night's Dream*, *Othello*, *The Taming of the Shrew*, and *The Merry Wives of Windsor*.

Haley has participated in four plays directed for television, including *Flashpoint '38*, about the Frome Riots in Jamaica. He expresses his pleasure in working with such Jamaican personalities as Ranny Williams, Louise Bennett Coverley, Lois Kelly

Miller, Reggie Carter, Oliver Samuels, Dennis Scott, Keith Sasso and Charles Hyatt, and to have been directed by persons like Maurice Harty, Reggie Carter, Douglas Prout, Paul Methuen, Norman Rae, Billy Pilgrim, Hugh Moss Solomon, Vibart Seaforth and others.

Brian Heap

Brian Starmer Heap grew up in the north of England, in the Lancashire town of Burnley, and was fortunate as a youngster to have had at his grammar school in the nearby town of Blackburn a series of excellent teachers through whom he was exposed to live theatre productions featuring actors of the calibre of Alec Guinness, Eileen Atkins, Hermione Gingold, Alan Bennett, John Gielgud, Hermione Baddeley, Vanessa Redgrave and Ian McKellan. In addition, he was encouraged to enter for the examinations of the English Speaking Board, which helped enormously in setting him on a path toward drama and theatre. His undergraduate years at the University of Leeds widened his cultural experiences in several areas – drama, opera, jazz, foreign-language and mainstream cinema, classical music, and musical theatre.

Brian Heap, actor, director. *Courtesy of LTM.*

When he first arrived in Jamaica in 1973, he discovered a vibrant theatre in Kingston, and retains fond memories of attending his first Jamaican pantomime, *Queenie's Daughter*, starring Louise Bennett Coverley and Ranny Williams. Not too long after that, he became involved in Jamaican theatre himself when he was invited to replace actor Bobb Kerr in Trevor Rhone's play *School's Out*, directed by Yvonne Brewster. Initially it was to have been for a six-week run, since the production had already been running at the Barn Theatre for about six months, but he remained with the play for a further six months. Other plays followed, including a very successful production of the drawing-room comedy *See How They Run*, directed by Claudette Henriques-Gentles.

Heap was then invited by actors Natalie Thompson and Bobb Kerr to assist them with the development of the Jamaica Children's Theatre Trust, which, during the late 1970s, produced a series of very successful Christmas shows for families, including an adaptation of *Mother Goose* by Barbara Gloudon, a Jamaican version of *Goody Two Shoes* entitled *Goody*, and an updated version of Cinderella called *Cindy*. It was as a result of being spotted in one of these shows by the late Shirley Aub that he was invited to replace her for a year at St Joseph's Teachers' College, where he was entrusted with the development of a drama course for primary school teachers. Being at St Joseph's in Cross Roads meant having increased proximity to both the Cultural Training Centre (now the Edna Manley College) and the Little Theatre.

By the late 1970s Brian Heap had also been asked by Dennis Scott, director of the School of Drama, to teach language and communication, and subsequently drama in education. He became involved in various projects of the institution, most notably a staff production in 1980 of Derek Walcott's play *Pantomime*, directed by Henry Muttoo, and co-starring Ancile Gloudon, alternating with the cast of Bobb Kerr and Keith Noel. Heap also appeared in the Trevor Nairne–directed production of Walcott's *Remembrance* at the Barn Theatre. In 1981 he was invited to appear in the pantomime *The Pirate Princess*, directed by Bobby Ghisays.

In 1982 Heap returned to England to pursue postgraduate studies at the University of Newcastle-upon-Tyne with drama educator Dorothy Heathcote. This also gave him a great deal of exposure to the theatre, particularly to productions by the Royal Shakespeare Company, which, that season, featured actors such as Helen Mirren, Derek Jacobi, Alun Armstrong, Michael Gambon, Alice Krige and Sinead Cusack. He also participated in a number of voice and speech workshops with Cicely Berry, voice coach for the Royal Shakespeare Company (RSC).

Heap eventually served as director of studies of the Jamaica School of Drama from 1984 to 1986. In 1984 he accompanied a group of students from the school to perform in the Newham International Festival of Theatre in Education, with a production entitled *Freedom to Be*, which was performed at the Theatre Royal in Stratford, East London, where Joan Littlewood had produced many of her ground-breaking productions.

During the summer of 1985, Jamaica's LTM invited theatre veteran Maurice Harty to conduct workshops with a core group of young people, with a view to establishing a National Pantomime Company. Heap was invited to direct the 1985 pantomime *Trash*, and almost by default became the founding artistic director of the Pantomime Company. There followed an almost unbroken run of directing fourteen pantomimes up until 2000. Heap's close relationship with the LTM has continued up to time of writing, particularly with the annual restaging of *Augus Mawnin*, both in Jamaica and overseas since 1997. This production was first staged to commemorate the reintroduction of Emancipation Day (1 August), as a national holiday in Jamaica and elsewhere in the Caribbean. Heap continues to direct the LTM pantomime from time to time, and conducted his fifteenth production as director with *Howzatt!!*, staged to coincide with the 2007 Cricket World Cup, which was hosted in the West Indies.

Heap's appointment in 1996 as staff tutor in drama at the Philip Sherlock Centre for the Creative Arts (formerly the Creative Arts Centre) of the UWI has presented many opportunities for further development of both his artistic and academic careers. He acted in the Norman Rae–directed production *Someone Who'll Watch Over Me*, and received a best actor award from the International Theatre Institute's (Jamaica Centre) annual Actor Boy Awards. In addition to his work with the University Dramatic Arts Society, which staged the world premiere of black British playwright Sol B. River's *The White Witch of Rose Hall* in 1998, and the Tallawah Student Drama competitions, he continues to nurture budding young playwrights, directors and actors at the UWI.

In 2003 Heap initiated the re-establishment of the University Players, the resident theatre company of the Philip Sherlock Centre, and has attempted in recent years to build on the pioneering work of people like Noel Vaz and the late Errol Hill. Heap was awarded the Actor Boy award for best director in 2006 for the third time, for staging Karl Williams's experimental work *The Black That I Am*. He is also co-author, with Pamela Bowell, of the book *Planning Process Drama*, which is currently used worldwide in the training of drama teachers. He has also worked with Dr Anthony Simpson on the use of process drama in promoting HIV/AIDS education in Jamaica and Zambia, and together they have produced a book on the subject, *Process Drama: A Way of Changing Attitudes*.

David Heron

David Heron, actor and playwright

David Heron, playwright, producer and actor, has been called one of Jamaica's most successful artists. He started his career early, as a student at Wolmer's Boys' School, when he won the best actor award for his one-act play *The Infidel* in 1985. As a student at the UWI, Heron won the best supporting actor award in the 1988 Tallawah Festival for his performance in *Children, Children*.

In 1994 Heron received acclaim for his first full-length play, *Ecstasy*, a work that dealt directly with social issues and breached middle-class norms. In the play, a brown-skinned, middle-class man marries a black, working-class nightclub dancer from the ghetto – a scenario not unfamiliar in Jamaican society – but Jewel, the go go dancer, will not accept the insults of the privileged and fights back in ways she learned from her life in the ghetto. The play ran for two years at the 120-seat Barn Theatre and closed only because its producers could not find other more suitable theatre space. During that time, *Ecstasy* toured thirteen towns outside of Kingston. It has since travelled to Miami, Fort Lauderdale, Coral Springs, New York (Bronx and Queens), Toronto, London, Birmingham, Manchester and Grand Cayman, making it the most travelled Jamaican play to date. It has also made return visits to some of these places.

To date, Heron has written five other stage plays, all of which have earned him much commercial and critical success, both in Jamaica and abroad: *Intermission* (1996), *Against His Will* (1998), *Love and Marriage and New York City* (1999), *Redemption* (2003), and *4Play* (2005). Among these works, *Intermission* is a play about friendships which get entangled in love and sex, class and race, and politics and drug trafficking in Jamaica. Five friends meet at intervals, pick up the strands of their lives and, in the process, deal with social influences such as education, ambition, eking out a living in the United States and, of course, sex.

The most successful of Heron's plays, to date, is the romantic comedy, *Love and Marriage and New York City*, which was written in 1999 and opened in Jamaica on Valentine's Day in 2000. The play was revived in 2006, and has since toured several cities in the United States, Canada and England. It treats the crucial issue of Jamaicans' trying to obtain the coveted American "green card" (permanent resident visa), honestly or otherwise, and the price some of them are prepared to pay for it. In 2002 and 2003 *Love and Marriage* played to packed houses in Britain and Toronto. In 2006 it played at the Billie Holiday Theater, off Broadway, New York, and this production received the prestigious AUDELCO Award, New York's highest accolade for off-Broadway black theatre. In 2007 it was selected as the official play for one of the largest festivals of its kind in the world, the National Black Theater Festival in Winston Salem, North Carolina. *Love and Marriage* was again revived in Toronto in 2008, where it received favourable reviews.

All Heron's other plays have had very successful runs in Jamaica. *Against His Will* was performed three hundred times, and toured the Eastern Caribbean and the United States, as well as Canada and Great Britain. Of *4Play*, critic Michael Edwards has said that the play "is provocative, thoughtful, funny, profane, and overall provides a night's entertainment that will linger in the mind long after the final bows".[13]

Heron is himself an actor of some talent, and has at times performed in his own

David Heron (*right*) in *Robinson Crusoe*, in New York. *Courtesy of David Heron.*

plays, including *Ecstasy*, *Intermission*, *Love and Marriage*, and *Redemption*. In plays by other playwrights Heron has appeared in *Children, Children*; *Cheaters*; the world premiere of *Robinson Crusoe* at the Orlando Shakespeare Festival; and *H* at the Bric Studio, New York.

In 2007 Heron made his Shakespearean debut as Laertes in *Hamlet* at the Workshop Theater, off Broadway, to excellent reviews. He also received excellent reviews in 2008 for his performances in Errol John's *Moon on a Rainbow Shawl*, which first appeared in 1958, and as the Messenger in *Medea* at the off-Broadway National Black Theater in Harlem. Heron's film credits include a role in *Zora's Dream* (Shango Films).

Frederick Hickling

Frederick William Elliot Hickling was born on 19 November 1944. Between the ages of six and ten, he received lessons in elocution from Alison Packer's Elocution School and was cast as the child lead in Benjamin Britten's *The Chimney Sweep*, directed by Roma Prosano Fitchett, a music teacher and retired opera singer. As a student at Wolmer's Boys' School, he won elocution contests in classes 1 and 2 of the All-Jamaica Elocution Contest, and became a member of the school's Dramatic Society, with which he performed in *Oedipus Rex*. As part of the 1962 independence celebrations, Hickling played the role of a priest in the presentation of T.S. Eliot's *Murder in the Cathedral* at Scot's Kirk, directed by Wycliffe Bennett. As a student of the UWI, he was president of the Dramatic Society from 1963 to 1964 and led the society on a tour of the Eastern Caribbean during the summer of 1963.

In 1963 Hickling was stage manager for *Star Boarder*, directed by Lloyd Reckord, and for seven other productions: the pantomime *Queenie's Daughter*, directed by Rex Nettleford; *Eight O'Clock Jamaica Time*, directed by Norman Rae; *Finian's Rainbow*, directed by Zackie Matalon; *Most Happy Fella*, directed by Norman Rae; *The Royal Hunt of the Sun*, directed by Norman Rae; *Stanley and Fay, Pularchie and P*, a radio serial for JBC directed by Norman Rae; and for the National Dance Theatre Company of Jamaica (NDTC), between 1963 and 1977. In 1964 Hickling played the male lead in Eugene Ionesco's *The Chairs*, directed by Noel Vaz, and, during the 1964–65 academic year, he was the drama critic for the Taylor Hall newspaper, *Rising Star*. Beginning in 1965, he served as stage director for the Jamaica Festival Office (a post that he held until 1971), and in 1966 he served as stage manager for *Marat/Sade*, directed by Noel Vaz. The next year, while a medical student, Hickling was producer and emcee for the Medical Smoker, an annual variety show. He was also a member of the Jamaica Festival Commission from 1967 to 1972.

Frederick Hickling, actor and playwright

Hickling also turned his attention to popular music and was artistic director for the Third World Band (1977–78); for Harold Butler and the Meek Jazz Band (1987–89); for the Black Safire Band (1988–89); and for Krossroads Band (1989–93). He has continued his acting career sporadically. In addition, he has written and produced twelve docudramas: *Explanitations*, written and produced for the Third World Band (January 1978); *Madnificent Irations*, for the Bellevue Hospital where he worked as psychiatrist (August 1978); *Visionated Penetrations*, also for Bellevue Hospital (August 1979); *Genesis of Ites*, for the Ministry of Culture, Government of Grenada (April 1980); *Madaptations*, for Bellevue Hospital (August 1980); *Cooling the Fires of Hell: Our Way*, for Provident Hospital in Baltimore, Maryland, United States (May 1981), with Pat Newton; *Irations Explosion*, for Bellevue Hospital (August 1981); *Forward Moses*, co-authored with Michael Smith for the Diaspora Cultural Movement, Jamaica (September 1981); *Mongrel Juice*, for the Belize Arts Council (October 1981); Harold Butler's *My Life, Part Two*, for Musical Associates Jamaica (November 1987); *Living on the Edge*, for the Black Safire Band, Jamaica (November 1988); *Krossroads: De Culcha Clash*, by Owen Ellis, produced for Musical Associates Ltd and Groundwork Theatre Company. Hickling is a psychiatrist who has also published extensively in his field.

Pablo Hoilett

Pablo Hoilett, theatre, television and radio producer, director, writer and actor

Pablo Hoilett is a professional theatre, television and radio producer, director, writer and actor whose career spans over thirty years. His vast directorial credits include diverse materials, ranging from Samuel Beckett's *Waiting for Godot* to Errol John's *Moon on a Rainbow Shawl*, and JBC-TV's *Lime Tree Lane*, for which he was director and producer, and sometimes writer and actor. In an effort to fill the void created by the shortage of interesting local plays in Jamaica, he has responded to the demand for fresh material with a mix of indigenous creations augmented by a series of smooth and seamless adaptations of foreign works, such as the British comedy *Key for Two*. Theatres in the United States, Canada, the Caribbean and the United Kingdom have presented his works, which from time to time showcase some of Jamaica's most extraordinary talents, including Oliver Samuels, Carl Bradshaw, Volier Johnson, Fae

Pablo Hoilett (*left*), Oliver Samuels and Bobby Clarke in *Come Blow Your Horn* (1980). *Photo by Monica DaSilva.*

Ellington, Audrey Reid, Munair Zacca and the Sistren Theatre Collective, of which he is a former chairman of the board.

Apart from working in major theatres in Jamaica and abroad, Hoilett is committed to educating Jamaicans about the safe use of pesticides. He has created a series of dramatic presentations on the subject which are mostly performed in rural farming communities across the island.

Hoilett studied theatre at the JSD, where he majored in acting and directing under the tutelage of Dennis Scott, Lloyd Reckord, Thom Cross and Honor Ford-Smith. Further studies took him to the Banff School of Fine Arts in Alberta, Canada, where he participated in numerous courses, workshops and seminars dealing with theatre, film, television and video productions. He has attended lectures and courses organized by the CPTC; by world-renowned documentary filmmaker Joan Shenton of Joan Shenton Films, London, England; by Merle Schreibman, noted Hollywood film director, producer, author and professor at the University of California at Los Angeles; and by Johanna Sophia, lecturer in screenwriting at Columbia University.

Discovering and developing new talents is one of Hoilett's major goals, and he hopes one day to be able to access funding to assist in the further development of indigenous Jamaican theatre and future professionals. His company, Hoilett Productions, was nominated for several Actor Boy awards in 2008. Hoilett is also founder and CEO of Mediaplanet, a creative entity designed to foster innovations for stage, screen and radio.

Father Richard Ho Lung

Father Richard Ho Lung, known for his years of philanthropy, is the founder and superior-general of the religious order the Missionaries of the Poor. Under his leadership, the Missionaries have, to date, opened five shelters for the homeless and indigent, orphaned and neglected children, and the physically and mentally challenged. Among the many ways he raises funds for his causes is by mounting large religious musicals, which he often writes and produces. Directors for these shows have included Cynthia Wilmot and Alwyn Bully.

Father Richard Ho Lung, actor and playwright. *Courtesy of Brothers of the Poor.*

According to a writer in the *Sunday Observer* (7 May 2006), "Father Ho Lung's life story is the stuff that the best biographies are made of. He has been a beloved 'ghetto priest', musician, singer, song writer and caregiver – perhaps his truest self of all." Born in St Mary on 17 September 1939, Ho Lung received his early education at St George's College. He then went on to Boston College in the United States and to a number of other universities, where he acquired, along the way, a PhD, an MLit, an MA in Theology and an MA in Philosophy, among other qualifications. He has been the recipient of seven Jamaica Music Industry Awards, for best original music in 1989, 1990, 1991, 1993, 1994 and 1995, and best music production in 1994. He also received the Actor Boy award for best musical drama and best original music for four years between 1993 and 2001. He has been honoured by many organizations and institutions, by the Government of Jamaica with the award of the Order of Distinction (OD), and by the Institute of Jamaica with the Silver Musgrave Medal for outstanding merit in the field of Literature and Arts – Liturgical Music (1997).

Father Ho Lung has published poems, written plays and musical productions, and published seventeen CDs, LP albums and cassette recordings. Among his fourteen original musical productions are *Take Up the Cross*; *Jesus*; *Rise Up*; *Praise Him*; *David*; *Run, Come*; *Jesus 2000*; *Amazing Grace*; *Moses*; and the Jam-reggae opera *Yes!* – all with very large casts. *Yes!* (2008), recounts the life of a man of faith and could be regarded as part autobiographical. Although the casts of Ho Lung's plays are primarily made up of members of the Roman Catholic congregation, artists may come from any denomination if they wish to participate and have the necessary talent and skills. All are volunteers.

Father Ho Lung has organized musical workshops in North America, England and the Caribbean. His *Diary of a Ghetto Priest*, a weekly column in the *Gleaner*, was serialized on EWTN (an American religious television station), and *Blessed*, a music video, was released in 2000. Father Ho Lung's musicals are always oversubscribed and play to vast audiences, totalling as many as 60,000 viewers over a run of approximately two weeks.

Charles Hyatt

Charles Hyatt, actor, broadcaster, writer. *Courtesy of Charles Hyatt Jr.*

The passing of Charles Hyatt in 2007, following so closely upon the deaths of Neville Willoughby and Perry Henzell, marked the end of an era in the growth and development of the performing arts in Jamaica. Hyatt, like Willoughby and Henzell, was a consummate artist at whatever he did, whether he was playing the porter, a role that lasts about two minutes in Shakespeare's *Macbeth*, or the role of Pa Ben, a part that covers two hours in Trevor Rhone's *Old Story Time*. As Hyatt would say, "There are no small roles, there are only small actors." One can triumph in two minutes but fail in two hours.

Hyatt lived for seventy-five years, and his genius embraced print, the stage, radio, film, television and the Internet. He was a mime and dramatic actor, a comedian, playwright, director and a producer. He was a raconteur, musicologist, journalist and a circus ringmaster (on one occasion). He owed a lot to Anthony Finn and the Caribbean Thespians Dramatic Society, which became an early source for the training of young actors, and one of the mainstays of the Adult Drama Festival and the Jamaica Drama League in the 1950s. Charles joined the Caribbean Thespians in 1946 and made his first appearance on stage at the Ward Theatre in the annual pantomime, *Aladdin*, in 1950. He performed in some thirteen other pantomimes. Before 1962 – that is, when the Jamaican pantomime began the transition towards becoming a Jamaican musical – he usually played the role of the dame.

In 1959 Hyatt was appointed presenter for the newly established JBC Radio service, for which he developed the widely popular series *Here Comes Charlie*. That same year, he received the actor of the year award for his role in Barry Reckord's *Miss Unusual*, and was awarded an Arts Council of Jamaica bursary to serve a six-month attachment at the Theatre Royal, Windsor. His stay in England lasted fourteen years. During that time, he was a much sought-after black actor, performing in productions by Barry Reckord and other West Indian playwrights. He appeared in many stage, television, film and radio productions, and was for many seasons resident actor at the Oxford Playhouse, where he appeared in Genet's *The Blacks*, and at the Phoenix Theatre, where he acted in Fugard's *Blood Knot*. He was cast as a West Indian doctor in the BBC's longest running radio serial, *Mrs Dale's Diary*, and played the role for nine months. He followed this performance with roles in the BBC TV series *A Book with Chapters in It* and in Jan Carew's *Day of the Fox*, which was produced for commercial television and starred Sammy Davis Jr.

During the 1962 independence celebrations, Hyatt was invited back to Jamaica to perform in the revival of *Carib Gold*. Afterwards, he returned to England and continued to play in Off West End shows in London and with Independent Television, Granada and London Weekend Television, BBC Radio Home, Third Light and Caribbean Radio Services programmes.

On his second return to Jamaica in the 1970s, he was appointed co-director, with Leonie Forbes, of the department of drama at the JBC, where he was responsible for the successful radio serial *Flora Lee*, among other shows. His performance, in Kingston and New York, with Grace McGhie in Trevor Rhone's *Two Can Play* (1982), a boisterous comedy about the battle of the sexes, seemed to get better with each performance. His major roles were as Pa Ben in Rhone's *Old Story Time* (1979);

Charles Hyatt as Pa Ben, with Pauline Cowan, in *Old Story Time*, by Trevor Rhone

as Lady Upper Crust, the Dame in the pantomime *Anancy and Pandora* (1973); as the drunken porter in *Macbeth* (1974); and in the role of Bedward in the first production of Louis Marriott's *The Shepherd* (1960), which was later renamed *Bedward* (1984). Hyatt reprised his role in the third production of this play in 2003–4.

A number of Hyatt's performances survive on film. Of his theatrical performances, *Old Story Time* and *Two Can Play* were recorded. His made his film debut in *A High Wind in Jamaica* (1965), starring Anthony Quinn, and among his other film highlights are *Club Paradise* (1986), starring Robin Williams, and *The Mighty Quinn* (1989), with Denzel Washington in the lead role. Hyatt's portrayal of the reluctant father in the film *Cool Runnings* (1993), about the Jamaican bobsled team that enters the Winter Olympics, and his dramatic reversal in that role are unforgettable.

Hyatt has created more memorable roles than most other artists in the history of the Jamaican theatre. He has been part of the great acting tradition of the twentieth century, which includes a galaxy of stars – Morton Tavares, who opened the twentieth century, having performed on both sides of the Atlantic and as far away as Australia in lead roles in *Macbeth* and *Othello*; Father Roy Campbell, SJ, of St George's College, a classic actor of such roles as Othello and Richelieu; E.M. Cupidon, comedian noted for acting in female roles, especially as Jane and Susan Proudleigh, characters which he adapted from H.G. DeLisser's novels; Mike Campbell, who played the Dame in the first LTM pantomime, *Jack and the Beanstalk* (1941); Stephen O.D. Hill as Shakespeare's *Hamlet* and Robert Browning in *Elizabeth Barrett Browning*; the incomparable Ranny Williams; the Guyanese actor Slade Hopkinson as King Lear and Prospero; and Lloyd Reckord, Reggie Carter and Oliver Samuels in a wide range of roles.

Other local productions in which Hyatt performed are *Brashana O!*, *Mother Courage* and *The Mouse Trap*. He also wrote, directed and produced *The Last of the*

Red Hot Lovers, and *Jesus Christ, Dem Kill Son Son*. In addition to numerous citations and awards, he has received the Silver Musgrave Medal and the Centenary Medal from the Institute of Jamaica, and the Order of Distinction from the Government of Jamaica. Hyatt generously shared his talents, his humour and his experience with his peers and his audiences, becoming in the process a source of emulation, inspiration and adoration to people in Jamaica and around the world. It is contributions of such measurably sterling worth that give Brand Jamaica its distinguished pedigree.

Beth Hyde

Beth Hyde, actress

Canadian Beth Hyde married Jamaican artist Eugene Hyde and made Jamaica her home. Her theatrical debut in 1964, playing the part of Louisa in Norman Rae's production of *The Fantasticks*, a delightful off-Broadway show running at the time, was enough to start her fascination with the theatre. In 1965 Norman Rae offered her the part of Honey in *Who's Afraid of Virginia Woolf*, this time in an emergency. Three days before the opening, the original actress had to drop out and Beth took up the challenge. For her it was an excellent learning experience, working with three more mature and experienced actors. This experience reinforced her desire to become involved in the theatre.

Then came the opportunity to play a completely different role, that of the Queen in *Once upon a Mattress* at the Ward Theatre. This meant playing opposite the great veteran of the Jamaican stage, Ranny Williams, as the King. Afterwards, Hyde was

Beth Hyde (*right*), with John Jones (*left*) and Richard Blazer, in *Slow Dance on the Killing Ground*, directed by Sheila Carter (1970). *Photo by Maria LaYacona.*

Marguerite Newland (*left*) and Beth Hyde (*right*) in a scene from *Royal Palm Estate* Courtesy of Mediamix.

offered the role of the Irish skivvy girl Theresa in Brendan Behan's play *The Hostage*, directed by Maurice Harty. Her next production was pure fun: the second in the series *Eight O'Clock Jamaica Time*. Hyde also had a small part in Trevor Rhone's comedy *Smile Orange*, which had a long run at the Barn Theatre and was invited to participate in the Eugene O'Neill Playwright Conference in Connecticut.

In 1968, for Jamaica Playhouse, Hyde tried out for the part of Rosie in William Hanley's dramatic play *Slow Dance on the Killing Ground*, directed by Sy Syna. Hyde says this was the most powerful and exhilarating production she has ever been associated with, and it left a lasting impression on her. Then came another *Eight O'Clock Jamaica Time* production, *Boonoonoos*, followed by two light and amusing plays, Noel Coward's *Blythe Spirit* and Philip King's *See How They Run*.

When Jamaica Playhouse was celebrating its tenth anniversary, its members chose to remount six of their best productions over the past ten years. One was *Slow Dance on the Killing Ground*, and Hyde was again invited to play Rosie, the same part she had played in the earlier production. She was the only member from the original cast. On this occasion the play was directed by Sheila Carter.

In 1981 Hyde performed in *Fling*, produced by Claude Clarke and directed by Lloyd Reckord. Some eleven years later, in 1992, she was invited by Lennie Little-White to play the role of Julia Blackburn, wife of a wealthy planter, in his new television soap opera, *Royal Palm Estate*. The part of husband Ted Blackburn was acted by Reggie Carter. The pilot was made and the show started on CVM-TV, where it is still running, sixteen years later. Over the course of the show, Ted Blackburn is killed (because of the death of actor Reggie Carter) and, at the time of writing, Hyde's character is now married to the notorious Sonny T, who uses every trick he knows to get hold of the Blackburn Estate. Beth Hyde is now a household name.

EASTON LEE

Easton Lee, actor, director, playwright, poet

Easton Lee has been a communications specialist for most of his life. He has been a radio and television announcer at the JBC, director of audio-visual programming at the Jamaica Information Service, and a public relations consultant and actor.

Lee was born in Wait-a-Bit, Trelawny, in 1931, and after attending elementary school he progressed through further training at the Jamaica School of Commerce, the Pasadena Playhouse (in California), the BBC and the Civil Service Senior Staff College. While at high school, Lee joined the Caribbean Thespians Society, established by Anthony Finn and mentored at that time by Errol Hill. He soon established himself as a major acting talent. For a long time he played characters much younger than his years. He was the little boy in Vidia Naipaul's *B Wordsworth*, directed by Keith Sasso in a Jamaica Drama League presentation in the 1950s, and again in *Once upon a Seaweed*, directed by Noel Vaz in 1960, when Lee was twenty-nine years old. He played the role of an apprentice in *The Matchmaker*, by Thornton Wilder, which opened the Little Theatre building on Tom Redcam Drive. He also acted in *Roshomon*, directed by Noel Vaz in the open-air theatre at Vale Royal.

Lee took these theatrical experiences to his job as drama officer with Jamaica Social Welfare Limited (later the Social Development Commission), a job which took him to every corner of the island and was a most valuable learning experience for him. Lee used this cultural exposure in rural Jamaica to form the backdrop for several very popular and creditable religious plays, such as *The Rope and the Cross*, which has been published and has toured extensively across the island. His other plays include *Once in a Manger*, *They That Mourn*, *Tarshan Lace and Velvet*, and *Man to Man*. Lee was awarded the Silver Musgrave Medal by the Institute of Jamaica in 1988, and the Commander of the Order of Distinction (CD) by the Government of Jamaica in 1990.

The Rope and the Cross, written and directed by Easton Lee, with Rooney Chambers and Grace McGhie (1980). *Photo by Monica DaSilva.*

Lennie Little-White

Lennie Little-White has earned a reputation for excellence in his work, starting with his stint at the Jamaica Information Service and in theatre during the 1960s. At nineteen years of age, he was the recipient of several awards for writing, producing and directing the play *That Golden Necklace*, which he entered in the Adult Drama section of the annual National Festival in 1965. The production won nine of eleven possible awards, including best drama, best director, best script, best set, best actress and best supporting actor. The same year, Little-White also received the Independence Festival of Jamaica's Commendation of Merit Trophy for presenting the Best Overall Drama. He founded the Fantasy Players theatrical group in 1964.

Lennie Little-White, director, writer, producer, media owner. *Photo courtesy of Mediamix.*

Little-White's reputation was enhanced during his sojourn at Ryerson Polytechnic University in Toronto, Canada, in the 1970s. In 1971, while a student there, he wrote and directed *Born Black*, the first ever film about black Canadians, in cooperation with Cheryl Ryman and other students of York University. The film was released in 1972. On graduating, he earned two gold medals: one as the "most outstanding student for the graduating class of 1972" and the other as "the most outstanding graduate in the film and television department" for the same year. His work since then has attested to the continuing quest for excellence in the areas of advertising, public relations, marketing, film and television. Public acclaim, various industry plaudits and awards speak to the achievement of this quest. With boldness and vision he equipped his company, Mediamix, with a million-dollar investment, constructing a multi-function media centre in 1983.

The Mediamix studio is equipped with state-of-the-art technology and produces Jamaican television programmes of the highest quality for distribution both locally and internationally. Some of these programmes include *Royal Palm Estate* (for over ten years and with nearly four hundred episodes produced); *Visions*, which showcases

Royal Palm Estate, written and produced by Lennie Little-White for CVM-TV, with Munair Zacca (*left*) as Sonny T, and Reggie Carter as Ted Blackburn. *Photo courtesy of Mediamix.*

positive and unusual achievements in Jamaica; *Jammin'*; *It's Showtime*; *Traxx*; *Star Search at Traxx*; and *Buzz*, a celebration of Jamaican and Caribbean musicians and artists. *Royal Palm Estate* deals with the lifestyle of a member of the Jamaican planter class and the piracy and corruption of the bosses of the underworld, one of whom believes he can buy his way into that society.

After a thirty-year television broadcasting monopoly in Jamaica, Lennie Little-White and Mediamix were central to realizing a long-cherished dream, to see Jamaica's second television station become a reality. CVM-TV – with Mediamix being the "M" in the station's name – was born in 1993. It was steered from the outset by the steady hand of Lennie Little-White as its project coordinator.

Little-White conceptualized, implemented and continues to lend critical support to Jamaica's (and the Caribbean's) first vehicle for recognizing excellence and outstanding contributions to the film and television industry, the Doctor Bird Awards, which he established in 1998. The Doctor Bird Awards in Film and Television also include a "Special Caribbean Award" as part of the regular categories for recognition. Little-White viewed the establishment of this prestigious award as the ideal way to celebrate his company's twenty-fifth year, and to give back to the industry and the country.

Royal Palm Estate, with Billy Wilmot and Berette Macauley. *Courtesy of Mediamix.*

Little-White has written, produced and directed the largest number of television programmes by the private or public sector in Jamaica's television history. The late Perry Henzell – an acclaimed filmmaker – repeatedly recommended him for a Doctor Bird Award (although Little-White is automatically disqualified by virtue of being the founder of the awards). Henzell's reasoning was that he is the most prolific film and television producer in Jamaica.

Little-White has incorporated Jamaican cultural forms and expressions into almost all of his work. He used an all-Jamaican cast and crew for the film he made from Derek Walcott's play *Children of Babylon*, an international full-length movie which features well-known artists like actress Leonie Forbes and reggae singer Bob Andy. The film boasts an original soundtrack in collaboration with Harold Butler and showcases the best of Jamaican talent, including Beresford Hammond, Pam Hall, Cynthia Schloss, the Mighty Diamonds and Delroy Wilson. The song "I Was Born a Woman", from the *Children of Babylon* soundtrack, written by Lennie Little-White and sung by Pam Hall, has become almost an anthem for women and Women's Day celebrations in Jamaica.

Little-White's latest major achievement is the direction and production of *Glory to Gloriana* (2006), a full-length movie based on the rags-to-riches life story of a Jamaican hotelier. The film is now playing internationally. *Royal Palm Estate* is but one example of his many productions that have become household staples for viewers at home and abroad. His Caribbean sensibilities are expressed in works like *Buzz* and *Traxx*, which have featured non-Jamaican artists from within the region. Under the direction and leadership of Little-White, Mediamix holds one of the most extensive privately owned Jamaican (and Caribbean) cultural archives on video dating back to 1974, and an equally extensive library of television products.

In addition to being a film and television producer, director and editor, Little-White is also a critic and journalist. He developed a regular column of critical reviews of film and television called *The Media Eye*, which appeared in the now defunct *Daily*

News newspaper of the 1970s. He has written short- and long-form film and television scripts and lyrics – in the latter case, the lyrics for the original soundtrack of *Children of Babylon*, as well as those for the *Royal Palm Estate* theme song. He has also provided a training environment for media specialists at all levels of the industry, through formal and informal programmes within and outside of his company. Some of these specialists include Brian St Juste, Trevor Johnson, Pam Grant, Carlington Silburn, Omar "Pili" Johnson and Susan Symes.

Mediamix and Lennie Little-White are, to date, the only Jamaican company and producer to be commissioned specifically to conceptualize, write and produce a film to market Jamaica as a tourism destination. In 2001, Little-White's work in advertising was recognized with the Dudley C. MacMillan Lifetime Achievement Peer Award, for his sustained and outstanding contribution to the advertising industry. Recognition for his media work, specifically in film and television, has come to include the former Soviet Union's Tashkent Film Festival's Best Film of the Festival Award in 1978 for the UWI film *Beginnings*. In 1979, Mediamix received the Red Stripe Award for Enterprise "in recognition of the high standard of initiative, originality and excellence of product displayed by the company in the manufacture of Film, Radio, Television and Press Productions". In 2000, he was awarded the Silver Musgrave Medal by the Institute of Jamaica "for outstanding merit in the field of Film and Television". In 2004, Mediamix (*Royal Palm Estate*) was presented with CVM-TV's tenth anniversary programme award for the company's contribution to the development of premier local programming. The award reads: "For bold, visionary and sustained creativity evidenced in the products and standards of excellence in the field of Communications and particularly in the area of Film and Television."

Glory to Gloriana, a full-length feature film by Lennie Little-White, with Marguerite Newland. *Courtesy of Mediamix.*

Amina Blackwood Meeks

Amina Blackwood Meeks is a political scientist and educator with a strong interest in the theatre. She studied at the UWI, Mona, where she is currently doing postgraduate research in the oral tradition. She has also worked as a lecturer in Caribbean aesthetics and Caribbean history and culture at the Edna Manley College and at the Exed School of Performing Arts. Her experience as a social and cultural policy research and development specialist is particularly useful in her job as director of the Culture in Education programme in the Ministry of Education, and as a member of the National Culture and Values Task Force. It is, however, for her work as a writer, performer and, above all, as a storyteller that she is known throughout the Caribbean and, indeed, internationally.

When Meeks's work as a storyteller first came to light in Antigua, where she lived for ten years, Dr Ermina Osoba, then resident tutor of the UWI School of Continuing Studies, described her as "a special and rare talent". That was after Tim Hector of the *Outlet* had described her as "a major talent in any theatre" and "a significant voice to be heard". It is not so much the excellent technical quality of her voice to

Amina Blackwood Meeks, actress, folklorist

which Hector referred, but the insightful and incisive social commentary for which that voice is employed that caused another Caribbean theatre luminary, Ken Corsbie, to describe her work as "an outrageous combination of education and entertainment, of glitz and thoughtfulness".

In Meeks's words, she was born September 1953 "hearing stories, born to tell stories and grew up believing that, like her parents, who were forever telling stories, everyone in the world spoke anecdotally, even if they didn't know how to conjugate it".[14] Her entry into St Andrew High School, one of the top girls' schools in Jamaica, came at a time when the Jamaican language was still reviled as a "dialect". And when it seemed that everyone else was watching the newly arrived television, her parents were still telling stories at night. She regards storytelling as the bedrock of humanity.

Meeks was the major writer for the theatre groups to which she belonged, including the Theatre Group for National Liberation in Jamaica, and Zebra, which she founded in Antigua. Her work with Antiguan children in the group Child's Play – which she also founded and ran for four years, in collaboration with the UWI School of Continuing Studies – brought storytelling to the fore as a tool for building self-esteem by empowering people with the knowledge of their glorious past that was embedded, sometimes hidden, in stories. An assignment for the members of Child's Play to research Anancy stories led to Caribbean oral tradition's becoming the main programme focus of the group, and subsequently to Meeks's MPhil and PhD research projects.

Meeks appeared at the first comedy festival in St Lucia in 1992, the first Caribbean Storytelling Festival, held in Barbados in 1996, and the first Gimme Story Festival in Cayman in 1998, and staged the first ever storytelling festival in Jamaica in 1998 as coordinator and founder of Jack Mandora, the Storytelling Association of Jamaica. She has also performed at storytelling festivals in the United Kingdom, Canada and the United States, where she appeared in 2007 as the featured international storyteller at the National Storytelling Festival in Tennessee. In 2008 she became the first international guest of the Rhode Island Black Storytellers Annual Festival, Fundafest. Along the way, she has conducted storytelling workshops for teachers, librarians and storytellers in all the places in which she has performed. In addition to these performances and workshops, she writes and performs a full-length storytelling revue every two years.

As an actress, Meeks has appeared in more than thirty full-length dramatic productions, and has performed throughout the Caribbean. In these productions, she has been directed by some of the Caribbean's stellar theatre lights. She has appeared in Trevor Rhone's *Two Can Play*, with Ron Robinson of the Theatre Company of Guyana, directed by Al Creighton; in the Antiguan production of *Fallen Angel and Devil Concubine*, directed by Michelle Barrow of Barbados; in Sylvia Wynter's *Maskarade*, directed by Jim Nelson; as Yemanja in *Obotala*, directed by Al Creighton; as the Mother in Brecht's *Mother Courage*, directed by Thom Cross, which went to the Eleventh World Festival of Youth and Students, in Cuba (1978); as Lawyer in the *Trial of One Short-Sighted Black Woman vs Mama Louise and Sapeeta Mae*, directed by Lloyd Reckord. She has also been directed by the late Earl Warner, Carroll Dawes and Keith Noel.

Meeks has won several awards for her work in radio, is a three-time best actress recipient, and a multi-medal winner in national creative writing competitions in Jamaica. She is the founder and artistic director of Ntukuma, the Storytelling Foundation of Jamaica, and remains, in her words, "dedicated to exploring the connections between the ancient wit and wisdom of the African ancestry and the ways in which this heritage has immediate redemptive applications for the growth, development and continuation of civilization".

Alma (Hylton) Mock Yen

Alma Mock Yen, dancer, actress and playwright

The name of Alma Mock Yen (*née* Hylton) is associated in Jamaica with many areas of the arts and culture: acting, dancing, broadcasting, journalism and teaching communications. She has co-authored communication texts and, to a lesser extent, works on political and environmental issues.

Mock Yen began her theatrical career in 1949 when, as a fifth-form student at Wolmer's Girls' School, she was cast as Naomi, wife of Ham, in the LTM production of Andre Obey's *Noah*, directed by Noel Vaz at the Ward Theatre. In 1960, she again teamed up with Vaz, when he produced Jamaica's first integrated musical, *Once upon a Seaweed*, for which Mock Yen wrote the libretto and lyrics. The music was composed by Eddy Thomas and orchestrated by Mapletoft Poulle. The production was to commemorate the tenth anniversary of Jamaica's first modern dance theatre company, the Ivy Baxter Dance Group; Mock Yen was a founding member of the group. She served as dancer, soloist, choreographer, and historian until 1962, when she left to pursue her own career.

In the newly created Harbour View housing estate where she then resided, Mock Yen established her own school of dance and, from 1962 to 1972, ran a successful teaching and touring company, the Harbour View Dancers. They won numerous trophies and produced a new set of leaders and artists to enrich the dance scene. Among these were L'Antoinette Stines, founder of the L'Acadco Dance Company, and Jackie Guy, who, after a distinguished career with the NDTC, in 2006 choreographed the successful stage version of the late Perry Henzell's cinematic cult classic *The Harder They Come*.

Alma Mock Yen's involvement with the theatre paralleled her training and performance in radio broadcasting, which dates back to 1959, when she became a household name as Putus, the role she played for four years opposite Ranny Williams, in the ground-breaking radio serial *Life with the Morgan Henrys*. In that series, broadcast on JBC Radio, Jamaicans heard their own Jamaican vernacular spoken on mainstream radio for the first time. It had a remarkable impact.

Mock Yen has trained most of the current radio producers and broadcasters who attended the Caribbean Institute of Mass Communication (CARIMAC) from 1981, when she began lecturing there. In 1985, along with Batiles Ulrico, Billy Hall and Leonie Forbes, she produced *Re-entry into Sound*, a four-part series for the training of radio practitioners which has been widely used not only in Jamaica but across the Caribbean region as well. In 1995, she again collaborated with Billy Hall, and Gladstone Wilson, to produce another four-part series, *Sound Advice*, directed at communications and media campaign management. In 2002 she published *Rewind: My*

Recollections of Radio and Broadcasting in Jamaica. She has worked with RJR and JBC, and served as a consultant with UNESCO. In 1987 she began working with the Radio Education Unit of the UWI, Mona, and created, in 1999, the Library of the Spoken Word, a research facility of audio materials.

Perhaps she will be best remembered for her role in the television version of *Tea Meetings*; in the play *Junction Village*, directed by Lloyd Reckord; and in the hilarious comedic part in the CPTC production *Uppers and Downers*, scripted by her and produced by Wycliffe Bennett.

Apart from acting, Mock Yen has served as a councillor for the Harbour View (East Kingston) division of the Kingston and St Andrew Corporation (1981–83). She has also published poetry, including *Potted Versions* (1992), and has had entries in various anthologies and local newspapers. Her latest collection of poetry, *Tafari Tuppence*, won the 2007 Jamaica Book Development Council's poetry prize. Although retired from the UWI since 2001, Mock Yen continues to lecture at the Mona campus and at other tertiary level institutions, as well as at several corporate entities, mainly on the topics of rhetorical competence and communication for industrial relations.

Henry Muttoo

Henry Muttoo, director, stage designer

Henry Muttoo, one of the Caribbean's foremost set, costume, and carnival designers and stage directors, joined the faculty of the School of Drama of the Edna Manley College in 1980 and went on to make a significant impact on Jamaican theatre. The philosophy of his art and his unapologetic Caribbean sensibility have been defined in his dynamic use of colour and movement, his attention to detail, and his passion for the imagery of the region's cultural traditions. The carnival traditions of the Caribbean remain a major source of his inspiration; so too does the rich multicultural ethos of Guyana, the country of his birth.

Muttoo's theatre experience in Guyana ranged from being an actor, director and set designer, to being an adjudicator in Guyana's National Festival of the Arts. As a member of the pioneering performing arts company *All ah We*, with Ken Corsbie and Marc Matthews, he was instrumental in the 1980s and 1990s in bringing, through performance, the literature of the region – poetry, plays and short stories – to school children and communities throughout the Caribbean. He received a series of awards for his outstanding work in these areas, and he went on to study at Croydon College of Design and Technology, London, from which he graduated with a diploma in theatre design.

Almost immediately upon graduation, Muttoo was invited to Jamaica to teach at the School of Drama. His work brought a fresh energy to production at the school, and before long he became a leading designer in the Jamaican professional theatre and in the annual costume competition produced by the JCDC. His outstanding sets, props and costume designs for the LTM Pantomime and other commercial productions helped to define the standards of artistic excellence and creative cohesion in local productions. His costume designs in the JCDC festival, for which he won several awards and unanimous critical praise, were compelling in their social commentary, aesthetic brilliance and structural ingenuity.

In 1989 Muttoo migrated to the Cayman Islands, where he is currently the artistic director of the Cayman National Cultural Foundation (CNCF). His continuing years of work there – seventeen, to date, at the artistic helm of the CNCF – have in large measure transformed the cultural landscape of the islands by revitalizing the arts, legitimizing traditional Caymanian re-enactments and educating government and the private sector about the usefulness of the arts in sustaining the community. His work with the CNCF has also brought for the Cayman Islands a new respectability within the Caribbean and international communities.

In Cayman, Muttoo founded the region's largest and most compelling storytelling festival, Gimistory. He has also edited and published several books and cultural journals on the arts, culture and heritage, and has directed and designed scores of stage productions, both Caribbean classics and new plays from the National Playwriting Workshops and Competition. This organization, Muttoo's brainchild, was created to inspire and motivate local writers. In addition to his theatre productions, Muttoo has promoted intellectual research and discourse on Caribbean performance, cultural diversity, cultural tolerance and cultural consumption, among other topics. To this end, he has been a special guest speaker and lecturer at events across the Caribbean. In 2007 he was the Macy's guest director at the University of South Florida, where he directed an award-winning production of the Errol John classic *Moon on a Rainbow Shawl*. And at Cayfest 2008, the Caymanian National Arts Festival, he presented the Distinguished Lecture. He continues to work for the full acceptance of the arts on par with other academic subjects in the school system in the Cayman Islands.

Muttoo's deeply held belief in artists as the unifiers of the region, and the mutual respect that he shares with many of the leading lights of the Caribbean arts, have resulted in his being able to draw to the Cayman Islands some of the most celebrated names in drama, poetry, music, design and arts education. Among those who have conducted workshops, presented papers, performed and inspired audiences in the Cayman Islands, at Muttoo's invitation, are Derek Walcott, Rex Nettleford, LeRoy Clarke, Peter Minshall, Earl Lovelace, Paul Keens Douglas, Trevor Rhone, Charles Hyatt, Oliver Samuels, Barbara Gloudon, Lorna Goodison, Honor Ford-Smith, Mervyn Morris, James Boodhoo, Eugene Williams, Rawle Gibbons, the Mighty Chalkdust (Dr Hollis Liverpool) and the Jamaican Folk Singers. This exposure has heightened many Caymanians' sensibility as Caribbean people and, likewise, has gained for the arts and culture of the Cayman Islands greater acceptance within the wider Caribbean community.

Mapletoft Poulle

Mapletoft Poulle, born 17 July 1923, was both a practising solicitor and a successful classical musician and popular band leader. One of his missions was to keep mento music alive, in the face of the growing popularity of calypso music. "Calypso music", he explained, "had a walking beat, which went well with carnival parades . . . The mento had a doubling of the bass similar to Samba music and actually came out of a dance step. Mento in fact was music to dance to."[15] He was convinced that mento was as attractive as calypso and that its traditions had deep roots.

Mapletoft Poulle, musican. *Courtesy of NLJ.*

Poulle studied piano with Doris Bird and violin with Vera Downes. In 1940, at seventeen years of age, he qualified as an LRSM on the pianoforte. Two years after leaving Wolmer's Boys' School, in 1942, he set up a trio with Johnnie Lopez and Lloyd Clark. The band grew from three members to five to fifteen, and soon they were playing at upscale nightclubs in the city, at royal occasions, and on cultural visits abroad.

When Ivy Baxter began her dance group in 1949, the Poulle band provided accompaniment, and this association lasted for twelve years, until the NDTC came into existence in 1962. The band toured with the Ivy Baxter Dance Group to the dance festival in Puerto Rico in 1952, to Trinidad for the launch of the West Indies Federation in 1958, and to Cuba in 1959, at Fidel Castro's invitation. They also toured with the Jamaica Company of Dancers and Singers, who visited Howard University and Morgan State University in the United States in 1961. Two years later, the Poulle band went with the NDTC to the Stratford Shakespeare Theatre in Ontario, Canada; in 1965 they went to the Commonwealth Festival of Arts in the United Kingdom.

In addition to touring with his band, Poulle composed music for four films, including *Jamaica Flavour* and *Songs of the World*. In 1953 he produced an LP titled *Jamaica Mento*, which introduced mento to Kingston's elite in night clubs. He co-composed, with Robert Lightbourne, the music for Jamaica's national anthem. His musical works also include *Folk Mass* (1973), which has a distinctive Jamaican flavour and was performed by the Diocesan Festival Choir for their fiftieth anniversary celebration. Parts of it continue to be performed in the Catholic mass. Poulle also produced, with Louise Bennett Coverley, *Carifesta Ring Ding*, a record of songs and verses. Other compositions include the *Twenty-third Psalm* and the very popular *Linstead Market Suite*, which was performed by the Sibthorpe Beckett Philharmonic Orchestra. Poulle worked with the LTM from 1955 to 1965, during which time he composed the music for *Queenie's Daughter* (1963) as well as a number of songs for other pantomimes, and composed *La Petite Madame* as a tribute to the life of the ballet teacher Madame May Soohih. Poulle died of a heart attack in February 1981.

George "Buddy" Pouyat, dancer, actor, director

George A. "Buddy" Pouyat

"Buddy" Pouyat was born in 1931 at a time when, except for the barnstorming of troubadours and comedians like E.M. Cupidon, Racca and Sandy, and their cronies, theatrical efforts were entirely voluntary. They nevertheless laid the foundations for what has now become a vibrant professional theatre. Pouyat stepped onto the boards of the Jamaican theatre in the 1950s and played in several pantomimes, as well as in local plays such as *Star Boarder*, *Dark of the Moon*, and *Stanley and Fay, Pularchie and P* (directed by Norman Rae). According to Pouyat, his love for the theatre dates to his early youth, when he entered and won a reading competition at his church and received as his prize a small part in the church play.

Pouyat was a founding member of the Ivy Baxter Dance Group – Jamaica's first modern dance studio – and danced in pieces Baxter choreographed for the annual pantomimes and in other locally staged productions, including *Danse Moderne*, *Once*

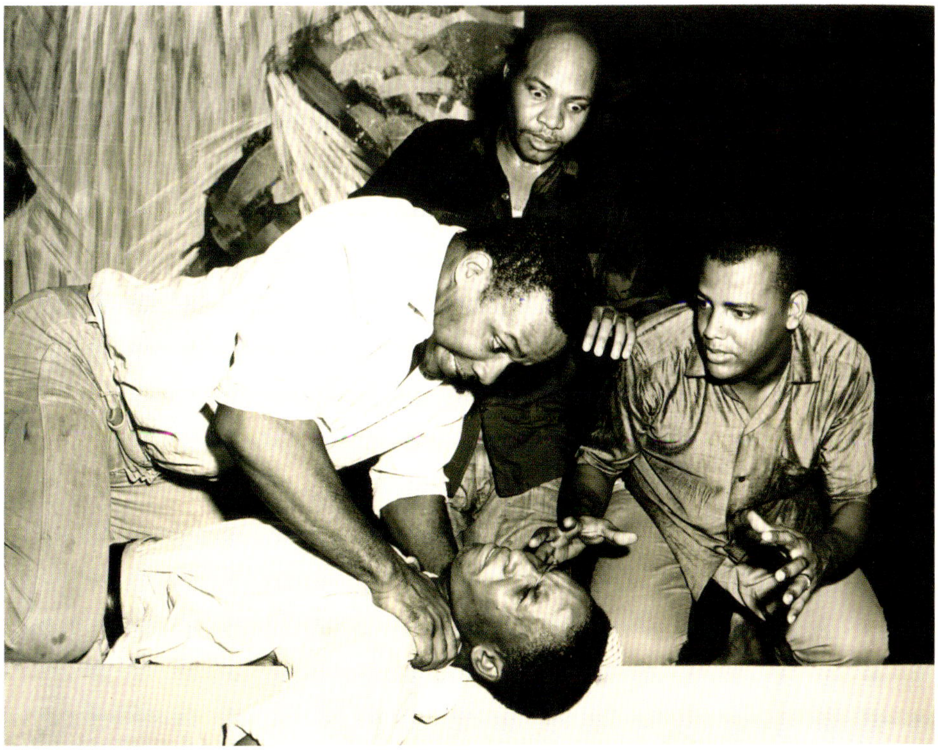

Buddy Pouyat (*left*) in a dramatic scene. *Courtesy of George Pouyat.*

upon a Seaweed and *A Raisin in the Sun*. He was an expert ballroom dancer and saw modern dance as an extension for displaying his talent.

He served as a member of the board of the LTM and the Ward Theatre Foundation, and produced the foundation's first Season of Excellence in 1988. He then began concentrating on directing and developed a most satisfactory series of collaborations with playwrights. At the time of writing, he has directed over thirty productions, including several of Basil Dawkins's works: *Feminine Justice*, *No Dirty Money*, *What the Hell Is Happening to Us, Dear?*, *A Gift for Mom* (awarded top honours in the 2004 Actor Boy Awards), *Toy Boy* and *Uptown Bangarang*. He has also directed David Heron's *Cheaters*, Anthony Winkler's *The Burglar*, and the comedy *Laugh Jamaica*, with some of Jamaica's foremost comedians: Tony Hendriks, Bello and Blacka (Winston Bell and Owen Ellis), and Joan-Andrea Hutchinson. According to Pouyat, what drives him to direct is the challenge he gets from taking the raw script, working with his actors and moulding it into a production which the audience can enjoy.

In 1958 Pouyat was a member of the Jamaican delegation that participated in the Trinidad Festival of Arts. He also toured with the Jamaican troupe which performed in Cuba at the invitation of the Cuban government. He has taught dancing and deportment at Shortwood Teachers' College and at the Mico Teachers' College. He was also a member of Errol Hill's group, the West Indian Players, at the University College of the West Indies. With this group, he performed in such productions as Roderick Walcott's *The Trouble with Albino Joe* and *Malfinis*; Slade Hopkinson's *The Blood of the Family*; and Derek Walcott's *Malcauchon*, for which he was also an actor and choreographer. He has acted in plays directed and produced by Ronald

Harrison, Carey Robinson and Lloyd Reckord, who, according to Pouyat, has directed some of the best productions of the period. In the 1960s and 1970s the preparation for each of these plays lasted over a month and a half, and the productions ran for two or three nights.

Among Pouyat's most endearing characteristics are his generosity of spirit and willingness to share his experience, skills and insights with younger practitioners. Efforts such as his have helped the Jamaican theatre to achieve its present sturdy growth.

Norman Rae

Norman Rae, director and theatre manager

Norman Rae was born in Kingston, Jamaica, on 5 December 1931. He was a career civil servant and held degrees from Oxford and London Universities. He was also a theatre critic for the press and for radio, a producer of radio programmes, and a theatre director. While at Oxford he directed Giraudoux's *The Enchanted* (1953) and a musical version of *The Candlelight Revue* which included the young Maggie Smith in the cast. In London he was also engaged in theatrical activities and undertook summer assignments – principally writing and recording scripts on topical subjects – for the BBC radio programme *Calling the West Indies*. On his return to Jamaica, he collaborated with Carmen Tipling on an adaptation of five biblical stories to contemporary Jamaican settings; these were then produced by Robin Midgely for JBC Radio. He produced the radio series *A Time to Remember* (1969–74), about the 1938 labour unrest in Jamaica. His idea was to present history palatably as soap opera.

A Time to Remember was broadcast three times weekly on RJR. Rae also produced Gloria Lannaman's prize-winning script, *The Heritage Now*, for RJR in 1969, and Lannaman's *Our Heritage in Perspective* to celebrate National Heritage Week in 1976, also for RJR. He was television host of *Very Special People*, and director of a number of amateur Jamaican and other productions, some of which toured in the United Kingdom between 2002 and 2003.

Before he was appointed to the Jamaica Foreign Service in 1974, Rae directed *The Fantasticks* at the New Arts Lecture Theatre, UWI. This production, coupled with Trevor Rhone's production of *Smile Orange* at the Barn, launched his intimate love affair with the Jamaican theatre. During these years, he also directed the farcical musical *A Funny Thing Happened on the Way to the Forum*, as well as John Whiting's *The Devils*, the pantomime *Hail Columbus*, Giraudoux's *Tiger at the Gates*, Lannaman's *Stanley and Fay, Pularchie and P*, Lannaman and Rae's *Dickance for Fippance*, and David Hare's *Slag*, a British comedy of the absurd. Between 1975 and 1978 he directed Simon Gray's *Butley*, Lannaman's pantomime *Brashana O!* and a Jamaican musical, *Don't Wake the Baby*, also by Lannaman.

Norman Rae contributed his time voluntarily organizing and programming work for the Ward Theatre Foundation, and produced *Music at the Ward* as well as *Season of Excellence* in 1995. He was made a Commander of the Order of Distinction (CD), and awarded the Institute of Jamaica's Silver Musgrave Medal for his work in the theatre. Norman Rae died on 19 June 2008 of a heart attack.

The Reckord Family and Theatre

Barry and Lloyd Reckord are among the pioneers of the modern Jamaican theatre. Their contributions have been significant, from the 1950s to the end of the century and well into the first decade of the 2000s. They produced many memorable plays for stage and other media which have enriched and expanded local cultural offerings, especially in the theatre, and have also introduced many memorable performers and performances to the Jamaican stage. With Barry Reckord's first play, *Della* (1953), and the founding of the National Theatre Trust by Lloyd (1968), Jamaican theatre has witnessed a procession of challenging, original and top-quality productions.

Barry Reckord was born on 19 November 1926 in Kingston. He grew up on Merrion Road in Vineyard Town with his three siblings under the watchful eye of a proud and protective mother. Barry, along with his elder brother Carol, enrolled early in nearby Kingston College, a high school for boys founded by Canon Percival Gibson, later Lord Bishop of Jamaica. Canon Gibson and his band of dedicated teachers soon recognized Barry's precocious talent and academic brilliance, and under their tutelage he won the Issa Scholarship that took him to Cambridge University in 1948.

Barry Reckford, playwright. *Courtesy of Yvonne Brewster.*

Reckord attended St Peter's College, then shifted to Emmanuel College, where he graduated with first-class honours in English Literature. On graduation, he took up a teaching job in London. It was this background in the comprehensive school system there that provided the material for his award-winning play, *Skyvers*, produced at the Royal Court Theatre in 1963.

Forty-three years later, in 2006, Reckord was recognized at a Royal Court reading of *Skyvers*, and the Royal Court presented this play for its fiftieth anniversary as one of its major productions that year. Critic Michael Billington commented on the play: "Reckord got there first! . . . While it is tempting to say that times have changed, new figures show that up to 16 million adults today have the reading and writing skills of primary school children. Pam Brighton's production also vividly captures the mutinous surliness of kids for whom school is little more than a prison."[16]

Barry Reckord returned to Jamaica with his wife, Mary, in the early 1950s and went immediately to his first love, the theatre. He wrote *Della*, which was produced for the Ward Theatre. The play was set in a Kingston tenement yard and was intended to portray Jamaican inner-city life, infrequently seen in local theatrical offerings up to that time. It was an ambitious and challenging production that brought together, in its cast, many performers who would go on to long and successful careers in theatre, film and television.

The whole Reckord family was involved. Supporting personnel often included the matriarch, Phygie, at the box office; Cynthia Reckord-Royal, doubling as secretary and administrator; Mary Reckord, stage manager; and Lloyd Reckord as actor and director. The younger generation, Michael, Margaret and Hilary – children of Carol – were actors.

Della confronted the harsh realities of Jamaican social life in its portrayal of inner-city living, and, possibly for these reasons, did not receive the audience support or the financial success it deserved. In spite of this, the Reckord brothers persisted in writing and staging challenging, provocative and exacting plays. The following year, in 1954, Barry Reckord produced the play under an altered title, *Adella*, in London. Four years later, the play, again retitled, *Flesh to a Tiger*, was mounted at the Royal Court Theatre, London. In 1962 Reckord's *You in Your Small Corner* was presented in Jamaica as an official item during the independence celebrations. That same year it was produced for television by Granada. Another of his plays, *In the Beautiful Caribbean*, was performed at the Ward Theatre in 1972 and was also produced by BBC TV. Barry Reckord's other plays include *I-man* (Jamaica, 1969); *Don't Gas the Blacks* (London, 1969); *A Liberated Woman* (Jamaica, London, New York, 1970); *White Witch* (London, 1985); *Let It All Hang Out, Daddy* (Kingston, 1988); and *Sugar D* (Kingston, 1988). His television dramas include *You in Your Small Corner* (Granada, 1962), *In the Beautiful Caribbean* (BBC, 1972) and *Club Havana* (BBC, 1975). He is also the author of two books: *Skyvers* (Penguin, 1966) and *Does Fidel Eat More Than Your Father?* (Praeger, 1971).[17]

Lloyd Reckord, Barry's brother, is an actor, director and writer for theatre, radio, film and television. Born on 26 May 1929, he spent some years working in the Jamaican theatre before he received a scholarship to the Bristol Old Vic Theatre School in England. He later joined the Old Vic Company, London, where he played in *Romeo and Juliet*, *The Merchant of Venice*, *Anna Lucastre* and in the Rogers and Hammerstein musical *South Pacific*. He directed and acted in brother Barry's play *Della* (later renamed *Flesh to a Tiger*) in London before he was awarded a Smith-Mundt Fellowship to the United States to study theatre at Howard University, Yale University and the American Theater Wing.

After five years of honing his craft in England, Reckord returned to Jamaica in 1956 and started the Actors Theatre Company, with which he directed and acted in

Lloyd Reckord (*left*), actor and director, in *Waiting for Godot*, with Thom Cross. *Courtesy of Lloyd Reckord.*

You in Your Small Corner, Barry Reckford's play about West Indians in England. This scene from the play shows Lois Kelly Barrow and Lloyd Reckord, who play the principal roles. The play was produced for the Arts Celebrations Committee by Noel Vaz. *Photo by Amador Pack.*

a number of original West Indian plays, as well as Arthur Miller's *The Crucible*. He returned to London to appear in *Flesh to a Tiger* at the Royal Court in 1958. He then performed in leading roles on stage and on television, including Ted Wills's *Hot Summer Night*. He directed plays at the Royal Court and at several other venues in and around London, and directed television documentaries for the BBC.

On his return to Jamaica in 1966, Lloyd Reckord directed and appeared in productions sponsored by the Jamaican government, including *1865: A Ballad for a Rebellion*, by Sylvia Wynter, as well as art programmes for television. He founded the National Theatre Trust, whose objectives were to promote West Indian theatre to the widest possible audience, as well as outstanding plays of world theatre. The Trust had an executive board of seven members plus a director. In 1968 it premiered with Barry Reckord's *You in Your Small Corner*, and for the next three years created an average of five productions annually. The majority of these were West Indian plays on themes relevant to West Indian audiences. The National Theatre Trust played in Kingston as well as in Montego Bay and St Ann's Bay. In 1971, they formed the National Theatre Company, using a nucleus of seasoned performers. The intention was to move towards professional theatre in Jamaica, but there was not sufficient financial support to sustain the company, and its members were soon known as the National Theatre Trust once more.

For the ensuing thirty-five years, the National Theatre Trust presented some forty plays and introduced to Jamaican audiences a festival of Cuban films in 1971, and the Harlem Dance Theater Company in 1973. With sponsorship from the business community, the National Theatre Trust organized a Theater for Schools programme which toured extensively throughout Jamaica, performing plays which had been chosen for the Cambridge School Certificate examinations in particular years. In this

Lloyd Reckord with Pauline Stone in *Junction Village*, by Charles Archibald; produced for Record Films Ltd. *Courtesy of Lloyd Reckord.*

way Lloyd Reckord's contribution to the understanding of the Shakespearean canon and other classical plays has been invaluable to students sitting the CXC and other high school examinations, as well as to other students at teachers' and community colleges.

Reckord directed *Rose Slip* in 1972 and again in 1982. His one-man show, *Beyond the Blues*, ran from 1979 into the early 1980s. It was a collection of black poetry and prose from Africa, the United States and the Caribbean, and he presented it at teachers' and community colleges and to the general public at the Creative Arts Centre at the UWI and at the Edna Manley College. These performances were sponsored by Grace, Kennedy Limited and by the host institutions. Reckord, with his one-man show, successfully toured six theatre centres on the east coast of the United States, among them the United Nations in New York, the Eugene O'Neill Center in Connecticut, the Smithsonian Institution's Museum of African Art in Washington DC and Dartmouth College in New Hampshire. He also undertook a three-month tour of the United Kingdom which culminated in six performances at the National Theatre of Great Britain's Cottesloe Theatre, and then made a ten-country tour of the English- and French-speaking Caribbean, ending in Barbados. A commentator in the *Daily Gleaner* noted that the presentation, which played at the ICA Centre in Kingston in 1981, was substantially different from the original presentation which opened in May 1979 at the UWI.[18]

Reckord also directed Sylvia Wynter's *Maskarade* (1988) – a fictional account of a leading Jonkonnu band in Kingston in the 1840s – and played three cameo roles in the production – as the mayor, as Mr Nathan and as the doctor. In film, his more recent documentaries deal with contemporary issues, and include *Cocaine Abuse: Jamaica* and *Fix*, about a teenaged drug addict. *Fix* was dramatized in 1987 and filmed in 1988. Both films have been shown locally as well as in the United Kingdom and the United States. The 1984–85 pantomime *Sipplesilver* was adapted from a scenario by Dennis Scott and was written by Pat Cumper, with input from Reckord.

In 1990 Reckord Films Limited was launched, for the production and distribution of films with Jamaican and Caribbean themes. To date, it has made three feature-length videos which are being marketed internationally: *Body Moves*, a Jamaican love story; *Junction Village* (stage script by Charles Archibald), a delightful Caribbean comedy; and *Miss Lou and Friends*, which presents a recital by Louise Bennett Coverley. These three videos have all been financial and artistic successes.[19] His early films, *Ten Bob in Winter* and *Dream a 40*, have been shown at international film festivals.

Michael Reckord

Michael Reckord, son of Carol and nephew of Barry and Lloyd, is a minister of religion as well as a playwright, short-story writer, journalist, theatre critic and lecturer in the performing arts. He has been a high school teacher, part-time university lecturer, and reporter and sub-editor of the *Daily Gleaner* since 1962. He was awarded best short play for the Jamaica 21 Playwriting Competition (1983) and won first prize (Caribbean region) in the Commonwealth Broadcasting Association's short story competition (1998).

Since his debut in *Della* in the 1950s Michael has performed in another of Barry's plays, *The White Witch of Rose Hall* (1975); in the pantomime *The Honourable All Purpus and the Dancing Princesses* (1979), from the script by Pat Cumper, for which he prepared the scenario; in *The Prisoner of Second Avenue*, written by Neil Simon and directed by Claude Clarke; *The Trial of the Cantonsville Nine*, directed by Lloyd Reckord for the JSD; and in his own play, *Nanny Meets the Wicked White Witch*. He has also written other short items for the Temple of Light Church of Religious Science, where he serves as a minister of religion. His theatrical writings include *Man with Machete*, anthologized in the third book of the series *Exploring English in the Caribbean* (Macmillan Caribbean, 1985); the book for the LTM pantomime *The Honourable All Purpus and the Dancing Princesses* (1979), from a fairytale adapted by Pat Cumper; several episodes of the radio serial *Lime Tree Lane* on JBC; *The Idiot and the Fool*, *Under the Law*, and several episodes of the radio series *Beverly Hills, Jamaica*.

Carole Reid

Carole Reid, soprano and NDTC singer

Carole Reid, soprano, has been a member and soloist of Christ Church, Vineyard Town, since she was twelve years old. In addition, she was a member and soloist of the "Y" Choral Group, and is currently a member of the Diocesan Festival Choir, the Jamaica Musical Theatre Company, the National Chorale, and the NDTC Singers.

Reid studied pianoforte at the ATCL and to the level of grade 8, RSM, at the Jamaica School of Music, where she also attained grade 8, with distinction, as a voice performer. Among her tutors at the Jamaica School of Music were Marian Nowakowski, Jeanette Cross, Robert Williams and Joyce Britton. She has also attended master classes conducted by Stephanie Scorbi, Professor Reuter and Sir Willard White.

She has given numerous solo recitals, locally and overseas. A few of the works which she has performed as soloist are: Bach, *St Matthew Passion*; Faure, *Requiem*; Gaul, *Holy City*; Gounod, *St Cecilia Mass*; Gabrielli, *Ecclesia*; Haydn, *Passion (Seven Last Words)*, *Creation* and *Mass*; Handel, *Messiah* and *Solomon*; Dettingen, *Te Deum*; Mapletoft Poulle, *Folk Mass*; Mendelssohn, *Elijah* and *Hymn of Praise*; Mozart, *Nozze de Figaro* and *La Grand Messe in C*; Schubert, *Mass in C*; Théodore DuBois, *Seven Last Words*; Vaughan William, *Serenade to Music*; Vivaldi, *Magnificat*; and Verdi, *Requiem*.

Reid's repertoire is extensive, ranging from classical to contemporary. She was a recipient of the JAMI Awards for best classical female performer in 1997 and 1998 among other numerous awards and honour certificates. In 1997 Reid participated in the Thirty-fifth International Eisteddfod of South Africa, in the category of classical recital (vocal), and attained two silver certificates for second place.

In addition to planning and coordinating large fund-raising events, especially for Christ Church, she performs as soloist at weddings and other special events and at numerous church functions and concerts. She was soloist at the funerals of two former prime ministers – the Honourable Michael Manley and the Honourable Hugh

Lawson Shearer – and also at the funeral of former governor general Sir Florizel Glasspole.

In 1999, Reid coached the international soprano Miss Kathleen Battle in a folk song of her choice for her performance at King's House, Jamaica. In addition, she has performed as a soloist for recitals in Ottawa (Canada) with the combined choirs of the National Chorale and the Bytown Singers. In her efforts to encourage classical music, she also has been guest soloist for the Jamaica College Chapel Choir, both in Jamaica and overseas.

Reid's first CD, entitled *Carole in Concert*, was launched by Jamaica's then-minister of finance, Dr Omar Davies, in December 2003. The disc was also launched in Long Island, New York, in April 2004 to a receptive audience, with guest accompanist Dr Stanley Ralph. On 13 December 2004, Carole launched her second album, entitled *A Gift of Carols*, fulfilling another dream that hopefully will bring joy to its listeners.

Apart from participating in various choirs, and being soloist at national and other prestigious events, Reid receives great satisfaction from working with young people. As former musical director for Probemaster Entertainment Limited, she was responsible for coaching teenagers and young adults in several original musicals, namely *Block 24*, *The Narrative*, *O Holy Night* and *The Glass Slipper*. A former director at the Bank of Jamaica and human resource and administration manager at the National Export-Import Bank of Jamaica, where she was assigned by the BOJ, Miss Reid is now a director of Alfrasure Structures and Roofing Limited.

David Reid

David Reid, choirmaster, conductor and tenor soloist

David Augustus Reid, choirmaster, conductor and tenor soloist, was born 18 January 1929. He has been a career civil servant, serving in local and overseas postings while devoting his spare time to musical endeavours. It was while on one of these assignments to England that he qualified as an Associate of the Royal College of Music (ARCM), gaining distinctions in every subject, both theoretical and practical. His repertoire comprises oratorio, opera, art songs, lieder, spirituals, folk songs, jazz, reggae and calypso.

Reid's first ever public appearance was in Jim Russell's *Showboat* at the Ward Theatre on 1 January 1940, at the age of eleven. He was a founding member of the Jamaica Musical Theatre Company in 1960 and continues to participate in their monthly concert series, which run from November to May each year. Over the years he has performed on a variety of occasions: at sacred concerts, variety concerts, fundraisers, special church services, banquets, tea parties and weddings.

David Reid was a member of the combined male voice choir drawn from the East Queen Street Baptist Fraternal Men's Choir (conducted by J.J. Williams), the Kingston Male Voice Choir (conducted by Eglon Fairweather) and the St George's Male Voice Choir (conducted by Easton Soutar), which sang at a reception for Queen Elizabeth II and Prince Philip at King's House in 1953. He was also a member of the male and mixed voice choirs for the 1955 Jamaica Bandwagon, which toured all parish capitals as Jamaica celebrated three hundred years of association with the

British. He has given solo performances at the funerals of two prime ministers, Sir Alexander Bustamante at the Roman Catholic cathedral in Kingston, and the Honourable Michael Manley at the lying-in-state at the National Arena. Reid's was the sole voice on an audition tape, singing the composition that was eventually chosen as Jamaica's national anthem. The tape was presented in 1962 to the committee responsible for selecting the anthem. The tune was retained as recorded but there were minor changes to the words.

In 1967, while on transfer to the Jamaica High Commission in England, Reid was a member of a cast, including professional West Indian singers and dancers, that supported Topol, star of London's West End production of *Fiddler on the Roof*, in the preparation and presentation of one of a series of eight Independent Television (ITV) shows featuring Topol. Reid has sung in a BBC broadcast to the Caribbean from the Anglican Church on Clapham Common, the church which William Wilberforce attended while he was championing the cause for the abolition of the slave trade. And he has been a soloist in a concert at St Paul's Cathedral, London.

Reid has been a member of the "Y" Choral Group since 1952, the St George's Anglican Church Choir since 1952 and conductor since 1984. His first and only pantomime performance was in *Anancy and Beeny Bud* (1956), in which he played the Young Lover Boy. (The music for the part was composed by the late Robert Lightbourne.) His first appearance as a principal in an oratorio was in *St Mark's Passion*, by Charles Wood, with the St Andrew Singers (1960). His first principal role in opera was in Gilbert and Sullivan's *The Pirates of Penzance* for the Jamaica Amateur Operatic Society, also in 1960. The show was conducted by Billy Pilgrim and directed by Fred Kench. Reid's first appearance as conductor of a major work – Mendelssohn's *Hymn of Praise* – was for the Methodist Chorale in 1986. Now, at seventy-nine years of age, Reid continues to be active in musical affairs.

Trevor Rhone

Trevor Rhone, playwright and actor. *Courtesy of Yvonne Brewster.*

If by "man of the theatre" we mean one who makes his living by the theatre and achieves distinction by that means alone, Trevor Rhone will be recognized immediately as one of the outstanding achievers in the history of the Jamaican theatre. Rhone has been successful as a playwright, actor, director and producer. Two other, but by no means minor, accomplishments are his superb speaking voice and his impeccable ear for Jamaican speech, whether in "received pronunciation" or in the vernacular. These factors have all contributed to the theatre-worthiness of his dramas, and his considerable talent embraces stage, radio, film, television and other manifestations of a rapidly globalizing industry.

Rhone was born in Kingston, Jamaica, on 24 March 1940. He received his secondary education at Beckford and Smith's High School (now St Jago High) in Spanish Town under the tuition of Mrs Doreen Freeman, and represented Beckford and Smith's in the annual Secondary Schools' Drama Festival, inaugurated in 1950. He studied theatre (1960–63) at Rose Bruford College in Kent, England, where he covered the regular drama school curriculum and built up a splendid reputation.

Back in Jamaica in 1965, he joined another Rose Bruford graduate, Yvonne Jones,

Old Story Time, written and directed by Trevor Rhone, with Keith Sasso, Karl Binger and Karen Ford Warner (1981). *Photo by Monica DaSilva.*

along with six others, to start Theatre 77. The young group hoped that, twelve years on, the foundations would have been truly laid for a national theatre, and they pursued their dreams modestly but intelligently. They organized workshops and staged their plays at the Barn Theatre, a garage which they had converted at Yvonne Jones's parents' home on Oxford Road in Kingston. But after a few years, only Rhone and Jones-Brewster, of the founding members, were still with Theatre 77.

To make a living, Rhone taught at high schools. He directed Molière's *The Miser* at Kingston College, and produced *Twelfth Night* and *Love Makes the Best Doctor*. At Kingston Technical High School in 1967, he staged two pantomimes, *Cinderella* and *Rip Van Winkle*. Rhone wrote and developed his first plays with the Theatre 77 group. One such effort was *The Gadget* (1969; renamed *Old Story Time*, 1979), which he wrote and directed with the assistance of Ancile Gloudon. In 1970 he co-authored, with Perry Henzell *The Harder They Come*, the film classic which helped to establish Jamaican reggae music on the international scene. In that same year, he was responsible for the book for the LTM pantomime *Music Boy*, performed at the Ward Theatre and directed by Thom Cross, another graduate of Rose Bruford College. He also wrote one of his most successful plays, *Smile Orange* (1971), which was mounted by Dennis Scott at the Barn. Then followed *Comic Strip* (1973), *Sleeper* (1974) and *School's Out* (1975). In 1975 he adapted, directed and produced *Smile Orange* as a film. This version won a major award at the Cork International Film Festival.

In 1979 Rhone premiered, with a Bahamian cast, his *Old Story Time* at the Dundas Centre for the Performing Arts in Nassau. The following year, he staged the Jamaican production at the Way Out Theatre at the Pegasus Hotel in Kingston. This version formed part of the Jamaican programme at Carifesta '81, the fourth Caribbean Festival of the Arts, which was held in Barbados. In Nassau, Kingston, Bridgetown, London and Toronto, wherever it has been performed, *Old Story Time* has triumphed.

In 1981 the Longman Group published *Old Story Time*, *School's Out* and *Smile Orange*. Yvonne Jones Brewster first staged *School's Out* at the Barn Theatre in 1975. A new production under the author's direction had an overflow run at the Way Out Theatre in 1983. These three plays, along with *Two Can Play*, establish Rhone's reputation among Jamaica's most successful playwrights to date. His most recent work is his one-man show *Bellas Gate Boy*, in which he relates his experiences growing up in rural Jamaica and his struggles as a student in England. Most of Rhone's plays deal with the effects of colonialism and post-colonialism on the Jamaican psyche.

The two-character comedy *Two Can Play* (1982), directed by Rhone himself with brilliant performances by Charles Hyatt and Grace McGhie in the two roles, demonstrates at once a theatrical flair, a gift for character individualization and an economy of dialogue that have seldom been equalled on the Jamaican stage. *Two Can Play* is a battle of the sexes set against the background of political violence and the feeling of doom that was the lot of many Jamaicans during the long, drawn-out election campaign of 1980. Notable in the play is the use of plastic values – the gun fire, sirens and other noises off, the blinding searchlight from without, and the hushed atmosphere and more subdued lighting within. The timing and control of stage business, and the on-stage movement betray the sureness of diction by a master craftsman. Wycliffe Bennett saw *Two Can Play* twice during its first run at the Way Out Theatre at the Pegasus Hotel in Kingston in 1982, and again in November 1983, when it came on a brief tour of New York. He liked it better each time.[20] So successful was the play that it won the National Theatre Critics Award, at the time sponsored by the JCDC; the Public Broadcasting Service (PBS) in the United States acquired the television rights. In order to appreciate fully Trevor Rhone's achievement and the special significance of *Two Can Play*, it is necessary to understand the changes which have taken place not only in the theatre, but also in the society that the theatre mirrors. An observer, for example, will note that, while the Jamaican theatre continues to reflect international trends, the major emphasis now is on the development of indigenous efforts.

Trevor Rhone's *Two Can Play*, directed by the playwright in 1982, with Grace McGhie and Charles Hyatt. *Photo by Monica DaSilva.*

Among Rhone's other plays are *It's Not My Fault, Baby*, a collaborative effort with members of the Barn Players (1967); *Everyman* (1980); *Pepper*, a family planning musical (1989); *The Power*, a radio play (1992); *One Stop Driver* (1992); *Dear Counsellor* (1997); and *Bellas Gate Boy* (2002). His films are *The Harder They* Come, with co-screenwriter Perry Henzell (released 1971); *Milk and Honey*, co-written with Glen Salzman and Rebecca Yates, and winner of the Canadian Genie award for best original screenplay (1974); *Smile Orange* (1976); and *One Love* (screenplay, 2003).

For Rhone's work as a playwright and for his contribution to the development of the Jamaican theatre, the Government of Jamaica honoured him in 1980 with the award of Commander of the Order of Distinction (CD). He also received the Musgrave Gold Medal (1988) from the Institute of Jamaica, and the Norman Manley Award for Excellence in the Theatre (1996). Rhone also acted in small parts in a number of films. Rhone died of a heart attack on 15 September 2009.

Carey Robinson

Carey Robinson, producer, director, writer, and former director and general manager of the JBC, was born in Port Antonio, Jamaica, on 26 November 1924. In his early adult years he worked on the editorial staff of the *Daily Gleaner* as a reporter and sub-editor, at *Spotlight News Magazine* as a reporter, and at Radio Jamaica (1953–57) as an announcer and producer. He entered the government service in July 1957 and was attached to the Public Relations Office (later the Jamaica Information Service, or JIS). As a broadcasting officer with the JIS, he reorganized the programmes of the Government Broadcasting Services to reflect the plans and policies of the government and to give general information of value to the citizenry. With the advent of television to Jamaica (1963), Robinson helped to set up the JIS television section. He was responsible for coordinating the film unit and for developing government television programming.

Carey Robinson, actor, producer, director, writer

Robinson is the author of *The Fighting Maroons*, *The Iron Thorn*, and *The Rise and Fall of Falmouth, Trelawny*. He has written several stage plays, three of which – *The Runaway*, *Mountain Lion* (based on the life of the Maroon Cudjoe) and *The Mantle of Spain* – have been produced and have won prizes in Jamaica Festival Drama Competitions. He has also written and directed the film *Time of Fury* (1965), the first full-length feature made in Jamaica by Jamaicans, for the centenary celebrations of the Morant Bay rebellion.

His work in the documentary genre includes the very popular *Hill and Gully Ride* series (begun 1989, still running in 2008), which profiles Jamaicans and Jamaican lifestyles. He has been a pioneer in docudramas, including *Spirit of Freedom* (1995) and *A Tale of Freedom* (1996), which celebrate the life of Nanny of the Maroons and her people. His documentary *Flashpoint '38*, co-authored with Louis Marriott, is based on the Frome Riots of 1938, and *Living Treasures of Jamaica* documents the lives of four distinguished Jamaican pioneers: Dr Thomas Philip Lecky, who developed the Jamaica Hope, the first breed of tropical cattle in one hundred years; Reverend Hugh Sherlock, a Methodist minister and social worker who founded Boys' Town; Cecil Baugh, a potter whose works are made from Jamaican clay; and Alvin Marriott, sculptor. All these were produced between 1991 and 1992.

Robinson's other documentaries include two features on Sir Philip Sherlock, social worker and first West Indian vice-chancellor of the University of the West Indies; *Visiting with Miss Lou* (Louise Bennett Coverley); *The Mission of Marcus Garvey* (2004); and several biographical features. Persons featured in Robinson's biographies include *Norman Manley* (1994), the founding father and first premier of Jamaica; *Sir Alexander Bustamante*, the labour leader and first prime minister;; *Sir Howard Cook*, governor general; *The Honourable Herb McKinley*, athlete (2006); and *Frank Gordon*, social worker (2007). Carey Robinson has been honoured by the Institute of Jamaica with the Gold and Silver Musgrave Medals, and has received the Government of Jamaica award of Commander of the Order of Distinction (CD).

Tony Robinson

From his early years, Tony Robinson seemed destined to end up in the media. His father, M.G. Robinson, was a pioneer in broadcasting on the technical side, and his mother was a teacher; both had great writing skills. The young Robinson, an avid reader, inherited these abilities.

An award-winning producer, director, videographer and writer, Tony "Teerob" Robinson began his professional career at the Jamaica Information Service (JIS) in 1970. While there, he learned the medium of film, scriptwriting, audio techniques, directing and producing from the ground up. He pulled cables, set microphones and held boom mikes for countless productions. He was a quick learner and had great teachers and mentors, such as Carey Robinson, Jean Barnes, Freddy Borrough and Don Lawrence, and was promoted to the position of television producer and director by 1972. During this period, he wrote, produced and directed numerous radio and television programmes which starred such Jamaican actors as Oliver Samuels, Volier Johnson and Teddy Price, before they became household names.

One notable series penned by Robinson was the nationally acclaimed television drama *Life with the Littles*, about a typical Jamaican family that struggled through the challenges of the times but always seemed to find a solution in the end. Robinson also wrote another television series, *Around the Browns*, which had a similar theme. Tony went on to further his studies at the BBC in England, where he graduated first in his class. In England, he was posted at various BBC stations in London, Birmingham, Manchester and Tottenham.

On returning to Jamaica, Robinson rejoined the JIS, but because of his recognized skills he was also called upon to direct major broadcasts for the JBC, now Television Jamaica (TVJ). These included the morning programme *Morning Time* (of which he and Lukee Chung were the first directors), and televised state visits, Musgrave Medal

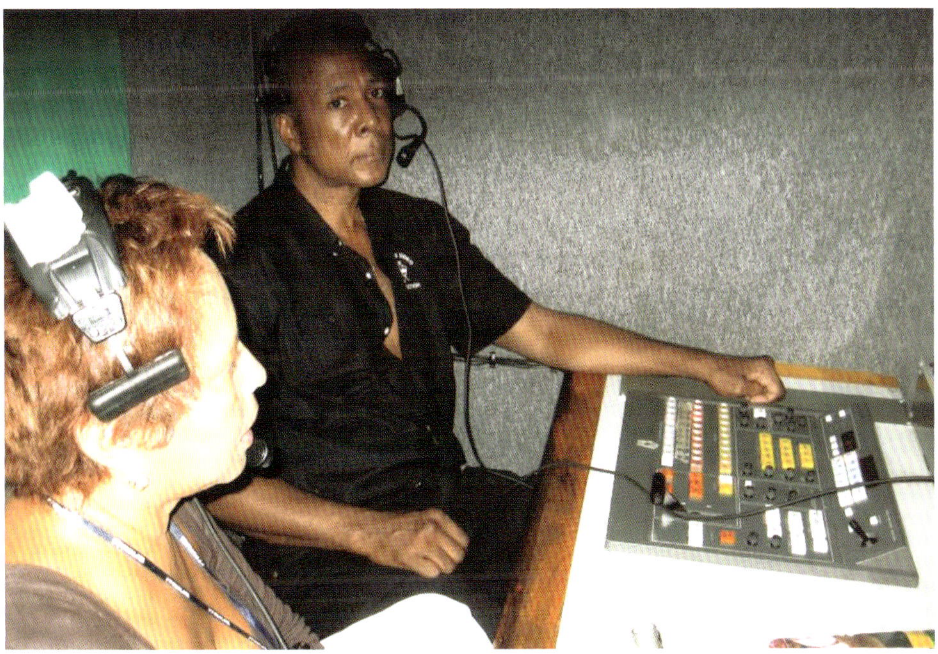

Tony Robinson, director, writer, producer and soundman

award ceremonies, parliamentary sessions, and musical and sports programmes. Many musical stars of the day had their first exposure on live television in these programmes. Robinson was also producer and director of the JIS *Sunday Playhouse* and remembers adapting Charles Dyer's *Rattle of a Simple Man* for Jamaican television, starring Oliver Samuels, as well as Strindberg's *The Stronger* and Chekhov's *Uncle Vanya*. These works were a challenge, as the language and culture of the originals was vastly different from anything in Jamaica. He also directed the filming of the major music festivals Sunsplash and Sumfest.

Robinson later became the senior producer and director for the JIS programme *Nightview*, which won the Press Association of Jamaica (PAJ) award for excellence. But he later resigned from JIS as the managing editor of the television department and ventured into the private sector, where he planned to earn a decent living and create more programmes for television. He found the move rewarding.

The CPTC has utilized Robinson's services as a freelancer, inviting him to direct many of their programmes, including *Today in Ja*, *Rappin'* and *Sunday Classics*. He has served as senior lecturer in production and directing techniques at the CPTC's television production courses. Robinson produced and directed *Flashpoint '38*, a five-part series with one-hour instalments that highlighted the labour unrest in Jamaica in 1938. To date this programme has been one of the most significant video productions ever undertaken in Jamaica, utilizing a cast of hundreds and shot over a six-month period. For many years, Robinson has also directed the annual Prime Minister's Independence Gala, which is broadcast live on TVJ and CVM stations.

With well over thirty years' expertise in the business, both locally and internationally, Robinson was chosen to direct broadcasts of the World Junior Games, as well as the World Netball Championships, both held in Jamaica. He utilized all-Jamaican crews with the World Junior Games, using twenty one cameras and an outside broadcast truck that had to be flown in from the United States. (At those same games, a young Jamaican named Usain Bolt made the world stand up and take notice with his phenomenal achievements.) Robinson also directed Jamaica's entry to the Commonwealth Music Video Vision Competition in London, which emerged as the first-place winner from a field of forty-seven entries.

He has worked as director with many renowned playwrights on various television dramas, including Trevor Rhone on the production *Safe Travel*, which won various awards in Jamaica and Canada. He has also worked for various government ministries, and won awards for many of those productions. He directed and edited the Jamalco video production *A Better Place*, which won an award of excellence in the Public Relations Society of Jamaica's (PRSJ) annual competition in 2000. Robinson directed the CVM-TV programmes *Our Voices* and *Let's Talk Health*. He also directed the award-winning, made-for-television movie *High Grade*, sponsored by UNESCO. He directed the Living with HIV-AIDS Awareness television commercials *Teenage Pregnancy and HIV* and *Get on with Life*, and has written and directed for the campaign *Pinch, Leave an Inch . . . Roll*. He has produced features and commercials for the cricket World Cup held in the Caribbean, and on subjects from agriculture to theology. He has produced a documentary, *Fruit Tree Crops in Jamaica*, for the Food and Agriculture Organization of the United Nations, and also a documentary for the United Theological College of the West Indies.

Robinson has also turned his skills to the newspapers, where he has been a humorous and controversial columnist for the *Jamaica Observer* for over fifteen years. For this he was recognized and rewarded in 1997 when he won the PAJ's award for journalism as a writer, for his opinion column *Daddy Oh*. For his first love, television, he earned the Doctor Bird Award in 2004 for his contribution to the film and television industry.

Although not known for his acting skills, Robinson has ventured before the cameras. A sixth-degree black belt in Seido karate, he has performed stunts for various movies, including *Countryman*, *Passion and Paradise*, and *Instinct*. He can say that he has bruised shoulders with actors the likes of Armand Assante and Anthony Hopkins. His stunts have included falling off tall buildings, taking hits, fighting bad guys, destroying entire villages, saving damsels in distress and other stuff that he only dreamt of doing as a young man. He was the stunt and fight coordinator for the movie *One Love*.

Tony Robinson has made his mark on the media landscape but, according to him, he is still learning, always honing his skills, forever trying to improve, for as the old saying goes, "You are only as good as your last production." He adds, "And when the phone stops ringing to ask for your skills, then that's it."

Cheryl Ryman

Cheryl Ryman, choreographer, dancer, researcher and writer

Cheryl Ryman is primarily a cultural specialist with a long and distinguished background in cultural research, documentation and dissemination, as well as in curriculum development and training since the 1970s. Her publications on various aspects of Jamaican and Caribbean history and culture, particularly on African retentions in traditional and popular performances, remain seminal works. She has been engaged in theatre as an actress, dancer and choreographer since 1960; and in film and television production as a project developer, screenwriter, producer and project manager. She acted with Theatre 77, and in several pantomimes, including the revival of *Queenie's Daughter*, *Anancy and Pandora*, and *Brashana O!*

Over a forty-year period, Ryman has developed skills in project development and management; personnel and human resource development; education; training; and oral, written and audio-visual communications. She co-founded and developed "start-up" operations for the African-Caribbean Institute of Jamaica (a branch of the Institute of Jamaica), where she was research fellow in dance from 1974 to 1989. She has produced seminal work for distribution to the media, and has written curricula for administration and general institution-building for the Jamaica School of Dance, CVM-TV, and, most recently, the Outameni Experience, a heritage park where Jamaican history is told through performance, exhibitions and multi-media presentations. The Mediamix group opened the Outameni Experience in Trelawny in September 2007.

Ryman holds a Bachelor of Arts (Honours) degree from York University, Toronto, where she majored in dance and studied the history of dance, dance therapy, dance notation (Laban method), and the techniques of ballet, jazz, modern contemporary dance, and Indian and Spanish dance. She has also earned a Master of Arts degree from Antioch International University, Ohio, and is currently pursuing a doctorate in cultural studies at the UWI, Mona.

Her first association with film and television was when she coordinated the production of *Born Black* (written, produced and directed by Lennie Little-White), the first film on blacks in Canada (released in 1972). From 1993 to 1995 she was operations manager for CVM-TV, where she was responsible for developing systems management, and for human resource development.

Apart from her work in film and television, she has been a consultant on cultural projects for such organizations as the Jamaica Information Service and the Institute of Jamaica, which she has assisted with publications and museum exhibits. She has also researched and designed a travelling exhibition on Jamaican culture for CARNEID–UNESCO, and has served as dance adjudicator and trainer for the JCDC. With Sheila Barnett, she designed and coordinated a workshop and exhibition for the Canadian University Service Organization (CUSO); and, acting as a consultant for Peter Minshall, the distinguished Trinidad Carnival costume designer, she provided critical commentary on the design elements of the Caribana Festival in Toronto. Also in Toronto, she choreographed and trained for the dance theatre company Chissamba Chiyuka. At the St Louis Art Museum, in the United States, Ryman was local facilitator of research, locations and costume makers for the Caribbean Festival of Arts exhibition and book project. Among her other activities, she wrote and produced an eight-part television Easter series for the CPTC, and guided and prepared project proposals for submission to international and local funding agencies in support of the Cultural Heritage Fund.

Ryman trained as a ballet dancer with Jenny Lyn Rodrigues (McIntosh) from 1957 to 1959; with the Eddy Thomas Dance Workshop (1965–69); with the Neville Black Dance Studio (1965–69), where she was a solo dancer; and with the NDTC of Jamaica (1967–83), where she was supporting dancer and principal dancer. Between 1972 and 1973 she was attached to the Institute of African Studies (University of Ghana, Legon), where she immersed herself in Ghanaian traditional dance, music forms and theatre, while at the same time carrying out field research. This research proved fruitful in the many activities she undertook for the Institute of Jamaica and its several cultural branches and committees.

Ryman choreographed the dance for *Maskarade*, written by Sylvia Wynter (Carew) and directed by Jim Nelson; and for the pantomime *River Mumma and the Golden Table*. She is co-founder, along with Sheila Barnett, Monica Campbell McFarlane, Alison Symes and Maria Smith, of DanceScape Jamaica Ltd. Since 1996 she has been engaged with Lennie Little-White and Mediamix/Palm Productions in marketing, public relations, promotion and script-writing for both film and television productions. With Little-White, she co-founded the Doctor Bird Awards in Film and Television in 1998 and continues to be the executive secretary for the foundation. She is also the Caribbean regional coordinator for International Public Television (INPUT), and has been responsible for staging a number of INPUT film festivals in Jamaica as well as representing the Caribbean region at the annual international INPUT film and television conferences and film festivals overseas since 2001. Ryman has been associated with Mediamix and its related companies as director and secretary since 1973.

Alwyn Scott

Alwyn Scott, actor

Alwyn Scott's odyssey with the stage began at the early age of six, with performances at Kingsgate Christian Church. He was encouraged by his first voice and elocution teacher, Frieda Reid. During his years at Half Way Tree Primary School, Alwyn excelled in speech and drama, and won many awards in Jamaica Festival competitions. At Jamaica College the young thespian was coached by poet, playwright and educator Dennis Scott, and won awards in the Jamaica Festival and the Secondary Schools' Drama Festival. Under Scott's direction Alwyn performed in his first stage play, as Sir Andrew Aguecheek in Shakespeare's *Twelfth Night*, to critical acclaim. Alwyn remembers Dennis remarking dramatically to him backstage after an exit, "Scott, I'm afraid you are an actor."

It was during Alwyn Scott's years at Jamaica College that he was selected to play a lead role in the BBC film *My Father Sun-Sun Johnson*, in which he performed alongside Lloyd Reckord, an up-and-coming Oliver Samuels, and Leonie Forbes, who was to become one of his lifelong mentors. Scott was also a founding member of the Children's Theatre Trust (spearheaded by Bob Kerr, Natalie Thompson and Brian Heap), for which he performed lead roles in *Mother Goose* and *Goody*. In high school Scott also won an OAS Fellowship to study acting at the Duke Ellington School of the Performing Arts in Washington DC.

After leaving high school, Scott entered the world of professional theatre. Among his credits are appearances or lead roles in classical and local plays, including *Labour Ward*; *Flatmate*; *Checkers*; the pantomime *Mansong*; *What the Butler Saw*; *The King and I*; *Flameheart*; *Hamlet*; *Marcus Garvey and the Captivity of Babylon*; *Old Story Time*; *The Rope and the Cross*; *The Tempest*; *Bellas Gate Boy*; *Once upon This Island*; *A Gift for Mom*; and *Dinner for Eleanor*. He has won four Actor Boy awards as best actor. Scott was also a member of the University Singers and performed many memorable solo parts. He still performs with the choir's alumni group.

Professionally, Scott is a radio and television producer and presenter. He has worked with JIS Radio and Television and was a founding member of the Fame FM fraternity. He has also done a stint with Radio Mona and is a regular voice on radio and television commercials and in documentaries. He is an experienced advertising executive, having been a member of the creative team at Grimax Advertising, and has operated his own advertising agency, Advertising Associates. He currently owns a group of media companies which include Global Media Services, Caribbean Retail Networks and Caribbean Television Network (Irie TV), which is aimed at providing Caribbean programming to the Caribbean diaspora via the Internet. Scott sees the Internet as the means by which local theatre and independent audio-visual producers as well as performers will begin the process of "reverse cultural colonization", where the Caribbean peoples have control over distributing the content of their creative efforts.

Dennis Scott

Dennis Scott, playwright, actor

Dennis Scott, poet, playwright, actor, educator, dancer and literary critic, was born on 16 December 1939. A graduate of the UWI, Scott was very actively involved in the University Drama Club during his undergraduate years. He first attracted attention with his one-act play *Terminus*, published in 1966 by the UWI Extra-Mural Department. That same year, he won the National Festival Literary Competition for his play *Chariots of Wrath*. Four years later he obtained a Schubert playwriting fellowship to the University of Georgia, where he completed his play *Echo in the Bone*, which relives the African Middle Passage and slave experience. As a playwright, he achieved international recognition for this play and two others, *Dog* and *Annabel Campbell*, an adaptation of the *Agamemnon* of Aeschylus. All three plays were performed in Jamaica, and *Echo in the Bone* and *Dog* were also performed in England.

Scott worked at the JSD in the early years, where he made a most valuable contribution to the students' search for a West Indian identity. When he directed classic works of theatre, he maintained the integrity of the texts but put a relevant local spin on them. This approach was later taken by other directors whom Scott taught, among them Rawle Gibbons of Trinidad in *The Tempest* and Eugene Williams of the School of Drama in Eugene O'Neill's *The Emperor Jones*.

In 1983 Scott was invited to become a visiting professor at the Yale School of Drama by Dean Lloyd Richards, where he was actively involved in the Yale Repertory Theatre and directed *A Raisin in the Sun* and *Othello*. He later became co-chairman of the Directing Department of the Yale School of Drama. In 1988, he directed the premiere of the Australian play *The Golden Age* for the Commonwealth of Letters,

Echo in the Bone, by Dennis Scott, in a production at the JSD, of which Scott was director for several years. *Photo by Monica DaSilva.*

an association of Yale Scholars. In 1990 he returned to acting, performing the part of the Griot in *The Warrior Ant* at the Spoleto and Philadelphia Music Festivals. Scott also played a small but significant role in *The Cosby Show* on television.

His first book of poetry, *Uncle Time*, appeared in 1973 and won the International Forum Prize and the Commonwealth Prize for Poetry the next year. His second collection, *Dreadwalk*, appeared in 1982, just before he left for Yale. *Strategies* appeared in 1989, and *After-Image* posthumously, in 2008. His poems have also appeared in *West Indian Poetry*, prepared for schools by Kenneth Ramchand and Cecil Gray in 1971, and in publications in Britain, the United States, the former Soviet Union, India, the Czech Republic and Cuba.

Before leaving Jamaica, Scott was a dancer with the NDTC. He taught drama and served as director of the JSD at what is now the Edna Manley College of the Visual and Performing Arts. He was a well-known art critic in the *Daily Gleaner*. He died 21 February 1991.

Godfrey Taylor

Godfrey Taylor, musican and musicologist

Godfrey Taylor was born in the Methodist manse at Port Morant, St Thomas, on 27 April 1954. His father, a Methodist minister, and his mother, a schoolteacher, lay preacher and church organist, had six children, of which Godfrey was fourth. At age four, he began learning to play the piano with his mother, who later introduced him to speech and drama in small church productions, which she often staged.

Godfrey attended York Castle and Titchfield High Schools, EXED Teachers' College (gaining a teacher's certificate) and the UWI, from which he received a Bachelor of Arts (Honours) degree in 1982. At York Castle High, he studied music with the late Mrs Enid Lewis. He started acting at Titchfield High, landing a leading role in *Sailors Ashore*, which was entered in the Schools' Drama Festival in 1970. At EXED, he studied drama and brass instruments, played in the Excelsior High School brass band, and was keyboardist with the Inner Circle band for a while. He was a founding member of the Carifolk Singers group, and in later years shared several seasons with them as guest director, composer, arranger, coach and accompanist.

While teaching at Ardenne High in the early 1970s, he was introduced by Jennifer Brownell to a new drama group, the Children's Theatre Workshop, based at the Barn Theatre. There he worked with one of its founders, Trevor Rhone, and with Carmen Tipling, among others. At Ardenne, he met musician Noel Dexter, with whom he collaborated on several concerts and theatrical productions over the years.

Taylor returned to Titchfield High as a teacher, where he worked with drama teachers Jennifer Brownell and Melissa Rafferty in school productions of *Oedipus Rex* and *African Slave . . . Play*, for which he composed the music. From 1975 to 1978 he was director for the Youth for Christ (YFC) Chorale in Port Antonio, where he encouraged the use of drama and music in evangelism, especially targeting the youth.

Upon entering the UWI in 1978, Taylor joined the University Singers and remained a member for many years, serving in several capacities – as singer, band member, guest conductor and composer. Among the songs he wrote are *Singers' Jazz*, *Singers'*

Dub, *Latin Scattin*, *The Creator* and *Black as Coal . . . Shotugo*. While at UWI he also directed the University and Colleges Christian Fellowship Choir and was musical director for Sounds of Love, a gospel group.

Taylor plays piano, organ, steel pan, guitar, French horn, trumpet, recorder, congas, and electric and double bass, and has played with school bands, pop bands and orchestras for both recorded and live events. Over the years he has been rehearsal pianist and band- and orchestra member for several plays and musicals, including *Godspel*, *Jumbie Jamboree* (written and produced by Jim Nelson), the Jamaica Music Theatre Company's production of *Jesus Christ Superstar*, Father Richard Ho Lung's *Christmas Oratorio*, and the LTM pantomime *Jack Mansong*.

From 1987 to 1997, Taylor was a member of the NDTC orchestra and performed with them locally and overseas as their bass guitarist. He composed all the music and was musical director for the Jambiz production of *Oliver and Pinocchio*. He was also musical director for *Once upon This Island* and for the Company Limited's production of *Dis Ting*. For *A Life Abundant*, an original Caribbean cantata for soloists, choir, steel band and electronic instruments, with lyrics and melodies by Michael R. Forbes, Taylor wrote the musical arrangements.

He has been church organist for several churches: Kensington Methodist (1969–71), Coke Methodist (1971–73), Lyndhurst Methodist (1973–75), Port Antonio Methodist (1975–78), UWI Chapel (1978 to present), Providence Methodist (1983 to present) and East Queen Street Baptist (2006 to present). He has been a music workshop developer and presenter as well as motivational speaker since 1981. He has worked with the annual Methodist Music Workshop since its inception and succeeded John Binns as its director of music in 1999. He is much sought-after as a musician who plays religious and contemporary music for small functions and large conventions. He is also a studio musician and vocal group coach.

Taylor has co-authored two publications, *Let Us Sing*, a worship songbook for Caribbean schools,[21] and *Mango Time*.[22] Since 2003 he has been the main host voice on *One Heart One Song*, a weekly radio programme featuring interviews with Jamaicans involved in the production of inspirational music. He is also involved in the planning and execution of the media ministry of the Methodist Church in Jamaica. Taylor attributes the development of his performing skills to the influences of Keith Gordon; Rollins Brown, drama director at Titchfield High; theatrical practitioners Trevor Rhone and Trevor Nairne; band master and orchestra leader Marjorie Whylie; teacher, collaborator, friend and critic Noel Dexter; and musicians Roger Williams and Audrey Wright.

Clive Thompson

Clive Thompson – a dancer, choreographer and teacher of distinction – is an artist of international renown. He began his performing career in revues and talent competitions as a child, along with his sister. At age sixteen he was exposed to Katherine Dunham's presentation of *Rites of Passage* in Kingston, and began his formal training in modern dance with Ivy Baxter, in ballet with May Soohih. During this period he represented his country at festivals in Cuba and Trinidad. He danced in Ivy Baxter's

Rat Passage and in *Once upon a Seaweed* before leaving Jamaica for New York in 1960.

Thompson was determined to meet and study with Martha Graham after seeing her film *A Dancer's World*. Within a week of applying he had obtained a scholarship with the Graham Company; six months later he had become a professional dancer with the company. For the next ten years he danced in leading roles with distinguished dancers, including Katherine Dunham, Yuriko, Walter Nicks and Geoffrey Holder.

In 1970 Thompson joined the Alvin Ailey American Dance Theater as a soloist, creating roles in works such as *Mary Lou's Mass*, *The Lark Ascending* and *Hidden Rites*. He performed most of the lead roles in the Ailey repertoire, including his signature piece, *Revelations*. Thompson later founded his own companies, Dance-Company and Dancecenter of Staten Island, which he ran for several years.

Thompson has performed at most major dance festivals, including the Festival d'Avignon in France and the Spoleto Festival in Italy. He has been in great demand as a master teacher at universities and colleges across the United States, Europe, Asia and Africa. He has also been hailed as a choreographer of ballet and modern dance genres in Japan, Brazil, Canada, Norway, France and his home country of Jamaica. For television he choreographed the dances for *The Pueblo Incident*, for which he won an Emmy Award. He also choreographed a Swedish production of *Othello*, and *Heartbreak House*, which featured Rex Harrison. Thompson has appeared on *Sesame Street* with his sons Christopher and Jason, along with noted jazz great Mary Lou Williams and Tina Yuan of the Ailey Company in a production that was conceived and co-produced by his wife, Elizabeth Thompson, who also choreographed *Electric Company* for the Children's Theater Workshop in the United States.

For the stage, Thompson has choreographed Leonard Bernstein's *Mass* for the Kansas City Philharmonic; *Othello* for the Norwegian Royal Opera Company; the world premiere of Thea Musgrave's opera *Harriet*; *A Woman Called Moses* for the Virginia Opera Association; and a new production of *Aida* for the Tulsa Opera.

Clive Thompson, dancer, choreographer

According to Eve, choreographed by John Butler, danced by Clive Thompson's Dance Company, Staten Island. *Courtesy of Clive Thompson.*

On his return to Jamaica in the early 1990s Thompson allied himself with the Edna Manley College, where he teaches and also choreographs with the NDTC. He is the recipient of the Institute of Jamaica's Gold Musgrave Medal (1988) and is an inductee into the Caribbean Hall of Fame.

Ouida Tomlinson Dunphy

Ouida Dunphy, musican and conductor

Ouida Dunphy (formerly Tomlinson), daughter of Bancroft Hylton, a merchant who sold musical instruments, is a musician by profession and an instrumental technology and media specialist. She plays the flute, the violin, the piano and the guitar, and holds the LRAM, GRSM and MA (Educational Technology) qualifications.

Dunphy taught for twelve years at the Excelsior and St Andrew High Schools before being appointed education officer in music in the Ministry of Education in 1969. She has directed and conducted workshops, seminars and festivals in African music and Caribbean and American folk music for the Ministry of Education in association with the UWI and the JCDC. She is a past adjudicator for the JCDC's annual festival, and was director of music for the Carifesta '76 Grand Gala, where she helped to train the ten-thousand-voice choir of young people who performed at the National Stadium. She has published a collection of folk songs, *Mango Walk*, which led to a series of workshops on African music, assisted by the famous Babatunde Olatunji Troupe of dancers. These workshops created a greater understanding of drumming and other aspects of African music as they relate to Caribbean music.

Noel Vaz

Noel Vaz, actor, director, producer and administrator

Noel Vaz gave long and distinguished service to the UWI from 1955, when he joined the staff as drama officer in the Extra-Mural Department and was assigned to Trinidad, until 1986, when he retired from the post of staff tutor in drama at the Creative Arts Centre (now the Philip Sherlock Centre for the Creative Arts) on the Mona campus.

Vaz was born in Clarendon in 1920. As a student at Calabar High School (1929–38), Vaz showed potential in drama with his end-of-term sketches and prize-giving-ceremony productions, one of which, *The Professor*, was about a local eccentric character often seen in the vicinity of the school. Some of his skits were also presented at fund-raising events at the nearby Jones Town Baptist Church. After leaving school he entered the Jamaican civil service, then went to work in the insurance industry before being invited by the British Council to join their staff and concentrate on drama. His first major production, in 1944, was Shakespeare's *A Midsummer Night's Dream*, which he co-produced and co-directed with Hazel Johnston and staged in an open-air setting on the grounds of Holy Cross Church at Half Way Tree for the LTM.

Primarily because of this production he was awarded a two-year scholarship by the British Council to study directorial skills at the Old Vic Theatre School, London.

There, Vaz worked in professional theatre and broadcasting in the United Kingdom and was offered a job as assistant to Michel Saint-Denis, the distinguished French director. He preferred to return to his native Jamaica, however.

Vaz directed the following productions for the LTM: *Vagabond King* (1944); *Arsenic and Old Lace* (1945); *Jupiter Laughs* (1945); the pantomime *Aladdin* (1946); *Beauty and the Beast* (1948), with dances choreographed by Anatole Soohih; Andre Obey's *Noah* (1950); Thornton Wilder's *Our Town* (1950, under the title *Give Us This Day*); the pantomime *Alice in Wonderland* (1950); and the pantomime *Bluebeard and Br'er Anancy* (1949), which he jointly devised and scripted with Louise Bennett Coverley, and which rejected, once and for all, reliance on the old, imported scripts. The music employed Jamaican folk songs, and one song in particular – "Evening Time", first sung by Joyce Lalor, with music specially composed for the show by Barbara Ferland, and lyrics by Louise Bennett Coverley – has become a Jamaican classic.

The LTM contracted Vaz for each show, and when they reduced the fees, Vaz returned to England. There he worked in repertory in the north of England with the occasional West End production, and on the BBC's radio programme *Caribbean Voices*. In 1955 he accepted an invitation to work with the Extra-Mural Department of the UWI and was based at St Augustine campus in Trinidad. His term there culminated with an open-air production of Derek Walcott's *Drums and Colours*, specially commissioned by the University to celebrate the inauguration of the first West Indian Federal Parliament in February 1958.

Vaz returned to the Mona campus in Jamaica in 1959 as staff tutor in drama. This position allowed him to travel through the islands of the Eastern Caribbean and Belize, where he helped to spread the gospel of the performing arts through seminars, summer schools, and festivals at which he adjudicated. He also directed special productions in Barbados, St Kitts, Dominica, Antigua, Nassau and Belize.

In 1963, along with Dennis Scott, he scripted the pantomime *Queenie's Daughter*, with input from Louise Bennett Coverley and Lois Kelly Miller. He directed Ionesco's *Chairs* in 1964, and when the Creative Arts Centre opened at the Mona campus in 1968, he was appointed staff tutor in drama. He now took on more administrative work and was involved in the academic teaching programme: to second- and third-year undergraduates he taught an introductory course on twentieth-century theatre. He inaugurated *Tallawah* in 1969, which drew teams of amateur actors from the four halls of residence on the Mona campus in a friendly, competitive spirit. He found time to direct *Marat/Sade* (1967) and Soyinka's *The Road* (1968), as well as Chekhov's *The Cherry Orchard* and Genet's *The Blacks*. He also helped to mount several West Indian works by Derek Walcott, Errol Hill and Dennis Scott.

As a tribute to Vaz on his retirement, the Creative Arts Centre produced Stafford Ashani's *Bar Jonah*, a ritualistic musical based on the life

Jean Genet's *The Blacks*, in a 1969 production directed by Noel Vaz. *Photo by Maria LaYacona.*

Marat/Sade, by Peter Weiss, produced and directed by Noel Vaz in 1967 at what was then the Creative Arts Centre, UWI, with Hugh Moss-Solomon. *Photo by Maria LaYacona.*

of Alexander Bedward, leader of a controversial religious sect who established a settlement in August Town not far from the present university campus. The university went all out to present a quality show. It invited Marjorie Whylie and Noel Dexter, two leading composers and arrangers, to work on the musical, and invited Henk Tjon, a well-known Surinamese theatre director versed in ritual, to direct the play.[23] Vaz himself has authored one full-length play, *The General: Alpha and Omega*, a study of the life of Simón Bolívar.

Maylynne Walton

Maylynne Walton, actress and dancer

Maylynne Walton is an actress and dancer who is very active in the Jamaican theatrical scene, acting with any group which requests her participation. To date she has acted in nine productions, including the Jambiz shows *Vibes* and *The Last Stand*; with the University Players in *Marahani's Misery*; at the Barn Theatre in *Making a Killing*; and in the Pantry Playhouse production of David Heron's *4Play*. In 2003 she was a member of the troupe that toured the United Kingdom with Heron's *Love and Marriage and New York City*.

She has acted in two local feature films, *Glory to Glorianna*, directed by Lennie Little White, and *Twang*, a Paul Bucknor production. She has also acted in the long running Lennie Little White television serial *Royal Palm Estate*, produced by Mediamix. She has acted in the Cathi Levy production *Applause*, and the Jamaica Musical Theatre Company's productions *Alladin* and *Cats*.

Walton was born 7 March 1976. She attended the Spence/Rowe Ballet School from 1980 to 1992 and 1996 to 1997, and the Tony Wilson School of Dance from 1990 to 1995 and in 2002. She received her theatrical training at Emerson College, Boston, and the American Academy of Performing Arts, New York City.

Earl Warner

Earl McDonald Warner (1952–98) has been described as "distinctly and unapologetically Caribbean" in his approach to interpreting work for the stage. His formal training included a bachelor's degree in drama as well as a postgraduate diploma in directing and theatre-in-education from the University of Manchester, England. Additionally, he gained the diploma in theatre arts from the JSD, where he later became a member of the faculty.

Among the major Caribbean works Warner directed are *Teacher, Teacher* (Anthony Hinkson); *An Echo in the Bone* (Dennis Scott); *In the Castle of My Skin* (George Lamming); *Sufferers Song* (Victor Questel); *A Branch of the Blue Nile*, *Remembrance* and *Ti Jean and His Brothers* (Derek Walcott); *I, Marcus Garvey*, *Three Kings Darkly* and *The Defense* (Edgar White); *Flame Heart*, on the life and work of Claude McKay (compiled by Maureen Warner-Lewis, Pat Cumper and Warner himself); *The Balmyard* (Don Kinch); *Buss Out* (Sistren); *I Lawah* (Rawle Gibbons); *Rock* (from four works by Kamau Brathwaite and Michael Gilkes); *Silver Web* (Glenville Lovell); *Growing up Stupid Under the Union Jack* (Austin Clarke);

Jane and Louisa (adapted by Pat Cumper, based on a novel by Erna Brodber); adaptations of *The Dragon Can't Dance* and *The Wine of Astonishment* (novels by Earl Lovelace); *Glory* (Felix Cross); and *McB* (Alwyn Bully).

Earl Warner was named a member of the prestigious World Consortium of Directors in 1993. He was the 1979–80 Granada fellow to the department of drama at the University of Manchester, and the Organization of American States' artist in residence at the Edna Manley College (1988–89). He died in February 1991 of a heart attack. He is remembered as a theatre practitioner who felt strongly that Caribbean people must rediscover their own flavour and distinctive traits: "We must sing our own song."

Marjorie Whylie

Marjorie Whylie was born in 1944 in a small, middle-class enclave known as the Beechwood Avenue–Collins Green area. She was sent to St Andrew High School as a boarder because her mother thought she needed discipline, and to learn to interact with other children, because her brother and sister were ten and more years older than she was. Hers was a very musical and artistic upbringing. On Collins Green Avenue were dancer Hugh Morrison and his siblings, musicians Roy Morrison and Flo Armstrong; across the street and just around the corner were the Barretts – Nerine, Elaine and Jean – all musically inclined. At the top of Beechwood Avenue were the Myrie daughters, whose father was a piano tuner. Miss Brenda Smythe was on Half Way Tree Road, and just around the corner was Miss Ena Helps – both well-known voice and piano teachers. There were also the Blondel Francis sisters, one of whom became known for speech and drama, and the other for ballet. Of the nearby Lumsden brothers, one went into radio. Close by were also Joyce Johns and Mrs Packer, both voice and piano teachers. Mrs Packer's two daughters, Valerie and Allison, were among the island's top elocutionists.

Wycliffe Bennett's interview July 2008 with Marjorie Whylie allows her to speak in her own voice:

Marjorie Whylie, musican and musicologist. *Photo by Peter Ferguson.*

WB: You could say Collins Green was a veritable Learning City.

MW: Yes, there was also Peter Hudson on the sax, with Mapletoft Poulle, who played in the big band for ladies of quality at the Glass Bucket Club. Poulle took Jamaican music into that sphere. He produced an LP called *Jamaica Mento* which set standards for other arrangers to follow. Poulle worked with the Pantomime for years. He brought legitimacy to local church music with his *Folk Mass* and he also set psalms and canticles to music.

WB: When did you start performing?

MW: By age fifteen years. By then I was well versed in classical music –

Beethoven, Bach and Shubert in particular – and very familiar with popular music of the day, which I played by ear. My debut as a pianist was at the Institute of Jamaica Junior Centre. Music has been my career. My latest position is as director of music at the UWI, Mona campus, where I also lecture in Introduction to Music.

WB: Where did you work in the earlier years?

MW: After completing a first degree at the UWI, I took a music education course at the Edna Manley College and then was appointed folk music research officer. I took over from Olive Lewin, who had done major research in the field over many years. I also taught at one of Jamaica's well-known high schools for boys, Kingston College, helping with the choir, directed by Barry Davis and later by the headmaster, Douglas Forest. From there I went to the Jamaica Social Welfare Commission and assisted Olive Lewin with music therapy classes at the Bellevue Hospital [a psychiatric hospital] and in the prisons.

WB: That was several years of hard labour.

MW: Yes. I began to feel the strain and so I left the Social Welfare Commission and freelanced for a while, playing in hotels, training persons in the tourism and entertainment field, [and] worked in Denver, Colorado, and with the Probation Board in England, teaching children with special needs, while performing at different places, including the Royal Festival Hall, London. At the present moment I am collaborating with Brian Heap, head of the drama unit at the Philip Sherlock Centre, UWI, hoping to convert a classical opera into Jamaican.

WB: How do you react to dancehall music?

MW: I do not dismiss dancehall out of hand. There are performers like Luciano, Tony Rebel and Buju Banton. Here are fine artists who carry a melody with intelligence, who couch their concerns about the ills of society in music, hoping to solve problems. As I have said, there is intelligence and melody in their songs.

However, there is another kind of dancehall artist who is listenable and danceable but without much substance; and there is a third kind who put rhythm scores together with little musical value. They create a "rydm" and ten to twelve artists sing over it. This melodic pattern appeals to the pelvic area and the feet. This group needs to get other parts of the body also responding. The length of time their sessions last – to four and five o'clock in the morning – is also damaging to the body. Dancehall has its good and bad features. Some artists are very good, some are mediocre, and some appeal to baseness in the society. The researcher now has to search among the dregs to find gems.

WB: What of the splendour of Bob Marley?

MW: Toots and the Maytals, Dennis Brown also. When Marley died his music was played for the whole day on [the] radio. For the first time I listened critically to the harmonic complexity, the use of backing voices and phrases.

WB: [I] heard "Redemption Song" on the radio in Germany . . .

MW: Artists sing his songs; orchestras arrange his works; Jamaican music is worldwide. Dancehall has been translated into Spanish. In Panama two years ago I heard Spanish arrangements of dancehall.

WB: What about Suriname, the Dutch Islands?

MW: Jamaican music is strong, going back to Marley. It is widespread throughout the Caribbean. Two years ago in Trinidad I heard Jamaican music blaring, and on enquiring learned that Trinidadian children won't go on a "maxi taxi" which does not play loud Jamaican music. Reggae has taken over from calypso. Soca fuels fêtes in Jamaica. Soca goes well with dancehall – the garments in particular.

WB: Is there anything more you would like to tell me?

MW: In my student days at the UWI, I formed a music society with the University Singers. I then moved on to the NDTC singers, where I have been engaged in arranging. It was at the School of Music under Tom Murray that I received my first exposure to arranging. There was the University Steel Band with ten to twelve members. I joined the band playing bass. I still use that training today. I arrange first the bass line, then add other arrangements.

WB: How did your interest in popular music come about?

MW: I was exposed to popular music through my big brother Dwight, when he was at the JBC and he started to record Jamaican music for such shows as Jamaica Hit Parade and Teenage Dance Party. I also met some overseas performers when he organized shows at the Regal Cinema, where he emceed or interviewed them. There was also the JBC Orchestra with Bertie King, Carlos Malcolm and Sonny Bradshaw.

Sonny Bradshaw organized a workshop at a house beside Champion House at the corner of Lyndhurst Road and Maxfield Avenue. Sonny Bradshaw taught me jazz harmony. Tony Mowatt taught me vibes. Miss Lou [Louise Bennett Coverley] introduced me to folk music. She was very generous with her material. She told me where to go, what to look for, how to approach people. "You have to give first and they will give after." She was the conduit.

WB: What sort of recognition have you received?

MW: I have received the Bronze Musgrave Medal and the Centenary Medal from the Institute of Jamaica; recognition from the City of Kingston; the Order of Distinction from the Government of Jamaica; the Pelican Award from the students of the UWI, among many others, including the Prime Minister's Medal of Appreciation and the Prime Minister's Award.

WB: When you look back on your life what do you see?

MW: I have lived a rich life. I have gained from the different areas in which I have worked. At KC I learned about church music, put canticles and psalms to music, some of which I have used in the NDTC Easter Morning presentations. In Educational Broadcasting for TV and Radio I have taught songs in the context of the music.

WB: Tell me more about your work with Miss Lou.

MW: I worked with Miss Lou for twelve years doing *Ring Ding*, and when the show was repeated in 2000 I was the host. I have also hosted a programme for children called *Vibrations*, for three years; the idea was that I would make myself redundant. I worked for two years and the regulars took over for one year. The subjects included nutrition, how to study and do homework, how to cross the street, how to use a toothbrush, among other things. The objective was also to let children show their creativity.

My life has been one of entertainment bound up with education, formal and informal. One person in London who understands this was my agent. In the daytime I would work on radio, in schools, give dance classes to teenagers in East London, use energy levels to warm the voice for voice production. I also incorporated Eastern practices in using breath.

WB: Your speech is remarkably clear.

MW: That was the way I was brought up. In the early years you could not speak creole in the home. I also come from a family of professionals, and at boarding school you were not allowed to speak creole.

WB: How do you see the NDTC today?

MW: For a while I was a little concerned, wondering where they would go from here, but there is Marlon Simms, dancer, choreographer and scholar, who commands respect of the younger dancers. He does not suffer fools gladly. Somehow the present dancers are not as committed. These youngsters do not understand the amount of experimentation that has been put into creating the dance vocabulary. Choreographers do not have to work as hard as in the past.

WB: How about the singers?

MW: There is need to find someone to take over from me. I have composed music and arranged music for the dance. I have given up time and energy to help develop the NDTC vocabulary.

WB: What about other departments?

MW: Barbara Kaufman, for example, is an encyclopaedia of costumes. She has organized the handling of costumes down to a fine point. Someone has to be trained to succeed her. Within an hour of the conclusion of a show, everything, including backdrops, is packed and ready to go. Performers are disciplined to put costumes immediately on the racks, so by the last item the earlier ones are dried and ready for packing.

WB: Thank you for so graciously giving up of your time to assist me.

Karl O'Brian Williams

Karl Williams's combined love for acting, writing and education has fuelled his pursuits and achievements over the years, and he has become somewhat of a renaissance man among his peers. With acting awards for memorable roles such as Ramses in Father Ho Lung and Friends' *Moses* (2004), and nominations for the characterization of Roman Henry in the restaging of Louis Marriott's epic *Bedward* (2003–4), and as Mr Rochester and Madox Ford in the University Players' *After Mrs Rochester* (2006), Williams continues to prove that dedication to one's craft can only bring success. Though still considered a young thespian by many, he has over a decade of stage experience, both in Jamaica and abroad.

His other awards include best director and best production (Campion College) for his adaptation of Shakespeare's *Macbeth* at the 2006 National Schools' Drama Festival. And in 2008, his direction of Karl Hart's commercial success, *Secrets . . . SHHH*, also received commendation. As playwright Williams has been two-time winner of the Actor Boy award for best new Jamaican play, with *The Black That I Am* (2005) and *Not About Eve* (2006).

He was trained in Shakespeare at the Royal Academy of Dramatic Art in London, and has performed with the Metropolitan Playhouse in Manhattan, the Jamaica Musical Theatre Company, the Pantomime Company, Jambiz International and the University Dramatic Arts Society. As a trained educator, he has taught English language, literature and drama at Campion College, where he reshaped the Drama Club to a level of distinction at national competitions and influenced the decision to make drama a legitimate subject on the school's curriculum. He has taught at the School of Drama at the Edna Manley College, and is an external examiner for the Council of Community Colleges of Jamaica. He is also a drama facilitator with Dream-a-World, a youth risk-reduction project sponsored by the Caribbean Institute for Mental Health and Substance Abuse (CARIMENSA).

Karl Williams, actor and director

Seamlessly moving throughout the worlds of drama and education, Williams is always attempting to improve and better that which he is involved in. With his company, MADKOW Productions, he aims to leave a legacy for others to follow, in keeping with the rich theatrical traditions that were handed down to him. MADKOW is the brainchild of Williams and Michael Anthony Daley. This team of artistic minds came together some years ago to think of creative ways of enhancing and adding to the already rich theatrical landscape of Jamaica. As individuals, both men have worked hard over the last decade at perfecting their skills and honing their craft in the world of performance – Williams as a stage actor and playwright, Daley as a director and producer. *Not about Eve* (2006) was the team's first major commercial effort. In 2008 MADKOW produced the first in a series of staged readings, "Work in Progress", at the Philip Sherlock Centre, aimed at showcasing new writers and their scripts for public viewing and critique.

MADKOW is also involved in artistic consultation and guidance of aspiring thespians, and plans to mount training workshops in all aspects of theatre. The ultimate goal of the organization is to procure a performance space for public entertainment as well as for the development of talent in the industry, including theatre and stage management, dramaturgy, technical theatre and theatre etiquette. The partners claim that they are not attempting to replace or compete with existing institutions already fostering the education of future performers, but to be an agent of support by creating an alternative space as well as an additional outlet for the creative and dramatic release of Jamaica's youth. MADKOW welcomes anyone who shares their vision to be a part of the journey as they go forth to build on the foundation laid by earlier Jamaican artists.

RANDOLPH SAMUEL WILLIAMS (RANNY, MAAS RAN)

Ranny Williams, actor and playwright

Ranny Williams was a man for all seasons. He was born in Colón, Panama, on 26 October 1912. His father, Thomas Samuel Williams, an engine driver, was born in Panama of Jamaican parents from the parish of St Thomas. On relocating to Jamaica, he worked in the same capacity with the Jamaica Railway Corporation. His mother, Frances Emeline Williams, was from the parish of Manchester, the granddaughter of a Maroon from Accompong. She met and married Thomas Williams while teaching West Indian children in the Canal Zone in Panama. She was a music teacher and a well-known singer and actress in her day.

The Williams family returned to Jamaica from Panama in 1918, when Ranny was six years old. He grew up on his parents' small farm near Riversdale in St Catherine, before moving to Kingston to attend Kingston Technical School. He also received private tutoring from the Reverend Ernest Price, headmaster of Calabar College, then on Slipe Pen Road, and he later gained a London Chamber of Commerce Certificate in Accounting.

With the help of his father, Ranny took correspondence courses in journalism and drama and in 1935 began contributing to the *Daily Gleaner*, the *Jamaica Standard* and other local newspapers, first as an unpaid writer, later as a professional. He wrote several articles on the theatre and other aspects of Jamaican life which have proved useful to researchers today. He was also a splendid communicator who, over the course of his life, kept a close watch on developments in radio, film and television. Ranny never failed to make the best possible use of these developments, whenever opportunity allowed. But it was primarily as a man of the theatre that he made his major contribution to Jamaica.

Williams began performing at the age of seven, at concerts presented by his mother. His ability as a comic was recognized early when, without any preparation, he treated an end-of-year audience at tutorial school to side-splitting jokes. After that, he was overwhelmed with invitations to perform in backyards, schoolrooms, church and lodge halls, and at garden parties and fairs all over Jamaica, often in aid of charity. By the time he left school he was well known as an amateur comedian and actor.

Ranny Williams became a professional entertainer about 1929, and in 1930 was invited by Marcus Garvey to become a member of the vaudeville group at Edelweiss Park. Williams wrote most of the skits, sketches and comedies in which he performed. It was Lee Gordon who introduced him to Professor Gerardo Leon, who was then in charge of entertainment at Edelweiss Park. Professor Leon encouraged both Williams and Gordon to develop their sketches and topicalities, and to make up little plays of their own, from which he would select those for presentation at the very popular weekly Saturday night shows.

Several productions at the park have been listed as originating from Ranny Williams, among them *Blacks Gone Wild* (1929), *King Belshazzar* (1930), *Landing the Landlord* (comedy, 1930), *Old Black Joe* (1930), *Perfectly Satisfied* (farce, 1930), *Say It Singing* (1930), *She Is a Sheba* (1930) and *Ugly but Good Looking* (sketch, 1930). The *New Jamaica* of July 1932 noted:

Ran Williams, the latest natural original comedian in Jamaica, has been given a chance to develop his skill at Edelweiss Park . . . [T]hat he has been getting on by leaps and bounds goes without saying . . . and if he should obtain the heights of Cupidon or become a local Harry Lauder, . . . he will have to thank Marcus Garvey for giving him the chance to make good.

Ranny Williams and Lee Gordon became a formidable duo. As "Amos and Andy", they performed at Christmas Morning concerts at the Ward Theatre in the 1930s and took their combined talents to the second LTM Pantomime, *Babes in the Wood*, which opened at the Ward Theatre, 26 December 1942. Ranny wrote the topicalities scenes each year, but his first attempt at writing the whole pantomime script was for *Quashie Lady* (1958). Inspired by his mother, he also wrote three plays based on religious themes, the first being *The Medes and the Persians*. After that he turned to comedy using Jamaican dialect and popular musical forms.[24]

With Lee Gordon and Archie Lindo, Ranny organized the show *Jamaica Night* once a month on ZQI Radio, Jamaica's first radio station, which began operating at the beginning of the Second World War in 1939. He developed the radio show *Life with the Morgan Henrys*, for which, for the first six months, he played five different characters before teaming up with Alma (Hylton) Mock Yen, who played Putus. This was the first time that Jamaicans were represented on radio by themselves, in their own language. Out of this programme developed the very popular *Ranny and Putus* radio serial. He also teamed up with Louise Bennett Coverley for a weekly broadcast from the Carib Theatre, known as *The Lou and Ranny Show*, for the opening of JBC Radio in 1959. He had another radio show called *Hello, You Out There*, and in 1963 premiered the *Ranny Williams Show* for JBC television.

Ranny and Lee Gordon, in the wake of Stanley Morand, E.M. Cupidon, Gene Martinez, Tony Ableton and Vere Johns, acquired a tremendous national reputation as entertainers. They provided a great deal of comic relief in the topicalities or "knockabout" sections, which facilitate scene changing in the pantomime. In this they were joined or succeeded by a number of talented players, including Louise Bennett Coverley, Lois Kelly Barrow (Miller), Charles Hyatt, and Oliver Samuels. Ranny Williams reached a defining moment in his career when he began playing Br'er Anancy, which started when Louise Bennett Coverley and Noel Vaz created *Bluebeard and Br'er Anancy* in 1949.

Williams played many aspects of the Anancy persona, the Ashanti spider god who is the folktale hero of Jamaica. He played Anancy in six pantomimes: *Bluebeard and Br'er Anancy*, *Anancy and the Magic Mirror*, *Anancy and Beeny Bud*, *Anancy and Doumbey*, *Rockstone Anancy*, and *Moonshine Anancy*. Indeed, "Maas Ran" created for the stage the iconic image of Bredda Anancy, complete with tail coat, top hat and spider's web, with the shuffling walk, the lisp and the laugh (which he had copied from old Jamaican storytellers). Overall, he played in twenty-nine pantomimes, thus enabling at least three generations of Jamaicans to enjoy live performances by him.

Williams's breadth and knowledge of the theatre was based on a rich, grassroots experience, nurtured by careful study and observation, during stints with the Government Census Department, as a delivery clerk on Kingston Wharves, in travelling road shows and through meaningful reading. His second pantomime script was *Jamaica Way* (1959). He adapted the English novel *Robinson Crusoe* for a pantomime, and co-authored *Queenie's Daughter* as well as the *Bredda Buck* pantomimes.

Ranny Williams was not limited to the Jamaican scene. He attended shows at the Ward Theatre by the Florence Glossop-Harris company and other touring companies from England and the United States until 1939, when the outbreak of the Second World War brought these visits to an end. As a performer, he was equally at home in the classics of the Western tradition, and he would play roles in these productions with as much flair as he did Br'er Anancy, whether the playwright were William Shakespeare, Thornton Wilder, Eugene O'Neill or any other. Williams's role as Lem in O'Neill's *The Emperor Jones*, for example, staged in 1949 by British Guianese director Robert Adams, invited to Jamaica for this purpose by the British Council, is memorable to this day. It was a play of undeniable theatricality: it told the story of a black dictator of a West Indian island, Brutus Jones, who had once been a citizen of the United States. As the play opens, Jones's subjects have rebelled, and Jones has reserved a silver bullet to kill himself. The production, which was staged at the Ward Theatre, was supported by such groups as the Surrey Players, Caribbean Thespians, Kingston Dramatic Club, the People's Theatre, Eric Coverley Concerts and Ivy Baxter and her dancers.

The play chosen to open the Little Theatre building in 1961 was Thornton Wilder's *The Matchmaker*. Ranny Williams was cast as Horace Vandergeler, a widower who owns a grocery store in Yonkers and was obviously in need of a wife. The play was directed by Arnold Moss, with Tess Thomas in the title role (as the matchmaker who wanted a man for herself), and included David D'Costa and Easton Lee in the roles of the two young clerks.

Williams also performed in a wide range of comic roles in Shakespeare's plays, directed by Paul Methuen at the Garden Theatre. He was Host of the Garter Inn in *The Merry Wives of Windsor*, and Bottom the weaver in *A Midsummer Night's Dream* (1971). Before this, he had appeared as Malvolio in *Twelfth Night*, directed by Orford St John at the Little Theatre, and as Trinculo in *The Tempest*, directed by Errol Hill and Hugh Morrison for the Jamaica 300 celebrations in 1955, on the grounds of St Andrew High School. He even played an Irishman, Finian, in the American musical *Finian's Rainbow* (1962), directed by Lloyd Reckord. *Finian's Rainbow* was used by the LTM that year to replace the pantomime. He made his final stage appearance in the title role of *The Honourable All Purpus and the Dancing Princesses*, the 1979 LTM pantomime. His films included *A High Wind in Jamaica*, *Oh Dad, Poor Dad*, *White Souls*, *Jamaica No Problem*, *Tropical Isles* and *The Marijuana Affair*.

Williams's work in the field of entertainment and drama earned him several awards, including the Jamaica Certificate and Badge of Honour in the Queen's New Year's Honours List (1968), the Institute of Jamaica Silver Musgrave Medal (1968) and the Centenary Medal (1979), and the Government of Jamaica award, Commander of the Order of Distinction (CD) "for outstanding services in the field of entertainment" (1976). The Ranny Williams Entertainment Centre in Kingston stands as a monument to his work.

Maas Ran had a comparatively small voice, but his voice projection was excellent – few other players could be heard as easily or comfortably in the Ward or Little Theatre, or in the open air without amplification. His breathing and breath control were excellent and he remained audible even when he whispered. He mastered the art of voice placement, of nuancing lines, of giving words their proper value and sustaining rhythm; and his timing was impeccable. He quickly captured the spine of any character he was called upon to play and had a genius for finding the right subtext.

He was a good community man who volunteered as a teacher at the Jamaica Movement for the Advancement of Literacy (JAMAL) and organized the Ranny Williams Youth Club and the Ranny Williams Jonkonnu Band. This band, supported by the School of Dance, performed in *Star Over Bethlehem*, the JBC's segment of a BBC broadcast from Hope Gardens in Kingston that aired live via satellite around the world on Christmas Eve in 1969. And as he was kind and generous in life, so was he among his fellow players on stage. As an actor, he helped to make other players in the same production look good. His name is often coupled with that of Miss Lou (Louise Bennett Coverley), as in *The Lou and Ranny Show*. They were both, individually and together, quintessential Jamaicans. Miss Lou has been given the high honours she justly deserves. But as a theatre personality Ranny was her co-equal and deserves no less. Like Miss Lou, he never failed to get us to lay aside our cares, make us laugh, think positively, and feel good about just being able to live. As Hamlet said of Yorick in that great play, "I knew him, Horatio. He was a man of infinite jest and most excellent fancy."

Munair Zacca

Munair Zacca claims that his interest in acting was undoubtedly stirred by the countless movies he was taken by his mother to see as a small boy growing up in Spanish Town. He was born there in 1945. At age eleven he was sent to Jamaica College in Kingston as a boarder, and although drama was not a subject on the school curriculum at the time, he remembers being congratulated by his headmaster for his performance in a school production.

Munair Zacca, actor and playwright

His headmaster's encouragement, combined with two memorable experiences at the theatre, strengthened his interest in acting. Zacca remembers seeing a production of *Twelfth Night* at the Ward Theatre, with Tony Watson, one of his teachers at Wolmer's Boys' School, in the role of Sir Toby Belch. He also recalls seeing Reggie Carter in the title role of *King Lear*, directed by Noel Vaz at the Little Theatre, with Judith Willoughby as Cordelia and Sheila Hill (later Carter) as Goneril. Both productions of *Twelfth Night* and *King Lear* had a lasting effect on him, and in time he came to work with Reggie and Sheila Carter.

Zacca got his start in professional theatre after meeting Trevor Rhone and Yvonne Jones (later Brewster), both graduates of the Rose Bruford College who were teaching drama at high schools in Kingston. With their encouragement and help he landed a minor role in the LTM pantomime *Morgan's Dream of Old Port Royal* (1965), written by Greta and Henry Fowler and starring Louise Bennett Coverley and Ranny Williams. The show was directed by Rex Nettleford, assisted by Trevor Rhone and Yvonne Jones.

Early in 1965 Rhone and Jones established Theatre 77, and Zacca joined them as the youngest member of the group. Theatre 77 soon moved from the University College of the West Indies campus to Oxford Road, where it was renamed the Barn Theatre. There Zacca honed his craft as resident actor for the next six years, with Jones and Rhone as artistic directors and producers.

Munair Zacca,with other members of cast in *Jamaica Rundown* by Aston Cooke, Barn Theatre, 1995

Zacca's first opportunity at directing came in 1970, when he was invited by Rhone, who was the drama tutor at St Andrew Technical High School, to direct the musical *Pinocchio* for the school's Christmas show. The play proved quite a success with students, parents and staff alike. Zacca went on to direct *The Shock of Recognition* (1971), one of four one-act plays by the American playwright Robert Anderson which were produced by Jamaica Playhouse at the Creative Arts Centre, UWI.

Zacca then directed Leonie Forbes and Claudia Robinson (alternating in the role of Mama) in the tragi-comedy *See Mama* (1972), by Edward Henry, at the Barn. The show ran for fifty-eight performances over a three-month period, which in 1972 was considered an achievement. He went on to direct Carmen Tipling's *Straightman* (1974) and the Cuban play *The Criminals* (1974), by Jose Triana. *The Criminals* was not a commercial success, although there was much potential for quality theatre and highly skilled acting. It had a short run and played to small houses. In the end it broke even. Soon thereafter Zacca became associated with Carroll Dawes, then-director of the JSD, who formed the National Festival Theatre of Jamaica (NFTJ) and took Dennis Scott's *Echo in the Bone* to FESTAC in Lagos, Nigeria, in 1976.

Zacca considers his role of Corporal Lestrade in Derek Walcott's *Dream on Monkey Mountain* (1975) to be among his best. The performance was directed by Carroll Dawes for the NFTJ at the Ward Theatre. In this role, Zacca created dubious history by being the first Jamaican actor to appear totally nude on stage. He says, "I was so wrapped up in the role I didn't even realize I had done it until after I had. Then I was in shock."

He was also associate director and production manager, with Carroll Dawes, for Wole Soyinka's *Bacchae of Euripides* (1975), which was mounted at the Little Theatre. Zacca recalls, "This is the only play I know of that actually started in the car park with the audience standing around and then following the action as it moved inside the theatre and onto the stage. They then took their seats in the auditorium for the rest of the presentation."[25] Another production in which he had an input was Dawes's staging of the battle-scene in *Macbeth* at the Ward Theatre, where the actors came swinging from the gallery down onto the stage on ropes.

Another of Zacca's major roles was that of Chief in the NFTJ production of Slade Hopkinson's *Summer Dread* (1976), a play about West Indian politics, directed by Dennis Scott and appropriately staged in the Garden Theatre of Jamaica House during a period when the country was undergoing radical political change and turmoil. Zacca also worked with the National Theatre Trust. He took part in *A Liberated Woman* (1970) and *The White Witch of Rose Hall* (1975), Barry Reckord's version of this well-known story. The central theme was, however, not about obeah, but about rebellion.

Zacca worked on and off with Reggie and Sheila Carter at the Jamaica Playhouse;

in *Othello* (1971) he played Cassio and had to take fencing lessons for the duel scene. The director was Sy Syna, an American from New York, who was associated with the Actors Studio and was a promoter of method acting. Through Syna's direction, method techniques had a positive impact on Zacca and helped develop his craft. Eventually, he concluded that there was no better or worse, right or wrong technique. If it worked, he used it; if it didn't, he dropped it. It was all a matter of individual needs.

Zacca also appeared in three other productions of the Playhouse: *The School For Wives* (1981), directed by Reggie Carter, in which he played the supporting role of Chrysalde, and for which he won an Actor Boy award; *The Miser* (1982), directed by Gillian Binns; and *The Imaginary Invalid* (1982), directed by Reggie Carter and Rooney Chambers. He also played in the musical satirical revues *A?* (1973), *E?* (1980) and *I?* (1981), all effortlessly directed by Reggie Carter, who also performed in them. These pieces were scripted in part by several writers, with contributions from Reggie Carter, Trevor Rhone, Morris Cargill and Tony Gambrill, among others.

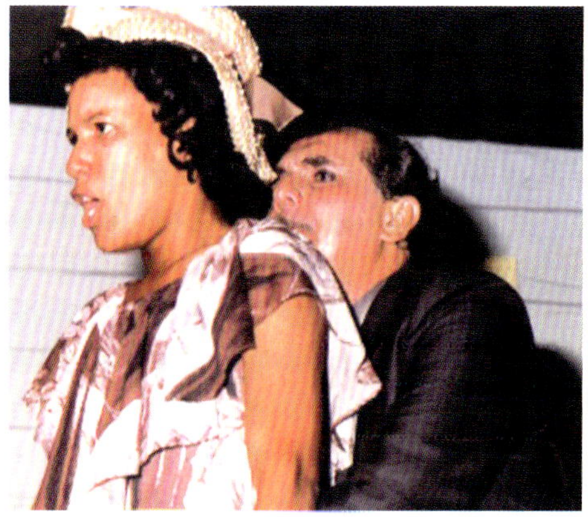

Munair Zacca, with Tulip Reid in *Irie Neighbours* by Myrna and Courtney Laughton, 1977

Zacca worked with Gambrill in the *Eight O'Clock Jamaica Time* series, and in the musical comedy *All That Glitters* (1976), a kind of English vaudeville-style production set in rural, old time Jamaica. It was a family show of sheer fun for both performers and audiences alike. Another play, *Gunfight at the Last Chance Saloon* (1978), was a Jamaican-style Western, staged at the Way-Out Theatre at the Jamaica Pegasus Hotel in the late 1970s. It was brilliantly directed by Bobby Ghisays, with music composed and performed by Peter Ashbourne. Zacca also took part in one of the last presentations of the *Eight O'Clock Jamaica Time* series (1986), also directed by Ghisays, with music by Peter Ashbourne. In this he played the role of Edward Seaga, then-prime minister of Jamaica, a role he had been playing for years opposite Reggie Carter's Michael Manley in the Jamaica Playhouse series of satirical revues.

Zacca played a supporting role in the Jambiz production of *Children, Children* (2000), written by Joan Andrea Hutchinson and Aston Cooke, and directed by Lenford Salmon at the Center Stage Theatre. It had a long run there and was followed by an extensive tour of rural Jamaica. According to Zacca, "I believe we went to every nook and cranny in addition to all the major country towns, and always played to packed houses."[26] For his role as Harry Cross in another Jambiz production, Patrick Brown's *Puppy Love* (1996), directed by Trevor Nairne, Zacca won an Actor Boy award for best supporting actor. The play later toured locally and overseas.

Munair Zacca, with Pauline Stone-Myrie in *Sweet Country Love*, 2004

As lead actor, Zacca won an award for his portrayal of Mel in Neil Simon's bittersweet comedy *The Prisoner of Second Avenue* (1982), produced by Claude Clarke at the New Kingston Theatre and directed by Pablo Hoilett, who subsequently became a producer. Munair worked with Hoilett in other plays too, such as *Hot Buns in Jam* and *The Making of a Millionaire*. Zacca won a second best actor award for his role as the abusive husband in Basil Dawkins's *Feminine Justice*, directed by Buddy Pouyat in a 2004 revival staged at the Little Theatre. He had played the same role when the play was first performed in 1997.

In 1987, the centenary of the birth of Marcus Garvey, Zacca acted in three productions based on the life of this Jamaican national hero: *Garvey: The Musical*, written, produced and directed by Perry Henzell at the Ward Theatre; *Mosiah*, written for television by Carey Robinson and produced by the CPTC; and *The Conflict*, written for television by Anthony Hall Ellis, produced by the Jamaica Information Service

CPTC production of *The Play's the Thing* by Munair Zacca. *From left:* Glen Campbell, Munair Zacca and Cathi Levy. *Courtesy of CPTC.*

and shot on location at Strawberry Hill when the property only consisted of a small, wooden colonial-style house. Zacca also performed in Carey Robinson's *Flashpoint '38*, in Edgar White's *Marcus Garvey and the Captivity of Babylon* (1991), directed by Earl Warner.

Zacca's film credits include small parts in the James Bond movie *Live and Let Die*, directed by Guy Hamilton; the BBC television miniseries *The Fight against Slavery*, written by Jamaican Evan Jones and directed by Christopher Ralling. He also made cameo appearances in the Walt Disney production of the television miniseries *Return to Treasure Island*, partially shot in Jamaica, and in the role of Perierra in Island Films' production of *Countryman*, written and directed by Dickie Jobson. More recently, Zacca had a supporting role as Mr Anderson in *Shottas*, written, produced and directed by Cecil Silvera. He played another politician in the film *Better Must Come*, produced and directed by Storm Saulter. (This film is yet to be completed although scenes were shown at the 2006 Flashpoint Film Festival in Negril, Jamaica.) Here Zacca plays the role of Henry Kissinger.

In addition to his work on film, Zacca has played in a number of other local stage plays: at the Center Stage, in the video series *Oliver and Titus* (1990); in the CPTC-produced *The Play's the Thing* (1994), directed by Wycliffe Bennett; and in a piece originally written and produced on stage by Zacca himself entitled *Play It* (1993). Some of his other performances have been in Cathi Levy's production of the macabre but funny *Three Little Witches* (1982); in Stafford Ashani's epic musical *Anancy and the Unsung Heroes Out West* (1978) at the Ward Theatre; and *Pillars in the Mud* (1973), by N. Niamtalli, about racial conflicts in Guyana, produced and directed by Lloyd Reckord at the Ward Theatre.

Munair Zacca, with Kerstin Pringle in *The Perfect Setup*, by Jack Sher, 2008

Zacca regards his participation in *Voices*, a presentation of poetry and excerpts from major dramatic works, produced and directed by Wycliffe Bennett at the Ward Theatre, to be among his most successful presentations. There was also *The Tempest*, staged outdoors in the Chapel Gardens of the UWI and directed by Gillian Binns. Zacca is also proud of his other performances: of Trevor Rhone's monologue poem "Look Two"; in *Its Not My Fault, Baby* (1967, 1989); as the friendly merchant Shifty in the LTM pantomime *Music Boy* (1972); in *The Game* (1982); and as the unethical realtor and banker, George, in *Old Story Time* (1981). The role for which Zacca is best known, however, is that of the guileful and flirtatious but cruel underworld character Sonny T in the local television series *Royal Palm Estate*, now in its twenty-sixth season (2008). At time of writing, he was also playing in *The Perfect Setup* at the Center Stage. He is among the most prolific actors the Jamaican stage has produced.

Notes

Acknowledgements

1. Francis Hanson, "Plays at a Publick Theatre", in *The Laws of Jamaica: Passed by the Assembly, and Confirmed by His Majesty in Council, Feb. 23, 1683. To Which Is Added A Short Account of the Island and Government Thereof, with an Exact Map of the Island* (London: printed for H. Hills by Charles Harper, 1683), 1:x.

Chapter 1

1. Philip Sherlock and Hazel Bennett, *The Story of the Jamaican People* (Kingston: Ian Randle, 1998), 2.
2. W.R. Inge, *The End of an Age: And Other Essays* (London: Putnam, 1949), 3.
3. R.N. Murray, letter to Wycliffe Bennett, April 1964.

Chapter 2

1. Maurice Bowra, introduction to "Poetry of the English Speaking Caribbean", ed. W.A. Roberts and W. Bennett (manuscript, 1951), cited from copy in the National Library of Jamaica.
2. Gloria Escoffery, "Monster of Anancyism", *Daily Gleaner*, 1 October 1982.
3. Richardson Wright, *Revels in Jamaica*, new ed. (Kingston: Bolivar, 1986), 2–3.
4. Errol Hill, *The Jamaican Stage, 1655–1900: Profile of a Colonial Theatre* (Amherst: University of Massachusetts Press, 1992), 126.
5. Ranny Williams, interview by Wycliffe Bennett, n.d.
6. Mrs. H. McPherson, letter and advertisement, *Daily Gleaner*, 8 January 1907.
7. Miss Bertram, notice, *Daily Gleaner*, October 1907.
8. The official figures for the racial mix for 1891, 1911, 1982 and 2001 are shown below.

	1891	1911	1982	2001
White	14,692	15,605	4,841	4,760
Mixed	121,955	163,201	278,015	161,234
Black	488,624	639,181	1,622,473	2,378,104

Continues

	1891	1911	1982	2001
East Indian	10,116	17,380	29,283	123,227
Chinese	481	2,111	5,320	5,153
Not rep./specified	3,623	2,905	206,169	21,411
Jews/Lebanese/Syrian			759	2,117
Other Mixed			24,818	
Other			1,206	
Totals	639,491	840,383	2,172,884	2,696,006

Source: The Census of Jamaica, years 1891 and 1911, in George Roberts, *Population of Jamaica* (Millwood, NY: Kraus Reprint Co., 1975), 65. Years 1982 and 2001 extracted from *Population of Jamaica Census*, vol. 10 (Kingston: Statistical Institute of Jamaica, 2001), 36–55.

9. H.S. Bunbury, letter to the *Daily Gleaner*, 21 December 1912.

Chapter 3

1. Basil Densham, comments prepared for theJamaica Library Service exhibition "Playing through the Ages" (1971).
2. Horace Vaz, "The Drama in Jamaica", *West Indian Review* 4, no. 2 (Spring 1947): 30–35, 47.
3. Tyrone Guthrie, *A Life in the Theatre* (New York: McGraw-Hill, 1959), 91–92.
4. Report of press conference given by George Bernard Shaw, *Daily Gleaner*, 12 January 1911.
5. Joan Grant, *Daily Gleaner*, 19 June 1937.
6. "Standards of Elocution in Jamaica", *Daily Gleaner*, 12 January 1937.
7. "After Dark", *Daily Gleaner*, 7 December 1937.
8. *Daily Gleaner*, 17 December 1945.
9. Ibid.
10. The writer was within earshot when the princess made her comments.
11. Sir Hugh Foot, letter to Doris Duperley, 3 November 1953.
12. Henry Popkin, ed., *The New British Drama* (New York: Grove, 1964), 11.
13. Ibid.

Chapter 4

1. Vaz, "Drama in Jamaica", 47.
2. Review, *Daily Gleaner*, 12 April 1937.
3. Ibid.
4. Ibid.
5. Ibid.
6. Wycliffe Bennett, "The Jamaican Theatre", *Jamaica Journal* 8 (September 1974): 3–9.
7. Ralph Thompson, interview by Wycliffe Bennett, n.d.

Chapter 5

1. *The Laws of Jamaica: Passed by the Assembly, and Confirmed by His Majesty in Council, Feb. 23, 1683. To Which Is Added A Short Account of the Island and Government Thereof, with an Exact Map of the Island* (London: printed for H. Hills by Charles Harper, 1683), 1:x.
2. From Puritan author William Prynne's well-known condemnation of the theatre in his 1632 treatise *Histrio-Mastix* (William Prynne, *Histrio-Mastix: The Player's Scourge, or Actor's Tragœdie*).
3. From the 29 May 1660 entry in John Evelyn's *Diary* (John Evelyn, *The Diary of John Evelyn*), on the return of Charles II to London.
4. G.M. Trevelyan, *English Social History: A Survey of Six Centuries from Chaucer to Queen Victoria* (New York: Longmans, Green and Co., 1942), 338.
5. Alexandre Beljame, *Men of Letters and the English Public in the Eighteenth Century, 1660–1744*, 2nd ed., trans. E.O. Lorimer (London: Kegan Paul, 1948).
6. Robert Mowbray Howard, ed., *Records and Letters of the Family of the Longs of Longville, Jamaica, and Hampton Lodge, Surrey*, 2 vols. (London: Simpkin, Marshall, Hamilton, Kent, 1925), 1:109–10, 1:184–94.
7. [Charles Leslie], *A New History of Jamaica, from the Earliest Accounts to the Taking of Porto Bello by Vice Admiral Edward Vernon* (London: printed for J. Hodges, 1740), letter 2.27.
8. John Oldmixon, *The British Empire in America*, 2nd ed. corrected and revised (London: Robertson, 1741), 2:416.
9. Wright, *Revels*, 21–22.

Chapter 6

1. One of the authors has seen all but three of the sixty-seven pantomimes staged by the LTM since 1941. He has checked the relevant newspapers and other publications, and has logged the pertinent items and interviewed as many persons as possible who have been involved, either as practitioners, critics or honest observers.
2. *The New Encyclopaedia Britannica*, 15th ed., s.v. "Pantomime".
3. Horace Vaz, "Jack and the Beanstalk", *Daily Gleaner*, 6 January 1942.
4. Henry Fowler, interview by Wycliffe Bennett, 1990.
5. Bennett, "Jamaican Theatre", 3–9.
6. Louise Bennett Coverley and Eric Coverley, interview by Wycliffe Bennett, n.d.
7. Louise Bennett Coverley, videotape interview, Creative Production and Training Centre, Kingston, Jamaica, n.d.
8. Ibid.
9. A.E. Wilson, *Christmas Pantomime: The Story of an English Institution* (London: Allen and Unwin, 1934).
10. Harry Milner, review, *Sunday Gleaner*, 10 January 1976.
11. Norman Rae, review, *Daily Gleaner*, 2 January 1974.
12. Harry Milner, in discussion with Wycliffe Bennett, n.d.
13. Sylvia Wynter and Alex Gradussov, *Rockstone Anancy* programme (1970).
14. Verena Reckord, *Sun Rays* (Kingston), 13 January 1980.
15. *Moonshine Anancy* programme note, "The Story of the Pantomome", 1981.
16. *Rockstone Anancy* programme (1970).

17. Neville Dawes, document in the authors' collection.
18. Henry Fowler, in discussion with Wycliffe Bennett, n.d.
19. Rex Nettleford, "Staging the Pantomime", *Sunday Gleaner*, 17 January 1988.
20. *Nuff an' Plenty* programme (2007).

Chapter 7

1. Ruth Benedict, *Patterns of Culture* (Boston: Houghton Mifflin, 1959), 17.
2. *You in Your Small Corner* programme (July 1968).
3. *Daily Gleaner*, 30 April 1976.
4. All quotes from Douglas Prout in this section have been taken from material he supplied to the author in 2008.

Chapter 8

1. "The Dramatic Society", *Pelican Annual* (1955): 106.
2. Ibid., 103.
3. Harry Milner, review, *Daily Gleaner*, 1 December 1953.
4. Ibid.
5. "Words and Music", *Pelican Annual* (1955): 105.
6. Harry Milner, review, *Daily Gleaner*, ca. 25 June 1955.
7. *Daily Gleaner*, 30 July 1956.
8. Review, *Pelican*, February 1957, 9.
9. *Pelican*, March 1957.
10. David Williams, "Preview", *Pelican*, March 1957.
11. Norman Rae, review, *Daily Gleaner*, 25 March 1957.
12. *Pelican Annual* (1959): 141.
13. Ibid.

Chapter 9

1. Rex Nettleford, "Report of an Exploratory Committee on the Arts" (mimeo, 1978), 88–89.
2. Ibid., 298.
3. Dennis Scott, graduation address, School of Drama, 1981
4. Thom Cross, interview by Honor Ford-Smith, n.d.

Chapter 10

1. *Daily Gleaner*, review, 28 December 1928.
2. Greta Bourke (Fowler), personal communication, n.d.
3. Lindsay Downer to Hazel Johnston, n.d., private collection of Wycliffe Bennett.
4. Greta Bourke (Fowler), personal communication, n.d.
5. Hazel Johnston, *Public Opinion*, June–September 1939.
6. J. McCulloch, *Caribbean Post*, March 1946, 16–17.
7. Orford St John, *West Indian Review*, August 1956.
8. Vic Reid, review, *New Day*, May 1960, 44.

Chapter 11

1. Maria Smith, "The Revival Iconography: Symbolic Language, Memory and the Performance of an Afro Jamaican Identity" (PhD dissertation, University of the West Indies, Jamaica, 2008).
2. *Encyclopaedia Britannica Micropaedia*, 7:75.

Chapter 12

1. Ivy Baxter, interview by Shivaun Hearne, Creative Production and Training Centre, Kingston, Jamaica, ca. 1991.
2. Tribute to Ivy Baxter, *Sunday Herald*, 17 January 1993.
3. Tribute to Ivy Baxter, *Gleaner*, 11 January 1993.
4. Ivy Baxter, *The Arts of an Island* (Metuchen, NJ: Scarecrow, 1970).

Chapter 13

1. Rex Nettleford, *Dance Jamaica* (New York: Grove, 1985), 137.
2. "NDTC for New York Performance", *Gleaner*, 2 March 2010.
3. This was the style used by Doris Humphrey and the Humphrey/Weidman group of Chicago. The technique influenced Neville Black, who passed it on to Jamaican modern dancers. Humphrey was a contemporary of Martha Graham.
4. Sheila Barnett, interview by Wycliffe Bennett, n.d.
5. Bert Rose, interview by Wycliffe Bennett, n.d.
6. NDTC programme (1982).
7. J.S. Mbiti, *Concepts of God in Africa* (New York: Anchor Books, 1970), 191.
8. Barnett, interview.
9. NDTC programme, 42nd season (2002).

Chapter 14

1. T.S. Reid, "Movements 26th Season of Dance", *Jamaica Observer*, 3 July 2007.
2. *Stolen Verses* programme (2004).

Chapter 15

1. O.G. Brockett, *History of the Theatre*, 3rd ed. (Boston: Allyn and Bacon, 1968).
2. Ibid.
3. Irving Rouse, quoted in Sherlock and Bennett, *Story of the Jamaican People*, 48.
4. R.N. Murray, ed., *J.J. Mills: His Own Account of His Life and Times* (Kingston: Collins and Sangster, 1969), 151–52.
5. Robert Fowler, tribute to Henry Fowler, given at a memorial service at the Little Theatre, Kingston, Jamaica, 26 March 2007.
6. D.T.M. Girvan, "History of the Jamaica Social Welfare Commission", *Welfare Reporter* 11, no. 3 (1950).

7. Eddie Burke [Uncle Newton, pseud.], *Newsy Wapps: The Ups and Downs of the Jamaican Boy* (Kingston: Jamaica Welfare Limited, 194–).
8. R. Harrison, "The Jamaica Drama League", part 2, *Daily Gleaner*, 25 June 1989.
9. Ibid.
10. Jamaica Cultural Development Commission, *Jamaica Festival Story* (1987): 9. (This publication was produced as the JCDC's twenty-fifth anniversary souvenir magazine.)
11. Ibid.
12. *Gleaner*, Festival Supplement, 12 August 2002.

Chapter 16

1. Murray, *J.J. Mills*, 108–9.
2. C.G.X. Henriques, Joan Grant and Douglas Judah, "The Standard of Elocution in Jamaica", *Daily Gleaner*, 12 January 1937.
3. Ibid.
4. Ibid.
5. Ibid.
6. Ibid.
7. Ibid.
8. W.A. Aikin, *The Voice: An Introduction to Practical Phonology* (London: Longmans, Green and Co., 1951).

Chapter 17

1. Linda Stockhausen, "The Story of the Cudjoe Minstrels", Jamaica, 11 March 1939.
2. Kingston Glee Singers, "Talented Musicians – No. 3", *Cosmopolitan*, August 1928, 110–19.
3. Percy Alfred Scholes, *Oxford Companion to Music*, 9th ed. (London: Oxford University Press, 1965).
4. Ethel Marson, *George Davis Goode: The Man and His Work* (Kingston: privately printed, 1964).
5. Ibid.
6. *Daily Gleaner*, 22 September 1913.
7. *Jamaica Times*, 28 September 1913.
8. Marson, *George Davis Goode*.
9. Ibid.
10. Kingston Glee Singers, "Talented Musicians", 110–19
11. *New Day*, January 1960.
12. Kingston Glee Singers, "Talented Musicians", 110–19.
13. Programme of the Jamaica Philharmonic Symphony Orchestra and Choral Group, 1982 Concert Season (May 1982).
14. Douglas Bennett, interview by Wycliffe Bennett, n.d.
15. From biographical information supplied by Shirley Thompson.
16. Ibid.
17. Ibid.
18. Citation read at the presentation of the Musgrave Medal to White.

Chapter 18

1. Pamela O'Gorman, "Reggae Has Achieved National Recognition", *Pepperpot*, December 1975, 33–35.
2. The "burru" is a family of three drums, originally small enough to be carried easily, and used to accompany Jonkonnu bands. The bass is a double-membraned drum made of wood and covered at both ends with goat skin. The smaller drums, the "fundeh" and the "repeater", are sometimes made of paint tins covered only at one end. The fundeh is covered with goat skin and the repeater with lamb skin, which gives it the highest pitch. The bass drum guides the metre of the rhythm and is played with a padded stick. The fundeh provides the steady, unbroken beat, and the repeater is the lead drum. The burru originated in the parishes of St Catherine (in the Old Harbour Bay area) and Clarendon. In time, the burru was adopted by the Rastafarians and the drums gradually became larger in size, so that the bass drum is now sometimes mounted on a stand. Marjorie Whylie, interview with Hazel Bennett, 2008.

Appendix

1. Wycliffe Bennett, remembrance given at service in honour of Reggie Carter, UWI Chapel, Kingston, Jamaica, 15 September 1995.
2. Sheila Hill-Carter, remembrance given at service in honour of Reggie Carter, UWI Chapel, Kingston, Jamaica, 15 September 1995.
3. Ibid.
4. *Sunday Gleaner* magazine, 27 April 1980.
5. *Sunday Gleaner*, Outlook magazine, 30 March 2008.
6. Ibid.
7. *Gleaner*, 18 February 2007.
8. Ibid.
9. Wycliffe Bennett, tribute to Henry Fowler at a memorial function, Little Theatre, Kingston, Jamaica, 26 March 2007.
10. Henry Fowler, interview by Wycliffe Bennett, n.d.
11. Robert Henry Fowler, tribute to Henry Fowler at a memorial function, Little Theatre, Kingston, Jamaica, 26 March 2007.
12. Bennett "Tribute to Henry Fowler".
13. Michael Edwards, *Sunday Gleaner*, 15 March 2001.
14. Amina Blackwood-Meeks, personal communication.
15. *Star*, 19 July 1963.
16. Michael Billington, "A Review of Skyvers at the Royal Court", *Guardian*, 25 January 2006.
17. Cynthia Reckord-Royal, "The Jamaica National Theatre Trust: A Local Theatre with a World View" (unpublished essay, 1983; updated by Margaret Reckord-Bernal in 2008).
18. " 'Beyond the Blues' for Kingston", *Daily Gleaner*, 6 August 1981.
19. Lloyd Reckord, *Adios Carenage* programme notes (2005).
20. Wycliffe Bennett, personal communication.
21. Godfrey Taylor, *Let Us Sing* (Kingston: Carlong, 2002).
22. Godfrey Taylor and Noel Dexter, *Mango Time* (Kingston: Ian Randle, 2007).
23. "Tribute to Noel Vaz", Philip Sherlock Centre for the Creative Arts, 1986.
24. Quoted in *West Indian Review*, 20 January 1951, 23.
25. From notes provided by Munair Zacca, 2008.
26. Ibid.

Selected Bibliography

Aikin, W.A. *The Voice: An Introduction to Practical Phonology*. London: Longmans, Green and Co., 1951.

Baxter, Ivy. *The Arts of an Island*. Metuchen, NJ: Scarecrow, 1970.

Beljame, Alexandre. *Men of Letters and the English Public in the Eighteenth Century, 1660–1744*. 2nd ed. Translated by E.O. Lorimer. London: Kegan Paul, 1948.

Benedict, Ruth. *Patterns of Culture*. Boston: Houghton Mifflin, 1959.

Bennett, Wycliffe. "The Jamaican Theatre". *Jamaica Journal* 8, nos. 2–3 (Summer 1974): 3–9.

Brockett, O.G. *History of the Theatre*. 3rd ed. Boston: Allyn and Bacon, 1968.

Bowra, Maurice. Introduction to *Poetry of the English Speaking Caribbean*. Edited by W.A. Roberts and W. Bennett. N.p., 1951.

Burke, Eddie [Uncle Newton, pseud.]. *Newsy Wapps: The Ups and Downs of the Jamaican Boy*. Kingston: Jamaica Welfare Ltd., 194–.

Evelyn, John. *The Diary of John Evelyn*. London: Macmillan, 1906.

Girvan, D.T.M. "History of the Jamaica Social Welfare Commission". *Welfare Reporter* 11, no. 3 (1950).

Guthrie, Tyrone. *A Life in the Theatre*. New York: McGraw-Hill, 1959.

Hanson, Francis. "Plays at a Publick Theatre". In *The Laws of Jamaica: Passed by the Assembly, and Confirmed by His Majesty in Council, Feb. 23, 1683. To Which Is Added A Short Account of the Island and Government Thereof, with an Exact Map of the Island*. London: printed for H. Hills by Charles Harper, 1683.

———. "A Short Account of the Island and Government of Jamaica". In *The Laws of Jamaica: Passed by the Assembly, and Confirmed by His Majesty in Council, Feb. 23, 1683. To Which Is Added A Short Account of the Island and Government Thereof, with an Exact Map of the Island*. London: printed for H. Hills by Charles Harper, 1683.

Hill, Errol. *The Jamaican Stage, 1655–1900: Profile of a Colonial Theatre*. Amherst: University of Massachusetts Press, 1992.

Howard, Robert Mowbray, ed. *Records and Letters of the Family of the Longs of Longville, Jamaica, and Hampton Lodge, Surrey*. 2 vols. London: Simpkin, Marshall, Hamilton, Kent, 1925.

Inge, W.R. *The End of an Age: And Other Essays*. London: Putnam, 1949.

[Leslie, Charles.] *A New History of Jamaica, from the Earliest Accounts to the Taking of Porto Bello by Vice Admiral Edward Vernon*. London: printed for J. Hodges, 1740.

Marson, Ethel. *George Davis Goode: The Man and His Work*. Kingston: privately printed, 1964.

Mbiti, J.S. *Concepts of God in Africa*. New York: Anchor Books, 1970.

Murray, R.N., ed. *J.J. Mills: His Own Account of His Life and Times*. Kingston: Collins and Sangster, 1969.

Nettleford, Rex. *Dance Jamaica*. New York: Grove, 1985.

O'Gorman, Pamela. "A Note on Their Music". *Jamaica Journal* (February–April 1989).

Oldmixon, John. *The British Empire in America*. 2nd ed., corrected and revised. London: Robertson, 1741.

Popkin, Henry, ed. *The New British Drama*. New York: Grove, 1964.

Prynne, William. *Histrio-Mastix: The Player's Scourge, or Actor's Tragœdie*. 1632.

Reckord-Royal, Cynthia. "The Jamaica National Theatre Trust: A Local Theatre with a World View". Unpublished paper, 1983. (Updated by Margaret Reckord-Bernal, 2008.)

Reyna, Ferdinando. *A Concise History of Ballet*. New York: Grosset and Dunlap, 1964.

Scholes, Percy Alfred. *Oxford Companion to Music*. 9th ed. London: Oxford University Press, 1965.

Sherlock, Philip, and Hazel Bennett. *The Story of the Jamaican People*. Kingston: Ian Randle, 1998.

Smith, Maria. "The Revival Iconography: Symbolic Language, Memory and the Performance of an Afro Jamaican Identity". PhD dissertation. University of the West Indies, Jamaica, 2008.

Stockhausen, Linda. "The Story of the Cudjoe Minstrels". *Jamaica*, 11 March 1939.

Taylor, Godfrey. *Let Us Sing*. Kingston: Carlong (Caribbean), 2002.

Taylor, Godfrey, and Noel Dexter. *Mango Time*. Kingston: Ian Randle, 2007.

Trevelyan, G.M. *English Social History: A Survey of Six Centuries from Chaucer to Queen Victoria*. New York: Longmans, Green and Co., 1942.

Vaz, Horace. "The Drama in Jamaica". *West Indian Review* (Spring 1947).

Wilson, A.E. *Christmas Pantomime: The Story of an English Institution*. London: Allen and Unwin, 1934.

Wright, Richardson. *Revels in Jamaica, 1682–1838*. New ed. Kingston: Bolivar, 1986.

Index

About the Authors

Co-author Wycliffe Bennett

Wycliffe Bennett was a company executive; a producer and director of theatre, radio, film and television; and a trainer in voice and speech. He was a pioneer organizer of the national arts festival movement (1943–63), and twice general manager of the JBC. He also served as chairman and executive chairman of the CPTC, and held chairships at the Jamaica School of Drama, Jamaica School of Music, Jamaica Drama League and Adult Drama Festival. He was chairman emeritus of the Ward Theatre Foundation and lifetime member of the LTM. He was born in Colón, Panama, on 19 May 1922, and came to Jamaica with his parents when he was two and a half years old. He was also a career civil servant with experience in administration, customs and town planning.

He held a Bachelor of Arts degree from Yale University, a Master of Fine Arts degree from Columbia University, the Diploma of the British Drama League and a Licentiateship of the Royal Academy of Music, among his other specialist training. He was a fellow of the Woodrow Wilson International Center for Scholars, and noted for some outstanding classical plays directed for the stage and television, including *Servant of Two Masters*, *Macbeth*, *Phaedra* and *The Good Woman of Setzuan*. He was also known for the grand spectaculars he produced on behalf of the Government of Jamaica: for the tercentenary celebrations (1955), the independence celebrations (1962), Kingston 100 (1972), the Jamaica Tribute (1974) and the Carifesta '76 Gala (1976).

He was executive producer and director of a set of five LP records of Caribbean poetry, prose and drama entitled *Voices from the Caribbean*, and a set of Jamaican classical, religious, traditional and popular music on eight LPs entitled *Music and Youth*, with eight half-hour films of the same name. While at the CPTC he was, for many years, executive producer of local plays and films for television, including the long-running programme *Rappin'*, which targeted young people. Bennett has received many honours and awards for his work in the arts, among them the Order of Distinction, Commander Class (CD) from the Government of Jamaica (1977), the Silver Musgrave Medal (1977), the Gold Musgrave Medal (2009) and the Centenary Medal (1979) from the Institute of Jamaica, and posthumously, the Order of Jamaica (2009).

Wycliffe Bennett, director, producer and broadcaster, co-author

Co-author Hazel Bennett

Hazel Bennett, educator, researcher, co-author

Hazel Bennett, educator, library pioneer and author, was married to Wycliffe Bennett for more than half a century. During that time they saw most theatrical productions in Jamaica together, so long as they were in the same place at the same time. She has worked on National Festival committees and on a National Library and Information Policy for Jamaica, and has worked behind the scenes at elocution contests and at rehearsals of plays and artistic performances which Wycliffe Bennett produced, whether as tutor to drama students or as director of national spectaculars. Hazel Bennett has been chauffeur, researcher, consultant, critic, costume maker and props maker at different times as the need has arisen. She has also researched, sorted, organized, assembled, written sections (as appropriate), edited and physically typed the body of material, collected over sixty years, which forms the substance of this book. Working alongside husband Wycliffe helped to fulfil the artistic and creative side of her life.

Among her many qualifications, Hazel Bennett holds a PhD in Library Science and an Master of Science in Literature. She was deputy director of the Jamaica Library Service during its pioneering years, established the Documentation Centre for the School of Education (UWI), was a member of the team which lobbied the UWI to establish a teaching department in Library Science, and was head of the Department for a period. She travelled the region promoting the need for professional librarians; advised on and guided the organization of teachers' college libraries in the Eastern Caribbean; recruited trainee librarians and technical assistants for the English-speaking Caribbean, Guyana and Belize; advised governments; and prepared draft library legislation for two countries.

Hazel Bennett is a lifetime member of the Library and Information Association of Jamaica (LIAJA). She was awarded the Institute of Jamaica Centenary Medal in 1979; the Silver Musgrave Medal for outstanding merit in the field of literature, library development and historical scholarship in 1998; the National Heritage Trust Award in 1998; and the Order of Distinction (OD) by the Government of Jamaica in 2007. Among her major works are *The Story of the Jamaican People* (1998), co-authored with Sir Philip Sherlock, and her doctoral dissertation, "A History of Libraries in Jamaica, 1697–1987".